Economic Adjustment and Exchange Rates in Developing Countries

A National Bureau
of Economic Research
Conference Report

Economic Adjustment and Exchange Rates in Developing Countries

Edited by Sebastian Edwards and Liaquat Ahamed

The University of Chicago Press

Chicago and London

SEBASTIAN EDWARDS is associate professor of economics at the
University of California at Los Angeles and a faculty research
fellow at the National Bureau of Economic Research.
LIAQUAT AHAMED is senior investment officer at the World Bank.

The University of Chicago Press, Chicago 60637
The University of Chicago Press, Ltd., London

Library of Congress Cataloging-in-Publication Data

Economic adjustment and exchange rates in developing
countries.

(A National Bureau of Economic Research conference
report)
"Papers . . . presented at a joint National Bureau of
Economic Research–World Bank conference held in Washing-
ton, D.C., 29 November through 1 December, 1984."—
Bibliography: p.
Includes index.
1. Foreign exchange administration—Developing
countries—Congresses. 2. Economic stabilization—
Developing countries—Congresses. I. Edwards, Sebastián.
II. Ahamed, Liaquat. III. National Bureau of Economic
Research. IV. World Bank. V. Series: Conference report
(National Bureau of Economic Research)

HG3877.E26 1986   332.4'5'091724   86-7045
ISBN 0-226-18469-2

Since this volume is a record of conference proceedings, it has been exempted from the rules governing critical review of manuscripts by the Board of Directors of the National Bureau (resolution adopted 8 June 1948, as revised 21 November 1949 and 20 April 1968).

This book is dedicated
to the memory of
Carlos F. Díaz-Alejandro

Contents

Acknowledgments

The papers and comments in this volume were presented at a joint National Bureau of Economic Research–World Bank conference held in Washington, D.C., 29 November through 1 December 1984. World Bank participation in the conference was organized by the Trade and Adjustment Division of its Country Policy Department. We would like to thank Armeane Choksi, the division's chief, for his help and encouragement. We also thank William Branson, director of international studies at the National Bureau, for his help in organizing the conference. Finally, we are grateful to Kirsten Foss and Jennifer Lewis, who made every effort to make the conference a big success.

This volume is dedicated to the memory of Carlos Diaz-Alejandro, whose untimely death in 1985 has robbed the profession of one of its most brilliant and eloquent members. Carlos played an important role in this conference. He gave an excellent comment on Arnold Harberger's paper. He also had a leading role in the roundtable discussion on "Exchange Rate Systems in Developing Countries" that took place during the conference. Carlos was a pioneer in the study of exchange rate problems in developing countries; his book *Exchange Rate Devaluation in a Semi-Industrialized Economy: The Experience of Argentina, 1955–1961* (MIT Press, 1966) has become a classic on the subject.

Any opinions expressed in this volume are those of the respective authors and do not necessarily reflect the views of the National Bureau of Economic Research, the World Bank, or any of the other sponsoring organizations.

Introduction

Sebastian Edwards and Liaquat Ahamed

In recent economic debates, the exchange rate has been singled out as one of the most important variables in the economies of developing countries. Some experts have argued, for example, that the exchange rate policies pursued by some developing countries in the late 1970s and early 1980s were inappropriate, resulting in acute real overvaluations of their currencies and contributing in an important way to the current debt crisis. According to the World Bank (1984), the dramatic deterioration in the agricultural sector of Africa during the last 15 years or so is due, to a large extent, to the unrealistic exchange rate policies followed in the majority of the countries in that continent. Moreover, the World Bank staff has forcefully argued that overvalued real exchange rates undermine exports, harm agriculture, and generate destabilizing capital outflows in the developing countries.[1]

At the more immediate policy level, policy makers and staff at the International Monetary Fund (IMF) and the World Bank are now regularly confronted with problems arising from exchange rate behavior. The following questions are commonly heard: Is the real exchange rate misaligned? How will the exchange rate policy affect the agricultural sector? How will a devaluation affect the country's ability to service its debt? Is nominal devaluation an effective tool to generate relative price changes and improvements in the balance of payments? In fact, nowadays it is difficult to tackle macroeconomic problems in the developing countries without addressing exchange rate issues.

Sebastian Edwards is an associate professor of economics at the University of California, Los Angeles, and a faculty research fellow at the National Bureau of Economic Research. Liaquat Ahamed is a senior investment analyst at the World Bank.

1

In spite of the very prominent role exchange rates have played in recent debates over the economies of developing countries, and in spite of the importance of the topic to policy, relatively few studies have systematically analyzed in detail the ramifications of exchange rate policy in these countries. The purpose of the essays and comments collected in this volume—which were presented at a joint National Bureau of Economic Research–World Bank conference in late 1984— is to provide a partial remedy to this situation. These papers cover issues ranging from the relationship between commercial policies and exchange rates, through the role of exchange rate policy in stabilization programs, to the effectiveness of devaluation as a policy tool and the interaction among exchange rates, the terms of trade, and capital flows.

The papers presented here concentrate on those exchange rate problems that are common among the developing countries. While there is a general recognition that in a number of respects all countries—poor and rich—face the same types of problems, it is also understood that some problems are more likely to occur in the developing countries. For example, very few developing nations have adopted floating exchange rates, pursuing instead a variety of exchange rate arrangements, such as fixed to a single currency, fixed to a basket of currencies, and a crawling peg. As a consequence of the exchange rate systems they have adopted, developing countries are more likely than developed countries to use abrupt devaluation as a component of a stabilization program. Furthermore, the economic structure of the poorer countries is vastly different from that of the richer countries. In the poorer countries there are many incomplete, or nonexistent, markets, including forward markets for foreign exchange and well-behaved financial markets.

In this introduction we first provide a reader's guide to the book, summarizing each chapter and its policy implications. We then outline a number of research issues raised in the general study of exchange rates in developing countries, issues we believe are still open and require additional attention by members of the profession.

Stabilization, Adjustment, and Exchange Rates

The first four papers in this volume deal with the role of exchange rate policy in stabilization programs and in the adjustment process. Although these papers address mainly analytical issues, they are all motivated by the desire to understand existing policy problems that are fairly common to the developing nations.

The first paper, by van Wijnbergen, focuses on the impact of currency devaluations on the levels of output and employment. In particular, this paper inquires into the conditions under which a devaluation will result in a decline in aggregate output. Traditional models, especially Keynesian models, have tended to focus on the expansionary effects of devaluations on output. According to this view, the increase in competitiveness following a devaluation tends to raise the demand for domestic goods by switching expenditures from imports to domestically produced goods. To the extent that nominal prices or wages are rigid, the devaluation leads to an increase in output in the domestic goods sector. For some time now, however, a number of economists have argued, contrary to the traditional view, that under certain circumstances a devaluation can be contractionary, resulting in reduced aggregate output and employment. It has long been recognized, for example, that there are a variety of channels through which a deflationary impact on aggregate demand may offset the expansionary effects of expenditure switching and thereby produce a contraction in output. These channels include distributional effects either within the private sector or through a fiscal transfer from the private sector to the public sector; the real balance effect; or the consequence of the income effect of initially large trade deficits. Nonetheless, the paper by van Wijnbergen focuses to a greater extent on the contractionary effects of devaluation on aggregate *supply* rather than on aggregate demand.

The author constructs a simple macroeconomic model to elucidate three alternative channels by which a devaluation can exert a contractionary effect on aggregate supply. The first channel arises when, as is typical in many developing countries, imported goods play a significant role in the production process. A devaluation raises the relative price of imported inputs versus domestic final goods. The ensuing rise in variable costs induces a fall in the output that firms are willing to produce. This contractionary effect may be partly offset by possibilities of substitution between imported inputs and domestic factors in production and by the expansionary effects of expenditure switching. A second contractionary channel is created when real wages are indexed to some index such as the consumer price index, that accounts for both domestic and foreign goods. An increase in competitiveness implies that foreign goods become more expensive than domestic goods. If real wages are indexed to a consumption basket that includes foreign goods, this implies that real product wages rise and that the improvement in competitiveness occurs at the expense of domestic production. The third contractionary channel is a result of the effect of the increase in the price level on the real volume of bank credit. In many developing countries, firms finance fixed and working capital requirements through bank loans. The rise in the price level associated with a devaluation leads to a rise in nominal demand for bank credit, which, given a fixed nominal money supply, leads in turn to a rise in real interest rates and thus a rise in the interest component costs.

In the second chapter Mussa develops a model that explicitly links budgetary policies, the real exchange rate, and the balance of payments. To highlight the significance of the linkage between aggregate spending and income as determinants of the balance of payments, he assumes that the economy is at full employment, output is exogenously determined, and all prices are flexible. Private expenditures relative to private disposable income is determined by the level of net foreign assets held by the private sector and by expected real interest rates, which in turn depend on expectations about future changes in the domestic price level relative to the foreign price level (that is, the real exchange rate). The excess of government expenditures over taxation is financed by foreign debt. The key innovation in Mussa's model is his incorporation of a variety of dynamic effects, including the effect of the current account balance on the growth of net foreign assets held by the private sector and the impact of the expected real exchange rate in the future on current expenditure decisions.

The implications of Mussa's framework can be illustrated in their starkest form by considering an economy in which the nominal exchange rate is fixed and in which the budget deficit is set at a level that is imcompatible with balance-of-payments equilibrium. Associated with the excess of expenditures over income are an appreciation in the real exchange rate and a consequent rise in nominal money balances to sustain the higher domestic price level.

This policy configuration—which has been quite common in a number of developing countries, most notably, Argentina in the late 1970s—is clearly not sustainable in the long run, since it requires a constantly expanding stock of government debt. The long-term instability of the policy is likely to be recognized by the private sector, which will come to anticipate a nominal devaluation. Expectations of a devaluation will in turn lead to rising domestic interest rates and a fall in the demand for domestic money balances, thus exacerbating the balance-of-payments disequilibrium and requiring even larger increases in foreign borrowing to support the nominal exchange rate. Mussa's paper traces through the dynamics associated with such cycles of crises followed by discrete devaluations, both in the case of fixed nominal exchange rates and under crawling peg regimes.

Mussa's model illustrates a recurring problem with devaluation crises in developing countries: the effects of speculation against the exchange rate. First, this speculation tends to create large shifts in the demand for money and thus poses considerable problems for monetary management. And second, speculative flows make it very difficult to assess the underlying balance-of-payments position, thereby complicating the task of determining the appropriate magnitude of the devaluation required to restore equilibrium.

The next paper, by Aizenman and Frenkel, examines the interaction among labor markets, real shocks, monetary policy, and exchange rates. The authors develop a one-good model with an imported intermediate input, to analyze the properties of alternative rules for wage rate indexation under different exchange rate regimes. The issue of wage indexation has become an important policy problem in many developing countries suffering from chronic inflation. For example, a number of observers have recently pointed out that the existence of 100 percent wage rate indexation in the presence of fixed exchange rates played a crucial role in the collapse of some of the recent economic liberalization attempts in the Southern Cone of Latin America.

In their model Aizenman and Frenkel assume that wages are set in advance by multiyear contracts. Consequently, once real shocks—which affect the demand for or supply of labor, or both—take place, the real wage cannot adjust and a welfare loss results. Within this context the authors develop a formal framework to analyze the optimality properties of indexation rules that link the nominal wage alternatively to the CPI, the value-added price index, and the nominal gross national product. They find that the relative ranking of these rules will depend on the relative elasticities of labor demand and supply.

Aizenman and Frenkel then establish that under flexible exchange rates, there is a dual relationship between wage rate indexation rules and monetary accommodation rules. This result has some important policy implications, since it suggests that, in this type of setting, economic authorities have to be careful not to implement monetary policies that would generate negative welfare consequences through their effect on the labor market. Policy makers should ensure, for example, that one policy does not undo what another policy is designed to achieve.

A particularly interesting aspect of Aizenman and Frenkel's analysis has to do with the joint determination of the optimal degree of exchange rate intervention and the optimal degree of wage indexation. The authors show that within the context of their model—characterized by real shocks, multiyear wage contracts, and imported intermediate inputs—a fully flexible or completely fixed exchange rate regime will almost never be optimal. This result, of course, has important policy implications for those developing countries that are trying to develop a more adequate exchange rate system.

In the fourth chapter Dornbusch analyzes the role of unconventional exchange rate systems in the adjustment process. In particular, he looks at the main properties of multiple exchange rates for commercial transactions. Even though Dornbusch concentrates on multiple rates for commercial transactions, unconventional exchange rate systems have in practice been applied to both commercial and financial transactions; in fact, systems of dual rates that differentiate between the current and capital accounts of the balance of payments have been historically important in a number of countries. Moreover, since the debt crisis arose these unconventional systems have experienced a relatively widespread revival among the less developed nations.

The principal question addressed by Dornbusch is whether there are circumstances under which—in spite of the distortions that they introduce—multiple exchange rate practices represent a desirable policy option. To tackle this question Dornbusch organizes his discussion around some of the more important fiscal and macroeconomic aspects of multiple rates. He first points out that by introducing a differential between buying and selling rates, a multiple exchange rate system is equivalent to an implicit tax-subsidy structure. Furthermore, to the extent that different exchange rates apply to inputs and to final goods, a multiple exchange rate system will result in a structure of differential rates of effective protection. To the extent that a multiple rate system is equivalent to an implicit system of tariffs, it will have the same efficiency costs as the implicit tariff system and thus will be only the second- or third-best device to achieve dometic objectives.

Dornbusch then moves on to analyze some of the macroeconomic effects of a system of multiple exchange rates. He posits that the imposition of multiple rates has the advantage that it can be aimed at those goods that have higher elasticities of demand. Thus, multiple rates may be a desirable policy option to address *temporary* balance-of-payments difficulties. To determine whether multiple rates are in fact desirable, the economic authorities should weigh the costs, which stem from the traditional efficiency losses, against the benefits, which are based on the ability to generate an adjustment that has a smaller impact on unemployment and income distribution than would otherwise be possible.

Economic Reform, Foreign Shocks, and Exchange Rates

The next two papers, by Calvo and by Obstfeld, analyze the effects of different exchange rate policies on economic liberalization attempts. For many years economists have advocated that the developing countries liberalize their economies, giving a more prominent role to market-determined prices. The opening up of these economies, both to trade in goods and to capital movements, has traditionally been an important component of reform proposals designed to liberalize these economies.

In the 1970s the countries in the Southern Cone of Latin America—Argentina, Chile, and Uruguay—initiated major efforts to liberalize their economies, implementing sweeping reforms that included creating active and rapidly growing domestic capital markets, reducing import tariffs, and eliminating capital controls. A decade later, the evidence indicated those efforts had to a large extent failed. In fact, in all three countries the reforms have been partially reversed. Severe financial crises arose that resulted in the collapse and virtual nationalization of the banking sectors of the countries. At this time there is no clear agreement among the experts on the primary causes for these failures. Nonetheless, many experts do agree that exchange rate management had an important effect on the outcome of these experiments.

This case of Southern Cone reforms, in which freer banking was associated with severe financial disruptions, serves as the grist for Calvo's analysis. The author develops an overlapping-generations model of an open economy to address a set of important questions regarding financial liberalization efforts. Using a formal welfare criterion, he examines the optimal rate of devaluation, the optimal rate of inflation, the optimal degree of capital mobility, and the optimal degree of "freeness" of the domestic banking sector. For the purposes of this investigation, Calvo develops increasingly complex versions of his model. In the simplest version he finds that with no banks and no distortions in the capital market, the optimal rate of devaluation is zero (that is, fixed rates are optimal); the optimal rate of inflation is also zero; and capital should be allowed to flow freely in and out of the country. When money and banks are introduced into the picture, and when currency and deposits are assumed to be perfect substitutes, the results indicating that zero rates of devaluation and inflation are optimal still hold, as long as there are no distortions in the capital market.

Calvo then considers the case of foreign demand for the small country's currency. He shows that, under the assumption that the central bank maintains its reserves in the form of an international bond, the complete liberalization of the domestic banking system is still optimal. But in order to attract foreign funds, the central bank may have to offer some type of deposit insurance. If the central bank provides this insurance by holding zero-interest bonds, a loss of resources will result. In turn, the bank may then find it advisable to discourage foreign deposits by reducing the rate of return on domestic bank deposits. Calvo argues that an alternative way to solve this problem would be to provide the deposit insurance by having the domestic banking system become a member of some international banking system or by allowing foreign banks to operate fully at home.

In his contribution, Obstfeld develops a model to analyze the dynamics of the real exchange rate following a program of liberalization with stabilization. As in the case of Calvo, Obstfeld's inquiry is motivated by the recent experience of the Southern Cone. His model considers a stabilization program that uses a preannounced rate of nominal devaluation as the principal tool to combat inflation.[2] The model emphasizes the importance of private portfolio shifts that accompany a decline in the preannounced nominal rate of depreciation. The economy analyzed is characterized by sluggish nominal wages that depend on inflationary expectations but adjust only gradually to labor market conditions. The budget deficit is financed by domestic credit creation; but to maintain the announced exchange rate, the central bank intervenes in the foreign exchange market. To keep his model simple, Obstfeld abstracts from the problems associated with an incompatibility between the exchange rate and monetary and fiscal policy by assuming that the budget deficit is set endogenously in such a manner that the resulting growth in domestic credit is adequate to accommodate the rate of depreciation. Thus, there remains only one key policy variable: the rate of depreciation.

Obstfeld uses the model to consider the effects of a reduction in the rate of depreciation in the two polar cases of capital immobility and perfect capital mobility. In a situation of capital immobility, the fall in the rate of inflation associated with a decline in the rate of devaluation results in higher real interest rates and thus a deflationary impact on demand. That impact in turn produces a real depreciation in the short run. In effect, the increased demand for domestic assets is met by cutting expenditures. Over the long run, however, the surplus in the balance of payments and the concomitant expansion in domestic liquidity tends to reflate the economy, eventually leading to a real appreciation. On the other hand, in a situation of capital mobility, the change in the rate of nominal depreciation is neutral and has no impact on the real exchange rate. The fall in the rate of nominal depreciation raises the demand for money. Nonetheless, the public can increase its nominal holdings by borrowing foreign exchange and selling it to the central bank. In effect, the ability of the private sector to borrow abroad implies that the central bank can fully accommodate the portfolio shift of the private sector by accumulating foreign reserves with no impact on spending.

Case Studies

Four of the papers collected in this volume are case studies of a varied array of countries: Colombia, Greece, Kenya, and the countries of the West African Monetary Union.

In the first of these case studies, Edwards develops a simple model for analyzing the macroeconomic interrelation among a commodity export sector, the real exchange rate, and the rest of the economy. The model, which is used to analyze the case of coffee in Colombia, emphasizes the importance of money creation and inflation during an export boom.

Edwards's model has two components: a real block and a monetary block. When permanent monetary equilibrium is assumed, the results obtained from the real block of the model correspond to the traditional Dutch-disease literature, which shows that an export boom will generate an equilibrium real exchange rate appreciation. But when monetary disequilibrium in the short run is assumed, a richer set of results emerges. Edwards's model points to the fact that under fixed or managed nominal exchange rates, an export boom usually results in the accumulation of international reserves, money creation, and inflation. In fact, this inflation can, in the short run, exceed what is required to generate the equilibrium real appreciation. According to Edwards this has been the case in a number of countries, including Colombia, where increases in the price of coffee have traditionally been associated with higher rates of base-money creation and with inflation. Moreover, according to Colombian authorities, one of that country's recurrent economic problems has been how to avoid an excessive real appreciation during coffee booms.

Edwards tests his model using annual data for Colombia for the years 1960–82. He finds that during that period changes in world coffee prices indeed resulted in important changes in the rates of money creation and inflation. In fact, his regression results suggest that the link between money creation and inflation has been one of the most important means by which changes in coffee prices have affected the real exchange rate in Colombia.

In the next study Branson develops a simple macro model of two sectors to analyze the effects of devaluations on stabilization programs. The model differs from more traditional approaches by incorporating intermediate inputs, wage indexation, and rigid prices. Branson then applies his model to the case of Kenya, comparing the macro effects of a devaluation with those of an "equivalent" cut in government expenditures. The issues he addresses are similar to those tackled by van Wijnbergen in the first chapter of this volume.

Branson emphasizes, in particular, intermediate inputs and wage indexing as factors contributing to a contractionary impact of devaluation. He also outlines some important policy implications in his comparison of the effects of a devaluation and a cut in government expenditures on the balance of payments and the real economy. Traditional monetary and Keynesian models have tended to view these two measures as complementary, balancing the expansionary effects of an improvement in competitiveness with the deflationary effects of fiscal restraint. When a devaluation has a contractionary effect, these two instruments become to some degree substitutes. But Branson argues that when elasticities of substitution in production are low, devaluation tends to have a more pronounced stagflationary effect than cuts in government expenditure for the same drop in the balance-of-payments deficit.

A nominal exchange rate devaluation will have a persistent effect on the real economy and on relative prices only if there is some stickiness or rigidity in the nominal prices. According to Branson, without nominal price or wage rigidity, center stage in a stabilization program moves away from the nominal exchange rate to those government policies that directly affect the overall level of spending relative to income—and, particularly in the context of developing countries, to budgetary policies. (The earlier paper by Mussa also emphasizes this issue.)

In the third case study, on Greece, Katseli analyzes the effects of alternative nominal exchange rate policies on the real exchange rate. In particular, she investigates whether the way in which a nominal devaluation is implemented—through a discrete stepwise adjustment or through small nominal devaluations à la a crawling peg— differentially affects the real exchange rate response. From a policy perspective this is an important question. One of the fundamental goals of a devaluation is to improve competitiveness in the tradable goods sector, by generating a real devaluation. Many times, however, and for different reasons, nominal devaluations fail to do this. A crucial question, then, is whether the way in which the nominal devaluation is carried out has anything to do with these failures.

Katseli's model, which draws on the recent industrial organization literature, focuses on the use of contracts in monopolistic pricing setting. The author indicates that both the magnitude and the frequency of nominal exchange rate adjustments are important determinants of real exchange rate behavior. More specifically, according to her model, discrete nominal exchange rate adjustments, by providing an "information signal," result in shorter contracts and faster price responses. As a consequence, under discrete and large nominal exchange rate adjustments, the real exchange rate response will be smaller than under payment and small crawling-peg types of adjustments.

Katseli tests the main implications of her model using aggregate, sectoral, and product-level monthly data for Greece. The results do offer some support for those implications; the data suggest that the nominal prices of nontraded goods adjust faster after a discrete nominal devaluation than they otherwise would. The interpretation of the results is somewhat difficult, however, because a number of products were subject to price controls in Greece during the period under study.

In the last case study, Macedo analyzes the functioning of the West African Monetary Union (UMOA). This paper has considerable policy importance, since it outlines the significant characteristics of one of the very few genuine monetary unions in the world. This paper will therefore serve as an important basis for future discussions of the desirability of alternative exchange and monetary regimes in the developing countries. The paper is organized in two parts. In the first the author develops a stylized four-country model of a monetary union, and in the second he analyzes the salient features of the UMOA.

It has long been recognized that fixed-peg exchange rate regimes do not impose adjustment costs when nominal domestic prices are fully flexible. But they hamper the adjustment to shock, whether real or monetary, when nominal prices or wages are not fully flexible. Macedo extends this analysis to the case of a small country that decides to peg not to some optimally chosen basket of foreign currencies but to the currency of a single large country, which in turn floats based on currencies in the rest of the world. He finds that when domestic prices are fully flexible, monetary disturbances do not affect the real exchange rate. On the other hand, when domestic prices are not fully flexible, the small economy becomes more subject to monetary shocks emanating from the large country to whose currency it is pegged.

The model provides another crucial insight into monetary unions such as the UMOA. A balance-of-payments deficit (surplus) in the union results in a transfer of resources from (to) the large country to whose currency the union is pegged. Even when domestic prices are fully flexible and monetary disturbances per se do not affect the real exchange rate of the countries in the union, the distribution of the transfer across countries can result in real exchange rate changes.

Although Macedo does not empirically test his model with UMOA data, the second part of his paper does discuss the behavior of the monetary union in light of the model's results. In particular, he finds that, as implied by his theoretical construct, the way in which the transfer from France has been distributed among the union countries during the last few years seems to have affected the behavior of the real exchange rate in those countries. The author also points out that any calculation of the costs and benefits of the UMOA should explicitly take into account the role of the transfer of resources, which, according to the current agreement, France has to make to the union when the union runs a deficit.

The Real Exchange Rate and Adjustment

The last paper in the volume, by Harberger, provides a general analytical survey of the role of the real exchange rate in the adjustment process. In some sense this chapter pulls together many of the topics addressed in the previous papers. Harberger formulates a framework for analyzing the way in which the equilibrium real exchange rate reacts to different exogenous and policy-induced shocks. His approach is general enough to allow most traditional models of exchange rate behavior as special cases.

The paper begins with a discussion of an appropriate definition of the equilibrium real exchange rate and an analysis of how this equilibrium rate is affected by alternative shocks, under both floating and fixed nominal rates. In particular, Harberger investigates how the equilibrium real exchange rate reacts to the imposition of an import tariff; the imposition of an export tax; a capital inflow spent on imports; a capital inflow spent on nontradables; a change in the world price of exports; and a change in the world price of imports. In fact, many of these disturbances are the subject of more detailed analyses in some of the other papers in the volume: Mussa and Dornbusch look at tariffs; Obstfeld and Calvo analyze the role of capital inflows; and Edwards focuses on the consequences of a change in the price of exports.

Harberger devotes an important part of his paper to discussing the concept of the real exchange rate. He notes that this concept has caused a great deal of confusion in economics; at least four or five competing definitions of the real exchange rate are employed on fairly regular basis. Harberger points out that it is important to clarify what is really meant by "the" real exchange rate. He argues that from an analytical perspective, the most useful definition of the real exchange rate is the nominal exchange rate deflated by a theoretical general price index. This is a novel proposition, since it does not correspond to any of the more common definitions used in the literature. Harberger avers that only when this definition is used does the real exchange rate react to all the different disturbances in the way the theory predicts. From a practical point of view, however, it is not easy to find the appropriate general price index. After discussing a number of alternatives, Harberger arrives at the conclusion that, given availability and periodicity, the consumer price index is the best real-world counterpart to the ideal theoretical price index.

Future Research

The papers collected in this volume examine a number of important issues regarding the role of exchange rates in the adjustment process of developing countries. Needless to say, the topics covered do not exhaust the subject. There are many important problems that have not been tackled in this volume, or elsewhere in the literature. We hope this book will encourage researchers to devote time and energy to better understanding the general topic of exchange rates in the developing countries.

The first obvious agenda for future research is to determine a set of general principles that could be used by policy makers in developing countries who must decide what type of nominal exchange rate system to adopt. Although there has already been some progress in this area, the roundtable discussion at the NBER–World Bank conference was a further reminder that economists are still far from agreeing on what this set of principles should be.[3]

A second important goal of future research should be to improve our empirical understanding of the effectiveness of nominal devaluations as tools of economic policy. We now have a fairly impressive set of theoretical models describing this subject, but the empirical verification of these models is lagging alarmingly behind. As Katseli points out in chapter 9, the primary policy objectives of nominal devaluations have been to generate a real devaluation or improvement in the international competitiveness of the country and to generate an improvement in the external position of the country. It will therefore be important to use historical data to analyze the extent to which these objectives have in fact been achieved. This type of analysis should, of course, account for the concomitant effects of other macroeconomic policies pursued alongside the nominal devaluations.

A related issue has to do with the empirical analysis of contractionary devaluation. A number of analytical papers, including the ones by van Wijnbergen and Branson in this volume, have pointed out that devaluation as a component of stabilization may reduce aggregate output and employment. To date, however, the empirical analysis of this topic has been quite sketchy and incomplete; most studies have taken the form of "before and after" analyses or simulation studies.

The determinants of real exchange rate variability also deserve further analysis. It is well established that "excessive" real exchange rate variability may result in nontrivial welfare costs. From an empirical point of view, however, our understanding of the determinants of real exchange rate movements in developing—and, for that matter, in developed countries—has been very limited. As Díaz-Alejandro pointed out in his comment on Harberger's paper, policy makers will greatly benefit from better information on how some of the theoretical determinants of the real exchange rate—such as the terms of trade and capital flows—have actually affected the real exchange rate in some of these countries.

Future research should also focus on the general issue of devaluation crises. Once again, the empirical analysis of this subject lags behind the theoretical developments. More specifically, it would be interesting to test the historical role played by different factors in devaluation crises. The developing countries present an extremely valuable sample, since many of them have gone through major exchange rate and balance-of-payments crises in the last three to four decades. One important factor in these crises has been the consistency, or lack thereof, among exchange rate, fiscal, and monetary policies. Argentina in 1981 offers perhaps the most dramatic recent example of clearly inconsistent fiscal and exchange rate policies eventually leading to a major economic crisis.

A final topic that deserves attention—especially in the aftermath of the international debt crisis—is the determination of an optimal policy mix to face external sector disequilibria. Theoretically, countries can address a balance-of-payments problem with four alternative strategies: they can reduce absorption; they can generate expenditure switching through commercial policy or a devaluation; they can run down their international reserves; or they can borrow from abroad. Since the debt crisis began, this last tool, borrowing from abroad, has been severely limited for most of the developing countries. Consequently, the use of exchange rate policy, international reserves, and commercial policy to face temporary balance-of-payments difficulties has become increasingly widespread. Work on this topic, at both the theoretical and the empirical level, would be most welcome. In particular, economists need to develop a general optimizing framework that can help determine the optimal rate of devaluation, reserves holdings, and use of commercial policy to adapt to different types of disturbances.

Notes

1. On the relation between exchange rate policies and the debt crisis, see Cline (1983). Pfefferman (1985) provides a general discussion of the interaction between exchange rate policies and the process of economic development.

2. A preannounced rate of devaluation (the so-called *tablita*) was used in Argentina, Chile, and Uruguay in the late 1970s as a way to reduce the inflation rate.

3. A roundtable discussion on appropriate exchange rate regimes for the developing countries took place at the NBER–World Bank conference. Manual Guitián chaired the discussion, and Carlos Díaz-Alejandro, Arnold Harberger, and Deepak Lal provided opening remarks.

References

Cline, W. 1983. *International debt and the stability of the world economy*. Washington, D.C.: Institute for International Economics.

Pfefferman, G. 1985. Overvalued exchange rates and development. *Finance and Development* 22 (March): 17–19.

World Bank. 1984. *Towards sustained development in Sub-Saharan Africa*. Washington, D.C.: World Bank.

I   Stabilization, Adjustment, and Exchange Rate Policy in Developing Countries

1   Exchange Rate Management and Stabilization Policies in Developing Countries

Sweder van Wijnbergen

1.1 Introduction

In a world without money illusion a nominal exchange rate devaluation per se will not have any persistent real effects. Under various plausible circumstances, however, a devaluation may speed up adjustment of the real economy to disturbances, be they exogenous or policy induced. It is in this vein that a devaluation is nearly always one of the major components of stabilization programs, such as those often administered by the International Monetary Fund.

Until quite recently the consensus among economists was that a devaluation, if it had any real effects at all, was expansionary: the resulting increase in competitiveness would switch foreign and domestic demand toward domestic goods. This switch, in the presence of idle factors of production, in turn would lead to an expansion in output, thus supporting one of the aims of stabilization policy (increasing output and, via output, employment).

In the economic development literature, early doubts were expressed by Hirschman (1949) and, especially, Díaz-Alejandro (1963). Krugman and Taylor lucidly summarized and extended that strand of research in a well-known paper (1978). All these contributions point out various channels (distributional effects, the effects of initial fiscal or current account deficits, and real balance effects) through which contractionary influences on aggregate *demand* may reverse the ex-

Sweder van Wijnbergen is a senior economist in the Country Policy Department of the World Bank and a research fellow of the Centre for Economic Policy Research in London.

This paper was written while I was a visitor at Development Economics Research Center, University of Warwick, which provided a congenial environment and financial support. I am indebted to Ed Buffie and Lance Taylor for helpful comments. This paper does not necessarily reflect the views of the institutions with which I am affiliated.

pansionary effects of the expenditure switching a devaluation is intended to achieve.

In this paper I first outline several mechanisms, substantially more likely to be of importance in less developed countries (LDCs) than elsewhere, through which a devaluation has a direct negative impact on *aggregate supply*. I then discuss the influence of a large foreign debt (obviously predominantly an LDC problem), first on the effects of discrete devaluation on output and then on the results to be expected from an anti-inflation policy used exclusively in LDCs—the exchange rate regime of a preannounced crawling peg.

I do not address floating exchange rates because financial institutions in most LDCs are insufficiently developed to make that a viable policy option. Nor do I discuss the interesting question of which "basket" to peg a country's exchange rate to if that country has decided on some sort of a fixed rate; this question has already been addressed in the existing literature (see, for example, Branson and Katseli 1980).

Section 1.2 presents a stylized model of a financial structure typical of many LDCs, one characterized by the absence of markets for primary securities (such as government bonds and equity), but flourishing curb markets. Bank credit and loans taken out on the curb market are used to finance firms' working capital, not consumer expenditure. This model provides a direct link between the financial system and the aggregate supply side of the economy that will play an important role at various stages of the analysis that follows.[1] Section 1.3 then employs variants of this model to illustrate several negative effects of a devaluation on aggregate supply. I discuss, in turn, the role of intermediate imports, real wage indexation based on imported wage goods (namely, food), and the link between the real volume of bank credit and aggregate commodity supply forged by the financing of working capital requirements. All three of these factors are shown to create working capital requirements. All three of these factors are shown to create a channel through which a nominal devaluation has a direct contractionary effect on aggregate supply, as opposed to the Díaz-Alejandro and the Krugman and Taylor contractionary effects on aggregate demand. This paper should therefore be seen as a complement to the work of those authors.[2] It should be noted that a fall in output induced by a backward shift in the aggregate supply schedule will be accompanied by upward pressure on inflation, contrary to a demand-induced contraction à la Díaz-Alejandro and Krugman and Taylor. It will therefore jeopardize the real depreciation a nominal devaluation is intended to achieve, also contrary to a demand-induced contraction.

Section 1.4 introduces private foreign borrowing and illustrates the consequences of the resulting foreign debt on the effects of a discrete devaluation and on the effects of a preannounced crawling-peg regime. Finally, section 1.5 provides a summary and conclusions.

1.2 The Basic Model

The model presented below is similar, though not identical, to the one used in van Wijnbergen (1983a); I will therefore describe it only briefly here. The reader interested in more detail than is provided here should consult that paper.

The model presented here incorporates several stylized character-istics of the financial structure of many LDCs. I assume the absence of markets for government bonds or equity. Intermediation between firms and private wealth holders takes place in the official banking system and in the unofficial money market (UMM), or curb market. Thus, firms finance fixed and working capital requirements by bank loans, by loans taken out at the UMM, or by retained earnings. Since firm owners can (and do) lend on the UMM, the opportunity cost of using retained earnings is the UMM rate. In fact, the use of retained earnings is modeled here as a loan from the owners of the firm to the firm and is lumped together with UMM loans.

Commercial banks are assumed not to hold free reserves. Reserve requirements and credit ceilings are thus mutually dependent instru-ments. The model assumes the use of credit ceilings. For simplicity, their sources of funds consist of demand deposits only. Although a more sophisticated liability structure can easily be constructed, it would add unneccessary detail to the model.

The private sector allocates its wealth, W (equal to the real value of the monetary base, MR, plus the capital stock) over loans made to firms through the UMM, deposits in banks, and cash. The model further assumes a fixed deposit rate and a fixed cash-bank deposit ration in private portfolios.

If a Tobin-type asset model is defined to govern the allocation of wealth or the UMM and other financial assets, a private supply of loans on the UMM, B_p, is created, such that:

$$(1) \qquad\qquad B_p = [1 - m(i, y)]W,$$

where B_p and W are real variables expressed in terms of domestic goods (nominal quantities are deflated by the price of domestic goods, p); and y is the real output of domestic goods. Since the private sector does not directly hold foreign assets, foreign interest rates and the expected rate of depreciation, θ, do not appear in equation (1).

Firms demand loans for working capital, D, to finance the variable costs of wages and payments for intermediate imports, namely, oil, for the sake of brevity. D depends positively on the real product wage (in terms of domestic goods), w; on the real price of imported oil, $p_O = \dfrac{ep_O^*}{p}$, where p_O^* is the "dollar price" of oil and e the exchange rate ("pesos per dollar"); and on domestic output, y, such that :

(2) $\qquad\qquad D = D(w, p_O, y), \qquad D_w, D_{pO}, D_y > 0.$

Firms will, of course, first try to satisfy their need for funds from official banks, since lending rates are invariably far below UMM rates, with loan quantities rationed as a consequence. Firms' net demand for loans at the curb market is therefore $D + K - B_b$, where K is the real value of the capital stock and B_b is the real volume of bank credit (deflated by p). This leads to an equilibrium condition for the UMM:

(3) $\qquad\qquad D\,(w, P_O, y) + K = B_b + [1 - m(i, y)]\,W.$

In what follows, K is suppressed for notational convenience; I will discuss only short-run phenomena, and so will ignore changes in the capital stock. By manipulating various budget constraints, it is straightforward to show that equation (3) also implies money market equilibrium. Equation (3) can be represented in $i - y$ space, or the asset market equilibrium locus, AM, in figure 1.1.

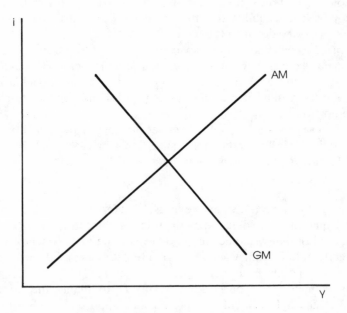

Fig. 1.1　　　　　Asset and goods market loci.

Along *AM*, equation (4) (presented below) holds that:

$$\frac{di}{dy} = \frac{(D_y + m_y W)}{m_i} > 0.$$

Because *AM* slopes upward ($m_i < 0!$); higher income, y, will increase private money demand, ($m_y > 0$), and therefore reduce the private supply of loans at the UMM; and at the same time, the demand for loans to finance working capital rises ($D_y > 0$). The resulting excess demand for funds necessitates an increase in the UMM rate, so that *AM* slopes upward.

Consider now the real part of the model. Production technology is assumed to be Cobb-Douglas in capital, on the one hand, and labor and energy, on the other. This allows us to write variable costs (which need to be financed by working capital) as:

$$D = g(w, P_O)\, y^a K^{(a-1)},$$

where $a = 1/(1 - \alpha)$, where α is a Cobb-Douglas share parameter. Total variable costs and inclusive costs of credit are accordingly $LC = D\,(1 + i - \hat{p})$. Firms maximize profits, $p(y - LC)$, which leads to an aggregate supply function:

(4) $$1 = ay^{a-1}\, g(w, p_O)\,(1 + i - \hat{p}),$$

where terms involving K are suppressed.

Aggregate demand for domestic goods, A_d, consists of foreign demand, $E(q)$, with $q = p/(ep^*)$; the relative price of domestic final goods in terms of foreign final goods and domestic consumption demand for domestic goods, $C_d\,(q,\, i - \hat{p},\, y - p_O O - \hat{p}MR,\, W)$; investment, $I(i - \hat{p},\, w,\, p_O)$; and government expenditure, G, such that:

$$A_d = C_d + I + E + G.$$

Disposable income equals output minus oil imports, $p_O O$, minus capital losses on nominal assets, $\hat{p}MR$ (equal to $\hat{p}MR$ rather than $C\hat{P}I.MR$ because income and MR are expressed in terms of domestic goods).

Finally, the price *level* is assumed to be sticky, and relative prices to change only gradually over time. The *inflation rate*, however, can change instantaneously in response to anticipated foreign inflation; $\hat{p}^*$; to the expected rate of devaluation, θ; or to excess demand for domestic goods, such that:

$$\hat{p} = \theta + \hat{p}^* + \lambda\,(A_d - y).$$

A microeconomic rationale for equations like (5) is presented in Barro (1972) and Sheshinsky and Weiss (1977). Gradual price adjustment implies the possibility of disequilibrium in the goods market. I will assume throughout that the country in question is under a regime of *classical* unemployment (that is, we start out in a position where $\hat{p} > \theta + \hat{p}^*$). This implies that output will be determined by supply. I make this assumption because most of the discussion to follow focuses on aggregate supply effects, which lose much of their relevance under a Keynesian regime. At any rate, the case of Keynesian unemployment has been more than adequately treated in Krugman and Taylor (1978).

The assumption of classical unemployment implies that output will be determined by the aggregate supply function in equation (4). Substituting $\hat{p}$ from equation (5) in equation (4) yields a goods market locus of GM in figure 1.1, such that:

$$\frac{di}{dy}\Big|_{GM} = -\frac{\lambda (1 - C_{dy}) + [1 + \lambda(C_{dy}MR + I_1)]\dfrac{(a - 1)}{y}(1 + i - \hat{p})}{l + \lambda C_{dy} MR}.$$

The denominator is always positive. The numerator will also be positive if $1 + \lambda (C_{dy}MR + I_1) > 0$, but this is not necessarily so, since $I_1 < 0$. The term plays a crucial role in the stability analysis of Keynes-Wicksell growth models, which have similar price dynamics (see Fischer 1972). If the term is positive, those models will have stable dynamics. An intuitive interpretation of the term is given and discussed in Fischer (1972) and in van Wijnbergen (1983a); I follow these two papers in assuming the term is positive. That assumption implies that $\dfrac{di}{dy}\Big|_{GM} < 0$, since there is a minus sign in front of the whole expression; GM slopes downward in figure 1.1. The reason for this is simple: higher production, y, will, other things equal, lead to a lower $\hat{p}$ in equation (5) because it leads to excess supply. Unless the interest rate, i, falls, the real rate will go up, which, from equation (4), can be seen to be incompatible with a higher y. In other words, higher output will, all else equal, lead to less inflation. Since the aggregate supply schedule tells us that the real interest rate $i - \hat{p}$ will have to fall before firms will increase output, given other factor costs, it follows that nominal rates of i will have to fall even lower than inflation, $\hat{p}$, or GM slopes downward.

1.3   The Contractionary Effects of a Discrete Devaluation on Aggregate Supply

In this section I will discuss three channels through which a devaluation exerts a contractionary effect on aggregate supply, namely, intermediate imports, real wage indexation based on a commodity bundle including foreign goods, and the real volume of bank credit available to the business sector. For the sake of clarity, I will address each channel in turn using slight variants of the model. In reality, of course, all three mechanisms work simultaneously in the economies of the countries in question.

1.3.1   Intermediate Imports

Let us consider the short-run impact of a devaluation within the context of the model outlined in the previous section. To simplify the analysis, assume that nominal wages are indexed on the price of domestic goods. This assumption will allow us to defer discussion of the role of wage indexation to the next subsection, where we will examine proper indexation on the consumer price index (CPI).

Under that assumption a devaluation will disturb two variables. The relative price of domestic goods in terms of foreign goods, q, will fall (and competitiveness increase); and the real price of oil in terms of domestic goods will rise, such that:

(6)
$$\frac{dp_O}{de} = \frac{p_O^*}{p} > 0, \text{ and } \frac{dq}{de} = -\frac{q}{e} < 0.$$

The effects of these disturbances can be seen in figure 1.2. The AM curve is not affected by q but does shift because of the devaluation-induced increase in p_O: higher oil prices raise variable costs and therefore working capital requirements. This will, for given output levels, lead to more demand on the UMM and thus to higher interest rates, and the AM curve shifts upward (as shown in the figure), such that:

(7)
$$\left. \frac{di}{dp_O} \right|_{\substack{AM \\ y=\bar{y}}} = \frac{-D_{p_O}}{m_i W} > 0.$$

The effects on the GM curve are more complicated. Consider first the effect of the change in p_O, the "structuralist" channel. Higher oil prices will directly reduce aggregate supply because they constitute an increase in the price of a factor of production. Added to that are deflationary effects on demand brought about by reduced investment and consumer spending, such that:

(8)
$$\left. \frac{di}{dp_O} \right|_{\substack{GM \\ y=\bar{y}}}$$

$$= \frac{\lambda \left[I_O - Cd_y (1 - \epsilon_{p_O}^O) 0 \right] - [1 + \lambda(Cd_y MR + I_1)] \psi_O (1 + i - \hat{p}) / p_O}{1 + \lambda Cd_y MR} < 0,$$

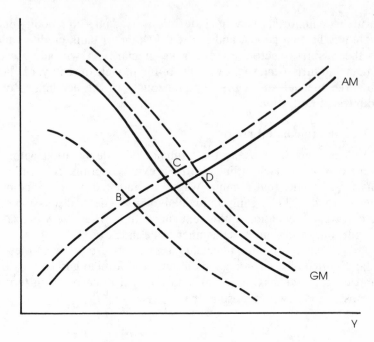

Fig. 1.2   The effects of devaluation through its impact on p_o and q.

where ψ_O is the share of intermediate imports in variable costs. We made the plausible assumption that the short-run price elasticity of energy demand is less than one $(1 - \epsilon^o_{p_O} > 0)$. Accordingly, the *GM* curve shifts downward, leading to a new short-run equilibrium at point *B*. At *B*, output has fallen but the curb market rate could go up or down (in figure 1.2 it falls); higher working capital requirements push *i* up but lower income pulls it down. The contractionary effect on output is unambiguous, however.

Of course, this is not the end of the story. There is still the standard expenditure-switching effect via $dq/de < 0$. A lower q switches world demand to the domestic goods, which in turn shifts the *GM* curve back up, such that:

$$(9) \qquad \left. \frac{di}{dq} \right|_{\substack{GM \\ y = \bar{y}}} = \frac{\lambda A d_q}{1 + \lambda\, C d_y\, MR} < 0.$$

This corresponds to an upward shift after a devaluation, since $dq/de = -q/e < 0$ as well.

Accordingly, we arrive at a point such as *C* in figure 1.2, with higher output and interest rates than would have resulted without the expenditure-switching effect. Without intermediate imports, *AM* would have stayed put and *GM* would have shifted upward because of expenditure switching, and an equilibrium such as point *D* in the figure would have resulted. It is straightforward to show that $y_C < y_D$:

(10)
$$\frac{dy}{de} = \frac{dy}{dq} \cdot \frac{dq}{de} + \frac{dy}{dp_o} \cdot \frac{dp_o}{de} \cdot$$

$$(\text{I; } +) \qquad (\text{II; } -)$$

Point *D* corresponds to the first term in equation (10), the positive expenditure switching effect. Point *C* results from adding the structuralist effect via intermediate inputs (term II in equation [10], which is always contractionary. Thus, $y_C < y_D$.

In summary, if the prices of final goods adjust only gradually (that is, they cannot ''jump''), a devaluation raises the real price of imported inputs in terms of domestic final goods. This result adds a contractionary element to a devaluation. Because intermediate goods typically make up the bulk of most LDC imports (50 to 60 percent is not an unreasonable estimate), the contractionary effect is likely to be more important in LDCs than in developed countries, the bulk of whose imports are typically consumer goods.

1.3.2 Real Wage Indexation

The second contractionary channel, real wage indexation, is in some sense a counterpart of the increase in competitiveness a successful devalation also needs to achieve. Consider again the basic model of section 1.2, with two changes. For a clearer focus I will ignore intermediate imports from now on; they have already been discussed in the previous section. The second change is the assumption of real wage indexation on the CPI, enforced by formal contracts, implicit arrangements, or social pressure. This change introduces a negative relationship between the real domestic product wage, *w*, and the terms of trade, *q*, such that:

(11)
$$w = q^{-\gamma},$$

where γ equals the share of foreign imports (food) in wage earners' consumption basket.

Furthermore, under the classical unemployment assumption of the model, real product-wage increases reduce output through two different channels. First, a higher *w* increases the demand for working capital (some of which is needed to finance wage payments), which in turn results in an upward shift of the *AM* curve, such that:

$$\left. \frac{d\bar{i}}{dw} \right|_{\substack{AM \\ y=\bar{y}}} = \frac{-D_w}{m_i W} > 0.$$

Second, a higher w also raises labor costs and therefore reduces aggregate supply, and the *GM* curve shifts to the left, such that:

$$\frac{dy}{dw}\bigg|_{\substack{GM \\ i=\bar{i}}} = \frac{\lambda I_w - [l + \lambda(Cd_y\, MR + I_1)]\, \psi_L\, (1 + i - \dot{p})/w}{\lambda\,(1 - Cd_y) + [1 + \lambda(Cd_y\, MR + I_1)]} < 0,$$

where ψ_L is the labor share in variable costs. The net result can be seen in figure 1.3: output will fall unambiguously. This, combined with the negative link between the terms of trade, q, and w because of indexation, is what causes problems after a devaluation that succeeds in lowering q (increasing competitiveness). Higher competitiveness implies that foreign goods are more expensive in terms of domestic goods. This is compatible with an unchanged real consumption wage only if real domestic product wages rise, which adds an aggregate supply shock effect to a devaluation, such that:

(12)
$$\frac{dy}{de} = \frac{\partial y}{\partial q} \cdot \frac{\partial q}{\partial e} + \frac{\partial y}{\partial w} \cdot \frac{\partial w}{\partial q} \cdot \frac{\partial q}{\partial e}.$$

$$\underset{(-)}{} \quad \underset{(-)}{} \quad \underset{(-)}{} \quad \underset{(-)}{} \quad \underset{(-)}{}$$

Expenditure
Switching   Effect via
Effect   Wage Indexing

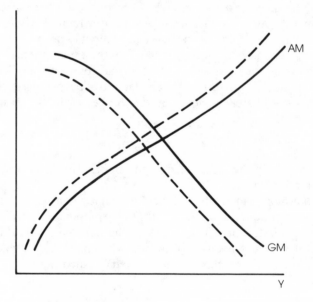

Fig. 1.3   The effects of an increase in w.

1.3.3   The Real Volume of Bank Credit

The final contractionary influence on aggregate supply is the real volume of bank credit, which is an important determinant of aggregate supply because of working capital requirements. Of course, given the sticky price-level assumptions made so far, this influence will come into play only gradually. Rather than engage in a full-fledged dynamic analysis,[3] I once again will slightly modify the model to eliminate the contractionary effects already discussed and focus on the contractionary effects of a decrease in the real volume of bank credit.

In particular, I will assume that through indexing arrangements the devaluation is passed on one-for-one in domestic prices and wages, thereby leaving q and w unaffected. This leads to a discrete change in p, of a proportion equal to the percentage increase in e. That in turn implies a reduction in B_p and MR, the real volume of bank credit and the monetary base. The contractionary effects of a lower real monetary base are, of course, well known and will, through standard monetary channels, be counteracted over time by a current account surplus.

Let us now consider the effects of a devaluation-induced reduction in the real volume of bank credit. There is no *direct* effect on the *GM* curve, since the real interest rate is the link between the financial system and the real part of the model, as shown in figure 1.4. The AM curve, however, is affected. A lower B_P means less bank credit for firms, which are therefore forced to rely more on the curb market for funds. This causes an incipient excess demand. To return to financial sector equilibrium, the interest rate on the curb market will have to rise, and the *AM* curve shifts up (as shown in the figure), such that:

$$(13) \qquad \left. \frac{di}{dB_p} \right|_{\substack{AM \\ y=\bar{y}}} = \frac{1}{m_i W} < 0.$$

Since we are discussing a decline in B_p, equation (13) implies an upward shift in AM.

The net effect of $dB_p/de < 0$ on output y is negative, as can be seen in figure 1.4. The cut in B_p pushes up the interest rate for a given rate of inflation, which raises the real rate that will reduce not only aggregate demand through traditional mechanisms, but also aggregate supply through the resulting higher cost of working capital. Whether inflation accelerates or declines depends on whether the aggregate supply effect via the costs of working capital dominates the additional effects reducing aggregate demand, such that:

$$(14) \qquad \frac{d\hat{p}}{dB_b} = \frac{I_1(a-1)(1+i-\hat{p})/y - \lambda(1-Cd_y)}{\Delta} \lessgtr 0.$$

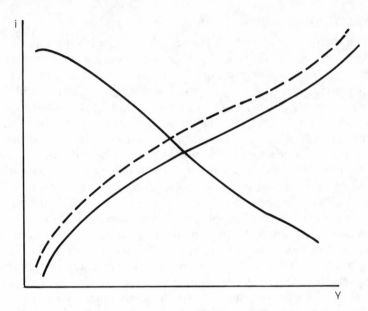

Fig. 1.4   The effects of a devaluation-induced reduction in the real volume of bank credit, B_p.

If $\hat{p}$ rises it will do so less than i does, however, so that the real rate $i - \hat{p}$ increases and, from the aggregate supply equation (4), y falls. For a more extensive discussion of the effects of changes in bank credit on inflation and output, see van Wijnbergen (1983a).

Empirical evidence for Argentina (Cavallo 1977) and South Korea (van Wijnbergen 1982) strongly supports the initial (say, two-quarters) dominance of the aggregate supply effect on inflation. That raises the intriguing possibility that inflation might accelerate on top of the one-for-one pass-through of the devaluation in the price level already incorporated, leading to the possibility of at least an initial, gradual, real appreciation after a nominal devaluation! Of course, standard deflationary effects on aggregate demand caused by a lower real monetary base will make this less likely to happen. Whether it will or not is an empirical issue, but the theoretical possibility is there in a stable model without money illusion.

1.4 Foreign Debt, Devaluation, and the Crawling Peg

In this section I will discuss another issue complicating exchange rate policy: the existence of a substantial foreign debt, bringing with it a debt service burden. This issue is substantially more important in LDCs (not counting most of the oil-exporting nations, of course) than it is in developed countries. To examine foreign borrowing, I first modify the simplest version of the model, that in section 1.2, by removing intermediate imports. I also make the no-immediate-pass-through assumption used in sections 1.3.1 and 1.3.2. Given this modified model I will then briefly discuss the effect of foreign debt on the impact of a devaluation. Finally, I will describe the consequences of foreign debt on an interesting policy experiment recently tried, without much success, in several Latin American countries: an attempt to curb inflation by a preannounced slowdown in the rate of depreciation of the exchange rate.

1.4.1 Foreign Debt Introduced

The bulk of private foreign debt in LDCs consists of the liabilities of commercial firms. That debt is moreover almost exclusively Eurodollar debt, since Western bond markets are by and large closed to LDCs. Thus, contrary to most previous research, I will not model capital mobility as foreign investors buying domestic bonds, or vice versa; this is not the way capital flows in and out of LDCs. Instead, I will assume that foreign borrowing is done by firms. Exchange risk is always borne by the borrower, and the borrower pays the foreign interest rate, i^*. The cost of a foreign loan is, accordingly, $i^* + \theta$, with θ the expected (and actual, in this perfect-foresight model) rate of devaluation. Substitution between foreign and domestic sources of funds is assumed to be imperfect: the larger the interest differential, $i - i^* - \theta$, the higher the (stock) demand for foreign loans by firms, B_f ($= e B_f^*/p$), where B_f^* is the dollar value of the debt, or:

$$B_f = e B_f^* (i - i^* - \theta)/p, \; B_f^{*\prime} > 0.$$

Dependence on y is easily introduced but adds only uninformative algebra. I will use $B_f^\prime$ for $e B_f^{*\prime}/p$ throughout, for notational convenience.

Introducing foreign borrowing as a third source of funds for firms modifies the financial sector equilibrium condition, equation (3), which now becomes:

(16) $D(w, y) + K = (1 - m(i, y)) W + B_p + B_f^*(i - i^* - \theta)e/p.$

Note that firms may take out foreign loans, but private wealth holders still do not hold foreign assets. The terms i^* and θ therefore do not appear as arguments of $m(\;)$. This assumption about portfolio structure is realistic for all but a few LDCs. Furthermore, MR is redefined to be equal to the real value of the monetary base minus private foreign debt: $MR = MB/P - B_f$. Since capital inflows cannot be sterilized (by assumption), MR in the new definition is fixed at any given time, since increases in B_f lead to one-for-one increases in M/B.

The only change needed in the real part of the model is in the definition of disposable income (an argument of c_d, domestic consumer demand for home goods). Disposable income now incorporates not only capital losses, $\hat{p}MR$, but also interest payments abroad and anticipated capital losses on foreign debt due to depreciation, such that:

$$(17) \qquad y_d = y - \hat{p}MR - (i^* + \theta)B_f.$$

The diagrammatic apparatus of figure 1.1 remain intact, although the algebraic expressions for slopes and shifts change somewhat (see the appendix).

1.4.2   Foreign Debt and Devaluation

A discrete devaluation in the presence of foreign debt raises a technical problem in the continuous time-instantaneous loans framework used here. Of course, $de > 0$ does not increase the amount of liquidity provided by existing debt; but the exchange rate at which the debt was contracted, say, e^-, is relevant where e^- is the old rate prevailing just before the devaluation. Accordingly, the AM curve is not affected, as shown in figure 1.5.

$$(18) \qquad \left.\frac{di}{de}\right|_{\substack{GM \\ y=\bar{y}}} = -\lambda Cd_y(i^* + \theta - \hat{p})B_f^*/p + \lambda Ad_q \cdot \frac{dq}{de}$$

$$\text{(I; } -) \qquad\qquad \text{(II; } +)$$

The first term, I, gives the contractionary effect of the debt service burden and is negative;[4] this is the shift indicated in figure 1.5. The second term, II, represents the standard expenditure-switching effect via the terms of trade, which was discussed in section 1.3.1.

The net effect on output is ambiguous, of course, since the expenditure-switching effect is expansionary, but the debt service effect adds a contractionary channel:

$$\frac{dy}{de} = (mB_f^{*\prime}/e - m_iMR)\,(-\lambda A_{dq}q/e + \lambda C_{dy}(i^* + \theta)B_f^*/p).$$

$$\text{(X; } +) \qquad\qquad \text{(Y; } -)$$

Because it operates on aggregate demand, this contractionary channel is more in the Krugman and Taylor vein than the three channels analyzed in section 1.3.

1.4.3   Inflation, Output, and the Crawling Peg

In the late 1970s several Latin American countries tried out an innovative policy to bring down inflation: a preannounced slowdown in the rate of devaluing the nominal exchange rate. (For an interesting

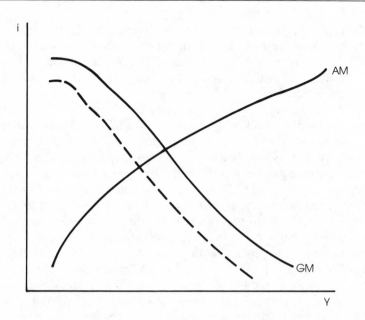

Fig. 1.5   The effects of a devaluation-induced increase in the debt
                    service burden.

discussion of the overall results, see Díaz-Alejandro 1981.) One of the
more puzzling outgrowths of these experiments was the huge real appreciation (around 40 percent in one year in Argentina, for example)
that resulted from the persistence of domestic inflation at a rate far
above foreign inflation plus the rate of crawl. In fact, domestic inflation
in Argentina actually accelerated in the first few months after its new
policy went into effect.

There is now an extensive literature on this subject (see, for example,
Calvo 1981; Obstfeld 1984; or Taylor 1981). The stories are essentially
similar: the slowdown in the rate of crawl causes an incipient excess
demand for domestic assets, which in turn causes an initial real appreciation that will disappear gradually as balance-of-payments surpluses augment the domestic money stock. The Argentine puzzle remains, however. Why was there an initial acceleration of the inflation
rate, rather than less than one-for-one slowdown that would also cause
a real appreciation? The following discussion will show that the existence of a large foreign debt may be the clue to solving the puzzle,
since a lower rate of crawl reduces the debt service burden for any
given volume of debt and so provides an expansionary stimulus.

Consider, then, what an announced (and, a nontrivial restriction,
believed) slowdown of the rate of devaluation, θ, does in the context
of the model presented above. As a hypothetical experiment, assume

that things would go as they were expected to go, that is, that inflation and the rate of interest would fall one-for-one with the slowdown in θ. Would this be a sustainable equilibrium, with an unchanged real interest rate and inflation down to the new value of $\hat{p}^* + \theta$? As we will see, this clearly would not.

Regarding the asset markets, the experiment would leave the interest differential, $i - i^* - \theta$, unchanged, so that B_f would remain unchanged. But at the lower interest rate, money velocity would fall; the private sector would increase its demand for domestic money; and therefore, as a consequence of the wealth constraint, the private sector would cut back on its supply of funds on the unregulated market. As a result, the interest rate would go back up, widening the gap $i - i^* - \theta$, making it more attractive for firms to borrow abroad, and thus leading to an inflow of foreign capital. The incipient excess demand for money would therefore be met partly by higher domestic interest rates (which reduce money demand) and partly by an inflow of foreign capital, which increases the money supply (if at least the inflow is not sterilized, a realistic assumption in LDCs). The net effect is that the AM curve will shift down after a reduction in θ, but less than one-for-one, such that:

$$(20) \qquad \left. \frac{di}{d\theta} \right|_{\substack{AM \\ y=\bar{y}}} = 1 - \frac{m_i MR}{m_i \, MR - mB_f'} = \epsilon, \, 0 < \epsilon < 1.$$

Note that we are reducing θ, and so a positive sign on expression (20) corresponds to a downward shift of the AM curve, as shown in figure 1.6. This part of the story is essentially similar to the analyses performed in Calvo (1981), Obstfeld (1981; 1984), Taylor (1983), and other papers in this volume.

But consider now what happens in the real part of the model. If our hypothetical experiment is followed again, i and $\hat{p}$ would decrease one-for-one with θ, and $i - \hat{p}$ would remain unchanged, as would real output. This case corresponds to a downward shift of GM one-for-one with the reduction in θ (note that i is on the vertical axis, so that dimensions are commensurate). At a lower inflation rate and rate of crawl, however, capital losses on the monetary base, MR, and the debt service burden, $(i^* + \theta) B_f$, would have decreased, which, other things equal, implies an increase in disposable income. That increase would put upward pressure on aggregate demand and shift the GM curve back up, so that this curve too would shift down less than one-for-one with θ. It is even possible that the GM curve would shift up rather than down, such that:

$$\left. \frac{di}{d\theta} \right|_{\substack{GM \\ y=\bar{y}}} = 1 - \frac{\lambda C_{dy} \, MR}{h} - \frac{\lambda C_{dy} \, B_f}{h},$$

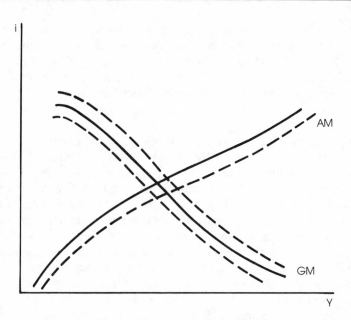

Fig. 1.6   The effects of a reduction in the rate of crawl, $d\theta < 0$, where both curves shift down less than $d\theta$.

where $h = 1 + \lambda(C_{dy}[MR + (i^* + \theta)B_f'] + C_{dw} B_f') > 0$. The second term is less than one, so $1 - \lambda C_{dy}MR/h > 0$; but if B_f is large enough the whole expression could turn negative, leading to an upward rather than a downward shift (keep in mind we are discussing a *reduction* in θ).

The appendix shows that what figure 1.6 suggests is indeed the case: interest rates will fall, but less than one-for-one with θ, leading to an increase in $i - i^* - \theta$ and a capital inflow. The most interesting results, however, are those for the inflation response. There are two reasons why, if it falls, it will fall less than one-for-one with θ, causing a real appreciation to develop over time.

First, consider what would happen if the inflation response fell one-for-one. Since, as we have seen, i will not fall all the way, the real rate, $i - \hat{p}$, would rise. This increase would lead to higher costs of working capital and therefore to a cut in aggregate supply, which in turn would push the inflation rate up. (The higher real rate would also cut demand. There is strong empirical evidence, however, that working capital effects on the supply side dominate in the short run. See Cavallo 1977; van Wijnbergen 1982.)

The second reason why inflation will not decrease one-for-one is the increase in disposable income due to the lower debt service on foreign debt, $(i^* + \theta) B_f$, triggered by the reduction in θ. In fact, if the foreign debt is large enough, the reduction in debt service may become so large, and the resulting demand expansion so big, that inflation will accelerate after the slowdown in θ. The debt service element is what distinguishes this discussion from the existing literature on the crawling peg, in which such an acceleration of inflation cannot occur.

1.5   Conclusions

This paper examined a variety of problems complicating exchange rate management and, especially, the use of the exchange rate as an instrument of stabilization policy in less developed countries. The first part of the paper outlined three channels through which a devaluation has a direct contractionary impact on the aggregate supply side of the economy: the domestic currency costs of intermediate imports; wage indexing (in the form of explicit contracts, implicit arrangements, or social pressure) with foreign goods present in wage earners' consumption bundles (namely, food imports); and a reduced volume of real credit to firms. The last channel has its impact on the supply side of the economy because firms in need of funds to finance working capital are pushed into the curb market if bank credit is reduced; as a result, interest rates increase and the aggregate supply curve shifts back. This last contractionary effect is obviously exacerbated if the devaluation is accompanied by a cut in the nominal volume of bank credit, as is often the case.

There is by now an extensive literature on contractionary devaluation, aptly summarized and extended by Krugman and Taylor (1978). They, as do most authors, focus on contractionary effects on aggregate demand (and, via Keynesian multiplier effects, only indirectly on aggregate supply). Both types of effects—the Krugman-Taylor demand contractions and the backward shifts in the aggregate supply curve described here—are deplorable, of course, since no country wants to incur unnecessarily the social costs of lost output and employment. Nonetheless, the contractionary effects of a devaluation on the supply side are more damaging than those on aggregate demand because a cut in aggregate supply leads to upward pressure on inflation, while a cut in aggregate demand tends to lower inflation. Over time, upward pressure on inflation may threaten the increase in competitiveness a nominal devaluation is usually also intended to achieve.

The second part of the paper discussed a second issue complicating exchange rate management in LDCs: the presence of a substantial foreign debt. It was demonstrated that if a devaluation succeeds in increasing competitiveness, it will also temporarily raise the real (in terms of domestic goods) burden of servicing that foreign debt, causing a Krugman-Taylor-like contractionary effect on aggregate demand.

The paper then proceeded to analyze the effects of a preannounced slowdown of the rate of depreciation. The analysis supported the evidence in previous work that interest rates and inflation will fall less than one-for-one with a slowdown in the rate of crawl, if at all, so that a real appreciation will emerge. The new point in this analysis is the demonstration that the existence of a substantial foreign debt (leading to a substantial decline in capital losses on foreign debt if the rate of devaluation falls) may lead to such an expansionary effect on aggregate demand that inflation actually accelerates in the early phases of the program. This is more than a theoretical cunosum; it is exactly what happened in the first few months after Argentina experimented with a slowdown in the rate of devaluation.

All of this does not imply that a devaluation should never be considered. It does suggest, however, that a devaluation is likely to be an ineffective tool for demand management because it may cut aggregate supply to an equal if not greater extent in the short run. Another conclusion suggested by the analysis is that if a devaluation is used to increase competitiveness by changing relative prices (to speed up adjustment to more fundamental reforms), special attention should be paid to compensate for the negative effects on aggregated supply, since these, contrary to the negative effects on aggregate demand, will exacerbate inflationary pressures that could well threaten any real depreciation that nominal devaluation might achieve initially.

Appendix

1. The model of section 1.2, without foreign borrowing in differentiated form, is as follows. If equation (4) is used to substitute out $\hat{p}$

$$\left[d\hat{p} = di + (a - 1)(1 + i - \hat{p})\frac{dy}{y} \right],$$ differentiation of the resulting

expressions gives:

$$
(2) \quad \begin{pmatrix} D_y + m_y\,MR & m_i\,MR \\ \\ (4,5) \quad \lambda(1 - C_{dy}) & 1 + C_{dy}MR \\ + (a - 1)(1 + i - \hat{p}) \\ [1 + \lambda(C_{dy}MR + I_1)] \end{pmatrix} \begin{pmatrix} dy \\ di \end{pmatrix} = \text{A.1}
$$

$$
\text{A.1} = \begin{pmatrix} [-D_o\,dp_o - D_w\,dw + (1 - m)dMR + dB_f] \\ \{[\lambda(I_O - C_{dy}\,(1 - \epsilon_{po}^O)\,O] \\ - \psi_o\,[1 + \lambda(C_{dy}MR + I_1)\,(1 + i - \hat{p})/p_o]dp_O \\ + (\lambda\,I_w - (1 + \lambda(C_{dy}MR + I_1))\,\psi_L\,(1 + i - \hat{p})\,dw \\ + \lambda A_{dq}\,dq + \lambda(C_{dw} - \hat{p}\,C_{dy})\,dMR\} \end{pmatrix}
$$

The expression Δ in equation (14) is the Jacobian of the system A.1:

$$\Delta = (D_y + m_y\,MR)(1 + \lambda\,C_{dy}MR) - m_i\,W(\lambda(1 - C_{dy})$$
$$+ (1 + \lambda(C_{dy}MR + I_1))\,[(a - 1)/y](1 + i - \hat{p}).$$

2. The model of section 1.2, without intermediate imports but with foreign borrowing, (as outlined in section 1.4) is as follows.

$$\begin{pmatrix} \begin{array}{ll} D_y + m_y\,MR & m_i\,MR - mB'_f \\ \lambda(1 - C_{dy}) & 1 + \lambda(C_{dy}\,(MR + (i^* + \theta)B'_f) \\ + (a - 1)(1 + i - \hat{p}) & + C_{dw}B'_f \\ (1 + \lambda(C_{dy}MR + I_1)) & \end{array} \end{pmatrix} \begin{pmatrix} dy \\ di \end{pmatrix}$$

$$= \left[\begin{array}{c} - mB'_f d\theta \\ (1 + \lambda\,C_{dy}(i^* + \theta)\,B_f + \lambda C_{dw}\,B_f \\ - \lambda C_{dy}B_f)d\theta \end{array} \right] \text{A.2}$$

The Jacobian of A.2, Δ_1, equals:

$$\Delta_1 = (D_y + m_y MR)(1 + \lambda C_{dy}(MR + (i^* + \theta)B'_f - (m_i\,MR - mB'_f)$$
$$\{\lambda(1 - C_{dy}) + (a - 1)\,(1 + i - \hat{p})[1 + \lambda(C_{dy}MR + I)]\} > 0.$$

After some algebra is performed, the assertions in the text can easily be seen to be true:

$$\frac{di}{d\theta} - 1 = (-(D_y + m_y MR)\,\lambda C_{dy}(B_f + MR) + m_i MR(\lambda(1 - C_{dy})$$
$$+ (a - 1)(1 + i - \hat{p})(1 + \lambda(C_y MR + I_1))))/\Delta_1 < 0.$$

$$\frac{d\hat{p}}{d\theta} - 1 = (m_i\,MR(\lambda(1 - C_{dy}) + (a - 1)(1 + i - \hat{p})$$

$$(I_1 - \lambda C_{dy}(i^* + \theta)B'_f - \lambda C_{dw}B'_f)$$

(A)

$$- (D_y + m_y\,MR + mB'_f\,\frac{(a - 1)}{y}\,(1 + i - \hat{p}))\lambda C_{dy}$$

$$(MR + B_f)))/\Delta_1.$$

(B)

The term A corresponds to the first reason for $\dfrac{d\hat{p}}{d\theta} < 1$ given in the text and is indeed negative if the aggregate supply effects of real interests rates via the cost of working capital (the "Cavallo effect") dominate the aggregate demand effects of higher real rates.

The term B corresponds to the second reason discussed there. $\left(\dfrac{di}{d\theta} - 1\right), \left(\dfrac{d\hat{p}}{d\theta} - 1\right) < 0$ corresponds to the claim in the text that both interest rates and inflation will fall less than one-for-one with a reduction in θ (if at all).

Notes

1. This link has been discussed extensively in recent work on the stagflationary effects of restrictive monetary policy in LDCs (Cavallo 1977; Bruno 1979; van Wijnbergen1982, 1983a, 1983b; Taylor 1981; and Buffie 1984).

2. The first contractionary effect on aggregate supply (via intermediate imports) has been formalized before by van Wijnbergen (1980), Buffie (1983), Gylfason and Schmid (1984), and Gylfason and Risager (1984). The other two effects, although frequently brought up in policy-making circles in LDCs, have not yet found their way into the theoretical literature, as far as I know. Cardoso (1981) presented related work but did not derive the contractionary effects on aggregate supply presented here.

3. The dynamics of a similar model are analyzed, albeit in a different context, in van Wijnbergen (1983a; 1983b).

4. This is assuming the real rate on foreign loans ($i^* + \theta - \hat{p}$) is positive, which may fail to hold true during a strong real appreciation ($\hat{p} > \theta + \hat{p}^*$).

References

Barro, R. 1972. A theory of monopolistic price adjustment. *Review of Economic Studies* 39, no. 1, 17–26.

Branson, W., and Katseli, L. 1980. Income instability, terms of trade and the choice of exchange rate regime. *Journal of Development Economics* 7: 49–69.

Bruno, M. 1979. Stabilization and stagflation in a semi-industrialized economy. In R. Dornbush and J.A. Frenkel (eds) *International Economic Policy* (Baltimore: Johns Hopkins University Press).

Buffie, E. 1983. Devaluation and imported inputs. Philadelphia: University of Pennsylvania. Photocopy.

———. 1984. Financial repression, the new structuralists and stabilization policy in semi-industrialized economies. *Journal of Development Economics* 14: 305–22.

Calvo, G. 1981. Trying to stabilize. Paper presented at an NBER conference on Financial Policies and the World Capital Market: The Problems of Latin American Countries, Mexico City, 1981.

Cardoso, E. 1981. Food supply and inflation. *Journal of Development Economy*.

Cavallo, D. 1977. Stagflationary effects of monetarist stabilization policies. Ph.D. dissertation. Cambridge: Harvard University.

Díaz-Alejandro, C. 1963. A note on the impact of devaluation and distributive effects. *Journal of Political Economy* 71: 577–80.

———. 1981. Southern Cone stabilization plans. In *Economic stabilization in developing countries,* ed. W.R. Cline and S. Weintraub. Washington, D.C.: Brookings Institution.

Fischer, S. 1972. Keynes-Wicksell neoclassical models of growth. *American-Economic Review* 62, no. 5 (December): 80–90.

Gylfason, T., and Schmid, M. 1983. Does devaluation cause stagflation? *Canadian Journal of Economics* 16: 641–54.

Gylfason, T., and Risager, O. 1984. Does devaluation improve the current account? *European Economic Review* 25: 37–64.

Hirschman, A.O. 1949. Devaluation and the trade balance: A note. *Review of Economic and Statistics* 16: 50–53.

Krugman, P., and Taylor, L. 1978. Contractionary effects of devaluation. *Journal of Development Economics* 8: 445–56.

Obstfeld, M. 1981. Capital mobility and devaluation in an optimizing model with rational expectations. *American Economic Review* 71: 217–21.

———. 1984. The capital inflows problem revisited: A stylized model of Southern Cone disinflation. NBER Working Paper no. 1456. Cambridge, Mass.: National Bureau of Economic Research.

Sheshinsky, E., and Weiss, Y. 1977. Inflation and the costs of price adjustment. *Review of Economic Studies* 44, no. 2, 287–303.

Taylor, L. 1981. IS/LM in the tropics: Diagrammatics of the new structuralist macro critique. In *Economic stabilization in developing countries*, ed. W. R. Cline and S. Weintraub. Washington, D.C.: Brookings Institution.

van Wijnbergen, S. 1980. Oil price shocks and the current account: An analysis of short term adjustment measures. *Weltwirtschaftliches Archiv* 120: 460–80.

———. 1982. Stagflationary effects of monetary stabilization policies: A quantitative analysis of South Korea. *Journal of Development Economics* 10: 133–69.

———. 1983a. Credit policy, inflation and growth in financially repressed economies. *Journal of Development Economics* 13: 45–65.

———. 1983b. Interest rate management in LDCs. *Journal of Monetary Economies* 12: 433–52.

Comment   James A. Hanson

For some time the international finance literature has included arguments that devaluation may reduce aggregate demand and output, depending on the sizes of appropriately defined price elasticities of demand for exports and imports. Recently, a new strand of literature on contractionary devaluations has argued that devaluation reduces ag-

James A. Hanson is senior financial economist in the Industry Department of the World Bank.

gregate supply by increasing the cost of imported inputs, including inputs consumed by domestic factors of production. The output effect of a devaluation thus depends on the algebraic sum of the usual expenditure-switching and expenditure-reducing effects, plus any supply-reducing effects.

In addition to examining these supply-reducing effects, the model used in van Wijnbergen's paper permits discussion of the effects of devaluation on the financial side of the economy and their links to the real economy, through both the demand side and the supply side. In the model, devaluation cuts real wealth and the real supply of credit. As a result, output tends to decline because of both the traditional real balance effect (the demand side) and the higher real cost of credit (the supply side).

According to the paper, one implication of the negative effect of devaluation on aggregate supply is that prices may increase proportionately more than a devaluation. The recent Argentine and Korean devaluations are cited as evidence of this possibility, but here I would argue that some care is needed in the interpretation. In many cases devaluations are accompanied by a substantial adjustment of public sector prices and controlled prices, which could easily result in the price index increasing faster than a devaluation, but not because of it. In fact, most empirical studies suggest that devaluation typically does result in a depreciation of the real exchange rate for at least one or two years; that is, the total price rise over that period does not fully offset the devaluation. Of course, immediately after a devaluation, prices typically do increase faster than the exchange rate unless the exchange rate is indexed to maintain purchasing power parity.

My quarrel with the paper is not with its results, but with what is left out. The omissions might lead a casual reader to move from the paper's argument that a devaluation can reduce supply to the conclusion that devaluation is a bad way to cure a payments deficit.

Drawing such a conclusion from the paper would reflect a common error in analyzing a devaluation based on its effect on the initial level of output. Most analyses of devaluation start from goods market and asset market (or money market) positions—output and interest rates—which do not represent a sustainable macroeconomic equilibrium. An economy with a balance-of-payments deficit is, by definition, running down a quite finite stock of international reserves in order to purchase more goods and assets than it can pay for with its current production and borrowing. Because the stocks of international reserves are finite, the flow rates of demand for foreign goods and assets simply cannot be maintained. In particular, the central bank is suffering an unsustainable change in its portfolio, but one that is behind the scenes in the usual models. Put in another, more traditional way, the underlying assumption regarding monetary policy often is not spelled out in models of devaluation; if it were, its unsustainability would be readily apparent.

Since an initial position with a payments deficit is unsustainable, it is difficult to argue that a movement away from it, toward a sustainable position, is bad. In other words, a devaluation may induce a fall in output in the supply-side models because real wages fall or interest rates rise. But if these real wages were excessive relative to the country's endowments or if interest rates were excessively low, it would be hard to argue that a devaluation that corrects these excesses is bad policy.

Once it is admitted that a balance-of-payments deficit cannot be sustained and that the economy therefore must institute a different output–interest rate combination, it becomes apparent that the appropriate way of judging a devaluation is not where it leaves the economy compared to the initial unsustainable position, but just how it does affect the economy in the transition period and how long the transition will last relative to alternative policies that would provide the same improvement in the balance of payments. This criterion is mentioned in the first paragraph of van Wijnbergen's paper, but in fact the paper discusses no alternatives. I would like to attempt one such comparison to give some idea of the difficulties involved.

Suppose monetary growth were allowed to fall to correct the balance-of-payments deficit instead of devaluing. As I understand the model, this policy would move the economy back along its aggregate supply curve because of the implied cut in aggregate demand, as with a devaluation. But a devaluation also has a relative price effect. A cut in monetary growth may or may not have such an effect; it would depend on how the increase in the central bank's domestic credit enters the economy. For example, if the government had been using newly created money to buy nontraded goods, a fall in the rate of money growth would tend to lower the relative price of those goods. This might affect aggregate supply, although just how it would do so is difficult to say.

Moreover, both a devaluation and a cut in money growth would affect the rate of interest and, according to the model, shift the aggregate supply curve backward. The size of the shift might be different, however, because of differences in the effects of the two policies on expectations and interest rates. Thus, a full comparison of these two policies would require a more complex treatment of the determination of expectations and their effect on interest rates than this model contains.

In addition, a proper comparison of the side effects of the two policies cannot be made until the magnitude the policies is adjusted to produce the same impact on the balance of payments. For example, suppose that a unit devaluation cuts real demand by the same amount as a unit cut in the money supply, but has larger negative effects on aggregate supply. Those supply effects would mean that the unit devaluation has a larger effect on the balance of payments than a unit cut in the money supply. Thus, a unit devaluation could be compared only with a larger-than-unit cut in the money stock.

Finally, I would like to add that even the foregoing comparisons may be irrelevant from the standpoint of a policy maker. Devaluation may be the only alternative for resolving a typical balance-of-payments deficit in a developing country; and comparisons with tighter monetary policy may not be germane given the lack of financial markets. The problem is simply that balance-of-payments deficits are often allowed to continue until the stock of international reserves becomes neglible and the required adjustment in the excess demand for foreign exchange is fairly large. As a result, it may be necessary to cut the real money stock to achieve the desired improvement in the balance of payments within the relevant time frame. Without financial markets in which to pursue open market operations, the best a government can achieve is a zero rate of domestic credit growth. This may not produce a very large cut in real money balances, despite the loss of international reserves and the continuance of inflation. Correspondingly, the excess private demand for foreign exchange may not fall to a level at which the stock of reserves at the beginning of the period can sustain the exchange rate for another period. Since the rate can no longer be propped up by the sale of reserves, a depreciation, through a floating rate, will be forced on the country. In sum, a devaluation, forced or not, is often the only feasible solution to a typical balance-of-payments deficit in an LDC. The country may simply have to accept any negative side effects that a devaluation may entail, because of the initial delay in adjustment and the lack of a full range of financial markets.

2 The Effects of Commercial, Fiscal, Monetary, and Exchange Rate Policies on the Real Exchange Rate

Michael Mussa

2.1 Introduction

Adjustments of nominal exchange rates provide a mechanism through which the general level of prices in one country may be modified to correspond to the general level of prices in other countries. This mechanism thus serves to neutralize the real effects of differential monetary disturbances in different countries. In contrast, the principal effect of commercial policies is on the relative prices of goods entering into international trade and hence on the allocation of real resources among sectors of the economy. Despite this fundamental difference between the prime mission and basic purpose of nominal exchange rate adjustments and commercial policies, it has long been recognized that exchange rates can, in some circumstances, be manipulated to affect relative commodity prices and thereby replicate many of the effects of commercial policies.

In the past, observers have recognized three important channels through which policies designed to modify exchange rates can influence relative commodity prices in a manner similar to that achieved by commercial policies. First, systems of multiple exchange rates in which different nominal exchange rates are applied to different categories of imports and exports are known to be essentially equivalent to a system of import and export taxes and subsidies. (The standard reference on this subject is Bhagwati 1968; see also Corden 1971, chap. 4; and Corden 1967.) Second, in the presence of rigidities or stickiness in the nominal prices of domestic goods or of goods entering into international

Michael Mussa is a professor of international business at the Graduate School of Business, University of Chicago, and a research associate of the National Bureau of Economic Research.

trade, or in the wages of factors employed in producing these goods, movements in the nominal exchange rate, even under a unified exchange rate regime, clearly have the capacity to affect relative commodity prices and influence the allocation of resources. This assumption is explicitly or implicitly employed in many of the earlier analyses of the effects of devaluation, including the classic contributions of Meade (1951), Harberger (1950), Machlup (1955), and Tsiang (1961). It is also the fundamental source of the real effects of nominal exchange rate changes in the more recent analyses that assume only temporary stickiness of nominal wages or prices, such as Dornbusch (1976; 1980), Buiter and Miller (1983), and Mussa (1977; 1982a; 1984). Third, even with a unified exchange rate and without nominal price or wage stickiness, government policies that affect either the distribution of expenditures among goods or the level of spending relative to income are known to have some capacity to influence the "real exchange rate," defined as the relative price of one country's output in terms of another country's output. This idea is clearly present in the work of Meade (1951), Pearce (1961), and Corden (1960), as well as in more recent contributions, such as Dornbusch (1975) and the literature on the "Dutch disease."

The purpose of this paper is to explore in a more explicitly dynamic framework the third of these channels. Section 2.2 describes and discusses the model of the real sector of the economy that is used as the basis for this exploration. This model is consistent both with the two-country, two-commodity model of real trade theory (modified to allow for differences between spending and income in the home country) and with the "dependent economy" model. The basic equations of this model are specified in a log-linear form that permits easier manipulation of the dynamic version of the model in the subsequent sections of the paper. In this model, as in the standard trade theory model, the equilibrium value of the (logarithm of the) relative price of domestic goods in terms of foreign goods is consistent with any given value of the trade balance of the home country, for given values of the exogenous parameters and policy variables that influence domestic and foreign demand for domestic and foreign goods. This relative price is identified with the concept of the real exchange rate. It is shown that the standard results of real trade theory apply with respect to the comparative statics effects of various government policies on this relative price. In particular, imposing a tariff on imported goods in the home country lowers the relative price of domestic goods in terms of foreign goods in that country. This result is taken as representative of the effects of commercial policy on the real exchange rate. A shift in spending by either domestic or foreign residents toward foreign goods at the expense of domestic goods (perhaps induced by government policy) has a similar qualitative effect on the real exchange rate. So, too, does a transfer of purchasing power from domestic residents to foreign residents, which results in a trade-balance surplus for the home country. This result reflects the assumption that domestic residents have a positive marginal propensity to spend on domestic goods, whereas foreign residents have a zero marginal propensity to spend on the home country's domestic goods.

In section 2.3 the model is extended to allow for the endogenous determination of differences between income and spending by domestic residents as a function of both their net asset holdings and the domestic real interest rate. Equilibrium in the balance of payments requires that this difference between income and spending by domestic residents equal the current-account balance, which is the trade balance determined by the real sector model of section 2.2 augmented by real interest income on net foreign asset holdings. This balance-of-payments equilibrium condition provides the basis for a comparative statics analysis of the effects of a variety of government policies on the real exchange rate. This comparative statics analysis, however, ignores the dynamic repercussions of expected changes in the real exchange rate and in the path of private net asset holdings.

In section 2.4 these dynamic considerations are taken into account and a solution is provided for the complete dynamic version of the model developed in the previous two sections. The solution reveals that the equilibrium value of the real exchange rate at any moment depends on expectations concerning the exogenous factors that will influence the trade balance in all future periods (including government commercial policies) and on expectations concerning the exogenous factors that will influence the desired relationship between income and spending in all future periods. For constant values of these exogenous influences, the dynamic behavior of the real exchange rate is driven by a process of adjusting the private stock of net foreign assets in a manner similar to that delineated in several recent models of the relationship between the exchange rate and the current account.

In section 2.5 this dynamic model is applied to an analysis of government fiscal policies. A temporary shift in government spending toward domestic goods at the expense of government spending on foreign goods initially appreciates the real exchange rate (raises the relative price of domestic goods), but to a smaller extent than would a permanent spending shift of the same magnitude. This temporary spending shift also induces a temporary current-account surplus and an increase in private net asset holdings, which in turn moderate the immediate effect of the spending shift on the real exchange rate by spreading some of its effect into periods after the spending shift itself has ended. A similar mechanism operates in the case of a permanent spending shift that is expected to occur at some future date. Because private agents anticipate the effect of this future spending shift on the real exchange rate, the actual real exchange rate and the level of private net asset holding react in advance of the actual start of the spending shift. A temporary general fiscal expansion, financed by an increase in government debt, is also shown to appreciate the real exchange rate in the short run, even though private agents may correctly forecast the future taxes that will be necessary to pay the interest on the expanded government debt. As with the temporary spending shift, this temporary fiscal expansion causes a temporary increase in private net asset holdings, which assists in spreading out over time the effects of this fiscal expansion on the real exchange rate. In the long run, the temporary fiscal expansion depresses the real exchange rate because the higher taxes necessary to finance the interest on the expanded government debt depress demand for domestic goods.

Section 2.6 considers the effects of capital controls. These controls can influence the real exchange rate by affecting the permissible difference between spending and income and hence the level of the current-account balance. It is argued, however, that capital controls have only a limited capacity to affect the long-run average level of the real exchange rate. Their principal effect is to influence the responsiveness of the real exchange rate to various forms of economic disturbances. In general, a capital control that fixes the permissible value of the current-account balance increases the sensitivity of the real exchange rate to disturbances (such as changes in commercial policies) that shift spending between domestic and foreign goods; but it reduces the sensitivity of the real exchange rate to disturbances that affect the general level of spending relative to income.

Section 2.7 presents an analysis of how monetary policy and nominal exchange rate policy can interact to influence the behavior of the real exchange rate. In the present model, which assumes full flexibility of all nominal prices, monetary policy cannot influence the real exchange rate when the nominal exchange rate is fully flexible. Similarly, nominal exchange rate policy cannot influence the real exchange rate when the domestic money supply is allowed full flexibility to adjust to official settlements surpluses and deficits. A policy that fixes a path for both the nominal money supply and the nominal exchange rate, however, can influence the real exchange rate and other real variables by affecting the behavior of the real money supply. To support such a combination of monetary policy and exchange rate policy, a government usually must intervene in the foreign exchange market on a sterilized basis. Such intervention necessarily implies differences between government spending and government revenue that are the fiscal effect of sterilized intervention. In the absence of full Ricardian equivalence between debt financing and tax financing of government expenditure, this fiscal effect of sterilized intervention provides a channel through which the combination of monetary and nominal exchange rate policies can affect the real sector of the economy and, in particular, the real exchange rate.

One example of such a combination of monetary and exchange rate policies is one that simultaneously fixes a level of the domestic money supply and pegs a value of the nominal exchange rate. In general, such a policy combination is dynamically unstable because the stock of government debt required to finance official intervention in support of the policy expands exponentially. This dynamic instability implies that a continued belief in the viability of such a policy combination by private asset holders is inconsistent with rational expectations—an assumption that is employed in the dynamic model developed in section 2.4. To deal with this difficulty, I assume that private agents foresee the possibility of a change in the nominal exchange rate and relate the probability of such a change and its expected magnitude to the cumulative extent of official intervention in support of the current nominal exchange rate. Under this assumption, it is shown that so long as the assessed probability of an immediate parity change remains negligible, the real exchange rate is influenced by the combination of fixed nominal money supply and the pegged nominal exchange rate in exactly the same way as if private agents never foresaw any prospect of a change in the exchange rate. When the cumulative extent of official intervention reaches the point at which people begin to suspect a significant probability of a parity change in the near future, the nature of the dynamic system is modified. The flow of intervention required to support the existing nominal exchange rate begins to accelerate, and the real exchange that was previously held constant by a constant money supply and nominal exchange rate begins to rise, in the case of a prospective devaluation, or fall, in the case of a prospective appreciation. Ultimately, there is a change in the nominal exchange rate and an adjustment of the real exchange rate to the level that is appropriate for the new nominal exchange rate and the size of the domestic money supply.

With slight modifications, this analysis also applies to a policy that fixes the rate of growth of the domestic money supply and the rate of crawl of the nominal exchange rate, with occasional major changes in the nominal exchange rate used to correct persistent payments imbalances. The behavior pattern of the real exchange rate, of the current-account balance, and of other related variables under this combination of policies is reminiscent of the experiences of some developing countries.

The paper concludes with a brief restatement of its main contribution to the literature and a discussion of the broader range of issues to which its analytical framework might be applied.

2.2 Goods Market Equilibrium, the Trade Balance, and the Real Exchange Rate

Consider a moderate-sized country that produces and consumes two goods: a domestic good that is different from goods produced in the rest of the world, and a traded good (sometimes referred to as the imported good or foreign good) that is identical to goods produced in the rest of the world. This country exports some of its domestic good to the rest of the world and imports some of the traded good from the rest of the world. In addition, the country trades securities, denominated in units of traded goods, with the rest of the world.

The country under consideration is assumed to be small with respect to world trade in traded goods and securities in the sense that it takes as given the real interest rate in the world securities market for securities denominated in traded goods, r^*. This interest rate is independent of the flow or stock amount of the borrowing and lending the country engages in to finance the difference between the value of its exports of the domestic good and the cost of its imports of the traded good. The country is not small, however, with respect to the market for its domestic good. Rather, it faces a foreign demand for this good that is less than infinitely elastic with respect to the relative price of this good in terms of the traded good. Specifically, the value of foreign excess demand for the domestic good (measured in units of the traded good) is given by:

$$(1) \qquad\qquad d^* = -\beta^* q^* + x^*,$$

where q^* is the (logarithm of the) relative price of the domestic good in terms of the traded goods available to foreign purchasers; $\beta^* > 0$ measures the sensitivity of foreign demand for the domestic good to variations in q^*; and x^* summarizes the exogenous factors affecting foreign demand for the domestic good. Since $\beta^* > 0$, the relative price elasticity of foreign demand for the domestic good, $\eta^* = d[\log(d^*)]/dq^* = -(\beta^*/d^*) - 1$ is negative.

Production possibilities in the home country are described by a smooth, convex transformation curve, with the implication that the supply of the domestic good is an increasing function of its relative price, whereas the supply of the traded good is a decreasing function of that relative price. Domestic demand for the domestic good is a decreasing function of its relative price, and domestic demand for the traded good is an increasing function of that relative price. Domestic demand for each good is an increasing function of total domestic spending. This standard specification of supply and demand conditions in the home country is consistent with the following log-linear specification of domestic excess demand for traded goods, f, and of the value (in terms of the traded good) of domestic excess demand for the domestic good, d, such that:

$$(2) \qquad\qquad f = \beta q - x + (1 - \sigma)\psi$$

$$(3) \qquad\qquad d = -\beta q + x + \sigma\psi.$$

In these excess demand functions, q denotes the logarithm of the price of the domestic good relative to the price paid for the traded good by domestic producers and consumers; $\beta > 0$ measures the sensitivity of these excess demands to changes in q; σ and $1 - \sigma$ are the shares of the domestic good and the traded good, respectively, in domestic spending; ψ is the excess of domestic spending over the value of the domestic product; and x summarizes the exogenous factors affecting domestic excess demands for the domestic and traded goods (including tastes, production possibilities, and government policies). Note that the total value of domestic excess demand for both goods, $d + f$, must equal the excess of domestic spending over the value of the domestic product, ψ. Note also that changes in q or x, holding ψ constant, must have offsetting effects on d and f. Note finally that since β is assumed to be positive, the relative price elasticity of domestic demand for imports of the traded good, $\eta = -\beta/f$, is negative.

The relative price of the domestic good confronting domestic residents differs from the relative price confronting foreign residents when the government of the home country imposes an ad valorem tariff on imports of traded goods or, equivalently, an ad valorem tax on exports of domestic goods. Formally, the effects of such commercial policies are indicated by the following relationship:

$$(4) \qquad\qquad q^* = q + \tau,$$

where τ is the logarithm of one (1) plus the ad valorem tax rate on either imports of the traded good or exports of the domestic good.

With this commercial policy in force, the condition for equilibrium in the market for the domestic good that must be satisfied at all times is expressed by:

$$(5) \qquad 0 = d + d^* = -(\beta + \beta^*)q + (x + x^* - \beta^*\tau) + \sigma\psi.$$

Further, at all times, the trade balance of the home country is the excess of the value of its exports of the domestic good, d^*, over the value of its imports of the traded good; that is:

$$(6) \qquad T = -(\beta + \beta^*)q + (x + x^* - \beta^*\tau) - (1 - \sigma)\psi.$$

From equations (5) and (6), we arrive at the conclusion:

$$(7) \qquad\qquad T = v(z - q) = -\psi,$$

where $v \equiv (\beta + \beta^*)/\sigma$, and $z = (x + x^* + \beta^*\tau)/(\beta + \beta^*)$. This result expresses the equivalence between the absorption and elasticities approaches to analyzing the trade balance. According to the elasticities approach, the trade balance depends on the terms of trade (represented by q) through the relationship $T = v(z - q)$. According to the absorption approach, the trade balance equals the excess of the value of the domestic product over the domestic expenditure, that is, $T = -\psi$.

It is worthwhile to emphasize that this result concerning the trade balance and the equations that underlie it are consistent with several possible specifications of the production structure of the economy. One specification is that of the standard two-country, two-commodity model described in the pure theory of international trade (summarized, for instance, by Mundell 1968, chaps. 1–3). In this specification, both the domestic good and the foreign good are produced (as well as consumed) in the home country, and the domestic good is distinguished only by the fact that it is exported by the home country. Another specification, one more commonly used in two-country, macroeconomic models (see Mussa 1979 and the references cited there), states that the home country produces only its domestic good and the rest of the world produces only the foreign good. A third specification is the "dependent economy" model developed by Salter (1959) and Swan (1960), which has been widely applied in both trade theory and open economy macroeconomics. In this specification, the domestic good is a nontraded good that is produced and consumed exclusively within the home country (d^* therefore is equal to zero), while the foreign good is an internationally traded good that is produced and consumed in the home country and may be either imported or exported depending on whether the home country has a trade deficit or a trade surplus. All of the analysis in this paper is consistent with all three of these specifications of production structure, though the interpretation of some results depends on the particular specification one has in mind.

The standard results of the real theory of international trade concerning the effects of import tariffs or export taxes and transfers paid to residents of the home country (usually derived in the standard two-country, two-commodity model) are obtained by applying implicit differentiation to equation (7) and evaluating the results where $T = 0$, such that:

$$(8) \qquad dq/d\tau = -\beta^*/(\beta + \beta^*); \quad dq^*/d\tau = \beta/(\beta + \beta^*)$$

$$(9) \qquad dq/d(-\psi) = dq^*/d(-\psi) = \sigma/(\beta + \beta^*).$$

The positive value of the denominator in (8) and (9), $\beta + \beta^*$, reflects the fact that the Marshall-Lerner condition is satisfied; that is, the sum of the import demand elasticities plus one (1) is negative, such that:

$$(10) \quad \eta + \eta^* + 1 = (-\beta/f) + [(-\beta^*/d^*) - 1] + 1$$
$$= -(\beta + \beta^*)/f < 0.$$

Equation (8) expresses the standard result that a tariff on traded goods imported into the home country reduces the relative domestic price of domestic goods (increases the relative domestic price of traded goods) and increases the relative foreign price of domestic goods. (See, for example, Mundell 1968, chap. 3.) Equation (9) says that a transfer received by residents of the home country (which allows an excess of domestic spending over domestic income, represented by a positive value of $-\psi$) pushes up the relative price of domestic goods. This positive effect of a transfer received (and spent) by domestic residents on the relative price of domestic goods reflects a determinate sign of the transfer problem criterion (see again Mundell 1968, chap. 2) that arises because the marginal propensity of domestic residents to spend on domestic goods is positive, whereas the marginal propensity of foreigners (who pay the transfer) to spend on domestic goods is zero.

For the purposes of this discussion, equation (8) is a key result that summarizes the basic mechanism through which commercial policy works its effects on the economy. Specifically, changes in commercial policy, represented by changes in τ, affect the relative price of domestic goods and thereby affect all of the production and consumption decisions that are influenced by this relative price. If the relative price of domestic goods is defined as the "real exchange rate," it follows that other policies can replicate the effects of commercial policy to the extent that they have similar effects on the real exchange rate.

There are two general mechanisms through which economic policies may have such effects on the real exchange rate. First, economic policies can affect the exogenous shift variable, x, that appears in the domestic excess demand functions and perhaps also the exogenous shift variable, x^*, that appears in the foreign excess demand function for the domestic good. Formally, the effects of changes in x and x^* on q are obtained by implicit differentiation of the trade balance equilibrium condition, $T = v \cdot (z - q) = 0$, such that:

$$(11) \quad dq/dx = dq^*/dx = 1/(\beta + \beta^*); \; dq/dx^* = dq^*/dx^* = 1/(\beta + \beta^*).$$

For example, a shift of government spending in the home country away from domestic goods and toward domestically produced traded goods induces a decrease in x and implies a decrease in q that is similar to that induced by an increase in the tariff rate. Alternatively, a tax-financed increase in government spending directed toward traded goods induces a decrease in x because the reduction in private sector spending resulting from the tax increase is spread over both domestic and traded goods. Second, as indicated by equation (9), economic policies can affect the real exchange rate by altering the difference between domestic spending and domestic income. Specifically, any policy that reduces domestic spending relative to domestic income (holding x, s^*, and τ constant) will reduce q and replicate the effects of an increase in the tariff rate on imports of traded goods. Further investigation of this mechanism through which economic policies can affect the real exchange rate and thereby replicate many of the effects of commercial policy is the principal subject of the remainder of paper.

2.3   Balance-of-Payments Equilibrium and Comparative Statics

To analyze policies that affect the real exchange rate by influencing the difference between spending and income, we must specify the determinants of differences between spending and income and describe the condition of balance-of-payments equilibrium. This equilibrium condition may then be employed to provide an initial comparative statics analysis of the effects of a variety of policies on the real exchange rate.

Suppose that the desired excess of private spending over private income for the country under consideration is given by:

$$(12) \qquad h = \mu A - \alpha r + u,$$

where h measures the excess of spending over income in terms of traded goods; A is the net stock of privately held assets denominated in traded goods; r is the real rate of return that domestic residents expect to earn on their net asset holdings; u summarizes the exogenous factors affecting h (including some government policies); and $\mu > 0$ and $\alpha > 0$ are parameters indicating the responsiveness of h to variations in A and r. Since privately issued securities net out against privately held securities, net private securities holdings must consist of securities issued by foreigners (or debts owed to foreigners if $A < 0$) or holdings of bonds issued by the domestic government. Since real interest income earned on private net asset holdings is included in private sector income, the positive value of the parameter μ implies that a rise in A increases desired private spending by more than it increases private income. Further, since excesses of private spending over private income must be financed at the expense of private net asset holdings, it follows that:

$$(13) \qquad D(A) = -h$$

where $D[A(t)] = A(t + 1) - A(t)$ is the forward difference in the level of A.

The excess of spending over income for the home country includes the excess of government spending over government revenue, g, as well as the excess of private spending over private income, h. Government spending includes the real interest that the government must pay on its outstanding stock of government debt, G. The excess of government spending over government revenue is financed by issuing (or retiring) government debt, that is:

$$(14) \qquad\qquad D(G) = g.$$

The net asset position of the home country as a whole, N, is equal to the excess of privately held net assets over the outstanding stock of government debt, such that:

$$(15) \qquad\qquad N = A - G.$$

The change in this net asset position corresponds to the total excess of income over spending, or:

$$(16) \qquad\qquad D(N) = -(h + g).$$

The desired change in net assets implied by equation (16) may be thought of as the desired capital outflow of the home country. For the economic system to be in equilibrium, this desired capital outflow must correspond to the current-account balance, which is the sum of the trade balance and the service-account balance. The trade balance is given by equation (7) as $T = v(z - q)$. The service-account balance is the real interest income that the home country earns on its net asset position, which is equal to the real interest rate prevailing in the world securities market, r^*, multiplied by $N = A - G$. If equation (12) is substituted into equation (16), the critical requirement for momentary equilibrium in the economic system may be expressed as the balance-of-payments equilibrium condition, or:

$$(17) \qquad v(z - q) + r^*(A - G) = \alpha r - \mu A - u - g.$$

In this condition, the expected real rate of return on private asset holdings is not identified with r^* because some government policies induce divergences between r and r^* and because expected changes in the relative price of domestic goods also imply such divergences.

Preliminary conclusions concerning the capacity of various policies to replicate the effects of commercial policy by influencing the real exchange rate may be obtained by applying implicit differentiation to the balance-of-payments equilibrium condition (17). These conclusions are only preliminary because they ignore the dynamic effects of induced changes in asset stocks and of changes in anticipations of future policies, which are examined in later sections. But they do apply (under appropriate assumptions and specifications) to the long-run effects of permanent changes in government policies when account is taken of these dynamic complications.

First, consider an increase in the outstanding stock of government debt. If z, A, r, u, and g are held constant, the change in q necessary to maintain balance-of-payments equilibrium in the face of an increase in G is given by:

$$(18) \qquad dq/DG = -r^*/v = -\sigma r^*/(\beta + \beta^*).$$

The explanation of this result is that a larger stock of government debt requires a higher flow of net interest payments to the foreigners who must be the holders of this debt if the net assets of the private sector are constant. With a constant desired capital outflow (or inflow), this increase in net interest payments requires an improvement in the trade balance, which in turn requires a lower relative price of domestic goods. This conclusion, it should be emphasized, does not depend on the assumption that the increased taxes necessary to finance the interest on the expanded government debt are ignored by the private sector. Since g is defined as the excess of government spending (including interest payments on government debt) over government revenue, and since g is held constant, the implicit assumption is that taxes are increased sufficiently to pay the increased interest on the expanded government debt. Private sector income falls by the amount of this increase in taxes. Since h is the excess of private sector spending over private sector income, and since h is held constant in the derivation of equation (18), this result embodies the assumption that private sector spending falls by the amount of the increased taxes necessary to finance interest payments on the expanded government debt. Indeed, the decline in the relative price of the domestic good in response to an increase in the outstanding stock of government debt is precisely the appropriate relative price response to a transfer of spending from domestic residents, who have a positive marginal propensity to spend on domestic goods, to foreigners (the recipients of the interest paid on the net government debt), who have a zero marginal propensity to spend on domestic goods.

Essential to equation (18) is an implicit assumption that the private sector does not view government debt as a liability, in the sense that the stock of such debt exerts a negative effect on the desired excess of private spending over private income that is equivalent to the positive effect, μA, exerted by privately held net assets. This assumption is consistent with the notion of Metzler (1951) and Mundell (1960) that marketable assets exert a positive effect on desired spending beyond the effect of their yield on income, but that future tax liabilities associated with government debt are not regarded as marketable liabilities that offset this effect of marketable assets. (An alternative approach to eliminating Ricardian equivalence between debt financing and tax financing of government expenditures is to assume an overlapping-generations model with no bequest motive. For a recent and elegant version of this model, see Blanchard 1984; see Frenkel and Razin 1984 for an application of this model in the context of an open economy.) Were this not the case, a term $-\mu G$ would have to be included among the factors affecting the desired excess of private spending over private income, so that equation (12) would become:

$$(12') \qquad h = \mu(A - G) - \alpha r + u.$$

This modification would add the term μG to the right-hand side of the balance-of-payments equilibrium condition (17) and would modify the result (18) to:

$$(18') \qquad dq/dG = -(r^* + \mu)/v.$$

This result, however, would not represent the long-run equilibrium effect of an increase in the stock of government debt because in equation (12') an increase in G implies a reduction in h and hence an increase in the rate of accumulation of privately held net assets. The long-run cumulative effect of this change in private asset accumulation is that privately held net assets would rise by exactly the amount of the increase in the stock of government debt. In the long run, therefore, there would be no reduction in domestic spending and an increase in foreign spending because the increased interest and associated taxes on the expanded government debt would be exactly offset by the increased interest received on privately held net assets. Consequently, under these conditions an increase in the stock of government debt would have no long-run effect on the relative price of domestic goods. (In Barro's [1974] terminology, there would be no long-run net wealth effect from changes in the stock of government debt because they would be fully offset by changes in private security holdings.)

Consider now a second dynamic complication: a temporary reduction in the general level of taxation. The short-run effect of this policy is a temporary increase in government expenditure relative to government revenue, that is, a temporary increase in g. Maintaining balance-of-payments equilibrium in the face of this increase in g, with given values of z, A, G, r, and u, requires an increase in the relative price of domestic goods, such that:

$$(19) \qquad dq/dg = 1/v = \sigma/(\beta + \beta^*).$$

This result embodies the assumption that the private sector does not forecast the future tax liability implicit in the flow of government debt that finances the current tax reduction. As a result, the excess of private spending over private income does not decline in response to the increase in government expenditure relative to government revenue; instead, private spending rises to the extent of the tax reduction. Part of this increase in private spending is for purchases of domestic goods and thus forces an increase in the relative price of those goods to maintain equilibrium in the domestic goods market. Over time, the temporary reduction in taxes enlarges the stock of government debt, and (under the assumptions of this analysis) this increase in the stock of government debt tends to offset the direct effect of the tax reduction in reducing q. Ultimately, when taxes are increased sufficiently to eliminate the government deficit, the long-run effect of the temporary tax reduction is to raise the long-run stock of government debt and the long-run level of taxes required to finance the interest on this debt. The long-term effect of the temporary tax reduction (again, under the assumptions of this analysis) is therefore to reduce the long-term equilibrium value of the real exchange rate for precisely the reasons discussed above in connection with the effects of an increase in the outstanding stock of government debt.

Third, consider a policy that permanently raises the expected real rate of return for private asset holders, such as a permanent reduction in the tax rate on interest income. At given values of A, G, g, u, and z, an increase in r reduces the desired excess of private spending over private income and requires a reduction in q to maintain balance-of-payments equilibrium, that is:

$$(20) \qquad dq/dr = -\alpha/v.$$

Over time, however, the reduction in h implied by an increase in r generates a higher net stock of privately held assets, and the effect of an increase in A on the relative price of domestic goods is given by:

$$(21) \qquad dq/dA = (\mu + r^*)/v.$$

The cumulative change in A necessary to offset the increase in r and return h to the zero value consistent with no further changes in A is given by $\Delta A = (\alpha/\mu)\Delta r$, where Δr is the policy-induced change in r. It is easily shown that the combined long-run effect of the increase in r and the induced increase in A on the relative price of domestic goods is given by:

$$(22) \quad \Delta q = (-\alpha/v)\Delta r + [(\mu + r^*)/v]\Delta A = (r^*/v)\Delta A = (\alpha r^*/v)\Delta r.$$

The reason for this increase in the long-run equilibrium value of q in response to a policy-induced increase in r is that the long-run level of income of domestic residents rises due to the increase in A and domestic residents spend a fraction of this increased income on domestic goods, thereby forcing an increase in their relative price. This example points to the importance of distinguishing between short-run and long-run effects when considering the consequences of government policies that affect the real exchange rate.

2.4   A Dynamic Model of the Real Exchange Rate

A complete, dynamic analysis of government policies that affect the real exchange rate must take account of endogenously determined changes in the net stock of privately held assets that occur as the counterpart of current-account imbalances. The analysis must also account for the influence of expected changes in the relative price of domestic goods on economic behavior. To provide a benchmark for such an analysis, it is useful first to examine the dynamic interactions among the real exchange rate, the net stock of privately held assets, and the current-account balance in the absence of any government interventions. For this purpose, it is assumed that the stock of government debt is constant at zero and that government expenditure and government revenue are also zero.

Since no tax is imposed on private security holdings, the interest rate earned on such holdings is the real interest rate, r^*, that prevails in the world securities market. The real rate of return that influences private spending and saving decisions, r, however, is equal to r^* only when no capital gains or losses on private security holdings are anticipated. More generally, the expected real rate of return for private security holders is given by:

$$(23) \qquad\qquad r = r^* - \sigma D^e(q),$$

where $D^e(q)$ denotes the expected rate of change in the relative price of domestic goods. The rationale for this relationship is that the real yield relevant for the spending and saving decisions of domestic residents is measured relative to a consumption basket that contains both domestic and traded goods. This real yield on a security with a fixed price and fixed interest rate in terms of traded goods is less than r^* to the extent of the expected growth rate of the relative price of domestic goods, multiplied by the share of domestic goods in the consumption basket. This assumption concerning the domestic real interest rate is a common feature of models that allow for changes in the real exchange rate, in particular, those in Dornbusch (1983), Mussa (1982a; 1984), and Obstfeld (1981a; 1983).

This specification of the domestic real interest rate, together with the assumptions that $G = 0$ and $g = 0$, implies that the balance-of-payments equilibrium condition (17) can be written as:

$$(24) \qquad\qquad v(z - q) + r^*A = w - \alpha\sigma D^e(q) - \mu A,$$

where $w \equiv \alpha r^* - u$ summarizes all of the exogenous factors (including the world real interest rate) that influence the desired excess of private income over private spending. Equation (26) is a dynamic equation because it specifies the expected rate of change of the relative price of domestic goods and because it specifies the net stock of privately held assets. That stock changes whenever private income differs from private spending. More specifically:

$$(25) \qquad D(A) = -h = w - \alpha\sigma D^e(q) - \mu A.$$

Under the assumption of the rationality of expectations, equations (24) and (25) constitute a dynamic system that constrains the expected evolution of the relative price of domestic goods and the net stock of privately held assets, conditional on the information available at a given date. In matrix form, this dynamic system may be written as:

$$(26) \qquad \begin{bmatrix} \alpha\sigma D^e - v & r^* + \mu \\ \alpha\sigma D^e & \mu + D^e \end{bmatrix} \begin{bmatrix} q \\ A \end{bmatrix} = \begin{bmatrix} w - vz \\ w \end{bmatrix}.$$

The economically appropriate solution of this dynamic system yields the following expression for the current expected equilibrium value of the real exchange rate, $q^e(t) = E[q(t); t]$:

$$(27) \qquad q^e(t) = \bar{q}(t) + \gamma[A^e(t) - \bar{A}(t)],$$

where $\bar{q}(t)$ is the current expected long-run equilibrium value of the real exchange rate; $A^e(t) = E[A(t); t]$ is the current expected level of net private asset holdings; $\bar{A}$ is the current expected long-run equilibrium level of net private asset holdings; and $\gamma > 0$ is a parameter that determines the responsiveness of $q^e(t)$ to deviations between $A^e(t)$ and $\bar{A}(t)$. The values of $\bar{q}(t)$, $\bar{A}(t)$, and γ are determined by:

$$(28) \qquad \bar{q}(t) = \bar{\bar{q}}(t) + (r^*/v)\bar{A}(t)$$

$$(29) \qquad \bar{\bar{q}}(t) = (1 - \theta)\left(\sum_{j=0}^{\infty}\theta^j\right)\{E[z(t + j); t]\}$$

$$(30) \qquad \bar{A}(t) = (1 - \theta)\left(\sum_{j=0}^{\infty}\theta^j\right)\{E[w(t + j)/\mu; t]\}$$

$$(31) \qquad \gamma = (\lambda/v) - (1/\alpha\sigma),$$

where the discount factor θ involved in the definitions of $\bar{A}(t)$ and $\bar{\bar{q}}(t)$ is given by:

$$(32) \qquad \theta = 1/(1 + \lambda),$$

and where λ is the positive characteristic root associated with the dynamic system (26), such that:

$$(33) \quad \lambda = (1/2)\{[r^* + (v/\alpha\sigma)] + \sqrt{[r^* + (v/\alpha\sigma)]^2 + 4(v\mu/\alpha\sigma)}\}.$$

The results (28) through (33) may be interpreted as follows. (For further discussion, see Mussa 1984.) Equation (16) states that the current expected long-run equilibrium real exchange rate, $\bar{q}(t)$, is the real exchange rate expected to make the present discounted value (using the discount factor θ) of trade imbalances equal to zero, namely, $\bar{\bar{q}}(t)$ as defined by (29), adjusted for the effect of expected net interest income on the current expected long-run equilibrium level of privately held net assets. According to equation (30), this expected long-run equilibrium level of privately held net assets is the expected present discounted value (using the discount factor θ) of the exogenous factors affecting the desired excess of private spending over private income, divided by the sensitivity of this excess of private income over private spending to the actual level of privately held net assets. Equation (31) defines the reduced-form parameter, γ, that appears in (27) in terms of the more basic parameters that appear in the balance-of-payments equilibrium condition (24). From (33), it is easily established that $\gamma > r^*/v$, which is necessarily positive. Equation (32) indicates that the positive characteristic root λ plays the role of the "discount rate" in the expressions that define $\bar{q}(t)$ and $\bar{A}(t)$. Equation (33) relates the value of this discount rate to the parameters that appear in the balance-of-payments equilibrium condition (24).

Because no restriction has been placed on the expected behavior of the exogenous factors affecting the trade balance (the z terms) or on the exogenous factors affecting the desired excess of private income over private spending (the w terms), these results provide a description of the determinants of the current expected equilibrium real exchange rate under a wide variety of possible assumptions about how economic conditions are expected to change over time. This generalizability has its costs: it increases the complexity of the model required for the analysis. But it also has important benefits: it allows an analysis of expected changes in government policies and other exogenous variables; it incorporates a variety of notions of permanent and transitory changes in government policies and other exogenous variables; and it distinguishes between the expected effects of expected changes in these exogenous variables and the unexpected effects attributable to new information about present and future government policies and other exogenous disturbances.

When the exogenous factors affecting the trade balance and the desired excess of private spending are known to have constant values (say, $z[s] = \bar{z}$ for all s terms and $w[s] = \bar{w}$ for all s terms), the dynamic process governing the expected evolution of the real exchange rate and the net stock of privately held assets can be described quite simply. Since there is no good reason to distinguish between the expected and the actual values of q and A when the z and w terms are equal to known constants, this description applies just as well to the actual evolution of q and A. The description is illustrated in those terms in figure 2.1. The dynamic process described in this figure embodies the essential features of a number of recent analyses of the dynamic interactions among the current-account balance, the level of net foreign assets, and the real exchange rate, in particular, those in Kouri (1976), Calvo and Rodriguez (1977), Dornbusch and Fischer (1980), and Obstfeld (1981a).

Suppose that the initial net level of privately held assets, A_0, is greater than the long-run equilibrium level, $\bar{A} = \bar{w}/\mu$. Then, as illustrated in the left-hand side of the figure, the initial equilibrium real exchange rate, $q_0 = \bar{q} + \gamma(A_0 - \bar{A})$, must be above the long-run equilibrium real exchange rate, $\bar{q} = \bar{z} + (r^*/v)\bar{A}$. As illustrated in the right-hand side of the figure, this initial real exchange rate implies an initial current-account deficit, $b_0 = v(\bar{z} - q_0) + r^*A_0 = (v\gamma - r^*)(\bar{A} - A_0) < 0$. This current-account deficit implies a decline in the net stock of privately held assets between period 0 and period 1, such that $D(A_0) = b_0 = (v\gamma - r^*)(A - A_0) < 0$. This decline in net assets implies that the real exchange rate in period 1, $q_1 = \bar{q} + \gamma(A_1 - \bar{A})$, as determined on the right side of the figure, must be below its previous value but still above its long-run equilibrium value. The fact that this decline in the real exchange rate, $D(q_0) - \gamma D(A_0) - \gamma b_0$, was anticipated in period 0 implies that the domestic real interest rate in that period, $r_0 = r^* - \sigma D(q_0)$, must have been above its long-run equilibrium value, r^*. In period 1, this process repeats, starting with a net stock of privately held assets, A_1, that is between A_0 and $\bar{A}$. Over time, the net stock of privately held assets, the real exchange rate, and the domestic real interest rate all gradually decline toward their respective long-run equilibrium values, and the current-account deficit is gradually eliminated.

The dynamic process illustrated in figure 2.1 is the process by which the economic system converges toward the fixed long-run equilibrium position determined by known constant values of the exogenous forcing variables z and w. The essential driving force in this adjustment process is the gradual adjustment of the net stock of privately held assets toward its long-run equilibrium level. There are limited circumstances in which this single element of a more complex dynamic system provides an essentially complete description of the dynamic response of the economic system to some change in economic conditions. In particular, consider a permanent (constant) increase in the tariff rate applied to imports of traded goods, $\Delta\tau > 0$. Such a tariff increase reduces the value of the exogenous forcing variable affecting the trade balance,

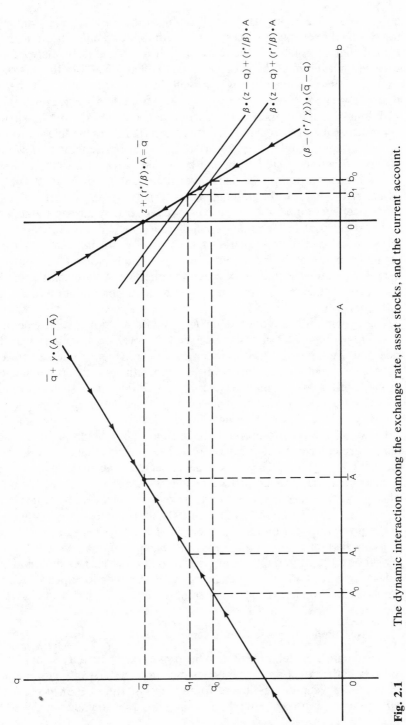

Fig. 2.1   The dynamic interaction among the exchange rate, asset stocks, and the current account.

$z = x + x^* - \beta^*\tau$, by a known constant amount, $\beta^*\Delta\tau$. This implies that the real exchange rate consistent with long-run equilibrium in the trade balance, $\bar{\bar{q}}$, falls by the amount $-\beta^*\Delta\tau$. If the tariff increase is assumed not to affect the exogenous factor that influences the desired excess of private spending over private income, it follows that there is no change in $\bar{A} = \bar{w}/\mu$ and hence that the real exchange rate consistent with long-run equilibrium in the current account, $\bar{q}$, falls by the same amount as $\bar{\bar{q}}$. In terms of figure 2.1, this means that the schedule showing $q(t)$ as a function of $A(t)$ on the right side and the schedule showing $b(t)$ as a function of $q(t)$ on the left both shift downward to the extent of the reduction in $\bar{\bar{q}}$ and $\bar{q}$. Whatever the net stock of privately held assets at the time of the permanent tariff increase, therefore, the immediate effect of the tariff increase is to reduce $q(t)$ by the same amount as the reductions in $\bar{\bar{q}}$ and $\bar{q}$. Depending on whether $A(t)$ is greater or less than $\bar{A}$, q will subsequently fall or rise toward its new long-run equilibrium value as A converges to $\bar{A}$. At each moment, q will be below the value it would have had in the absence of the tariff increase by precisely the amount that measures the long-run equilibrium effect of the tariff increase.

The dynamic system of equation (26) and its solution given by equations (28) through (33) may also be used to analyze changes in the tariff rate that are expected to be temporary or permanent at some future date. Such commercial policy changes imply either a temporary change in the level of the forcing variable, z, that will occur at some specific future date. These changes may also imply changes in the exogenous forcing variable, w, that accounts for the desired spending and saving behavior of the private sector. The reason w may be affected is that temporary changes in commercial policy or changes that are expected to occur at a future date affect the expected time path of the real exchange rate and hence private incentives for spending and saving. This point has recently been emphasized by Razin and Svennsson (1983) (see also Svennsson and Razin 1983) and is represented formally in the present model by allowing for changes in the path of w as well as in the path of z. Given the prescribed changes in the paths of these exogenous forcing variables, the general solution of the model provides a description of how the real exchange rate responds to expected temporary or future changes in commercial policy.

2.5   Fiscal Policy and the Real Exchange Rate

The dynamic model presented in the previous section may be applied to analyze the effect on the real exchange rate of shifts of government spending between domestic and foreign goods. Recall that in section 2.2 an increase in government spending on domestic goods at the expense of government spending on foreign goods is represented by an increase in the exogenous factor x that enters positively into the value of excess demand for domestic goods and negatively into the value of excess demand for foreign goods. In the dynamic model of section 2.4, such an increase in x translates into a corresponding increase in the exogenous forcing variable, z. It follows that an unexpected permanent shift in government spending away from foreign goods and toward domestic goods, $\Delta x > 0$, will increase the equilibrium real exchange rate given by equation (27) by a constant amount, $\Delta q = (\sigma/v)\Delta x$, at every moment, relative to the value it would have had in the absence of this government spending shift. This result is, of course, the same as the one obtained in the initial comparative statics analysis of a government spending shift described in section 2.2.

The virtue of the dynamic model of section 2.4 is that it permits analysis of any more complicated shift in the actual or expected distribution of government spending between domestic and foreign goods. In particular, consider an unexpected shift of government spending toward domestic goods, Δx, at time t that is expected to last only T periods. The effect of this unexpected temporary spending shift on the real exchange rate in period t is $\Delta q(t) = (\sigma/v)(\Delta x)(1 - \theta^T)$, which is smaller than the effect of a permanent spending shift of the same magnitude. As the time when the spending shift will be terminated approaches, the effect of the shift on the real exchange rate consistent with long-run trade-balance equilibrium diminishes, with $\Delta \bar{\bar{q}}(s) = (\sigma/v)(\Delta x)(1 - \theta^{T+t-s})$ for $t < s < (T + t)$. The effect on $\bar{\bar{q}}$, however, is not the only effect of the temporary spending shift on the real exchange rate. Because private asset holders know that the spending shift is temporary, they anticipate that q will change in period $t + T$ when the temporary spending shifts ends. This anticipated change in q affects the expected real interest rate for domestic residents who consume both domestic and foreign goods and thereby affects their spending and saving behavior. Between period t and period $t + T$, domestic residents expect future declines in q and therefore save more than they otherwise would. This implies that the private net stock of foreign assets, $A(s)$, rises above the level it would otherwise have for $t < s < (t + T)$. It follows that $\Delta q(s) > \Delta \bar{\bar{q}}(s)$ for $t < s < (t + T)$. Moreover, since $A(t + T)$ is greater than the value it would have in the absence of the temporary spending shift, it follows that $q(s)$ remains somewhat above the level it would have in the absence of the temporary spending shift for $s \geq (T + t)$ and only gradually converges back toward its previous path, as the increase in A built up between t and $t + T$ is gradually run down.

Another application of the dynamic model is in the analysis of a shift in government spending expected to occur at date $s = t + T$ that lies

T periods in the future. Suppose that private agents first learn of this spending shift in period t and that they expect it will be permanent once it starts in period $t + T$. Even though this expected future spending shift has no immediate direct effect on excess demands for domestic and foreign goods, it does have an immediate effect on the real exchange rate equal to $\Delta q(t) = (\sigma/v)(\Delta x)(\theta^T)$, where Δx is the size of the permanent spending shift that is expected to occur at $t + T$. The source of this change in $q(t)$ is the change in the real exchange rate anticipated to be consistent with long-run equilibrium in the trade balance, $\Delta \bar{\bar{q}}(t)$. Over the period between t and $t + T$, the real exchange rate is also affected by induced changes in private net asset holdings, which are reduced relative to their previously expected path because private agents anticipate increases in q as the moment of the spending shift approaches. The decrease in $A(t + T)$ relative to the level it would have had in the absence of anticipations of the spending shift implies that $q(t + T)$ as determined by equation (27) is below the level it would have if the spending shift suddenly became known at $T + t$. Thus, the effect of spending shift being anticipated in period t, rather than becoming known in period $t + T$, is that the adjustment of the real exchange rate to this spending shift is spread out over time, rather than occurring all at once in period $t + T$. Some of the adjustment of q takes place immediately when the spending shift is first anticipated in period t. Further adjustment of q happens between t and $t + T$, and some adjustment takes place after $t + T$, as private net asset holdings are raised back to the path they would have followed in the absence of anticipations of the spending shift.

With slight modification, the dynamic model of section 2.4 may also be used to analyze the effects on the real exchange rate of general fiscal policy, defined as variations in the debt-financed difference between government expenditure and government revenue, g. To deal with general fiscal policy, the balance-of-payments equilibrium condition must be modified from equation (24) to:

$$(34) \qquad v(z - q) + r^*(A - G) = w - \alpha\sigma D^e(q) - \mu A - g,$$

where G is the stock of government debt, and g is the excess of government spending (including interest payments on outstanding debt) over government revenue. With this modification, the dynamic system determining the expected future evolution of q and A is given by:

$$(35) \qquad \begin{bmatrix} \alpha\sigma D^e - v & r^* + \mu \\ D^e & \mu + D^e \end{bmatrix} \begin{bmatrix} q \\ A \end{bmatrix} \begin{bmatrix} w - vz - g + r^*G \\ w \end{bmatrix}.$$

The only difference between this dynamic system and the dynamic system in (26) is that the exogenous forcing variable in the top equation is now $w - vz - g + r^*G$, whereas before it was simply $w - vz$. The additional term $(r^*G - g)$ in this forcing variable accounts for the effects of general fiscal policy. The solution of the dynamic system (35) is the same as the solution of the dynamic system (26), as given by (27) through (33), except that the expression for the real exchange rate consistent with long-run equilibrium in the trade balance, $\bar{q}(t)$, given by (29) must be modified by replacing the forcing variable $z(t + j)$ with $y(t + j) = z(t + j) + (1/v)[g(t + j) - r^*G(t + j)]$.

With this modification in mind, consider now an unexpected temporary fiscal expansion in which lump-sum taxes are cut by a constant amount for T periods, starting in the current period t, without any tax increases to finance the increased interest payments on the expanding government debt until period $t + T$, when taxes are raised sufficiently to eliminate the deficit. This policy translates into a constant unexpected increase in $y(s)$ for $t \leq s < (t + T)$ and a constant unexpected decrease in $y(s)$ for $s \geq (t + T)$ equal to the interest on the increase in the government debt between t and $t + T$. The effect of this fiscal policy on the real exchange rate at time t is given by:

$$(36) \quad \Delta q(t) = \Delta\bar{q}(t) = (1 - \theta)[1 - \theta^T(1 + r^*)^T](\Delta\kappa/v) > 0,$$

where $\Delta\kappa > 0$ is the amount of the reduction in lump-sum taxes (relative to their previously expected path) between t and $t + T$. This effect on the real exchange rate is positive because the discount rate λ used in calculating $\bar{q}(t)$, as given by (33), is larger than r^* and therefore implies that $\theta^T(1 + r^*)^T = [(1 + r^*)/(1 + \lambda)]^T$ is less than one. As time goes by, the size of the increase in $\bar{q}(s)$ for $t < s < (t + T)$ diminishes and ultimately turns negative because the number of future periods in which taxes will be lower is diminishing and the date at which taxes will be raised to cover the deficit is approaching. After time $t + T$, $\bar{q}(s)$ is reduced permanently by the amount $(\Delta\kappa/v)[(1 + r^*)^T - 1]$, which represents the long-run equilibrium effect on $\bar{q}$ of the increased taxes that are imposed to finance the increased interest on the expanded stock of government debt.

Except in period t, the response of $q(s)$ to the fiscal policy does not mirror exactly the response of $\bar{q}(s)$ because the expectations of changes in q induced by the policy influence private saving behavior and hence the path of the private net stock of foreign assets. Specifically, since q is expected to decline after its initial upward jump in period t, $A(s)$ rises above its level in the absence of the fiscal policy for $t < s < (t + T)$ and gradually falls back to its previous path for $s \geq (t + T)$. In accord with equation (27), this increase in $A(s)$ relative to its previous path results in an increase in $q(s)$ relative to $\bar{q}(s)$. The overall result, as illustrated in figure 2.2, is that during the interval between t and $t + T$, $\Delta q(s)$ remains positive even after $\Delta\bar{q}(s)$ has become negative. By period $t + T$, $\Delta q(s)$ is negative but smaller in absolute value than $\Delta\bar{q}(s)$. Only as the increased net stock of private asset holdings built up between t and $t + T$ is run down does $\Delta q(s)$ fall to the long-run equilibrium level of $\Delta\bar{q}(s)$.

This analysis of the effects of general fiscal policy can be extended to other examples embodying alternative specifications of the paths of g and G and hence of the exogenous forcing variable $y = z + (1/v)(g - r^*G)$. Rather than pursuing such examples, however, it is more useful

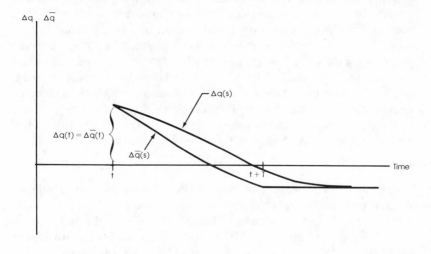

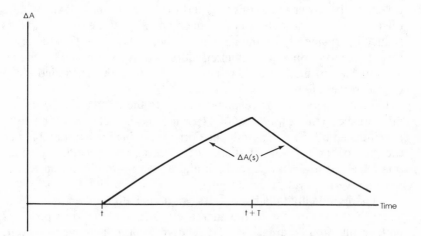

Fig. 2.2   The effects of a temporary fiscal expansion on the real exchange rate and on private net holdings of foreign assets.

to investigate the elements of the specification of the present model that allow general fiscal policy to influence the behavior of the real exchange rate.

The short-run effect of expansionary fiscal policy in raising the real exchange rate does not depend on the failure of private asset holders to forecast future tax liabilities correctly or on the failure of the government to impose taxes sufficient to pay the interest on the government debt. It does depend, however, on the absence of full Ricardian equivalence between debt-financed and tax-financed government spending. In the example just considered (as should be the case in any well-specified example of fiscal policy), the government's intertemporal budget constraint is satisfied because the government ultimately (starting in period $t + T$) raises taxes sufficiently to pay the interest on the expanded stock of government debt. Private agents foresee this tax increase starting in period t when the policy is introduced, and the reaction of the real exchange rate to the new policy, as given by equation (36), reflects the anticipation of these future taxes. The effect of the anticipated increase in future taxes reduces but does not eliminate the expansionary effect of the government deficit because the discount rate, λ, that is applied to determine the effect of future taxes on the current real exchange rate is greater than the interest rate, r^*, on government debt. If private saving responded immediately to the government deficit in the manner required to maintain Ricardian equivalence between debt financing and tax financing of government spending, there would be no such expansionary effect of fiscal policy. In this case, the exogenous variable, w, which accounts for the exogenous factors affecting the desired excess of private income over private spending, would rise immediately to offset any increase in g and leave no room for government deficits to affect the aggregate level of desired spending. The present analysis, which excludes such an offsetting effect of private saving, implicitly assumes that general fiscal policy operates in the same way as do shifts in the desired intertemporal distribution of private spending. This assumption would be entirely appropriate even under the conditions of Ricardian equivalence, if the government always acted in the interests of its country's private asset holders, with its budget deficits and surpluses reflecting private preferences regarding the intertemporal distribution of spending relative to income.

2.6   Capital Controls and the Real Exchange Rate

In the preceding analysis of the behavior of the real exchange rate, it has been assumed that private agents can borrow and lend in the world market whatever amount they want (denominated in terms of foreign goods) at the prevailing real interest rate, r^*. Through capital controls policies a government may limit the extent of private credit flows and thereby influence the behavior of the real exchange rate. Specifically, looking back at the expression for the trade balance given in equation (7), $T = v(z - q) = -\psi$, it follows that any policy that affects $-\psi$ (the excess of domestic income over the value of domestic output) by controlling international capital flows must, for a given value of z, affect the level of q.

Formally, there are a variety of ways in which capital controls can be introduced into the model used to determine the behavior of the real exchange rate. By far the simplest is to specify that the international flow of net private capital (the change in the net private stock of foreign securities) is controlled directly by the government during each period. The policy-determined net outflow of capital (that is, the increase in private net holdings of foreign assets) in period t is denoted by $a(t)$. Returning to the base-case assumptions that government revenue is equal to government expenditure ($g = 0$) and that there is no outstanding government debt ($G = 0$), the condition for balance-of-payments equilibrium in the presence of capital controls is expressed by the requirement:

$$(37) \qquad v(z(t) - q(t)) + r^*A(t) = a(t).$$

Solving this condition for $q(t)$, it follows that the (logarithm of the) real exchange rate is given by:

$$(38) \qquad q(t) = z(t) + (1/v)[r^*A(t) - a(t)].$$

It is apparent that a higher permissible capital outflow or a lower permissible capital inflow in the current period (that is, a lower value of $a[t]$) implies a lower current real exchange rate (a lower value of $q[t]$). But since greater current capital outflows or smaller current capital inflows mean larger future private net holdings of foreign assets (higher future values of $A[s]$ for $s > t$), a higher current value of $a(t)$ implies lower future values of $q(s)$ for $s > t$.

In considering the effects of capital controls on the real exchange rate, it is useful to distinguish between persistent effects on the level of the real exchange rate and effects on the variability of the real exchange rate in response to different types of economic disturbances. The capacity of capital controls to maintain a long-run average value of the real exchange rate different from the long-run average that would prevail in the absence of such controls is limited to the ability of such controls to maintain a long-run average value of A that differs from its long-run equilibrium value in the absence of controls. Specifically, comparing the long-run average value of q determined by equation (38) (denoted by $\bar{q}_c$ for the average with controls) with the long-run average value of q determined by (27) (denoted by $\bar{q}_n$ for the average with no controls), under the assumption that the processes generating the z terms and the w terms are stationary, we find that:

$$(39) \qquad \bar{q}_c - \bar{q}_n = (r^*/v)(\bar{A}_c - \bar{A}_n),$$

where $\bar{A}_c$ and $\bar{A}_n$ are the long-run average values of A with and without controls, respectively. This result reflects the fact that interest income earned on private net foreign asset holdings is spent partly on domestic goods, thereby implying that a higher long-run average level of private net foreign asset holdings requires a higher long-run average level of q to maintain equilibrium in the market for domestic goods. For relevant sizes of the parameters r^* and v, it is apparent that for capital controls to have a substantial long-run effect on the average value of the real exchange rate, they must have a large effect on the long-run average level of private net holdings of foreign assets.

In contrast to their limited capacity to affect the long-run average level of the real exchange rate, capital controls can substantially affect the responsiveness of the real exchange rate to temporary disturbances. Again, a comparison of equations (38) and (27) shows that under capital controls, with a fixed value of $a(t)$, the current value of $q(t)$ responds one-for-one with variations in $z(t)$, whereas in the absence of controls, $q(t)$ depends on the discounted present value of the current z and all expected future values of z. It follows that a temporary, one-period disturbance to $z(t)$ will have a much stronger effect on $q(t)$ under capital controls (with $a[t]$ fixed) than in the absence of controls. This is because in the absence of controls the capital flow will adjust to accommodate part of the current disturbance to $z(t)$ and thereby spread the effect of the disturbance over time. More generally, this principle applies to any form of temporary disturbance to the value of z: capital controls (with a fixed path of $a[t]$) tend to accentuate the effects of such disturbances on the real exchange rate.

The other side of the coin is that capital controls reduce the sensitivity of the real exchange rate to disturbances in the values of w, that is, to disturbances that affect the desired excess of income over spending. Equation (27) reveals that disturbances to w affect $q(t)$ in the absence of capital controls because $q(t)$ depends on $\bar{A}(t)$, and $\bar{A}(t)$ depends on a discounted sum of the present and expected future values of w. Looking at (38), however, we find that neither the current w nor any expected future value of w affects the current value of $q(t)$. Thus, capital controls, with a fixed value of $a(t)$, insulate $q(t)$ from disturbances to the value of w.

There is no necessity, of course, for capital controls to maintain a fixed value of $a(t)$ in the face of all forms of economic disturbances. In particular, if a government wanted to stabilize the behavior of the real exchange rate (over and above the stability resulting from the absence of capital controls), it would seek to increase or reduce the value of $a(t)$ to offset positive or negative disturbances to $z(t)$, while holding $a(t)$ constant in the face of disturbances to the value of w.

A special circumstance in which a government might wish to manipulate the international flow of capital is if it is pursuing other policies designed to affect the real exchange rate. In particular, consider the unexpected temporary shift of government spending toward domestic goods and away from foreign goods discussed at the beginning of section 2.5. Because private asset holders anticipate declining values of q subsequent to the impact of this spending shift, the rate at which they accumulate net foreign assets will increase in the absence of capital controls. Later on, especially after period $t + T$ when the spending shift ends, the increase in private net holdings of foreign assets maintains q at a level somewhat higher than it would otherwise be. But in period t and in the periods immediately following, the increase in private saving diminishes the effect of the spending shift in raising the relative price of domestic goods. If the government wished to maximize the effect of the spending shift in raising $q(t)$, it would limit the extent of the capital outflow (the purchase of foreign assets by domestic residents) in order to bottle up the effect of the spending shift toward domestic goods. A similar capital controls policy would also be pursued by a government that wished to maximize the effect on the real exchange rate of the unexpected temporary fiscal expansion discussed at the end of section 2.5.

Much of this analysis of capital controls carries over to the analysis of exchange rate systems in which governments maintain two separate nominal exchange rates: one for current-account transactions, and one for capital-account transactions. (See Dornbusch 1984 and the references cited there for an analysis of these systems.) Dual exchange rate systems are usually designed so that the current-account rate is fixed or determined by a crawling peg, while the capital-account rate is allowed to be determined by market forces. The effect, indeed the purpose, of such a system is to control the extent of private international capital flows, with the differential between the capital-account and the current-account exchange rates measuring the effective rationing price of whatever net amount of foreign exchange is allowed to become available for financing private capital flows.

2.7 The Combined Effects of Monetary and Exchange Rate Policy

An especially important mechanism through which economic policies affect the real exchange rate and thereby replicate some of the effects of commercial policies is through the interaction of monetary policies and policies designed to influence the nominal exchange rate. To analyze the implications of this combination of policies, it is necessary to broaden the model introduced in the earlier sections by introducing appropriate monetary elements. The condition for equilibrium in the domestic money market is expressed by the requirement:

$$(40) \qquad m = k + p^* + e + lq - \xi D^e(e),$$

where m denotes the logarithm of the nominal money supply; k summarizes the exogenous factors affecting the logarithm of the demand for domestic money; e denotes the logarithm of the nominal exchange rate (defined as the price of a unit of world money in terms of domestic money); p^* denotes the logarithm of the world money price of traded goods; $l > 0$ is the elasticity of money demand with respect to the relative price of domestic goods; and $\xi > 0$ is the semielasticity of money demand with respect to the expected rate of change in the nominal exchange rate. The unitary coefficients on p^* and e in (40) are justified by the assumption that the demand for domestic money is unit elastic with respect to the general level of domestic prices. The positive coefficient of q in (40) reflects the effect of increases in q in raising the demand for domestic money, both by raising the general level of domestic prices (given p^* and e) and by increasing the real value of domestic output measured in terms of traded goods. The negative coefficient of $D^e(e)$ in (40) reflects the negative effect on domestic money demand of an increase in the domestic nominal interest rate that results from an increase in the expected depreciation rate of the foreign exchange value of domestic money.

When the nominal exchange rate is freely flexible, and when goods prices adjust instantaneously to maintain equilibrium in the goods markets, monetary policy exerts no influence on the real exchange rate, q, or on any other variable in the real sector of the economy. (See Mussa 1984 for further discussion.) This conclusion is based on the assumption that the behavioral equations and equilibrium conditions for the real sector of the economy that were described and analyzed in the preceding sections of this paper require no modification to accommodate the condition of domestic money market equilibrium given in equation (40). Specifically, this means that we abstract from any real balance effect through which the real value of domestic money balances might affect the desired excess of domestic real spending over domestic real income. We also assume that under a freely flexible exchange rate, the real sector of the economy is not affected by the fiscal effects of money creation and destruction. The revenue that the government derives from money creation is redistributed to the private sector through lump-sum transfers. The private sector then uses these transfers to pay the inflation tax on its real money balances that results from domestic money creation under a flexible exchange rate. Private sector spending on domestic and foreign goods is therefore assumed to be unaffected by the fiscal effects of money creation under a flexible exchange rate.

Given the conclusion that the real sector of the economy is not affected by monetary policy under a flexible exchange rate, the money market equilibrium condition of equation (40) may be used to determine the behavior of the nominal exchange rate, treating the behavior of the money supply and of the determinants of money demand as exogenous. Specifically, treating (40) as a forward-looking difference equation in the expected level of e (and ruling out "bubbles" in the solution), it follows that:

$$(41) \quad E[e(s); t] = (1 - \phi)\left(\sum_{j=0}^{\infty} \phi^j\right)\{E[m(s + j) - \kappa(s + j); t]\},$$

where $\phi = \xi/(1 + \xi)$, and $\kappa(u) = k(u) + p^*(u) + lq(u)$. This result, which is familiar from monetary models of exchange rate determination (see Mussa 1976; 1982a; 1982b; or 1984), states that the (logarithm of the) expected nominal exchange rate is a discounted sum of expected present and future differences between the (logarithm of the) nominal money supply and the (logarithm of the) component of money demand that does not depend on the exchange rate. Included in this component of money demand is the influence of the behavior of the (logarithm of the) relative price of domestic goods, which is determined independently of the behavior of the domestic money supply.

The real exchange rate and other real sector variables are not influenced by the behavior of the money supply or by the nominal exchange rate under a flexible exchange rate regime because under this regime the nominal exchange rate always adjusts to offset variations in the money supply and preserve monetary neutrality. This neutrality breaks down, even in the absence of real balance effects or nominal price stickiness, when the exchange rate is not freely flexible. To see why this is so and how monetary policy and nominal exchange rate policy may interact to influence the real exchange rate, it is useful to consider the specific case in which the (logarithm of the) money supply is held constant at $\bar{m}$ and the (logarithm of the) nominal exchange rate is pegged at $\bar{e}$. A similar analysis applies to the case in which the rate of money supply growth is held constant and the rate of change in the nominal exchange rate is fixed by some predetermined rate of crawl.

With e pegged at $\bar{e}$ and m fixed at $\bar{m}$, and if private asset holders expect no change in the nominal exchange rate (so that $D^e[e] = 0$), the only variable that is free to adjust to satisfy the money market equilibrium in equation (40) is the (logarithm of the) real exchange rate. Specifically, the value of q that is consistent with (40) is given by:

$$(42) \quad q = (1/l)[\bar{m} - \bar{e} - p^* - k].$$

This relationship indicates that for any given value of k and p^*, the greater the level of $\bar{m}$, the greater the level of q required to maintain money market equilibrium; and the greater the level of $\bar{e}$, the lower the level of q required to maintain money market equilibrium. It follows that with a pegged exchange rate, the real exchange rate is not independent of the policy-determined level of the money supply; and with a policy-determined level of the money supply, the real exchange rate is not independent of the policy-determined value of the nominal exchange rate.

To maintain e at $\bar{e}$ and simultaneously keep m at $\bar{m}$, the government of the home country will generally need to intervene in the foreign exchange market and sterilize the effects of its interventions on the domestic money supply. Analytically, it is simplest to deal with such sterilized intervention by assuming that the government keeps the domestic credit component of the money supply constant and finances necessary interventions in the foreign exchange market by borrowing and lending on the world capital market. The required extent of government borrowing is determined by the balance-of-payments equilibrium condition:

$$(43) \qquad v(z - q) + r^*(A - G) = w - \alpha\sigma D^e(q) - \mu A - g,$$

where G represents the outstanding stock of government debt, and g represents the flow of government borrowing to finance intervention. Interest in G is assumed to be financed by lump-sum taxes.

The flow of government intervention is represented by the same variable, g, as was previously used to denote the excess of government spending over government revenue. This specification is appropriate because when the government borrows in the world capital market to finance its foreign exchange intervention, it is necessarily financing an excess of spending over revenue. This is the fiscal effect of sterilized intervention in the foreign exchange market. Specifically, if government spending on goods and services is constant (as will be assumed throughout this discussion), there must be a reduction in lump-sum taxes to correspond to government borrowing to finance intervention in the support of the foreign exchange value of domestic money; and there must be an increase in lump-sum taxes to correspond to the government lending (or repayment of past borrowings) that occurs when the government intervenes to prevent appreciation of the foreign exchange value of domestic money.

The fiscal effect of foreign exchange market intervention has important implications for the spending behavior of the private sector. If the government must intervene to support the foreign exchange value of domestic money, the domestic money market is in "quasi-equilibrium" in the sense that the current demand for the stock of domestic money is equal to the current supply, but domestic money holders wish to run down their money balance over time. This running down of money balances over time implies an incipient excess of private sector spending over private sector income that private agents plan to finance at the expense of money holdings, without any effect on the rate of change in the net foreign asset holdings of the private sector. Under a flexible exchange rate, this incipient excess of private spending over private income financed out of money balances would not emerge because the exchange rate would adjust to the level at which the stock of money is willingly held, and the planned rate of money accumulation corresponds to the expected rate of monetary expansion (both of which are zero when m is held constant at $\bar{m}$). When the exchange rate is pegged at a value that necessitates intervention in support of the foreign exchange value of domestic money, the incipient excess of private sector spending over income corresponding to the planned rate of reduction in money balances is offset by the reduction in lump-sum taxes associated with the fiscal effect of government intervention in the foreign exchange market. This result must be so because with sterilized intervention, the actual level of domestic money balances does not decline, implying that the private sector does not succeed in spending in excess of its actual income (taking account of reduced lump-sum taxes) at the expense of its money balances. The actual excess of private sector spending over private sector income therefore corresponds to the desired rate of decumulation of private net holdings of foreign assets, $-D(A) = -w + \alpha\sigma D^e(q) + \mu A$, which is determined by exactly the same factors as those analyzed in the earlier sections of this paper.

It should be emphasized that this analysis of the interaction between private sector spending behavior and the fiscal effect of sterilized intervention in the foreign exchange market does not rely on a traditional real balance effect, in which the level of real money balances influences the desired level of private spending. With a given nominal money supply, incipient differences between spending and income that the private sector plans to finance out of money balances arise only when the government pegs the nominal exchange rate at a value different from that which would prevail under a flexible exchange rate regime.

On the other hand, it should also be emphasized that the analysis of this interaction does rely on the assumption that the private sector fails to foresee the effect of current government borrowing and lending (carried out in support of foreign exchange market intervention) on the future tax liabilities of the private sector. If there were a full Ricardian offset of private sector saving for government borrowing, there would be no mechanism through which the flow to government borrowing or the stock of government debt would influence the real sector of the economy. Thus, there would be no way (at least in the context of the present model) for a policy of sterilized intervention to maintain the real exchange rate at the level determined by equation (42) if the pegged value of the nominal exchange rate differs from the nominal exchange rate that would prevail under exchange rate flexibility. (In a portfolio balance model in which asset holders have distinct demands for securities denominated in different national monies, however, there is some latitude for sterilized intervention to affect the exchange rate; see for example, Kenen 1981 and Henderson 1984.)

If the conditions for the fiscal effect of sterilized intervention to influence the real exchange rate are assumed to be satisfied, the behavior of the real exchange rate becomes sensitive to monetary policy and exchange rate policy. Specifically, a fixed nominal money supply, $\bar{m}$, and a fixed nominal exchange rate, $\bar{e}$, maintained by a policy of sterilized intervention, determine the level of the real exchange rate through the relationship in equation (42). Given this value of the real exchange rate, the balance-of-payments equilibrium condition (43) determines the extent of official intervention (financed by government borrowing in the world capital market) that is required to maintain this value of the real exchange rate, such that:

$$(44) \quad g = r^*G - (r^* + \mu)A - \alpha\sigma D^e(q) + w - vz \\ + (v/l)[\bar{m} - \bar{e} - p^* - k + \xi D^e(e)].$$

Since $D(G) = g$, and under the assumption that no change is expected in the nominal exchange rate or in the real exchange rate, the dynamic law governing the evolution of the stock of government debt is given by:

$$(45) \quad D(G) = r^*G - (r^* + \mu)A + w - vz \\ + (v/l)(\bar{m} - \bar{e} - p^* - k).$$

The dynamic law governing the evolution of the stock of privately held foreign assets (again under the assumption of no expected change in q) is given by:

$$(46) \quad D(A) = w - \mu A.$$

Together, (45) and (46) constitute the dynamic system that determines the joint evolution of G and A with a fixed money supply and a pegged nominal exchange rate, under the assumption that no change is expected in either the nominal or the real exchange rate.

This dynamic system has two characteristic roots: a stable one, $\lambda_1 = -\mu < 0$; and an unstable one, $\lambda_2 = r^*$. The stable characteristic root is associated with the dynamic process that governs the evolution of the private stock of net foreign assets. With a fixed value of the forcing variable, w, which measures exogenous influences on private sector desired saving, the stock of privately held foreign assets necessarily converges to a long-run equilibrium level of w/μ. The unstable characteristic root is associated with the dynamic process governing the evolution of the stock of government debt. With fixed values of the forcing variables, w, z, p^*, and k and of the policy-determined variables, $\bar{m}$ and $\bar{e}$, there is for each initial stock of private net foreign assets a unique initial stock of government debt for which the subsequent stock of government debt converges to a finite steady-state level. Specifically, if A is initially at its long-run equilibrium level, w/μ, the stock of government debt must be:

(47) $$\bar{G} = (w/\mu) + (v/r^*)(z - q),$$

where q is given by equation (42). At this level of G, and only at this level of G, the flow of government intervention required to maintain the pegged nominal exchange rate and the fixed nominal money supply will be zero, implying that the outstanding stock of government debt will not be changing. If $G > \bar{G}$ (with $A = w/\mu$), the required flow of intervention will be positive, implying an explosively expanding stock of government debt. If $G < \bar{G}$ (with $A = w/\mu$), the required flow of intervention will be negative, implying an explosively contracting stock of government debt (or explosively expanding stock of government lending).

This dynamic instability in the behavior of the stock of government debt applies for any assumed behavior of the exogenous forcing variables. It reflects the fundamental economic instability of a policy that seeks to maintain a constant nominal exchange rate and a constant nominal money stock by means of sterilized intervention. For any path of the exogenous forcing variables z, w, p^* and k, and for any policy-determined value of $\bar{m}$, there is only one fixed value of $\bar{e}$ that can be sustained by sterilized intervention (with a finite bound on government borrowing and lending). In general, therefore, a policy of fixing the nominal money supply and pegging the nominal exchange rate is not viable and cannot permanently sustain an arbitrary value of the real exchange rate.

Rationality of expectations presumably implies that private asset holders recognize the long-run nonviability of a policy that fixes the nominal money supply and pegs the nominal exchange rate. If a government must persistently intervene to support the foreign exchange value of domestic money, private agents will suspect that at some point the money supply will need to be contracted or domestic money will need to be devalued (an increase in $\bar{e}$). Conversely, if a government must persistently intervene to prevent appreciation of the foreign exchange value of domestic money, private agents will suspect either a money supply increase or an exchange rate appreciation (a reduction in $\bar{e}$). For purposes of the present discussion of the real exchange rate, it is useful to focus on the case of persistent intervention in support of the foreign exchange value of domestic money, whereby adjustment is expected to come through a nominal exchange rate devaluation (an increase in $\bar{e}$). This case has been a common pattern of economic policy in a number of developing countries.

It is possible to model expectations of a devaluation in several ways, each of which will yield somewhat different implications. The approach adopted here will be to assume that expectations of a devaluation are based, at least in part, on the cumulative extent of past intervention in support of the current nominal exchange rate. Specifically, assuming that G was zero when the current exchange rate was established, suppose that G must reach some critical level, $\hat{G}$, before private asset holders begin to expect any significant probability of a parity change in the near future. This implies that $D^e(e) = 0$, so long as $G < \hat{G}$. It follows that so long as $G < \hat{G}$, q will be determined by equation (42). Thus, so long as cumulative intervention in support of the current nominal exchange rate remains below the critical level, $\hat{G}$, the real exchange rate will be at the level dictated by money market equilibrium for the policy-determined values of $\bar{m}$ and $\bar{e}$. Under this assumption about expectations of devaluation, the combination of monetary policy and nominal exchange rate policy therefore has the capacity to influence the real exchange rate, at least over some finite time period.

When G rises above $\hat{G}$, the expected rate of devaluation is assumed to be given by:

$$(48) \qquad D^e(e) = \rho(G - \hat{G}).$$

The factor ρ reflects both the expected probability of devaluation (during the next brief time interval) and the expected extent of devaluation if a parity change occurs (during this brief interval). Given this assumption about $D^e(e)$, the level of q consistent with money market equilibrium is still given by equation (42) when $G < \hat{G}$, whereas when $G > \hat{G}$, the level of q is given by:

$$(49) \qquad q = (1/l)[\bar{m} - \bar{e} - p^* - k + \xi\rho(G - \hat{G})].$$

When $G < \hat{G}$, the expected rate of change in q, $D^e(q)$, is zero. When $G > \hat{G}$, the expected rate of change in q is given by:

$$(50) \qquad D^e(q) = -\epsilon(G - \hat{G}) + (\xi\rho/l)[D(G)],$$

where $\epsilon = (1 + \xi)(\rho/l) > 0$, and $D(G) = g$ is the flow of intervention when no devaluation takes place. This result reflects the assumption that if a devaluation occurs during the next brief time interval, the expectation of a further devaluation during the following brief time interval falls to zero.

With these assumptions, it follows that during the period between devaluations, when $G < \hat{G}$, q is constant at the level q determined by (42), and the evolution of A and G are determined by the dynamic system of (45) and (46). The comments previously made about this dynamic system apply here as well, except for the fact that in this case, the intervention tends to support the foreign exchange value of domestic money, and G is generally growing over time. When G reaches $\hat{G}$ and before the devaluation actually occurs, q is determined by (49) and the evolution of A and G are determined by the dynamic system:

(51) $\quad D(A) = w - \mu A + \alpha \sigma \epsilon (G - \hat{G}) - (\alpha \sigma \xi \rho / l)[D(G)]$

(52) $\quad D(G) = r^*G - (r^* + \mu)A + w - vz + \alpha \sigma \epsilon (G - \hat{G})$
$\qquad - (\alpha \sigma \xi \rho / l)[D(G)] + (v/l)[\bar{m} - \bar{e} - p^* - k + \xi \rho (G - \hat{G})].$

This dynamic system has one negative characteristic root, $\lambda_1 > -\mu$, and one positive characteristic root, $\lambda_2 > r^*$. As in the previous case, the negative root is associated with the process of convergence of the private stock of net foreign assets toward its steady-state level; and the positive root is associated with the explosive behavior of the stock of government debt. The fact that the positive characteristic root is now greater than its previous value of r^* indicates that private agents' anticipation of a devaluation contributes to the explosive tendency of the dynamic system. The economic explanation of this result is the following. As private agents come to expect a significant probability of a devaluation of the nominal exchange rate, the domestic nominal interest rate must rise and the demand for domestic money must decline. To offset this factor tending to reduce the demand for domestic money and thus maintain money market equilibrium, q must rise. This rise in q implies an increase in the flow of intervention required to maintain the nominal exchange rate and the nominal money supply and sustain balance-of-payments equilibrium. In turn, this larger flow of intervention accelerates the growth of the outstanding stock of government debt and thereby further accelerates the explosive tendency of the dynamic system. Moreover, as $D^e(e)$ rises as the result of increases in the assessed probability of devaluation and in the expected magnitude of devaluation, private agents no longer expect a zero rate of change in the real exchange rate. Initially, when G is near $\hat{G}$, $D^e(q)$ is negative because the expected effect of the growth of G (conditional on no devaluation), $(\xi \rho / l)[D(G)]$, outweighs the expected effect of devaluation (conditional on its occurrence), $- \epsilon(G - \hat{G})$. This initial negative value of $D^e(q)$ tends to reduce the extent of intervention required to maintain balance-of-payments equilibrium and partially offsets the acceleration of the growth of G induced by the higher level of q. Later, when G grows large relative to $\hat{G}$, $D^e(q)$ will become positive and thus become yet another factor contributing to the explosive tendency of the dynamic system.

The behavior of the real exchange rate and the nominal and real interest rates in this dynamic process are as follows. So long as G remains below $\hat{G}$, q is constant at the level determined by equation (42), which is above the value that q would have if the nominal exchange rate was not sustained by intervention in support of the pegged foreign exchange value of domestic money. Indeed, as shown in section 2.2, the excess of spending over income that is financed by the fiscal effect of intervention in the foreign exchange market may be thought of as the proximate cause of the higher level of q. Since $D^e(e) = 0$ and $D^e(q) = 0$ while G remains below $\hat{G}$, the domestic nominal interest rate remains at the level of the world nominal interest rate, i^*, and the domestic real interest rate remains at the level of the world real interest rate, r^*. As G rises above $\hat{G}$, the level of q determined by equation (49) is forced higher and higher by rising assessments of the probability and likely extent of devaluation, as summarized by the increasing value of $D^e(e) = \rho(G - \hat{G})$. As $D^e(e)$ rises, the domestic nominal interest rate rises further and further above the world nominal interest rate.

The domestic real interest rate follows a somewhat different pattern. When G initially rises just above $\hat{G}$, the expected real domestic interest rate, $r = r^* - \sigma D^e(q)$, falls below r^* because the positive effect of expected growth in G (conditional on no devaluation) on $D^e(q)$, $(\xi\rho/l)$ $[D(G)]$, outweighs the negative effect associated with the expectation of devaluation, $-\epsilon(G - \hat{G})$. Later on, the factor $-\epsilon(G - \hat{G})$ tending to induce a negative value of $D^e(q)$ outweighs the positive factor $(\xi\rho/l)[D(G)]$ tending to induce a positive value of $D^e(q)$, and $D^e(q)$ becomes negative. At this point the domestic real interest rate, $r^* - [\sigma D^e(q)]$, rises above the world real interest rate, r^*, and it continues to rise until the moment of devaluation.

The general features of this description of real exchange rate behavior and domestic nominal and real interest rate behavior apply under a broader range of assumptions about the conduct of monetary policy and exchange rate policy. Specifically, consider a policy under which the nominal exchange rate is depreciated at a predetermined rate of crawl, supplemented by occasional major devaluations, and the money supply is made to grow at a rate greater than the growth in the demand for money at the predetermined rate of crawl of the exchange rate. Suppose that when major devaluations occur under this general policy regime, they are of sufficient magnitude that for some time afterward private agents do not expect another major devaluation. Also suppose that the extent of the major devaluation is such that for some time afterward there is a balance-of-payments surplus (on an official settlements basis) that allows the government to repay loans used to finance the intervention in support of the exchange rate prior to the last major devaluation. Under these assumptions, the path of the real exchange rate and of other relevant variables will be something like the following.

In the initial period following a major devaluation, during which private agents do not predict another immediate major devaluation, the level of q is determined by the money market equilibrium condition to be:

$$(53) \qquad q = (1/l)(m - e - p^* - k),$$

where m and e are the policy-determined (but not constant) values of the (logarithm of the) money supply and the (logarithm of the) price of foreign exchange; and, for simplicity, p^* and k are assumed constant. By assumption, the rate of growth of the money supply, $D(m)$, is greater than the rate of crawl of the nominal exchange rate, $D(e)$. Thus, the level of q determined by (53) will be rising over time at the rate:

$$(54) \qquad D(q) = (1/l)[D(m) - D(e)].$$

The extent of the major devaluation is assumed to be such that the level of q for some period after the devaluation is consistent with an official settlements surplus, the magnitude of which is given by:

$$(55) \quad D(G) = r^*G - (r^* + \mu)A - (\alpha\sigma/l)[D(m) - D(e)]$$
$$+ (v/l)(m - e - p^* - k).$$

The dynamic behavior of the private stock of net foreign assets during this period is given by:

$$(56) \qquad D(A) = w - \mu A - (\alpha\sigma/l)[D(m) - D(e)].$$

Assuming that private asset holders correctly anticipate the increase in q determined by (54), the domestic real interest rate, $r^* - \sigma D^e(q)$, remains below the world real interest rate during this period.

With the passage of time, the level of q determined by (53) rises sufficiently that the official settlements balance shifts from surplus to deficit. The repayment of government debt during the period of surplus, however, is assumed to restore confidence that there will not be an immediate major devaluation. Accordingly, the level of q, its rate of change, the extent of intervention required to maintain balance-of-payments equilibrium, and the rate of change in private net holdings of foreign assets continue to be determined by (53) through (56). When the cumulative effect of official settlements deficits pushes government borrowings above the critical level $\hat{G}$ at which private agents begin to suspect a significant probability of a major devaluation, these equations need to be modified along the lines previously discussed. The rate of increase in q is accelerated by rising expectations of the probability and likely magnitude of a major devaluation. The ex ante domestic real interest rate, $r = r^* - \sigma D^e(q)$ initially declines relative to the value it would have in the absence of anticipations of a major devaluation, but later r rises as G rises significantly above $\hat{G}$. The official settlements deficit and the rate of government borrowing to finance this deficit rise more rapidly as a consequence of anticipations of a major devaluation, thereby contributing to the explosive tendency of the dynamic system.

When the major devaluation occurs, the nominal price of foreign exchange (an increase in e) jumps up, and the real exchange rate (a reduction in q) jumps down. Subsequently, the just-described patterns of behavior of the real exchange rate, the domestic real interest rate, and the official settlements balance all repeat themselves until the next major devaluation.

Alternative assumptions about the conduct of monetary policy and exchange rate policy will yield different conclusions concerning the behavior of the real exchange rate and other related variables. Given the general purpose of this paper, the important general conclusion of this analysis is that the combination of a policy that controls the nominal money supply and a policy that controls the nominal exchange rate, supported by a policy of official intervention in the foreign exchange market, has some capacity to influence the behavior of the real exchange rate and other real economic variables. This capacity arises from two sources. First, the policy combination inevitably influences the behavior of the real value of the money supply, and this behavior should be expected to influence the behavior of other real variables, including the real exchange rate. Second, so long as the private sector does not adjust its spending relative to its income to offset fully the debt-financed difference between government spending and government revenue, the fiscal effect of sterilized intervention in the foreign exchange market will affect the aggregate difference between spending and income for the economy as a whole. It is through this channel that the intervention will affect the relative prices that sustain equilibrium in the goods markets. For this effect to be present, it is not essential that private asset holders totally disregard the future tax liabilities implicit in the current flow of government borrowing. But it is essential that they not reduce their own spending relative to their income to offset fully the government borrowing used to finance the intervention in the foreign exchange market. Of course, in order for this effect to be substantial, the flow of borrowing to finance the intervention must be large, and the offset of private sector spending in response to government borrowing must not be too great.

2.8   Conclusion

This paper has developed a general analytical framework that may be used to analyze how a variety of government policies and other exogenous disturbances can affect the real exchange rate and thereby influence the allocation of resources in ways similar to the effects of commercial policy. Two broad classes of government policies and exogenous disturbances can have such effects: policies and disturbances that affect the distribution of domestic spending between domestic goods and foreign (or traded) goods; and policies and disturbances that affect the level of domestic spending relative to domestic income. In some cases, the effects of such policies and disturbances on the real exchange rate and on the allocation of resources may be quite transparent, as is the case, for instance, when a government shifts its own spending from purchasing military equipment in the world arms market to pursuing domestic development projects that employ primarily domestic labor. In other cases, the mechanisms through which the real exchange rate is affected may be more obscure. They may be obscure, for example, in the case of capital controls that depress the relative price of domestic goods in terms of foreign goods by limiting the excess of domestic spending over domestic income that can be financed by an inflow of foreign capital. Another example is the case of a combined policy of pegging the path of the nominal exchange rate and fixing the path of the domestic nominal money supply, whereby the excess of government spending over government revenue appears under the guise of reserve losses or official foreign borrowing to support sterilized intervention in the foreign exchange market.

The model developed in this paper has essentially the same static structure as the two basic models that have traditionally been applied in the theory of international trade and in analyses of the effects of commercial policies. These are the standard two-country, two-commodity model summarized by Mundell (1968) and the dependent economy model of Salter (1959) and Swan (1960). The key innovation of the present analysis is that these models are made dynamic by taking account both of changes in net foreign asset positions caused by current-account imbalances and of the effects of changes in net asset positions and anticipated changes in relative prices on the relationship between spending and income. This innovation allows an analysis of policies and disturbances the effects of which cannot be fully appreciated within the context of a wholly static model. It permits analysis of, for example, temporary changes in commercial policies or changes in commercial policies that are anticipated to occur at a future date. It also allows us to examine temporary or anticipated future changes in either the level or the distribution of government spending, of capital controls, and of nonsustainable policies that fix, for some period of time, both the path of the nominal exchange rate and the path of the nominal money supply.

Finally, it is worthwhile emphasizing that the analytical framework developed in this paper can be applied to a wider set of issues than those examined here. For example, it is often suggested that some

Latin American countries suffered severe economic disturbances in the late 1970s and early 1980s, first, as a consequence of a sudden influx of foreign capital and, then, from an even more sudden curtailment of their capacity to borrow in the world capital market. This type of disturbance can easily be analyzed in the framework developed in this paper by specifying an appropriate path for the actual and expected evolution of the exogenous forcing variable, w, that influences the difference between income and spending. The influx of foreign capital would be represented by a downward shift in the actual and expected future values of w, which implies an increase in the real exchange rate (the relative price of domestic goods in terms of foreign goods) and a current-account deficit financed by the inflow of foreign capital. The sudden, unanticipated curtailment of access to foreign credit corresponds to an upward shift in the actual and expected future value of w to above the level it had before the influx of foreign credit. This shift induces a decline in the real exchange rate to below its level prior to the influx of foreign credit and an improvement in the trade balance of sufficient magnitude to allow the country to pay the interest on its expanded stock of foreign debt. The analysis carried out in this paper would suggest that a policy limiting international capital flows would reduce the sensitivity of the real exchange rate to this type of disturbance. The present framework is capable of analyzing any other form of disturbance that can be described as an alteration in the actual and expected time paths of either the exogenous variable that affects the desired distribution of spending or the exogenous variable that affects the relationship between spending and income.

References

Barro, Robert. 1974. Are government bonds net wealth? *Journal of Political Economy* 82 (November/December): 1095–1117.

Bhagwati, Jagdish N. 1968. The theory and practice of commercial policy: Departures from unified exchange rates. *Special Papers in International Economics* no. 8. Princeton: International Finance Section, Princeton University.

Blanchard, Olivier. 1984. Debt, deficits and finite horizons. Cambridge, Mass.: Photocopy. Department of Economics, Massachusetts Institute of Technology.

Buiter, Willem, and Miller, Marcus. 1983. Real exchange rate overshooting and the cost of bringing down inflation. In *Exchange rates and international macroeconomics*, ed. J. A. Frenkel, 317–58. Chicago: University of Chicago Press.

Calvo, Guillermo, and Rodriquez, Carlos. 1977. A model of exchange rate determination under currency substitution and rational expectations. *Journal of Political Economy* 85 (June): 617–25.

Corden, W. Max. 1960. The geometric representation of policies to attain external and internal balance. *Review of Economic Studies* 28 (February): 1–22.

———. 1967. The exchange rate system and the taxation of trade. In *Thailand: Social and economic studies in development*, ed. T. H. Silcock. Canberra: Australian National University Press.

———. 1971. *The theory of protection*. London: Oxford University Press.

Dornbusch, Rudiger. 1975. Alternative price stabilization rules and the effects of exchange rate changes. *Manchester School of Economic and Social Studies* 43 (September): 275–92.

———. 1976. Expectations and exchange rate dynamics. *Journal of Political Economy* 84 (November/December): 1161–76.

———. 1980. *Open economy macroeconomics*. New York: Basic Books.

———. 1983. Real interest rates, home goods and optimal external borrowing. *Journal of Political Economy* 91 (February): 141–53.

———. 1984. Exotic exchange rate arrangements. Paper presented at the NBER–World Bank conference on Structural Adjustment and the Real Exchange Rate in Developing Countries, Washington, D.C., November 29–December 1.

Dornbusch, Rudiger, and Fischer, Stanley. 1980. Exchange rates and the current account. *American Economic Review* 70 (December): 960–71.

Frenkel, Jacob A., and Razin, Asaf. 1984. Fiscal policies in the world economy. Chicago: Department of Economics, University of Chicago. Photocopy.

Harberger, Arnold C. 1950. Currency depreciation, income and the balance of payments. *Journal of Political Economy* 58 (February): 47–60.

Henderson, Dale W. 1984. Exchange market intervention operations: Their effects and their role in financial policy. In *Exchange rate theory and policy*, ed. J. Bilson and R. Marston. Chicago: University of Chicago Press.

Kenen, Peter B. 1981. Effects of intervention and sterilization in the short run and the long run. In *The international monetary system under exchange rates: Global, regional and national*, ed. R. N. Cooper. Cambridge, Mass.: Ballinger.

Kouri, Pentti. 1976. The exchange rate and the balance of payments on the short run and the long run. *Scandinavian Journal of Economics* 78 (May): 280–304.

Machlup, Fritz. 1955. Relative prices and aggregate expenditure in the analysis of devaluation. *American Economic Review* 45 (June): 255–78.

Meade, James E. 1951. *The theory of international economic policy*, vol. 1: *The balance of payments*. London: Oxford University Press.

Metzler, Lloyd A. 1951. Wealth, saving and the rate of interest. *Journal of Political Economy* 59 (April): 93–116.

Mundell, Robert A. 1960. The public debt, corporate income taxes and the rate of interest. *Journal of Political Economy* 68 (December): 622–26.

———. 1968. *International economics*. New York: Macmillan.

Mussa, Michael. 1976. The exchange rate, the balance of payments and monetary and fiscal policy under a regime of controlled floating. *Scandinavian Journal of Economics* 78 (May): 229–48.

———. 1977. A dynamic theory of foreign exchange. In *Studies in modern economic analysis: Proceedings of the University Teachers of Economics*, eds. M. Artis and A. R. Nobay. Oxford: Basil Blackwell.

———. 1979. Macroeconomic interdependence and the exchange rate regime. In *International economic policy: Theory and evidence*, eds. R. Dornbusch and J. Frenkel. Baltimore: Johns Hopkins University Press.

———. 1982a. A model of exchange rate dynamics. *Journal of Political Economy* 90 (February): 74–104.

———. 1982b. Exchange rate and price level dynamics in a simple monetary model. In *Exchange rate determination and adjustment*, J. S. Bhandari. New York: Praeger.

———. 1984. The theory of exchange rate determination. In *Exchange rate theory and practice*, ed. J. Bilson and R. Marston. Chicago: University of Chicago Press.

Obstfeld, Maurice. 1981a. Macroeconomic policy, exchange rate dynamics and optimal asset accumulation. *Journal of Political Economy* 89 (December): 1142–61.

———. 1981b. Transitory terms of trade shocks and the current account: The case of constant time preference. *International Finance Discussion Paper* no. 194. Washington, D.C.: Board of Governors of the Federal Reserve System.

———. 1983. Intertemporal price speculation and the optimal current-account deficit. *Journal of International Monetary Economics* 12 (August): 135–45.

Pearce, Ivor F. 1961. The problem of the balance of payments. *International Economic Review* 2 (February): 1–28.

Razin, Asaf, and Svennsson, Lars. 1983. Trade taxes and the current account. *Economic Letters* 13: 55–57.

Salter, W. 1959. Internal and external balance: The role of price and expenditure effects. *Economic Record* 35 (August): 226–38.

Svennsson, Lars, and Razin, Asaf. 1983. The terms of trade and the current account: The Harberger-Laursen-Metzler effect. *Journal of Political Economy* 91 (February): 97–175.

Swan, Trevor. 1960. Economic control in a dependent economy. *Economic Record* 36 (March): 51–66.

Tsiang, S. C. 1961. The role of money in trade balance stability. *American Economic Review* 51 (December): 912–36.

Comment   Jeffrey A. Frankel

Mussa's paper is a masterful tour de force. Armed with a clean log-linear model and his usual clear expository style, Mussa sets out to conquer a veritable universe of macroeconomic questions. He examines the effects of shifts in the composition of government spending, tax cuts, capital controls, and some combinations of monetary policy and exchange rate policy, including a crawl with occasional major devaluations. Throughout he keeps track not only of the accumulating stock of foreign assets, as Pentti Kouri did in his classic exchange rate model, but also of the interest rate, interest payments in the international service account, the accumulating stock of government debt, and government interest payments. Furthermore, he also assumes perfect foresight and distinguishes between temporary and permanent policy changes.

My only reservations about the paper concern truth in advertising. First, the term *real exchange rate* is somewhat misleading because it is used for the price of domestic goods in terms of traded goods (q), whereas the more common usage is the inverse of this. Second, the terms *traded good* and *domestic good* are themselves misleading because *both* goods are in fact internationally traded, as I understand it. They should instead be called the "importable" and the "exportable" goods.

Third, it could be considered misleading to call the country under analysis "medium sized" instead of "large." The country produces some of each good, whereas the rest of the world produces only one, the importable good. There is therefore one sense in which the domestic country is bigger than the rest of the countries in the world. Finally, it is also misleading to present this paper at a conference on "Structural

Jeffrey A. Frankel is an associate professor of economics at the University of California, Berkeley, and a research associate of the National Bureau of Economic Research.

Adjustment and the Real Exchange Rate in Developing Countries'' because the model has little to do with LDCs. Aside from the fact that the country in question is not a minor participant in the goods markets, it is a country with sufficiently developed financial markets that the government practices sterilized foreign exchange intervention and that the effect of a fiscal expansion is to cause a real appreciation of the currency. This characterization sounds more like the United States than Brazil.

I cannot resist recalling what they say about the Holy Roman Empire: It wasn't holy, it wasn't Roman, and it wasn't an empire.

My complaint that the paper is not particularly relevant to developing countries applies equally to several of the other papers presented here. We hear hardly anything about the international debt situation, for example. These are countries with serious problems—problems that have serious economic and political implications for the citizens of these countries and that are of serious intellectual interest for economists worldwide. To address these problems, we who in the past have worked primarily on the macroeconomics of the industrialized countries must do more than simply change the name of one of our jump variables.

Comment   Kathie L. Krumm

In his very comprehensive paper, Mussa has examined a range of macroeconomic policies that affect the real exchange rate in a manner similar to the effects of commercial policy. In defining the discussion of any policy that affects the real exchange rate as equivalent to a discussion of the exchange rate as a tool of commercial policy, the paper is perhaps too broad ranging and not sufficiently focused.

Before returning to commercial policy and the topics I believe need more examination, I want to compliment the author on the integrated framework in which he has examined various policies. His handling of some of the dynamics is elegant, once I got used to the upside-down definition of the real exchange rate. I found a number of the results interesting. The modeling of capital controls, for example, illustrated the ways in which the macro economy and the real exchange rate respond quite differently to shocks in the presence of such controls; and the model is rich enough to allow for various formulations of capital controls. Furthermore, the shift of government expenditures between

Kathie L. Krumm is an economist in the Country Policy Department of the World Bank.

sectors is an interesting policy instrument to consider in theory, though it may not be a feasible instrument in practice, given the difficulties in identifying the degree of tradability of a sector, in integrating such an instrument into a budgeting framework, and in divorcing other sectoral concerns from the analysis.

This leads to me reason why this paper may not be relevant to most commercial policy concerns. Usually, commercial policy is not designed to affect the general relative price level, or we would see more uniform tariff rates and more effective protection rates. Instead, the policies are aimed at prices in particular sectors, either output prices or the prices of factors intensively used in a sector. If that is the case, it might be interesting to analyze which other macroeconomic policies have similar sectoral effects, such as sector-specific government expenditures, be they temporary or permanent, and capital controls favoring certain sectors. Another limitation of the paper for evaluating the role of the exchange rate as a tool of commercial policy is the absence of some framework for welfare analysis. For example, since both policies affect the real exchange rate in the same direction, when should the government shift expenditures to tradables rather than impose tariffs?

This paper seems to be motivated mainly by the adverse effects an appreciated real exchange rate is claimed to have on international trade competitiveness and employment, as appears to be the current situation in the United States, for instance. Mussa states at the outset his assumption of full employment, making it difficult to address a general concern with an appreciated real exchange rate as long as this has limited employment effects.

Finally, it is not clear how this analysis incorporates any features of the economy that are viewed as more critical for poor countries than for richer countries. Mussa's initial comment that governments often attempt to manipulate the real exchange rate for commercial policy purposes seems more relevant to developed than to developing countries. Nonetheless, the clean framework presented in this paper demonstrates the importance of understanding the interdependent effects of macroeconomic policies in both developing and developed countries and could be used to handle a number of issues raised in the study of macroeconomic adjustment packages.

3　Wage Indexation, Supply Shocks, and Monetary Policy in a Small, Open Economy

Joshua Aizenman and Jacob A. Frenkel

3.1　Introduction

The energy crises of the 1970s stimulated a renewed interest in questions concerning the proper adjustment to external supply shocks. In general, restoring equilibrium in response to shocks necessitates the adjustment of both quantities and prices. When applied to labor markets, various proposals for policy rules attempting to restore labor market equilibrium may be classified in terms of their impact on the division of adjustment between quantities (the level of employment) and prices (the real wage). The design of optimal policies provides for the appropriate division of this adjustment.

This paper develops a unified framework for the analysis of wage indexation and monetary policy. The analytical framework is then applied to determine the optimal policy rules in the presence of supply shocks, as well as to evaluate the welfare consequences and ranking of alternative (suboptimal) policy rules. To set the stage for an evaluation of the welfare implications of alternative policy rules, we first analyze two extreme cases: a rule that stabilizes employment, and a rule that stabilizes the real wage. The analysis of these two extreme cases provides the ingredients for evaluating various rules for wage indexation and monetary targeting. We examine the implications of indexing wages to the nominal gross national product (GNP), the consumer price index (CPI), and the value-added price index. The dis-

Joshua Aizenman is an associate professor of business economics at the Graduate School of Business, University of Chicago, and a faculty research fellow of the National Bureau of Economic Research. Jacob A. Frenkel is the David Rockefeller Professor of International Economics at the Department of Economics, University of Chicago and a research associate of the National Bureau of Economic Research.

tinction between the CPI and the value-added price index is of special importance in the study of supply shocks. We also look at the implications of targeting the money supply to these three alternative indicators.

Our analysis demonstrates that, on the formal level, the various indexation rules bear a dual relationship to the various monetary targeting rules. We show that the welfare ranking of the various rules depends on whether the elasticity of the demand for labor exceeds or falls short of the elasticity of labor supply. Specifically, if the demand for labor is more elastic than the supply of labor, policy rules that stabilize employment are preferable to those that stabilize the real wage, and vice-versa. Accordingly, using this principle we demonstrate that if the elasticity of labor demand exceeds the elasticity of labor supply, indexing wages to the nominal GNP is preferable to indexing to the value-added price index, which in turn is preferable to indexing to the CPI. Likewise, because of the dual relationship between monetary policy and wage indexation, it follows that under the same circumstances, monetary policy that targets the nominal GNP is preferable to policy that targets the value-added price index, which in turn is preferable to the policy that targets the CPI. This ranking is reversed when the elasticity of labor supply exceeds the elasticity of labor demand.

Our analysis has implications for both theoretical and policy debates over wage indexation and monetary rules. Specifically, great attention has been given to the question whether the monetary authority, when faced with a higher price of imported energy, should follow an accommodative policy and expand the money supply to "finance" the higher energy price or whether it should be unaccommodating and contract the money supply to lower inflation. The key question has been whether, in the absence of an active monetary response, labor markets can adjust without costly deviations from full employment (see, for example, Gordon 1975; 1984; Phelps 1978; Blinder 1981; Rasche and Tatom 1981; and Fischer 1985). Our analysis deals with these questions as part of the more general analytical framework.

Section 3.2 describes the building blocks of the model, including a specification of the stochastic shocks and a determination of output and employment. Section 3.3 introduces the objective function that is designed to minimize the expected value of labor market distortions. In our model, as in Gray (1976) and Fischer (1977a; 1977c), the need for wage indexation and monetary policy arises from the existence of labor market contracts according to which wages are set in advance of the realization of the stochastic shocks. This labor market convention results in some stickiness of wages. Wage indexation and monetary policies are designed to reduce the undesirable consequences of this stickiness. With the aid of the objective function, we derive the optimal wage indexation rule that eliminates the welfare cost. The key characteristic of the optimal indexation rule is that it distinguishes between the effects of monetary shocks and the effects of real shocks on the wage.

In section 3.4 we examine the implications of departures from the optimal indexation rule. In this context we develop a general criterion for comparing rules that stabilize employment and rules that stabilize real wages. We then apply this criterion to determine the welfare ranking of alternative proposals for wage indexation rules.

The question of monetary accommodation is addressed in section 3.5. We start by specifying the conditions for monetary equilibrium. We then determine the optimal money-supply rule and analyze its dependence on the nature of the stochastic shocks, on the parameters of the demand for money, on the elasticities of the demand for and supply of labor, and on the degree of wage indexation. The section concludes with an analysis of various targeting rules for monetary policies. Analogously to the comparisons of the wage indexation rules, the monetary rules are analyzed in terms of their relative impact on stabilizing quantities (employment) versus stabilizing prices (the real wage).

In section 3.6 we apply the analytical framework to investigate the welfare implications of other departures from the optimal wage indexation rule. For this purpose we examine two alternative simple formulas representing different degrees of departure from the optimal rule, and we modify the money-supply process to allow for exchange rate intervention. We thus are able to determine the optimal managed float in conjunction with the optimal wage indexation coefficients. These (second-best) solutions are determined subject to the constraints limiting the form of the money-supply process and the constraints limiting the variables that govern the wage indexation formulas. Finally, section 3.7 offers our concluding remarks.

Before turning to the formal analysis a word of caution is in order, especially to the casual reader. This paper develops a theoretical framework, and its arguments are therefore based on the formal logic of economic theorizing. Our purpose is to formulate in what we hope is a useful and revealing way a complex structure of a small, open economy that is subject to a variety of stochastic shocks. Since the analysis is formal (containing some algebra), we anticipate that the more practically inclined reader might wonder where the algebra leads. This question cannot, of course, be answered in the abstract. Rather, it should be examined in the context of the insights yielded by the theoretical model. We believe that the analytical framework developed in this paper is sufficiently robust to accommodate some changes in specifications. We illustrate this point in a brief discussion in the final section of the paper.

3.2   The Model

In this section we outline the structure of the model, which includes a specification of the productive technology and a determination of the levels of output, employment, and wages.

3.2.1   Output and Employment

Output is assumed to be produced by a Cobb-Douglas production function using labor and imported energy as variable inputs. Thus, for period t:

$$(1) \quad \log Y_t = \log B + \beta \log L_t + \lambda \log V_t + \mu_t,$$
$$0 \leq \beta < 1, \, 0 \leq \lambda < 1,$$

where Y_t denotes the level of output; L_t and V_t denote, respectively, the inputs of labor and energy; B denotes a parameter including all fixed factors of production; and μ_t denotes a productivity shock. The productivity shock is assumed to be distributed independently and normally with a zero mean and a known variance of σ_μ^2. In competitive equilibrium the parameters β and λ denote, respectively, the relative shares of labor income and the energy bill in the GNP. Throughout the analysis we assume that current information is complete; thus, producers and others in the economy know the realized values of the stochastic shocks.[1]

Producers, who are assumed to maximize profits, demand labor and energy so as to equate the real wage and the relative price of energy to the marginal products of labor and energy. Expressed logarithmically, these equalities are:

$$(2) \quad \log\left(\frac{W}{P}\right)_t = \log \beta B - (1 - \beta)\log L_t + \lambda \log V_t + \mu_t$$

$$(3) \quad \log\left(\frac{P_v}{P}\right)_t = \log \lambda B + \beta \log L_t - (1 - \lambda)\log V_t + \mu_t,$$

where W denotes the nominal wage; P_v denotes the nominal price of energy; and P denotes the price level.

Equations (1) through (3) characterize the levels of output and factor inputs for a given realization of the stochastic productivity shock μ_t. In the absence of stochastic shocks, the corresponding levels of output and factor inputs are denoted by Y_0, L_0, and V_0, and the corresponding real factor prices are $(W/P)_0$ and $(P_v/P)_0$. For subsequent use we denote by lowercase letters the percentage discrepancy of a variable from the value obtained in the absence of shocks. Thus, $x = \log X - \log X_0$. Accordingly, the percentage deviation of output from its nonstochastic level is:

$$(1') \quad\quad\quad y = \beta l + \lambda v + \mu,$$

where $y = \log Y_t - \log Y_0$, $l = \log L_t - \log L_0$, and $v = \log V_t - \log V_0$. Analogously, subtracting from equations (2) and (3) the corresponding equations for the nonstochastic equilibrium yields:

$$(2') \qquad w - p = -(1 - \beta)l + \lambda v + \mu$$

$$(3') \qquad p_v - p = \beta l - (1 - \lambda)v + \mu,$$

where, for simplicity, the time subscript has been omitted. From equations $(2')$ and $(3')$ the demands for labor and energy (or, more precisely, the percentage discrepancy of the demands for labor and energy from their nonstochastic levels) are:

$$(4) \qquad l = \sigma[(1 - \lambda)(p - w) - \lambda(p_v - p) + \mu]$$

$$(5) \qquad v = \sigma[\beta(p - w) - (1 - \beta)(p_v - p) + \mu],$$

where $\sigma = \dfrac{1}{1 - \beta - \lambda}$.

Assuming that producers are always able to satisfy their demands for labor and energy inputs, we substitute equations (4) and (5) into $(1')$ and obtain:

$$(6) \qquad y = \sigma[\beta(p - w) - \lambda(p_v - p) + \mu].$$

Equation (6), which may be viewed as the aggregate supply function, shows that the percentage deviation of output from its deterministic level depends on the percentage deviations of the real wage and of the relative price of energy from their deterministic levels, as well as on the real productivity shock μ. Higher values of the real wage and of the real energy price operate like negative supply shocks and result in lower output, whereas a positive productivity shock raises output.

We assume that the economy is small in the world energy market and that it faces an exogenously given energy price that is distributed normally around a given mean. To simplify the notations we define an *effective* real shock, u, as the sum of the positive supply shocks arising from shocks to productivity and to the price of imported energy. Thus, $u = \mu - \lambda(p_v - p)$. With this definition of the effective real shock, the demand for labor in equation (4) and the supply of output in equation (6) can be written as:

$$(4') \qquad l = \eta(p - w) + \sigma u$$

$$(6') \qquad y = \sigma[\beta(p - w) + u],$$

where $\eta = \sigma(1 - \lambda)$ denotes the (absolute value of the) elasticity of the demand for labor with respect to the real wage. This specification of employment and output (or, more precisely, the percentage discrepancy of employment and output from their nonstochastic levels) reflects the assumption that l and y are determined exclusively by the demand for labor rather than by the interaction between the labor demand and labor supply.[2] The resultant disequilibrium in the labor market induces a welfare cost, which can be minimized in ways outlined in our subsequent analysis. To obtain a benchmark for assessing the implications of distortions in the labor market, we turn first to an analysis of the equilibrium that would exist in the absence of distortions.

3.2.2 The Undistorted Equilibrium

Under the condition of undistorted equilibrium, labor demand equals labor supply. Let the supply of labor be:

$$(7) \qquad \log L_t^s = \log A + \epsilon \log\left(\frac{W}{P}\right)_t,$$

where ϵ denotes the elasticity of labor supply. As before, using lowercase letters to denote the percentage deviation of labor supply from the nonstochastic level, we obtain:

$$(7') \qquad l^s = \epsilon(w - p).$$

Equating the demand for labor, equation (4'), with the supply of labor, equation (7'), yields the undistorted *equilibrium employment,* $\tilde{l}$ and the undistorted *equilibrium real wages,* $(\widetilde{w - p})$, such that:

$$(8) \qquad \tilde{l} = \frac{\epsilon\sigma}{\epsilon + \eta} u$$

$$(9) \qquad (\widetilde{w - p}) = \frac{\sigma}{\epsilon + \eta} u.$$

Using equation (9) in (6') yields the undistorted *equilibrium output* $\tilde{y}$:

$$(10) \qquad \tilde{y} = \frac{(1 + \epsilon)\sigma}{\epsilon + \eta} u.$$

When this equilibrium exists, the demand for labor equals the supply of labor, and, in the absence of other distortions, efficiency is maximized.

3.3 The Measure of Welfare Loss and Optimal Indexation

The foregoing analysis determined the undistorted equilibrium levels of output, employment, and real wages. It was assumed that the flexibility of wages and prices yielded an undistorted labor market equilibrium. The values of the key variables in the undistorted equilibrium serve as benchmarks against which the actual levels of output, employment, and real wages can be compared. These comparisons provide the basis for computing the welfare loss caused by labor market distortions. In this section we outline a measure of the welfare loss and discuss the optimal policies to eliminate this loss. A more formal derivation of the measure of welfare loss is presented in the appendix.

3.3.1   The Welfare Loss

We assume that, because of contract negotiation costs, nominal wages are set in advance at their expected market-clearing level and that employment is determined by the demand for labor. For a given realization of the effective real shock, u, the resulting level of employment is l, as given by equation (4'). The corresponding equilibrium level of employment is $\bar{l}$, as given by equation (4'') below, which is obtained by substituting into (4') the equilibrium real wage $(\widetilde{w - p})$ for the actual real wage.

$$(4'') \qquad \bar{l} = \eta(\widetilde{p - w}) + \sigma u.$$

The discrepancy between $\bar{l}$ and l is responsible for the welfare loss. That discrepancy is:

$$(11) \qquad \bar{l} - l = \eta[-(w - p) + (\widetilde{w - p})].$$

To compute the welfare loss associated with this discrepancy, we need to multiply the discrepancy by one-half of the difference between the demand and the supply prices at the actual level of employment. As illustrated in figure 3.1, $\bar{l}$ and $(\widetilde{w - p})$ designate the equilibrium values of employment and real wages, whereas l designates actual employment. At the actual employment level, l, the demand price for labor, $(w - p)^d$, exceeds the corresponding supply price, $(w - p)^s$. The welfare loss is represented by Δ, which measures the area of the triangle ABC. This triangle expresses the welfare loss in terms of consumer and producer surpluses. Thus:

$$(12) \qquad \Delta = \frac{1}{2}[(w - p)^d - (w - p)^s](\bar{l} - l).$$

By using the definitions of the elasticities of labor demand and labor supply, we note that $(w - p)^d - (w - p)^s = \left(\dfrac{1}{\epsilon} + \dfrac{1}{\eta}\right)(\bar{l} - l)$. Substituting this into equation (12) and recalling that the equilibrium real wage, $(\widetilde{w - p})$, is specified by equation (9), we find that:

$$(13) \qquad \Delta = \frac{1}{2}\eta\left(\frac{\epsilon + \eta}{\epsilon}\right)\left(-w + p + \frac{\sigma}{\epsilon + \eta}u\right)^2.$$

Equation (13) measures the area of the triangle ABC in figure 3.1. In what follows we assume that the objective of policy is to minimize the expected value of the welfare loss, and we denote the loss function by H, where $H = E(\Delta)$.[3]

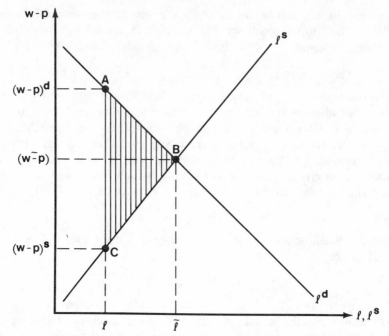

Fig. 3.1   The welfare loss caused by labor market distortions.

As is evident by inspection of (13), a policy that is capable of generating a real wage, $w - p$, that is equal to the equilibrium wage, $\sigma u/(\epsilon + \eta)$, will eliminate the welfare loss. In what follows we determine the optimal wage indexation formula that eliminates the welfare loss. We then use the loss function to evaluate the welfare implications of alternative formulas for wage indexation and for money-supply rules.

3.3.2   Optimal Wage Indexation

As we already indicated, we assume that, because of negotiation costs, nominal wages are set in advance and are adjusted over time according to a simple, time-invariant indexation rule. Let the indexation rule be:

$$(14) \qquad \log W_t = \log W_0 + b_0(\log P_t - \log P_0) + b_1 u_t.$$

Equation (14) specifies the wage at period t as a function of three variables: W_0, the equilibrium wage that is obtained in the absence of shocks;[4] the percentage deviation of the price from its nonstochastic equilibrium; and the effective real shock u. Expressing the wage rule in terms of lowercase letters, recalling that the effective real shock is composed of productivity and energy-price shocks (that is, $u = \mu - \lambda q$), and allowing for different coefficients of indexation to μ and q, we find that:

$$(15) \qquad w = b_0 p + b_1 \mu + b_2 q.$$

Equation (15) specifies an indexation rule by which the nominal wage adjusts in response to the price, p; to the productivity shock, μ; and to the energy-price shock, q. The optimal values of b_0, b_1, and b_2 are chosen so as to eliminate the discrepancy between actual and equilibrium real wages. Inspection of the last parenthetical term in equation (13) reveals that the nominal wage that eliminates the welfare loss is:

$$\tilde{w} = p + \frac{\sigma}{\epsilon + \eta} \mu - \frac{\lambda \sigma}{\epsilon + \eta} q,$$

where $\mu - \lambda q$ has been substituted for the effective real shock u. Thus, the optimal values of the coefficients in the indexation rule of equation (15) are:

$$(16) \qquad \bar{b}_0 = 1; \bar{b}_1 = \frac{\sigma}{\epsilon + \eta} ; \text{ and } \bar{b}_2 = -\lambda \bar{b}_1.$$

This formulation of the indexation rule is analogous to that of Karni (1983), who showed (in the context of a closed economy without an energy input) that at the optimum, the nominal wage must adjust to the price level by an indexation coefficient of unity, whereas, in general, its adjustment to the productivity shock differs from unity.[5]

The magnitude of the indexation coefficient $\bar{b}_1$ depends on the structure of the economy as reflected by the elasticities of labor demand and labor supply. For example, a lower elasticity of labor supply raises the absolute values of the optimal coefficients of indexation to the real shocks (that is, to productivity and energy-price shocks). When the elasticity of labor supply approaches zero, $\bar{b}_1$ approaches $[1/(1 - \lambda)] > 1$, and $\bar{b}_2$ approaches $-\lambda/(1 - \lambda)$. Likewise, the magnitude of the coefficients of indexation to real shocks depends on the relative share of the energy cost in output. As shown in equation (16), a higher share of the energy cost raises $\bar{b}_1$ as well as the absolute values of $\bar{b}_2$. In general, $\bar{b}_1$ will be positive and $\bar{b}_2$ will be negative.

The key point to emphasize here is that by altering the nominal wage, the optimal indexation rule *eliminates* the welfare loss associated with the distortion to the real wage. The equilibrium that is obtained with optimal indexation replicates the equilibrium that would have been obtained if the labor market cleared *after* realizing the stochastic shocks. The optimal indexation formula thus serves to nullify the distortions arising from the assumption that, because of labor contracts, nominal wages are predetermined.[6] Further, if economic policy was only concerned with the efficiency of resource allocation, then, in the absence of other distortions, there would be no need to undertake additional macroeconomic policies once the optimal indexation formula was adopted.

The essence of the optimal indexation rule lies in the distinction between the coefficients of indexation to nominal shocks and those to real shocks. In the specification of equation (14), nominal shocks were represented by p and real shocks were represented by u. It was shown that with optimal indexation, wages should be indexed to p with a coefficient of unity, whereas the magnitude of the optimal indexation to u would depend on the elasticities of labor demand and labor supply. Since the real shocks are ultimately manifested in the realized level of output, we may also include the level of output directly in the indexation rule and thereby obtain an alternative formulation. The alternative expresses the wage indexation rule in terms of the response of nominal wages to the price and to the level of output, such that:

$$(17) \qquad\qquad w = p + b_y y,$$

where b_y denotes the coefficient of indexation of nominal wages to real output. Substituting $b_y y$ for $(w - p)$ in equation (6') yields the realized value of y; and equating this realization with the equilibrium value $\bar{y}$ from equation (10) yields the optimal indexation coefficient:

$$\tilde{b}_y = \frac{1}{1 + \epsilon}.$$

Thus, the optimal indexation rule expressed in terms of prices and output is:

$$(17') \qquad\qquad w = p + \frac{1}{1 + \epsilon} y.^{7}$$

The advantage of this alternative (but equivalent) formulation is its simplicity. Here the wage rule is specified in terms of the observable variables p and y, about which data are readily available.

3.4   Alternative Wage Indexation Rules

In the previous section we specified the optimal wage indexation formula. In this section we apply the analytical framework to evaluate specific proposals for indexation rules, including the indexation of nominal wages to nominal income, to the CPI, and to the domestic value-added price index.[8] In general, restoring labor market equilibrium in response to a shock necessitates some adjustment of employment and some adjustment of real wages. The optimal indexation formula provides for the optimal division of the adjustment between changes in employment and changes in real wages. The various proposals that depart from the optimal indexation rule differ in allocating the adjustment between employment and real wages. To evaluate the relative merits and welfare costs of such alternative allocations, we start with an analysis of two extreme indexation rules: a rule that stabilizes the real wage, and a rule that stabilizes employment. Because the various proposals for wage rules generally involve some combination of these two rules, the analysis of the two extreme cases provides the necessary ingredients for an evaluation of the various proposals.

3.4.1 Stable Real Wages Versus Stable Employment

In general, as was shown above, the expected welfare loss, H, is proportional to the expected squared discrepancy between the actual wage and the equilibrium real wage, such that:

$$(18) \qquad H = aE[-(w - p) + \widehat{(w - p)}]^2,$$

where a denotes the proportionality factor implied by equation (13). Consider first the indexation rule that stabilizes the real wage. With this indexation rule, $w - p = 0$. Substituting the equilibrium real wage from equation (9) into (18) implies that in this case the welfare loss is:

$$(19) \qquad H_{w=p} = a\left(\frac{\sigma}{\epsilon + \eta}\right)^2 \sigma_u^2.$$

Here, $H_{w=p}$ indicates that this loss results from the stabilization of real wages. Thus, equation (19) shows the welfare loss resulting from an indexation rule by which nominal wages are indexed to the CPI with a coefficient of unity.

Consider next the other extreme indexation rule, which stabilizes employment and thereby ensures that $l = 0$. In that case it follows from equation (4′) that the actual real wage is $u/(1 - \lambda)$. Substituting this wage into (18) implies that if $l = 0$, the welfare loss is:

$$(20) \quad H_{l=0} = aE\left(-\frac{u}{1 - \lambda} + \frac{\sigma u}{\epsilon + \eta}\right)^2 = a\left(\frac{\epsilon}{(1 - \lambda)(\epsilon + \eta)}\right)^2 \sigma_u^2.$$

Here the notation indicates that this welfare loss results from the stabilization of employment.

These two measures of the welfare loss are described diagramatically in figure 3.2. The schedules l^d and l^s portray the demand for and the supply of labor, as specified by equations (4′) and (7′) in section 3.2. The slopes of l^d and l^s are $-1/\eta$ and $1/\epsilon$, respectively; that is, the slopes are the inverse of the corresponding elasticities. The initial equilibrium is described by point 0, at which the initial demand curve (not drawn) intersected with the supply. Thus, initially, $(\widetilde{w - p}) = 0$. The demand schedule shown here corresponds to a situation in which there was a positive realization of the effective real shock, u. As indicated by equation (4'), this shock induces an upward displacement of the demand schedule by $u/(1 - \lambda)$ and results in a new equilibrium real wage, $\sigma u/(\epsilon + \eta)$, and correspondingly in a new equilibrium level of employment.

When the indexation rule stipulates that real wages must not change, the real wage remains at point 0 and employment increases to l_1 at point C. In that case the welfare loss is proportional to the area of the triangle CEB, and its expected value is $H_{w = p}$, as specified by equation (19). In the other extreme, when the indexation rule stipulates that employment must not change, the level of employment remains at point 0 and the real wage rises to $u/(1 - \lambda)$ at point A. In that case the welfare loss is proportional to the area of the triangle OAB, and its expected value is $H_{l=0}$, as specified by equation (20). Since the various expressions illustrate percentage deviations from the nonstochastic

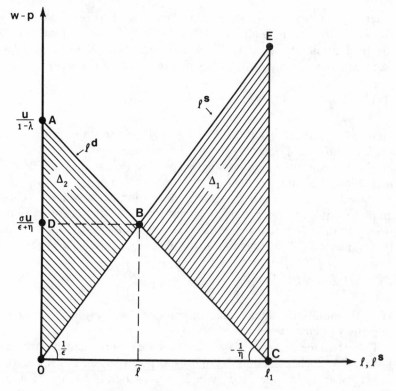

Fig. 3.2   The welfare losses caused by indexation rules that stabilize the real wage and by indexation rules that stabilize employment.

equilibrium, the actual welfare loss expressed in units of output is obtained by multiplying (19) and (20) by the equilibrium nonstochastic wage bill.

To determine the relationship between the extent of the welfare losses in the two cases, we need to compare the areas of the two triangles CEB (denoted by Δ_1) and OAB (denoted by Δ_2). We first note from the geometry that the two triangles are similar in shape and that the ratio AD/DO (where point D indicates the equilibrium real wage) equals the ratio AB/BC. It follows, therefore, that the ratio of the two areas Δ_2/Δ_1 equals $(AD/DO)^2$. As can been seen in figure 3.2:

$$AD = \left(\frac{1}{1 - \lambda} - \frac{\sigma}{\epsilon + \eta}\right)u = \frac{\sigma\epsilon}{\eta(\epsilon + \eta)}u$$

and

$$DO = \left(\frac{\sigma}{\epsilon + \eta}\right)u;$$

therefore:

(21)
$$\frac{\Delta_2}{\Delta_1} = \left(\frac{\epsilon}{\eta}\right)^2.$$

Thus, if the elasticity of labor supply, ϵ, is smaller than the elasticity of labor demand, η, an indexation rule that fixes employment induces a lower welfare loss than that induced by an indexation rule that fixes the real wage. This is the case illustrated in figure 3.2. On the other hand, if the elasticity of the labor supply exceeds the elasticity of labor demand, $\Delta_2 > \Delta_1$. Under these circumstances rules that stabilize employment inflict a higher welfare loss than that inflicted by rules that stabilize the real wage.

Now that we have analyzed the two extreme indexation rules in preparation for evaluating the various proposals that combine elements of the two rules, we turn next to examine the properties of the proposal of linking the nominal wage to nominal income.

3.4.2 Indexation to Nominal Income

When the nominal wage is indexed to nominal income with a unit coefficient, $w = p + y$. In this case the coefficients of indexation to the price and to real output are both unity. We should first note with reference to equation (17') that as long as the elasticity of labor supply, ϵ, differs from zero, full indexation to nominal income entails a welfare loss. Only when $\epsilon = 0$ does the optimal indexation rule require that wages be indexed to nominal income with a coefficient of unity.

To evaluate the welfare loss induced by a departure from the optimal indexation rule, we must stipulate that with indexation to nominal income, $w - p = y$. Substituting $w - p$ for y in equation (6') and solving for the realized real wage yields:

$$(22) \qquad (w - p)\Big|_{w = p + y} = \frac{1}{1 - \lambda}u.$$

Here the notation indicates that this wage is obtained under the rule by which nominal wages are indexed to nominal income with a coefficient of unity. With this real wage the level of employment can be read from equation (4'). Substituting (22) for the real wage in (4') shows that in this case $l = 0$. Thus, an indexation rule that links the nominal wage to nominal income through an indexation coefficient of unity results in stable employment. The resulting welfare loss corresponds to the area of the triangle OAB in figure 3.2 and is expressed by equation (20). Thus, it follows that:

$$(23) \qquad H_{w=p+y} = H_{l=0}.$$

3.4.3 Indexation to the Value-Added Price Index

An alternative proposal that received especially wide attention following the energy shocks of the 1970s links wages to the domestic value-added price index. This proposal was analyzed recently by Marston and Turnovsky (1985). In what follows we explore further the implications of this indexation rule.

Let the price of final output, p, be a weighted average of the domestic value-added price index, p_d, and the price of imported energy input, p_v; and let the weights correspond to the relative shares of value added and energy in output. Thus:

$$p = (1 - \lambda)p_d + \lambda p_v.$$

It follows that the domestic value-added price index is:

$$(24) \qquad p_d = \frac{1}{1 - \lambda}p - \frac{\lambda}{1 - \lambda}p_v.$$

An indexation rule that links the nominal wage to this index through a coefficient of unity sets w equal to p_d. By the definition of p_d from (24), the implied real wage is:

$$(25) \qquad (w - p)\Big|_{w = p_d} = -\frac{\lambda}{1 - \lambda}q,$$

where the notation indicates that this wage is obtained under the rule by which nominal wages are indexed to p_d with a coefficient of unity.

A comparison of equations (25) and (22) reveals that in the special case in which $\mu = 0$ (so that shocks to the imported energy price constitute the only component of the effective real shock), $u = -\lambda q$ and the indexation of wages to the domestic value-added price index is equivalent to the indexation of wages to nominal income. Furthermore, as was shown above, in this case such indexation results in stable employment, and the corresponding welfare loss is also represented by equations (20).

In the more general case, however, with nonzero productivity shocks the indexation to p_d does not stabilize employment, and the welfare loss differs from the one represented by equations (20). The expression for the welfare loss in that case is obtained by substituting the equilibrium real wage from (9) and the actual real wage from (25) into (18), such that:

$$(26) \quad H_{w=p_d} = a\left(\frac{\epsilon}{(1 - \lambda)(\epsilon + \eta)}\right)^2 \lambda^2\sigma_q^2 + a\left(\frac{\eta}{(1 - \lambda)(\epsilon + \eta)}\right)^2 \sigma_\mu^2.$$

Here the notation indicates that this welfare loss results from adopting the rule by which nominal wages are indexed to p_d with a coefficient of unity.

3.4.4   Ranking the Indexation Rules

The preceding discussion implies that, in general, the choice between indexing to nominal income and indexing to the domestic value-added price index depends on the difference between the expressions measuring the losses $H_{w=p_d}$ in (26) and $H_{l=0}$ in (20). To facilitate this comparison we can usefully rewrite equation (20) somewhat differently by decomposing the effective real shock into its two components. Thus:

$$(20') \quad H_{l=0} = a\left[\frac{\epsilon}{(1 - \lambda)(\epsilon + \eta)}\right]^2 (\sigma_\mu^2 + \lambda^2\sigma_q^2).$$

Since the terms involving the variance of q are identical in both of the expressions in (26) and (20'), differences in the welfare losses arise only from the terms involving the variance of μ. Subtracting (20') from (26) and denoting the difference by D yields:

$$(27) \quad D = \frac{a(\eta^2 - \epsilon^2)}{[(1 - \lambda)(\epsilon + \eta)]^2}.$$

Thus, the sign of D depends on whether the elasticity of the demand for labor exceeds or falls short of the corresponding elasticity of supply. Since $\eta = (1 - \lambda)\sigma$ exceeds unity (in practice, with typical relative shares the magnitude of η is likely to be around 3), and since estimates of the elasticity of labor supply are typically small, indexation to nominal income is likely to be preferable to indexation to the domestic value-added price index. The opposite holds, however, for cases in which the elasticity of supply exceeds the elasticity of demand.

A comparison of (20') and (26) shows that when $\epsilon = 0$, indexation to nominal income is optimal, since in that case the value of the loss function in (20') is zero. In contrast, as shown in equation (26), the welfare loss associated with indexation to the domestic value-added price index is positive, even though $\epsilon = 0$. In this case the expression in (26) is reduced to $a[1/(1 - \lambda)]^2\sigma_\mu^2$. As argued above, only when the variance of the productivity shock, μ, is zero do the two indexation rules yield identical outcomes.[9]

To gain a broader perspective over the issues raised by comparing the two forms of indexation, we observe that the condition determining the sign of D in (27) is the same as the condition determining whether the cost of indexation rules that stabilize the real wage exceeds or falls short of the cost of indexation rules that stabilize employment. These relative costs are reflected in the relative sizes of the triangles in figure 3.2. As shown in equation (21), when the elasticity of labor demand exceeds the elasticity of labor supply, indexation rules that stabilize employment are preferable to those that stabilize real wages. These are also the circumstances under which the indexation of wages to nominal income is preferable to indexation to the domestic value-added price index.

The equivalence between the condition under which stable employment is preferable is stable real wages and the condition under which indexation to nominal income is preferable to indexation to the value-added price index is interpreted by reference to equations (22) and (25). When wages are indexed to the value-added price index, then, as shown in equation (25), any given realization of the productivity shock, μ, does not alter the real wage. Thus, when the effective real shock consists only of productivity shocks, this rule stabilizes the real wage. On the other hand, when wages are indexed to nominal income, then, as shown in equation (22), any given realization of the productivity shock alters the real wage by $\mu/(1 - \lambda)$. This change in the real wage corresponds precisely to the vertical displacement of the demand for labor arising from the productivity shock and therefore results in stable employment. Finally, as indicated above, when the effective real shock consists only of shocks to the price of imported energy, then, as can be seen from equations (22) and (25), the two rules yield identical outcomes in terms of real wages, employment, and welfare.

The following analysis of the various wage indexation rules is summarized in table 3.1, which reports the coefficients of indexation to the price (b_0), to the productivity shock (b_1), and to the energy-price shock (b_2) that are implied by the alternative indexation rules. For example, as indicated by the second line of the table, indexing wages to p_d implies an indexation to p with a coefficient $b_0 = 1$ and an indexation to q with a coefficient $b_2 = -\lambda/(1 - \lambda)$. This rule follows from equation (25). Likewise, the third line of the table specifies the coefficients implied by an indexation rule by which nominal wages are indexed to nominal income with a coefficient of unity. These coefficients follow from equation (22). The optimal indexation formula corresponds to the fourth line in the table, which follows from equation (16). It is a weighted average of the first and the third lines with weights $\epsilon/(\epsilon + \eta)$ and $\eta/(\epsilon + \eta)$, respectively.

Our analysis also determines the welfare cost associated with the various indexation rules. Accordingly, as shown in table 3.1, if the elasticity of the labor supply is smaller than the elasticity of the labor demand, the welfare ranking of the alternative rules is:

$$(28) \qquad \bar{b} > (p + y) > p_d > p,$$

where the symbol $x > y$ indicates that x is preferred to y. Thus, it follows that under this assumption, full indexation to nominal income is preferred to full indexation to the domestic value-added price index, which in turn is preferred to full indexation to the CPI. Of course, the optimal indexation rule, $\bar{b}$, is preferred to all of the other alternatives. On the other hand, in cases in which the elasticity of the labor supply exceeds the elasticity of the labor demand, the welfare ordering of the suboptimal rules is reversed. In that case:

$$(28') \qquad \bar{b} > p > p_d > (p + y).$$

3.5 Monetary Equilibrium and Optimal Accommodation

Up to this point the monetary sector has played no explicit role in our analysis of the wage indexation rules. Detailed considerations of

Table 3.1   **Alternative Wage Rules, where $w = b_0 p + b_1 \mu + b_2 q$**

	Indexation Coefficients		
	b_0	b_1	b_2
Wages Indexed to			
CPI(p)	1	0	0
Value-added deflator (p_d)	1	0	$-\dfrac{\lambda}{1 - \lambda}$
Nominal income ($p + y$)	1	$\dfrac{1}{1 - \lambda}$	$-\dfrac{\lambda}{1 - \lambda}$
Optimal indexation ($\bar{b}$)	1	$\dfrac{\sigma}{\epsilon + \eta}$	$\dfrac{-\lambda\sigma}{\epsilon + \eta}$

Conclusion: If $\epsilon < \eta$, the welfare ranking of the alternative rules is $\bar{b} > p + y > p_d > p$; and if $\epsilon > \eta$, the welfare ranking is $b > p > p_d > (p + y)$.

the money market could be left in the background, since in all the rules we have examined, the wages were indexed to the CPI with a coefficient of unity. Furthermore, as shown in Aizenman and Frenkel (1985a), the specification of the model implies that there is a redundancy of policy instruments. Thus, in the absence of other distortions, once the optimal indexation rule is adopted there is no need to undertake additional macroeconomic policies. On the other hand, it also follows that if wages are not indexed optimally, there may be room for other policies designed to restore labor market equilibrium. In this section we introduce the monetary sector and analyze the optimal money-supply rule.

3.5.1   The Monetary Sector

To determine the equilibrium levels of the nominal quantities such as the price level, we need to introduce the conditions of money market equilibrium. Let the demand for money be:

$$(29) \qquad \log M_t^d = \log k + \log P_t + \xi \log Y_t - \alpha i_t,$$

where M denotes nominal balances; i denotes the nominal rate of interest; α denotes the (semi)elasticity of the demand for money with respect to the rate of interest; and ξ denotes the income elasticity of the demand. The domestic price level is assumed to be linked to the foreign price through purchasing power parity. Thus:

$$(30) \qquad \log P_t = \log S_t + \log P_t',$$

where S_t denotes the exchange rate (the price of foreign currency in terms of domestic currency); and P_t' denotes the foreign price. Let the foreign price be:

$$(31) \qquad \log P_t' = \log \bar{P}' + \chi_t,$$

where a prime ($'$) denotes a foreign variable, and a bar over a variable denotes the value of its fixed component. In equation (31) χ_t denotes the stochastic component of the foreign price, which is assumed to be distributed normally with a mean of zero and a fixed known variance. Using (31) for $\log P_t'$ yields:

$$(32) \qquad \log P_t = \log S_t + \log \bar{P}' + \chi_t.$$

In principle, the random component of P_t may also include stochastic deviations from the purchasing power parity relation of equation (32). When all shocks are zero, the domestic price is:

$$(32') \qquad \log P_0 = \log S_0 + \log \bar{P}';$$

and subtracting (32') from (32) yields:

$$(33) \qquad p = s + \chi,$$

where, as before, we suppress the time subscripts.

The nominal rate of interest is linked to the foreign rate of interest, i'. Arbitrage by investors, who are assumed to be risk neutral, assures that uncovered interest parity holds, such that:

$$(34) \qquad i_t = i'_t + E_t(\log S_{t+1} - \log S_t),$$

where $E_t \log S_{t+1}$ denotes the expected exchange rate for period $t + 1$ based on the information available at period t. The foreign rate of interest is also subject to a random shock, ρ, which is distributed normally with a mean of zero and a fixed known variance. Thus:

$$(35) \qquad i'_t = \bar{i}' + \rho_t.$$

The specification of the stochastic shocks implies that the expected exchange rate for period $t + 1$ is S_0 (the level obtained in the absence of shocks) and therefore $E_t(\log S_{t+1} - \log S_t) = -s_t$. Thus, from equations (34) and (35), it follows that:

$$(36) \qquad i_t - \bar{i}' = \rho - s.[10]$$

In the absence of stochastic shocks, $i = \bar{i}'$ and therefore:

$$(29') \qquad \log M_0^d = \log K + \log P_0 + \xi\log Y_0 - \alpha\bar{i}'.$$

Subtracting (29') from (29), omitting the time subscript, and recalling that, from (33), $s = p - \chi$ yields:

$$(37) \qquad m^d = (1 + \alpha)p + \xi y - \alpha(\rho + \chi).$$

The supply of money (or, more precisely, the percentage deviation of the supply of money from its nonstochastic level) is denoted by m. Monetary equilibrium is obtained when the demand for money equals the supply of money. We turn next to an analysis of the optimal money supply.

3.5.2   Optimal Monetary Policy

The analysis of section 3.3 derived the optimal wage indexation rule. In this section we focus on the determinants of a money-supply rule that is designed to achieve the same goal of eliminating labor market disequilibrium. To determine the optimal money supply and to contrast the results with those of the previous sections, we assume that wages are completely unindexed, so that $w = 0$. The question that is being addressed concerns the optimal response of monetary policy in the face of exogenously given shocks. This question is not new. It has been addressed by various authors in the context of the energy-supply shocks of the 1970s.[11] The key question has been whether monetary policy should be accommodative and expend the money supply to "finance" the higher energy price or whether it should be nonaccommodative and contract the money supply to lower inflation. Many observers have, of course, recognized that a real shock that lowers the potential level of output cannot be combated successfully by monetary policy. Instead, the question has been whether monetary policy can be designed so as to prevent the additional costs arising from departures from the new (lower) level of potential output. In what follows we reexamine this question.

To determine the optimal money supply we first equate the demand for money, m^d (from [37]), with the supply of money, m, and by using equation (10) for the equilibrium level of output, we obtain the equilibrium price level $\bar{p}$, such that:

$$(38) \qquad \bar{p} = \frac{1}{1 + \alpha} \left[m + \alpha(\rho + \chi) - \frac{(1 + \epsilon)\xi\sigma}{\epsilon + \eta} u \right].$$

From equation (9) it is evident that when $w = 0$ (as is the case when nominal wages are unindexed), the value of p that yields the equilibrium real wage and thereby eliminates labor market disequilibrium is:

$$(9') \qquad \bar{p} = - \frac{\sigma}{\epsilon + \eta} u.$$

Equating the value of p that clears the money market (from equation [38]) with the corresponding value of p that clears the labor market (from equation [9']) and solving for m yields the optimal monetary rule:

$$(39) \qquad \hat{m} = - \alpha(\rho + \chi) + \frac{[\xi(1 + \epsilon) - (1 + \alpha)]\sigma}{\epsilon + \eta} (\mu - \lambda q),$$

where $\mu - \lambda q$ has been instituted for the effective real shock u.

An inspection of equation (39) reveals that when the income elasticity of the demand for money, ξ, is unity, while the elasticity of the supply of labor, ϵ, and the interest (semi)elasticity of the demand for money, α, are zero, $\hat{m} = 0$. This is the case analyzed in detail by Fischer (1985). In this special case the price generated by the condition of money market equilibrium is precisely the price needed to yield the equilibrium real wage, and therefore no accommodation is necessary. In fact, any attempt to alter the money supply in response to the supply shock would result in suboptimal employment and would inflict a welfare loss. In general, however, as long as α or ϵ differs from zero and ξ differs from unity, there is justification for an active monetary policy.[12]

In interpreting the rule specified by (39), we should note that a positive foreign interest rate shock, ρ, and a positive foreign price shock, χ, lower the demand for money; the interest shock operates through its direct effect on the domestic rate of interest, while the price shock operates through its influence on exchange rate expectations. When both shocks are present, their effect is to reduce the demand for money by $\alpha(\rho + \chi)$.[13] The proper response should reduce the money supply by the same amount and thereby prevent further spillovers of the effects of these shocks to other segments of the economy. The second term on the right-hand side of equation (39) specifies the optimal response to shocks to productivity, μ, and to the imported energy price, q. Both of these shocks alter the equilibrium level of output and result in a new equilibrium real wage. In addition, the new equilibrium level of output alters the demand for money. Without changes in the money supply, the conditions of money market equilibrium yield a new price level and thereby a new real wage. As shown in equation (39) the induced change in the real wage will be just sufficient to restore labor market equilibrium only if $\xi(1 + \epsilon)$ equals $(1 + \alpha)$. In general, a rise in the price of imported energy should induce an expansionary monetary policy if $(1 + \alpha) > \xi(1 + \epsilon)$, and vice versa. It is also relevant to note that in general the optimal monetary response to the effective real shock depends on the relative share of imported energy in output. A higher value of the energy share, λ, raises the (absolute value of) the optimal response.

The preceding analysis demonstrated that when wages are unindexed, monetary policy can be designed to ensure labor market equilibrium. Furthermore, it was shown that when $\xi = 1$ and $\epsilon = \alpha = 0$, monetary policy should not accommodate supply shocks. Before we conclude this section, it is worth reexamining these results for situations in which wages are indexed according to an arbitrary rule by which $w = b_0 p$. Recalling the equilibrium real wage from equation (9) and using the assumed indexation rule yields the equilibrium price that clears the labor market:

$$(9'') \qquad \bar{p} = - \frac{\sigma}{(1 - b_0)(\epsilon + \eta)} u.$$

Following the same procedure as before, we equate this price with the price that clears the money market and obtain the optimal money-supply rule:

$$(39') \quad \bar{m} = -\alpha(\rho + \chi) + \frac{[\xi(1 - b_0)(1 + \epsilon) - (1 + \alpha)]\sigma}{(1 - b_0)(\epsilon + \eta)}(\mu - \lambda q).$$

Two points are worth noting with reference to equation (39'). First, in contrast with the discussion of equation (39), in which nominal wages were unindexed, here even if $\xi = 1$ and $\epsilon = \alpha = 0$, $\bar{m}$ does *not* equal zero, and a real shock calls for an active monetary response. In that case the optimal money-supply rule becomes:

$$(39'') \qquad \bar{m} = \frac{-b_0}{(1 - b_0)(1 - \lambda)}(\mu - \lambda q).$$

Thus, with a partial wage indexation, a rise in the price of energy and a negative productivity shock require an expansionary monetary policy.

Second, with one important exception, the welfare loss induced by the choice of a suboptimal value of b_0 could be eliminated through the monetary rule prescribed by equation (39'). The important exception occurs when b_0 is arbitrarily set to equal unity. In that case the indexation rule prevents changes in the real wage and results in an absolute real wage rigidity. Any real shock that alters the equilibrium real wage therefore results in labor market disequilibrium and induces a welfare loss. And monetary policy cannot reduce that loss.

Equation (9'') specified the value of the equilibrium price $\bar{p}$ that is obtained when monetary policy adopts the optimal rule $\tilde{m}$. It follows that the variance of the equilibrium price is:

$$(40) \qquad \sigma_{\bar{p}}^2 = \left[\frac{\sigma}{(1 - b_0)(\epsilon + \eta)} \right]^2 \sigma_u^2.$$

Further, since at the optimum the domestic price is independent of the foreign price shock, χ, it follows that:

$$(41) \qquad \sigma_{\bar{s}}^2 = \sigma_{\bar{p}}^2 + \sigma_{\chi}^2.$$

Thus, when monetary policy follows an optimal rule, the variance of the exchange rate exceeds the variance of domestic prices.

Finally, from the specification of $\tilde{m}$ in equation (39'), we can note that the variance of the optimal money supply is:

$$(42) \qquad \sigma_{\tilde{m}}^2 = \alpha^2 \, \sigma_{\rho+\chi}^2 + \left\{ \frac{[\xi(1 - b_0)(1 + \epsilon) - (1 + \alpha)]\sigma}{(1 - b_0)(\epsilon + \eta)} \right\}^2 \sigma_u^2.$$

Thus, in general, the variance of the optimal money supply depends positively on the variance of the foreign interest and price shocks (ρ and χ), as well as on the variance of the effective real shock, u. Using equation (40) we can also express the variance of $\tilde{m}$ as:

$$(42') \qquad \sigma_{\tilde{m}}^2 = \alpha^2 \, \sigma_{\rho+\chi}^2 + [\xi(1 - b_0)(1 + \epsilon) - (1 + \alpha)]^2 \, \sigma_{\bar{p}}^2.$$

Equation (42') shows that at the optimum the relative magnitude of the variances of money and prices depends on whether $[\xi(1 - b_0)(1 + \epsilon) - (1 + \alpha)]^2$ exceeds or falls short of unity. In general, if this quantity is larger than unity, the variance of money will exceed that of prices, whereas if it is smaller than unity, the relationship between the variances will depend on the magnitude of $\alpha^2 \sigma_{\rho+\chi}$.[14]

3.5.3 Alternative Monetary Rules

The preceding discussion specified the optimal money-supply rule. In practice, various alternative rules for monetary targets have been proposed, with special attention given recently to the proposal that monetary policy target nominal income.[15] In this section we apply the analytical framework to the evaluation of alternative proposals. For this purpose we substitute equation (6') for y into the demand-for-money equation (37); and recalling that with zero wage indexation ($w = 0$), the demand for money can be written as:

$$(37') \qquad m^d = (1 + \alpha + \xi\sigma\beta)p + \xi\sigma u - \alpha(\rho + \chi).$$

Consider first a monetary rule that targets the CPI. With such a rule, $p = 0$ in equation (37'), and the resulting money supply is:

$$(43) \qquad m\Big|_{p\,=\,0} = \xi\sigma u - \alpha(\rho + \chi).$$

This monetary rule assures that $p = 0$ and that, in the absence of wage indexation, the real wage is stabilized. The welfare loss associated with CPI targeting is the same as the loss resulting from a full indexation of wages to the CPI, since both stabilize the real wage. This loss is specified in equation (19).

Consider next the monetary rule that targets nominal income, such that $p + y = 0$. In this case, from equation (6'), the value of output is $y = \sigma u/(1 + \beta\sigma)$. If we substitute this into equation (37') and recall that $p = -y$, the resulting money supply is:

$$(44) \qquad m\Big|_{p\,+\,y\,=\,0} = \frac{[\xi - (1 + \alpha)]\sigma}{1 + \beta\sigma}\,u = \frac{\xi - (1 + \alpha)}{1 - \lambda}\,u.$$

To evaluate the welfare loss associated with this monetary rule, we observe that in this case, with $w = 0$, the real wage ($w - p$) equals y; and from equation (6'), $y = [1/(1 - \lambda)]u$. With this real wage the level of employment remains unchanged (as can be seen from equation [4']), and, therefore, the resulting welfare loss is specified in equation (23).

Consider next a third monetary rule that targets the domestic value-added price index. With this rule, $p_d = 0$; and from the definition of p_d in (24), it follows that $p = [\lambda/(1 - \lambda)]q$. Substituting this into (37') yields a money supply of:

$$(45) \qquad m\Big|_{p_d\,=\,0} = \xi\sigma\mu - \frac{[\xi - (1 + \alpha)]}{1 - \lambda}\,\lambda q - \alpha(\rho + \chi).$$

With this targeting rule and with unindexed wages, $w = p_d = 0$ and the resulting welfare loss is specified by equation (26).

The equivalence between the measures of the welfare losses associated with the different targeting rules for monetary policy and with the indexation rules for nominal wages implies that the welfare rankings of the various rules is also the same as those in equations (28) and (28'). It follows that if $\epsilon < \eta$, the welfare ranking is:

$$(46) \qquad \tilde{m} > m\bigg|_{p + y = 0} > m\bigg|_{p_d = 0} > m\bigg|_{p = 0} \quad ;$$

and if $\epsilon > \eta$, the welfare ranking is:

$$(46') \qquad \tilde{m} > m\bigg|_{p = 0} > m\bigg|_{p_d = 0} > m\bigg|_{p + y = 0} \quad .$$

It is interesting to note that the ranking provided by (46) is also consistent with that in Tobin (1983), where the targeting of nominal income (with annual revisions) is supported and the targeting of price indexes is criticized. In discussing the choice between targeting p and targeting p_d Tobin concluded, however, that "if any price index were to be a policy target, it should surely not be the CPI, subject as that index is to fluctuations from specific commodity prices, taxes, exchange rates, import costs, interest rates, and other idiosyncracies. It should be some index of domestic value added at factor cost" (Tobin 1983, 119). Our analysis shows that this ranking is not robust. As revealed by the comparison of (46) and (46'), the ranking of the various alternatives depends on the relative magnitudes of the elasticities of the demand for and the supply of labor.

In this section we have considered three specific targeting rules. A similar analysis can be applied to the evaluation of other rules, such as targeting the exchange rate (setting s equal to 0), targeting the interest rate (setting $i - \bar{i}'$ equal to 0), targeting the money supply (setting m equal to 0), or Hall's (1984) "elastic price rule." Each of these alternatives inflicts a welfare loss, but in general, the welfare ranking of the various rules depends on the values of the parameters. It can be shown, however, that:

$$(47) \qquad m\bigg|_{p = 0} > m\bigg|_{s = 0} > m\bigg|_{i - \bar{i}' = 0} \quad .$$

Thus, in the present model, a monetary rule that targets the CPI is preferable to a rule that targets the exchange rate, which in turn is preferable to a rule that targets the rate of interest. Furthermore, in the special case in which $\epsilon = 0$, the targeting of the nominal GNP is optimal, and it therefore is the most preferred of all the policy rules, including the rule specifying a constant money growth.

Finally, we should note that when there are no real shocks (so that $\mu = q = y = 0$), $p + y = p = p_d$. In this special case all of the targeting rules (including the optimal rule, $\tilde{m}$) yield identical money-supply responses. Those responses ensure that the real wage remains intact, that changes in the money supply exactly offset shock-induced changes in the money demand, and that the welfare loss is eliminated.

3.6 Other Departures from Optimal Indexation Rules

In section 3.4 we analyze the welfare implications of alternative rules for wage indexation. The rules we considered ensured that either the level of employment or the real wage was kept constant. In this section we examine the welfare implications of other departures from the optimal wage indexation rule. For this purpose suppose that instead of the sophisticated wage indexation rule specified in equation (15), the actual rule adjusts the nominal wage according to simpler formulas. We consider in this section two alternative simple formulas representing different degrees of departure from the optimal rule. To allow for exchange rate intervention, we let the money supply be:

$$(48) \qquad \log M_t^s = \log \bar{M} + \delta_t - \gamma s_t,$$

where $\bar{M}$ denotes the mean value of the nominal money stock; δ_t denotes a random money-supply shock that is assumed to be distributed with a mean of zero and a fixed known variance; and the parameter γ denotes the elasticity of the money supply with respect to s—the percentage deviation of the exchange rate from its deterministic value. As is evident, when $\gamma = 0$, the supply of money does not respond to s and the exchange rate is fully flexible; on the other hand, when $\gamma = \infty$ the exchange rate is fixed. Between these two extremes there is a wide range of intermediate exchange rate regimes. Expressing equation (48) in terms of lowercase letters and suppressing the time subscripts yields:

$$(48'') \qquad m = \delta - \gamma s.$$

3.6.1   Indexation to the Price Level

Suppose that wages are indexed only to the observed price level. Also suppose that the coefficients b_1 and b_2 in equation (15) are set equal to zero. Thus:

$$(15') \qquad w = b_0 p.$$

In addition, suppose that the monetary authority can adjust the money supply in response to the information conveyed by the exchange rate according to equation (48'). What should be the optimal values of b_0 and γ?

To find these values, we incorporate the constraints on the forms of the wage indexation and the money-supply rules into the measure of the welfare loss. With the indexation rule the real wage, $w - p$, is $(1 - b_0)p$. To compute the value of p, we equate the supply of money from equation (48″) with the demand for money from equation (37); and to simplify, we assume for the rest of this section (without sacrificing any great insights) that the income elasticity of the demand for money, ξ, is unity. Recalling that $s = p - \chi$ and that from equation (6′) $y = \sigma[\beta(p - w) + u]$, we find that the value of p that clears the money market is:

$$(49) \qquad p = \frac{\delta + \alpha\rho + (\alpha + \gamma)\chi - \sigma u}{1 + (1 - b_0)\beta\sigma + \alpha + \gamma} .$$

Using equation (49), we can write the negative of the real wage, $-(w - p)$, as:

$$(50) \qquad\qquad (1 - b_0)p = \phi\theta,$$

where $\phi = \dfrac{1 - b_0}{1 + (1 - b_0)\beta\sigma + \alpha + \gamma}$ and $\theta = [\delta + \alpha\rho + (\alpha + \gamma)\chi - \sigma u]$. Substituting equation (50) for the real wage into the measure of the welfare loss, Δ, in equation (13) yields:

$$(13') \qquad\qquad \Delta = \frac{1}{2}\eta\left(\frac{\eta + \epsilon}{\epsilon}\right)\left(\phi\theta + \frac{\sigma}{\epsilon + \eta}u\right)^2 ;$$

and computing the expected value of the loss yields the loss function H:

$$(51) \quad H = \frac{1}{2}\eta\left(\frac{\eta + \epsilon}{\epsilon}\right)\left[\phi^2\sigma_\theta^2 - 2\phi\frac{\sigma^2}{\epsilon + \eta}\sigma_u^2 + \left(\frac{\sigma}{\epsilon + \eta}\right)^2\sigma_u^2\right],$$

where $\sigma_\theta^2 = \sigma_\delta^2 + \alpha^2\sigma_\rho^2 + (\alpha + \gamma)^2\sigma_\chi^2 + \sigma^2\sigma_u^2$. To find the optimal value of the indexation coefficient, we should note that in (13′) and in the loss function (51), b_0 appears only in ϕ; therefore, minimization of Δ in (13′) or of H in (51) with respect to b_0 is equivalent to minimization with respect to ϕ (holding γ constant). This procedure yields the optimal value of ϕ,[16] such that:

$$(52) \qquad\qquad \phi^* = \frac{\sigma^2}{\epsilon + \eta}\frac{\sigma_u^2}{\sigma_\theta^2} .$$

Equating ϕ^* with the definition of ϕ in (50) yields the optimal value of the indexation coefficient b_0;

$$(53)$$

$$b_0^*\bigg|_{\substack{b_1 = 0 \\ b_2 = 0}} = 1 - \frac{1 + \alpha + \gamma}{\dfrac{1}{\sigma_u^2}[\sigma_\delta^2 + \alpha^2\sigma_\rho^2 + (\alpha + \gamma)^2\sigma_\chi^2]\left[\dfrac{\epsilon + \eta}{\sigma^2}\right] + (1 + \epsilon)} ,$$

where the notation on the left-hand side indicates that the optimization is performed under the constraints that the coefficients b_1 and b_2 in the general indexation rule of equation (15) are set equal to zero.

Equation (53) suggests that the optimal indexation coefficient b_0^* depends on three groups of parameters. The first contains the structural parameters of the economy, such as the interest (semi)elasticity of the demand for money (α); the elasticity of the supply of labor (ϵ); and the elasticity of the demand for labor (η), which also embodies the elasticities of output with respect to labor and energy (β and λ). The second group contains the stochastic structure of the various shocks (δ, ρ, χ, μ, and q); and the third contains parameters of other prevailing policies, such as the degree of foreign exchange intervention represented by γ. In general, the dependence of b_0^* on the various parameters is:

$$\frac{\partial b_0^*}{\partial \epsilon} > 0, \; \frac{\partial b_0^*}{\partial \beta} < 0, \; \frac{\partial b_0^*}{\partial \lambda} < 0$$

$$\frac{\partial b_0^*}{\partial \sigma_u^2} < 0, \; \frac{\partial b_0^*}{\partial \sigma_\delta^2} > 0, \; \frac{\partial b_0^*}{\partial \sigma_\rho^2} > 0, \; \frac{\partial b_0^*}{\partial \sigma_\chi^2} > 0.$$

Equation (53) specifies the optimal value of the indexation coefficient under the assumption that the value of γ is set at an arbitrary level. Later on, we will also set γ at its optimal level, but before we do so, it might be instructive to examine the implications of two extreme exchange rate regimes. First, we observe that when $\gamma = \infty$, that is, when the exchange rate is completely fixed, the optimal indexation coefficient is unity. This can be verified by noting that in the measure of the welfare loss (13'), when $\gamma = \infty$ the negative of the real wage $\phi\theta$ is $(1 - b_0)\chi$. Thus, to minimize the value of the last term in parentheses on the right-hand side of (13'), we need to set b_0^* equal to unity. On the other hand, when $\gamma = 0$, that is, when the exchange rate is completely flexible, the optimal indexation coefficient is given in equation (53) after setting γ equal to zero. As can be seen, in that case, when the ratio of $\sigma_\delta^2 + \alpha^2(\sigma_\rho^2 + \sigma_\chi^2)$ to σ_u^2 approaches infinity, as would be the case in the absence of supply shocks, the optimal indexation coefficient approaches unity. On the other hand, when this ratio approaches zero, as would be the case when supply shocks constitute the only disturbances, the optimal indexation coefficient approaches $(\epsilon - \alpha)/(1 + \epsilon)$. (Recall that in deriving this expression we have assumed a unit income elasticity of the demand for money.)

To compute the welfare implications of the departures from the optimal wage indexation rule of section 3.3, we substitute (52) for ϕ into the loss function (51) and obtain:

(54)

$$H(b_0^*;\gamma)\bigg|_{\substack{b_1 = 0 \\ b_2 = 0}} = \frac{1}{2}\left[\frac{\sigma^2\eta\sigma_u^2}{\epsilon(\epsilon + \eta)}\right]\left[\frac{\sigma_\delta^2 + \alpha^2\sigma_\rho^2 + (\alpha + \gamma)^2\sigma_\chi^2}{\sigma_\rho^2 + \alpha^2\sigma_\rho^2 + (\alpha + \gamma)^2\sigma_\chi^2 + \sigma^2\sigma_u^2}\right],$$

where the notation on the left-hand side indicates that the loss is evaluated under the condition that only b_0 is set optimally, while the coefficients b_1 and b_2 in the wage indexation rule (15) are zero and the coefficient γ in the money-supply rule (48″) is set at an arbitrary level. As can be seen, in general (except for the special cases in which the variance of the effective real shock is zero or the second bracketed term in (54) is zero), the indexation to the price level alone cannot eliminate the welfare loss.

It is also of some interest to examine the welfare implications of alternative magnitudes of the production elasticities, λ and β, which are embodied in σ, where $\sigma = 1/(1 - \beta - \lambda)$. It can be shown that when $b_1 = b_2 = 0, \dfrac{\partial H(b_0^*;\gamma)}{\partial\beta} > 0$ and $\dfrac{\partial H(b_0^*;\gamma)}{\partial\lambda} > 0$. Thus, if wages are constrained to be indexed only to the price level, then, for a given configuration of the stochastic shocks, the optimal welfare loss is higher in economies in which the relative shares of labor and energy in the GNP are higher. Equation (54) reveals the channels through which these shares affect the welfare loss. The size of the labor share, β, affects the loss function through its direct impact on σ. On the other hand, the size of the energy share, λ, affects the loss function through its direct effect on σ, as well as through its impact on the stochastic structure itself. Since $u = \mu - \lambda q$ and $\sigma_u^2 = \sigma_\mu^2 + \lambda^2\sigma_q^2$, a higher value of λ will increase the variance of the effective real shock.

Equation (54) can also be used to assess the welfare implications of adopting two extreme exchange rate regimes. When the exchange rate is completely fixed, $\gamma = \infty$ and (54) becomes:

(54′)

$$H(b_0^*;\gamma)\bigg|_{\substack{b_1 = 0 \\ b_2 = 0 \\ \gamma = \infty}} = \frac{1}{2}\left[\frac{\sigma^2\eta\,\sigma_u^2}{\epsilon(\epsilon + \eta)}\right].$$

In that case, the welfare loss depends only on the productive technology, on the elasticity of labor supply, and on the effective real shock. The adoption of the optimal value of b_0 eliminates the welfare implications of the money-supply shock, δ; the foreign interest shock, ρ; and the foreign price shock, χ. In that case, the value of α therefore does not influence the measure of the welfare cost. On the other hand, when the exchange rate is completely flexible, $\gamma = 0$ and the loss function becomes:

$$(54'')\quad H(b_0^*;\gamma)\Bigg|_{\substack{b_1 = 0 \\ b_2 = 0 \\ \gamma = 0}} = \frac{1}{2}\left[\frac{\sigma^2\eta\sigma_u^2}{\epsilon(\epsilon + \eta)}\right]\left[\frac{\sigma_\delta^2 + \alpha^2(\sigma_p^2 + \sigma_x^2)}{\sigma_\delta^2 + \alpha^2(\sigma_p^2 + \sigma_x^2) + \sigma^2\sigma_u^2}\right].$$

A comparison of equations (54') and (54'') shows that:

$$(55)\quad H(b_0^*;\gamma)\Bigg|_{\substack{b_1 = 0 \\ b_2 = 0 \\ \gamma = \infty}} \geq H(b_0^*;\gamma)\Bigg|_{\substack{b_1 = 0 \\ b_2 = 0 \\ \gamma = 0}}$$

Thus, unless the effective real shock is zero, an economy that can only set b_0 optimally should prefer flexible exchange rates over fixed exchange rates. This result confirms the proposition established by Flood and Marion (1982).

Finally, it can be shown that for a given elasticity of the demand for labor, the difference between (54') and (54'') depends on the share of energy in output. The higher the value of λ, the greater the advantage of flexible exchange rates over fixed exchange rates as long as b_0 is set optimally.

The foregoing discussion presumed that the value of γ is set at an arbitrary level. Inspection of the loss function (54) reveals that to minimize the loss function, the value of γ must be set equal to $-\alpha$. Intuitively, a rise in s (through its impact on expectations) raises the demand for money by αs; and therefore, to restore money market equilibrium, the supply of money must adjust by the same amount. Substituting $-\alpha$ for γ in equation (53) yields the optimal indexation coefficient:

$$(53')\quad b_0^*\Bigg|_{\substack{b_1 = 0 \\ b_2 = 0 \\ \gamma = -\alpha}} = 1 - \frac{1}{\dfrac{1}{\sigma_u^2}(\sigma_\delta^2 + \alpha^2\sigma_p^2)\dfrac{(\epsilon + \eta)}{\sigma^2} + 1 + \epsilon},$$

where the notation indicates that the optimization is performed under the assumption that b_1 and b_2 are constrained to equal zero *and* that γ is set optimally at the level $-\alpha$.[17]

As is evident from (53'), in this case the optimal coefficient of indexation depends positively on the interest (semi)elasticity of the demand for money. A comparison of (53) and (53') shows that adopting an optimal exchange rate policy eliminates the effects of the variance of foreign price shocks, σ_χ^2.

Equation (53′) indicates that, in general, as the ratio of $\sigma_\delta^2 + \alpha^2\sigma_\rho^2$ to σ_u^2 approaches infinity, as would be the case when there are no real shocks, the optimal indexation coefficient approaches unity. On the other hand, when this ratio approaches zero, as would be the case when there are only real shocks, the optimal indexation coefficient approaches the fraction $\epsilon/(1 + \epsilon)$.

Substituting $-\alpha$ for γ in the loss function (54) yields:

$$(56) \quad H(b_0^*,\gamma^*)\bigg|_{\substack{b_1 = 0 \\ b_2 = 0}} = \frac{1}{2}\left[\frac{\sigma^2\eta\sigma_u^2}{\epsilon(\epsilon + \eta)}\right]\left[\frac{\sigma_\delta^2 + \alpha^2\sigma_\rho^2}{\sigma_\delta^2 + \alpha^2\sigma_\rho^2 + \sigma^2\sigma_u^2}\right],$$

where the left-hand side indicates that the loss is evaluated under the conditions that both b_0 and γ are set optimally and that b_1 and b_2 are constrained to equal zero.

3.6.2 Indexation to the Price Level and to the Relative Price of Imported Energy

Consider now an alternative indexation rule that comes closer to the general rule of equation (15). Suppose that only the coefficient b_1 in equation (15) is constrained to be zero. Thus, wages are assumed to be indexed to the price, p, and to the relative price of energy, q, according to the following:

$$(15'') \qquad\qquad w = b_0 p + b_2 q.$$

With this indexation rule the measure of the welfare loss is:

$$(13'') \qquad \Delta = \frac{1}{2}\,\eta\!\left(\frac{\eta + \epsilon}{\epsilon}\right)\left[(1 - b_0)p - b_2 q + \frac{\sigma}{\epsilon + \eta}\right]^2,$$

and the policy problem is to determine the optimal values of b_0 and b_2 so as to minimize the expected value of the welfare loss. As is evident, minimizing the loss function is equivalent to minimizing the expected value of the last (squared) term in (13″), which measures the difference between the actual real wage and the equilibrium real wage. In what follows we focus on this term.

Proceeding along similar lines as in section 3.5.1, we find that the equilibrium price that clears the money market is:

$$(49') \qquad p = \frac{\delta + \alpha\rho + (\alpha + \gamma)\chi - \sigma(u - \beta b_2 q)}{1 + (1 - b_0)\beta\sigma + \alpha + \gamma}.$$

After substituting this expression for p into (13″) and collecting terms, we can write the loss function (or, more precisely, the expected value of the squared difference between the actual and the equilibrium real wage) as:

$$(57) \quad E\left\{\left[\phi\sigma(\beta b_2 + \lambda) - b_2 - \frac{1 - \eta}{\epsilon + \eta}\right]q + \phi\theta_1 + \frac{\sigma}{\epsilon + \eta}\mu\right\}^2,$$

where $\theta_1 = \delta + \alpha\rho + (\alpha + \gamma)\chi - \sigma\mu = \theta - \sigma\lambda q$, and θ and ϕ are as defined in equation (50).

In minimizing the loss function we first equate the coefficient of q to zero and substitute the optimal value of ϕ (analogous to equation [52]) into (57). This yields the optimal value of b_2, such that:

$$(58) \quad b_2^* = -\frac{\lambda}{\sigma}\left\{\frac{\sigma_{(\theta_1 + \sigma\mu)}^2/\sigma_\mu^2}{\left[\dfrac{\sigma_{(\theta_1 + \sigma\mu)}^2}{\sigma_\mu^2}\right]\left(\dfrac{\epsilon + \eta}{\sigma^2}\right) + 1 + \epsilon}\right\} < 0.$$

Thus, a higher relative price of imported energy must lower the wage.
The dependence of b_2^* on the various parameters is:

$$-\frac{\partial b_2^*}{\partial\epsilon} < 0, \quad -\frac{\partial b_2^*}{\partial\beta} > 0, \quad -\frac{\partial b_2^*}{\partial\lambda} > 0, \quad -\frac{\partial b_2^*}{\partial\left[\dfrac{\sigma_{(\theta_1 + \sigma\mu)}^2}{\sigma_\mu^2}\right]} > 0.$$

Furthermore, it is noteworthy that the elasticity of $-b_2^*$ with respect to the size of the energy share, λ, exceeds unity.

Once b_2 has been set at its optimal level, the coefficient of q in the loss function vanishes and the expression in (57) reduces to the following:

$$(57') \quad E\left(\phi\theta_1 + \frac{\sigma}{\epsilon + \eta}\mu\right)^2.$$

Since the optimal value of b_2 serves to eliminate the impact of imported energy-price shocks on labor market disequilibrium, it is evident that from now on the formal structure of the optimization problem is identical to that in section 3.6.1. The only difference between the two is that the expression in (57') does not include terms involving q. Thus, (57') contains θ_1 and μ, whereas the expression in (51) contains θ and u. It follows that the optimal value of b_0 is the same as in equations (53) and (53') except for the substitution of σ_μ^2 for σ_u^2.

A comparison of the optimal value of b_2^* in (58) and the corresponding value of b_0^* shows that the two components of the wage indexation rule are related to each other through a simple link. For example, when γ is set at its optimal value, b_0^* is described by equation (53') (modified to include σ_μ^2, instead of σ_u^2), and the two indexation coefficients are related to each other according to the following:

$$(59) \qquad b_2^* = \frac{\lambda}{\sigma} \left(\frac{\sigma_\delta^2 + \alpha^2 \sigma_\rho^2}{\sigma_\mu^2} \right) (b_0^* - 1).$$

Thus, the ratio $b_2^*/(b_0^* - 1)$ is higher, the higher the relative share of imported energy in output. Likewise, this ratio is higher, the higher the variances of the monetary shock, δ, and the foreign interest shock, ρ, and the lower the variance of the productivity shock, μ.

The formal similarity between the structure of the optimization problem in equation (57') and that of section 3.6.1 also implies that all the expressions developed in that section for the purpose of measuring the welfare loss resulting from alternative second-best situations continue to apply. The only modification requires the substitution of the variance of the productivity shock, σ_μ^2, for the variance of the effective real shock, σ_u^2. Furthermore, since σ_μ^2 is smaller than σ_u^2 (which also contains the variance of the imported energy price), it follows from (53) that the optimal value of b_0 is higher when the indexation rule allows for the application of an optimal response to q than when it does not.

The foregoing discussion, together with the results obtained in section 3.3, implies that:

$$(60) \qquad \left. b_0^* \right|_{\substack{b_1 = 0 \\ b_2 = 0}} \leq \left. b_0^* \right|_{\substack{b_1 = 0 \\ b_2 = b_2^*}} \leq \left. b_0^* \right|_{\substack{b_1 = b_1^* \\ b_2 = b_2^*}} = 1.$$

This chain of inequalities demonstrates that the optimal degree to which wages should be indexed to the price level depends critically on the precise form of the constraints that are imposed on the indexation rule. In the absence of constraints on the degree of sophistication of the wage rule, the optimal coefficient of indexation to the price level is unity. This ensures that monetary shocks, which should not affect the equilibrium real wage, are prevented from inducing changes in the real wage. At the optimum, real shocks are allowed to alter the real wage through separate indexation coefficients. Once such a separation is not allowed, successive departures from the sophisticated indexation rule result in successive reductions in the degree to which wages ought to be indexed to prices.[18]

3.7   Concluding Remarks

In this paper we analyzed the interactions among supply shocks, wage indexation, and monetary policy. We developed an analytical framework for determining the optimal wage indexation and monetary policy. This framework was then applied to analyze the implications of suboptimal policy rules. The welfare ranking of those rules was based on the relative magnitudes of the deadweight losses associated with the various policies. The main results of our analysis are summarized in the introduction to this paper. In this section we outline some of the limitations of the study and possible further extensions of this line of research.

In our framework labor market contracts stipulate the nominal wage rule for the length of the contract period. Those contracts reflect the cost of negotiations. Since the wage rule is set in advance of the realization of the stochastic shocks, it may give rise to deadweight losses associated with disequilibrium real wages. Our analysis employs this specific form of wage contracts as a stylized description of conventional labor market arrangements. Implicit in our formulation is the assumption that workers and employers are risk neutral. A useful extension would allow for risk aversion that would rationalize contracts in terms of the insurance function (see, for example, Azariadis 1978).

Further, in our specification the welfare loss arises only from a suboptimal employment level. Implicit in this specification is the assumption that all other markets are undistorted. An extension would allow for other distortions. In that case the welfare loss caused by suboptimal money holdings would be added to the loss associated with labor market distortions and would depend on both the level and the variance of inflation.

Although we have assumed in the main analysis that the stochastic shocks are identically and independently distributed with a mean of zero and a fixed variance, we have outlined the way by which one could allow for more general time-series properties of the stochastic shocks. An explicit elaboration of such an extension would highlight the important distinction between permanent and transitory shocks and would generate a profile of wage dynamics. In addition to the distinction between permanent (long-lived) and transitory (short-lived) shocks, one could also allow for lags in the implementation of the indexation rules. With such lags, as indicated by Fischer in his accompanying comment, optimal policies would index wages to the long-lived shocks but would not index wages to the short-lived shocks. To clarify the above prescription, we should note that "long-lived" shocks are those that are in effect during the period in which indexation can be implemented but that have not yet been incorporated into the determination of the contractual base wage. On the other hand, "short-lived" shocks are those that are in effect for a length of time shorter than the indexation lag. With this distinction, our formulas for optimal wage indexation rules are fully applicable. They may be interpreted as providing a guide for the necessary adjustment of the nominal wage in the presence of long-lived shocks. Richer and more complicated dynamics could also be induced by staggered contracts and by capital accumulation (see, for example, Fischer 1977c; 1985) and Taylor 1980).

Our analysis assumed that there is one composite good that is traded internationally at a (stochastically) given world price. With this level of aggregation we demonstrated that wage indexation rules bear an exact dual relationship to monetary targeting rules. This duality implied that there was no fundamental difference between the outcomes of various wage indexation rules and the outcomes of the corresponding monetary targeting rules. Thus, when there is a single composite commodity, the choice between wage indexation and monetary policy is governed by additional considerations such as the relative costs and complexities associated with the implementation of the two alternatives rules. In the more general case, however, when there are many sectors producing a variety of goods, the exact duality between wage indexation and monetary policy breaks down. Specifically, as shown by Blinder and Mankiw (1984), it is clear that monetary policy, being an aggregative policy, is not a suitable response to sector-specific shocks. Under such circumstances it is evident that optimal sector-specific policies are called for instead. A natural extension of our analysis would be to apply the analytical framework to determine the optimal sector-specific wage indexation formulas that would eliminate the welfare loss resulting from labor market distortions (for a sketch of such a framework, see Aizenman and Frenkel 1986b).

Appendix: The Computation of the Welfare Loss

In this appendix we provide a formal derivation of the welfare loss that is used in the text.

Consider a two-period model and let the present value of utility U be:

$$(A1) \qquad U = u(C_1, L_1) + \bar{\rho}u(C_2, L_2),$$

where $\bar{\rho}$ designates the subjective discount factor; C_i and L_i ($i = 1, 2$) denote the levels of consumption and labor in period i; and the subscripts 1 and 2 designate periods 1 and 2, respectively. The value of assets not consumed in period 1 is A_1, and their value in period 2 is $(1 + r)A_1$, where r designates the exogenously given (stochastic) world rate of interest on internationally traded bonds. Profits are denoted by R and are assumed to be redistributed as lump-sum transfers. The value of profits in each period is the corresponding value of output, Y_t, minus payments to labor and energy inputs, such that:

(A2) $R_t = Y_t(L_t, V_t) - \left(\dfrac{W}{P}\right)_t L_t - \left(\dfrac{P_v}{P}\right)_t V_t,$ $(t = 1, 2),$

where W, P_v, and P denote the nominal wage, the price of energy, and the price of output, respectively. Producers are assumed to maximize profits subject to the given real wage and the given relative price of energy. In equilibrium the real wage and the relative price of energy are equated to the marginal products of labor and energy, respectively, such that:

(A3) $$\dfrac{\partial Y(L, V)}{\partial L} = \dfrac{W}{P}$$

(A4) $$\dfrac{\partial Y(L, V)}{\partial V} = \dfrac{P_v}{P}.$$

These conditions yield the demands for labor and energy inputs. The *equilibrium* real wage that clears the labor market is defined by $(\tilde{W}/P)$, and $\bar{L}$ and $\tilde{V}$ denote the corresponding equilibrium levels of employment and energy utilization. At this general equilibrium all markets clear.

We turn now to the formal maximization problem, starting with the maximization of second-period utility. Denoting by R_i^* $(i = 1, 2)$ the solution to the producers' profit maximization problem in period i, as implied by the solutions to (A3) and (A4), we can write the maximization problem in period 2 as:

(A5) $\max u(C_2, L_2)$

s.t. $C_2 = (1 + r)A_1 + \left(\dfrac{W}{P}\right)_2 L_2 + R_2^*.$

The solution to this problem yields C_2^* and L_2^* as the optimal values of consumption and labor supply in period 2. These optimal values are conditional, of course, on the historically given value of A_1. Thus, we can define a function $u^*(A_1)$, which denotes the expected value of optimal utility in the second period. Thus, $u^*(A_1) = E[u(C_2^*, L_2^*)]$. The maximization problem for period 1 can then be presented as:

(A6) $\max u(C_1, L_1) + \bar{\rho}\, u^*(A_1)$

s.t. $C_1 = Q + \left(\dfrac{W}{P}\right)_1 L_1 + R_1^* - A_1,$

where Q denotes the given initial endowment. The solution to (A6) yields the optimal values $\tilde{C}_1$, $\bar{L}_1$, and $\tilde{A}_1$. For subsequent use we note that the optimal value of A_1 is chosen so as to satisfy the first-order condition requiring that:

(A7) $$\bar{\rho}\, \partial u^*(A_1)/\partial A_1 = \partial u(C_1, L_1)/\partial C_1.$$

The value of utility in the general equilibrium is denoted by $U(\tilde{L}_1)$, where it is understood that this level of utility is obtained when C_1, L_1 and A_1 are set at their unconstrained optimal values, $\tilde{C}_1$, $\tilde{L}_1$ and $\tilde{A}_1$. In practice, because of the existence of contracts, the level of employment might be constrained to L_1. The resulting level of utility would be $U(L_1)$, where it is understood that C_1 and A_1 are still chosen optimally subject to the constraint that the maximization of profits and the given nominal wage yield labor demand (and therefore employment) at the level L_1. The welfare loss caused by the constrained employment (L_1) in terms of first-period consumption is:

(A8) $$\frac{\Delta U}{\Theta} = \frac{U(\tilde{L}_1) - U(L_1)}{\partial u(\tilde{C}_1, \tilde{L}_1)/\partial \tilde{C}_1},$$

where $\Delta U = U(\tilde{L}_1) - U(L_1)$, and $\Theta = \partial u(\tilde{C}_1, \tilde{L}_1)/\partial \tilde{C}_1$ denotes the marginal utility of consumption during the first period evaluated around the general equilibrium.

To obtain an expression measuring the welfare loss, we first compute the change in welfare associated with a marginal change in employment around an initial arbitrary level L. In what follows we compute the welfare loss for period 1, and we suppress the corresponding time subscript. Using equation (A6), the first-order approximation of the change in welfare resulting from a marginal change in employment is:

(A9) $U(L + \Delta L) - U(L)$
$$= [\partial u(C, L)/\partial C]\Delta C + [\partial u(C, L)/\partial L]\Delta L + \bar{\rho}[\partial u^*(A)/\partial A]\Delta A.$$

Using equation (A7) and expressing (A9) in terms of first-period consumption yields:

(A10) $$\frac{U(L + \Delta L) - U(L)}{\partial u(C, L)/\partial C} = \Delta C - \left(\frac{W}{P}\right)^s \Delta L + \Delta A,$$

where $(W/P)^s = -\partial u(C, L)/\partial L$ denotes the real wage as measured along the *supply* of labor. From the definition of profits in (A2) and the budget constraint in (A6) we can see that:

$$C + A - Q = Y(L, V) - \frac{P_v}{P}V$$

and therefore:

(A11) $$\Delta C + \Delta A = \frac{\partial Y}{\partial L}\Delta L + \frac{\partial Y}{\partial V}\Delta V - \frac{P_v}{P}\Delta V.$$

Since producers always maximize profits, we may substitute the first-order conditions (A3) and (A4) into (A11) to obtain:

(A10′) $$\Delta C + \Delta A = \left(\frac{W}{P}\right)^{d} \Delta L,$$

where $(W/P)^d$ denotes the real wage as measured along the *demand* for labor. Substituting (A10′) into (A10) yields:

(A12) $$\frac{[U(L + \Delta L) - U(L)]/\Delta L}{\partial u(C, L)/\partial C} = \left(\frac{W}{P}\right)^{d} - \left(\frac{W}{P}\right)^{s}.$$

Finally we note that as $\Delta L \to 0$, (A12) becomes:

(A12′) $$\frac{dU(L)/dL}{\partial u(C, L)/\partial C} = \left(\frac{W}{P}\right)^{d} - \left(\frac{W}{P}\right)^{s}.$$

In computing the welfare loss, we note that:

$$U(\tilde{L}_1) - U(L_1) = \int_{L_1}^{\tilde{L}_1} \frac{dU}{dL}\, dL.$$

Substituting this expression, together with (A12′), into (A8) yields:

(A13) $$\frac{\Delta U}{\Theta} = \frac{1}{\partial u(\tilde{C}_1, \tilde{L}_1)/\partial \tilde{C}_1} \int_{L_1}^{\tilde{L}_1} \frac{\partial u(C, L)}{\partial C}\left[\left(\frac{W}{P}\right)^{d} - \left(\frac{W}{P}\right)^{s}\right] dL.$$

Finally, if we assume a constant marginal utility of consumption (that is, risk neutrality), (A12) can be written as:

(A13′) $$\frac{\Delta U}{\Theta} = \int_{L_1}^{\tilde{L}_1}\left[\left(\frac{W}{P}\right)^{d} - \left(\frac{W}{P}\right)^{s}\right] dL.$$

To obtain a more useful expression for the welfare loss, we first express $\left(\frac{W}{P}\right)^{d}$ and $\left(\frac{W}{P}\right)^{s}$ in terms of the elasticities of labor supply and labor demand. Using the definitions of the elasticities, we can express the values of $\left(\frac{W}{P}\right)^{d}$ and $\left(\frac{W}{P}\right)^{s}$ around the general equilibrium as:

$$\left(\frac{W}{P}\right)^{d} = \left(\frac{\tilde{W}}{P}\right)\left(1 - \frac{\Delta L}{\tilde{L}\eta}\right)$$

$$\left(\frac{W}{P}\right)^{s} = \left(\frac{\tilde{W}}{P}\right)\left(1 + \frac{\Delta L}{\tilde{L}\epsilon}\right),$$

where $\Delta L = L - \tilde{L}$, and ϵ and η denote the elasticities of labor supply and demand, respectively. Substituting these expressions into (A13′) yields:

$$(A14) \qquad \frac{\Delta U}{\Theta} = \int_{L_1}^{\tilde{L}_1} \left(\frac{\tilde{W}}{P}\right)\frac{1}{\tilde{L}}\left(\frac{1}{\epsilon} + \frac{1}{\eta}\right)(\tilde{L} - L)dL.$$

Integrating the expression in (A14) yields:

$$(A15) \qquad \frac{\Delta U}{\Theta} = \left(\frac{\tilde{W}}{P}\right)\frac{1}{\tilde{L}}\left(\frac{1}{\epsilon} + \frac{1}{\eta}\right)\frac{(\tilde{L} - L)^2}{2}.$$

The loss function H is the expected value of (A15). Denoting by Y_0 and L_0 the equilibrium levels of output and employment obtained in the absence of stochastic shocks, we note that:

$$\Delta L = L - \tilde{L} = L_0\left[\frac{(L - L_0) - (\tilde{L} - L_0)}{L_0}\right] = L_0(l - \tilde{l})$$

and

$$\frac{\tilde{L}}{L_0} = (1 - \tilde{l}).$$

We also note that from the first-order condition:

$$\left(\frac{\tilde{W}}{P}\right)\tilde{L} = \beta\tilde{Y} = \beta Y_0(1 + \tilde{y}).$$

Substituting these expressions into (A15), ignoring terms higher than the second-order terms of Taylor expansion, and computing the expected value yields:

$$(A16) \qquad E\left(\frac{\Delta U}{\Theta}\right) = E\left[\left(\frac{W}{P}\right)_0 L_0 \left(\frac{1}{\epsilon} + \frac{1}{\eta}\right)\frac{(\tilde{l} - l)^2}{2}\right].$$

Finally, substituting equation (11) of the text for $(\tilde{l} - l)$ yields the loss function:

$$(A17) \quad H = E\left\{\frac{1}{2}\eta\frac{\epsilon + \eta}{\epsilon}\left(\frac{1}{\epsilon} + \frac{1}{\eta}\right)[-(w - p) + (\widetilde{w - p})]^2\right\},$$

where H is the approximation to $\dfrac{\Delta U}{\Theta}\bigg/\left(\dfrac{W}{P}\right)_0 L_0$. The expression in (A17) is the expected value of equation (13) in the text.

Notes

1. This assumption is relaxed in Aizenman and Frenkel (1985a), where it is assumed (in the context of a model without energy) that the value of the stochastic shock is not known at each point in time. In that case behavior is governed by the conditional expectations of the shocks based on the available information.

2. The question concerning the efficiency of the assumed wage contract is addressed in section 3.3.2, note 6.

3. This expression corresponds to equation (A17) in the appendix. To obtain the welfare loss in units of output, we need to multiply equation (13) by the equilibrium (nonstochastic) wage bill, $(W/P)_0 L_0$. For a useful discussion of welfare loss measurement, see Harberger (1971).

4. We assume that the initial contractual nominal wage is set at W_0—the level that would have prevailed in equilibrium in the absence of shocks. Any other initial wage would not minimize the *expected* value of the welfare loss. In making this statement we use the approximation $\log E_{t-1}(e^{u_t}) \simeq E_{t-1}(u_t)$. This approximation is valid for small values of the variance and of the realization of the stochastic shock u.

5. For an analysis of optimal indexation rules, see Fischer (1977a; 1977b).

6. The assumption that employment is determined by the demand for labor was challenged by Cukierman (1980), who examined alternative specifications of employment. As is evident with optimal policies, these issues become inconsequential since, at the optimum, labor demand and labor supply are equal. Likewise, at the optimum, the conceptual difficulties raised by Barro (1977) concerning the existence of suboptimal contracts are also inconsequential, since with optimal policies these contracts are in fact optimal. For a further discussion and rationalization of labor contracts, see Hall and Lazear (1984) and Fischer (1977b).

7. The specification in equation (17) constrained the coefficient of p to be unity. More formally, let the coefficient of p in (17) be b_p; in that case the real wage is $w - p = (b_p - 1)p + b_y y$, and the level of output (using 6') is $y = [-(b_p - 1)p + \sigma u]/(1 + \beta \sigma b_y)$. Substituting this expression into the real wage equation and using equation (13) reveals that to equate the realized real wage with the equilibrium real wage, the coefficient of p must be unity and the coefficient of y must be $1/(1 + \epsilon)$. It is also relevant to note that equation (17') corresponds to equation (15) in Karni (1983, 286). The precise analogy may not be apparent because there is a typographical error in Karni's equation (15). Using Karni's notations his coefficient of indexation to real output should read $\eta/(w + \eta + \delta w \eta)$.

8. For analyses of alternative proposals, see Fischer (1977a), Eden (1979), Marston and Turnovsky (1985), and Marston (1984). For an analysis of alternative compensation systems and for a related discussion of employment versus real wage stabilization, see Weitzman (1983).

9. It is relevant to note that with a Cobb-Douglas production function, indexing nominal wages to nominal income is equivalent to indexing real wages to the real value of value added in terms of units of final output. To verify, define the real value added by $Y - (P_v/P)V$ and the percentage change thereof by $\dfrac{y}{1 - \lambda} - \dfrac{\lambda}{1 - \lambda}(q + v)$. From the first-order conditions, $\lambda Y/V = P_v/P$ and therefore $y = q + v$. It thus follows that $\dfrac{y}{1 - \lambda} - \dfrac{\lambda}{1 - \lambda}y = y$. Marston and Turnovsky (1985) argued that the rule according to which nominal wages are indexed to the value-added price index produces equivalent results to those produced by the rule by which real wages are indexed to the real GNP. Our analysis shows that this equivalence holds only as long as there are no productivity shocks. Further, if the two rules are equivalent, they will be optimal only if, in addition, $\epsilon = 0$.

10. The implicit assumption underlying this formulation is that all variables are stationary, that is, that there are no trends and that $E_t \log S_{t+1}$ is not influenced by the observed price. Thus, in the absence of shocks, $i = \bar{i}'$. Our assumption about the absence of trend allows us to focus on the properties of the stationary equilibrium for which the

current values of the stochastic shocks do not affect expectations about future values of the variables. In general, the stochastic shocks need not be identically and independently distributed with a mean of zero and a fixed variance. Allowing for a more general specification requires a modification of the definition of the benchmark equilibrium that is obtained in the absence of shocks. With a more general specification of the stochastic shocks we let lowercase letters denote an *innovation* of a given variable. Thus, $x_t = \log X_t - E_{t-1} \log X_t$, instead of the specification adopted in the text according to which $x_t = \log X_t - \log X_0$. Obviously, in the special case discussed in the text, the assumed properties of the stochastic shocks imply that $E_{t-1} \log X_t = \log X_0$. With this interpretation of x_t (as the innovation of $\log X_t$), the analysis can allow for trends in the various series, and the various shocks may include permanent and transitory components. It is also relevant to note that the specification of equation (36) also embodies the assumption that the equilibrium is unique. The choice of the unique equilibrium is consistent with the criterion suggested by McCallum (1983). On the issue of uniqueness, see Calvo (1979) and Turnovsky (1983b).

11. Relevant early references are Gordon (1975) and Phelps (1978). The focus on the question of accommodation in the presence of supply shocks is contained in Blinder (1981), Gordon (1984), and Fischer (1985); and various structural issues concerning adjustment to external shocks in an international setting are found in Bruno (1984), Bruno and Sachs (1982), Findlay and Rodriguez (1977), and Marion and Svensson (1982).

12. Phelps (1978) emphasized the implications of an income elasticity differing from unity.

13. In the more general specification of the stochastic shocks (which are described in note 10), the term $(\rho + \chi)$ in equation (37) would be replaced by the innovation in $i_t + \log P_t$, which can also be expressed as $i_t' + E_t \log S_{t+1} + \log P_t'$. Thus, the innovation of this term is $(i_t' - E_{t-1}i_t') + E_t s_{t+1} + p_t'$, where $E_t s_{t+1} = E_t \log S_{t+1} - E_{t-1} \log S_{t+1}$, and $p_t' = \log P_t' - E_{t-1} \log P_t'$. To obtain this expression for the innovation we first substitute equation (34) into the demand for money (in equation [29]) and replace $\bar{i}'$ (in equation [29']) with $E_{t-1}i_t'$. Subtracting the resulting two equations from each other yields the more general expression corresponding to equation (37).

14. We should note that the formulation of the objective function in terms of the minimization of the welfare loss from labor market distortions presumes that other markets are undistorted. Within this framework the variances of prices and of the money supply are reported in equations (40) and (42) only as informative statistics. A more general formulation would recognize that the productivity (or the utility yield) of money depends on these variances. Optimal policies would then minimize the welfare loss from labor market distortions along with the loss from suboptimal inflation and price variability.

15. For analyses of nominal income targeting, see, for example, Meade (1978), Poole (1980), Tobin (1980; 1983), Hall (1983), Bean (1983), Taylor (1985), and Aizenman and Frenkel (1986a). For discussions of a close variant of nominal income targeting see McCallum (1984) and Mishkin (1984); and for other rules see Phelps and Taylor (1977).

16. Minimizing the expected value of (13') with respect to ϕ amounts to computing the ordinary-least-squares estimate of a regression of $\sigma u/(\epsilon + \eta)$ on $-\theta$. It follows that the optimal value of ϕ is:

$$\phi^* = - \frac{\text{cov}(u, \theta)[\sigma/(\epsilon + \eta)]}{\sigma_\theta^2} ;$$

and when the stochastic shocks are independent of each other, this expression reduces to equation (52) in the text.

17. For a related analysis of the relationship between optimal wage indexation and optimal foreign exchange intervention, see Aizenman and Frenkel (1985a), Bhandari (1982), Marston (1982), and Turnovsky (1983a).

18. It can be shown that if the constraint on the indexation rule sets $b_2 = 0$ but allows for the optimal determination of b_0 and b_1, then:

$$\left. b_0^* \right|_{\substack{b_1 = b_1^* \\ b_2 = 0}} \gtrless \left. b_0^* \right|_{\substack{b_1 = 0 \\ b_2 = b_2^*}} \quad \text{as } \sigma_\mu^* \gtrless \sigma_{\lambda q}^2.$$

References

Aizenman, Joshua, and Frenkel, Jabob A. 1985. Optimal wage indexation, foreign exchange intervention and monetary policy. *American Economic Review* 75, no. 3 (June): 402–23.

————. 1986a. Targeting rules for monetary policy. *Economics Letters* 21.

————. 1986b. Sectorial wages and the real exchange rate. NBER Working Paper Series, no. 18 (January). Forthcoming in *Journal of International Economics*.

Azariadis, Costas. 1978. Escalator clauses and the allocation of cyclical risks. *Journal of Economic Theory* 18, no. 1 (June): 119–55.

Barro, Robert J. 1977. Long-term contracting, sticky prices, and monetary policy. *Journal of Monetary Economics* 3, no. 3 (July): 305–16.

Bean, Charles R. 1983. Targeting nominal income: An appraisal. *Economic Journal* 93, no. 4 (December): 806–19.

Bhandari, Jagdeep S. 1982. Staggered wage setting and exchange rate policy in an economy with capital assets. *Journal of International Money and Finance* 1, no. 3 (December): 275–92.

Blinder, Alan S. 1981. Monetary accommodation of supply shocks under rational expectations. *Journal of Money, Credit and Banking* 13, no. 4 (November): 425–38.

Blinder, Alan S., and Mankiw, Gregory N. 1984. Aggregation and stabilization policy in a multi-contract economy. *Journal of Monetary Economics* 13, no. 1 (January): 67–86.

Bruno, Michael. 1984. Raw materials, profits, and the productivity slowdown. *Quarterly Journal of Economics* 99, no. 1 (February): 1–30.

Bruno, Michael, and Sachs, Jeffrey. 1982. Input price shocks and the slowdown in economic growth: The case of U. K. Manufacturing. *Review of Economic Studies* 5 (special issue): 679–706.

Calvo, Guillermo A. 1979. On models of money and perfect foresight. *International Economic Review* 20, no. 1 (February): 83–102.

Cukierman, Alex. 1980. The effects of wage indexation on macroeconomic fluctuations: A generalization. *Journal of Monetary Economics* 6, no. 2 (April): 147–70.

Eden, Benjamin. 1979. The nominal system: Linkage to the quantity of money or to nominal income. *Revue Economique* 30, no. 1 (January): 121–43.

Findlay, Ronald, and Rodriguez, Carlos A. 1977. Intermediate imports and macroeconomic policy under flexible exchange rates. *Canadian Journal of Economics* 10 (May): 208–17.

Fischer, Stanley. 1977a. Wage indexation and macroeconomic stability. In *Stabilization of domestic and international economy,* ed. Karl Brunner and Allan Meltzer. Carnegie-Rochester Conference Series on Public Policy, vol. 5, a supplementary series to the *Journal of Monetary Economics* 3: 107–47.

———. 1977b. Long term contracting, sticky prices and monetary policy: A comment. *Journal of Monetary Economics* 3, no. 3 (July): 317–23.

———. 1977c. Long-term contracts, rational expectations, and the optimal money supply rule. *Journal of Political Economy* 85, no. 1 (February): 191–205.

———. 1985. Supply shocks, wage stickiness, and accommodation. *Journal of Money, Credit and Banking,* 17, no. 1 (February): 1–15.

Flood, Robert P., and Marion, Nancy P. 1982. The transmission of disturbance under alternative exchange-rate regimes with optimal indexation. *Quarterly Journal of Economics* 97, no. 1 (February): 43–66.

Gordon, Robert J. 1975. Alternative responses of policy to external supply shocks. *Brookings Papers on Economic Activity* (no. 1): 183–206.

———. 1984. Supply shocks and monetary policy revisited. *American Economic Review* 74, no. 2 (May): 38–43.

Gray, Jo Anna. 1976. Wage indexation: A macroeconomic approach. *Journal of Monetary Economics* 2, no. 2 (April): 221–35.

Hall, Robert E. 1983. Macroeconomic policy under structural change. In *Industrial change and public policy,* 85–111. Federal Reserve Bank of Kansas City.

———. 1984. Monetary Strategy with an Elastic Price Standard. In *Price stability and public policy,* 137–59. Federal Reserve Bank of Kansas City.

Hall, Robert E., and Lazear, Edward P. 1984. The excess sensitivity of quits and layoffs to demand. *Journal of Labor Economics* 2, no. 2 (April): 233–57.

Harberger, Arnold C. 1971. Three basic postulates for applied welfare economics: An interpretive essay. *Journal of Economic Literature* 9, no. 3 (September): 785–97.

Karni, Edi. 1983. On optimal wage indexation. *Journal of Political Economy* 91, no. 2 (April): 282–92.

Marion, Nancy P., and Svensson, Lars E. O. 1982. Adjustment to expected and unexpected oil price increases. NBER Working Paper no. 997. Cambridge, Mass.: National Bureau of Economic Research, October.

Marston, Richard C. 1982. Wages, relative prices and the choice between fixed and flexible exchange rates. *Canadian Journal of Economics* 15, no. 1 (February): 87–103.

———. 1984. Real wages and the terms of trade: Alternative indexation rules for an open economy. *Journal of Money, Credit and Banking* 16, no. 3 (August): 285–301.

Marston, Richard C., and Turnovsky, Stephen J. 1985. Imported material prices, wage policy and macroeconomic stabilization. *Canadian Journal of Economics* 19, no. 2 (May): 273–84.

McCallum, Bennett T. 1983. On non-uniqueness in rational expectations models: An attempt at perspective. *Journal of Monetary Economics* 11, no. 2 (March): 139–68.

———. 1984. Monetarist rules in the light of recent experiences. *American Economic Review* 74, no. 2 (May): 388–91.

Meade, James E. 1978. The meaning of internal balance. *Economic Journal* 88, no. 3 (September): 423–35.

Mishkin, Frederic S. 1984. The causes of inflation. In *Price stability and public policy,* 1–24. Federal Reserve Bank of Kansas City.

Phelps, Edmund S. 1978. Commodity-supply shock and full-employment monetary policy. *Journal of Money, Credit and Banking* 10, no. 2 (May): 206–21.

Phelps, Edmund S., and Taylor, John B. 1977. Stabilizing powers of monetary policy under rational expectations. *Journal of Political Economy* 85, no. 1 (February): 163–90.

Poole, William. 1980. Comments on paper by Tobin. *Brookings Papers on Economic Activity* (no. 1): 79–85.

Rasche, Robert H., and Tatom, John A. 1981. Energy price shocks, aggregate supply and monetary policy: The theory and the international evidence. In *Supply shocks, incentives and national wealth,* ed. Karl Brunner and Allan Meltzer, 9–13. Carnegie-Rochester Conference Series on Public Policy, vol. 14, Amsterdam: North-Holland.

Taylor, John B. 1980. Aggregate dynamics and staggered contracts. *Journal of Political Economy* 88, no. 1 (February): 1–23.

———. 1985. What would nominal GNP targeting do to the business cycle? In *Understanding Monetary Regimes,* ed. Karl Brunner and Allan Meltzer, 61–84. Carnegie-Rochester Conference Series on Public Policy, vol. 22. Amsterdam: North-Holland.

Tobin, James. 1980. Stabilization policy ten years after. *Brookings Papers on Economic Activity* (no. 1): 19–71.

———. 1983. Commentary. In *Industrial change and public policy,* 113–22. Federal Reserve Bank of Kansas City.

Turnovsky, Stephen J. 1983a. Wage indexation and exchange market intervention in a small open economy. *Canadian Journal of Economics* 16, no. 4 (November): 574–92.

———. 1983b. Exchange market intervention policies in a small open economy. In *Economic interdependence and flexible exchange rates,* ed. J. Bhandari and B. Putnam, 286–311.

Weitzman, Martin L. 1983. Some macroeconomic implications of alternative compensation systems. *Economic Journal* 93, no. 4 (December): 763–83.

Comment   Stanley Fischer

My comments on this useful paper start with an alternative graphic presentation of the model, continue by highlighting the main results, and end by noting the limitations and potential extensions of the analysis.

The paper derives optimal and some second-best wage-indexing formulas and their implications for the macro economy. Wages or the wage indexation formulas are fixed one period in advance of the shock to the economy, and firms determine the level of employment according to their demand functions for labor. The optimality criterion is the minimization of the welfare-triangle loss in the labor market that results from the difference between the actual real wage and the real wage that would clear the labor market. Because Aizenman and Frenkel's welfare criterion does not include the behavior of the price level, they are unable to discuss analytically the trade-off between inflation and unemployment that is the essence of the accommodation issue.

The most valuable section of the paper, 3.4, examines the well-known proposals that wages be indexed to the domestic value-added deflator or to the nominal GNP. The interest in this section comes both from the fact that the proposed indexation formulas have attracted much support and from the fact that this section examines indexation formulas that tie wages to directly observable macro aggregates such as the price level and the GNP, as they have to be tied in practice, rather than to disturbances.[1] The authors' general conclusion is that indexing to nominal income is likely to be better than indexing to the domestic value-added deflator or to the price level.

The Model

Aizenman and Frenkel (A & F) concentrate their graphic presentation on the labor market. This makes it easy to see labor market welfare triangles. An alternative exposition of the same model focuses on the goods market, drawing aggregate supply and demand curves as in figure C3.1.

The aggregate supply curve (AS) is derived from A & F's equation (6'). It is:

$$(6'') \qquad p = w + \frac{1}{\sigma\beta} y - \frac{u}{\beta} .$$

Stanley Fischer is a professor of economics at the Massachusetts Institute of Technology and a research associate of the National Bureau of Economic Research.

I am grateful to Joshua Aizenman and Jacob Frenkel for their comments on this paper.

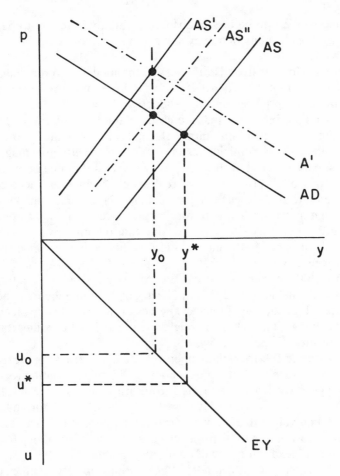

Fig. C3.1 Indexation and aggregate supply: The view from the goods market.

The slope of the curve is likely to be less than one, since $(1/\sigma\beta)$ is equal to $(1 - \beta - \lambda)/\beta$ and β, the share of labor, is well above one-half. The condition that $(1 - \beta - \lambda)/\beta$ is less than unity plays a role in ranking the different indexation formulas.

In this model $\sigma\beta$ is the elasticity of the supply of real output with respect to the real wage. The relevant concept here is the short-run supply elasticity, based entirely on the production function, since in the short run (the contract period) the firm is assumed to be able to employ as much labor as it demands.

The aggregate demand curve (AD) is equation (37'), which can be derived from A & F's (37), such that:

(37') $$p = (1 + \alpha)^{-1}[m - \xi y - \alpha(\rho + \chi)].$$

Its slope is likely to be less in absolute value than one, both because ξ, the income elasticity of money demand, is not above one and because α is positive.

There are four or five disturbances in the model: two real and three nominal. The real disturbances are to the price of energy, an input in the production process, and to productivity. The difference between these two disturbances is that increases in the price of energy lead to offsetting reductions (with unitary elasticity) in the quantity of energy demanded. This economizing response reduces the effective magnitude of the supply shock, but there is otherwise no difference between the implications of the two types of real shocks, which are accordingly combined into the aggregate supply shock. The nominal shocks are to the foreign interest rate and to foreign prices (equivalently to the Purchasing Power Parity (PPP) relationship that determines the exchange rate); a disturbance in the money-supply function makes an occasional appearance as well.

Although the nominal disturbances are described as foreign, they are not distinguishable in their impact from domestic money-demand disturbances. Indeed, one of the weaknesses of the model is that its structure ends up giving very little weight to international considerations. I will return to this point below.

The disturbances are serially uncorrelated. An increase in the foreign price level in turn leads to an expectation of foreign deflation (because the foreign price level is expected to return to its average level) and thus, through an analysis developed in equations (32) through (37), becomes equivalent to a shock to the foreign interest rate. The absence of a serial correlation of disturbances has serious implications for both policy and indexation that will be discussed below.

The third element of the model is the relationship between the supply shock and the appropriate level of output, shown in the lower half of figure C3.1, which is equation (10). Equilibrium output is an increasing function of the real shock (defined as the favorable productivity shock minus the unfavorable energy price shock, adjusted for the response of energy demand to the shock). Given the level of the shock, the appropriate level of output is read from the EY (equilibrium output) locus. Note the key and not surprising result that the appropriate level of output is a function only of the real and not the nominal shock.[2]

When an adverse supply shock strikes, the appropriate level of output falls. All that then has to be done is to realign the AS and AD curves to intersect at the appropriate level of y. For instance, suppose u^* is the expected level of the supply disturbance[3] and that the nominal wage is set to clear the market at y^*, the corresponding level of output. Then let the realized value of u be u_0, with the appropriate level of output y_0.

The economy can attain y_0 through shifts in either the AS or the AD curves. There is an automatic upward shift of the aggregate supply curve in response to an adverse supply shock, but the shift appears a priori unlikely to take the intersection precisely to the correct level of output without either indexation or a change in the money stock.

One of the contributions of A & F's analysis is to clarify the conditions under which the automatic shift of the AS curve, with nominal wage fixity and without an accommodating monetary policy, leads to the optimal level of output. In their model that happens only if the coefficient of the supply shock in (39) is zero, that is, if:

$$\xi(1 + \epsilon) = 1 + \alpha.$$

ξ is the income elasticity of money demand; ϵ, the labor-supply elasticity; and α, the interest elasticity of money demand. With $\xi = 1$, $\epsilon = 0$, and $\alpha = 0$, the condition is satisfied.[4] But it is, of course, a singular event for the condition to be satisfied, and it is unlikely that it would ever be met exactly in practice.

It has frequently been argued on a priori grounds by equilibrium business cycle theorists that the elasticity of labor supply in response to transitory real wage increases is large. If it were, so that $\xi(1 + \epsilon) > 1 + \alpha$, an adverse supply shock would be followed by overemployment unless the money stock were reduced. With ϵ large, the EY locus would be relatively flat, implying that the intersection of the new AS schedule following a supply shock and AD would be to the right of y_0. Since the problem of supply shocks seems instead to be one of unemployment, we assume that the full employment level of output falls by less than the reduction implied by the intersection of AD and the new AS curve and that the maintenance of full employment requires an expansion and not a contraction of aggregate demand. The demand curve should therefore shift to AD'.

Of course, shifting the curves to ensure that a supply shock creates a recession does not explain why in fact adverse supply shocks are associated with high unemployment. More careful modeling of the employment decision, of the links between output and employment, and of the reallocation of labor would be needed to go more deeply into this issue.

Optimal monetary policy when wages are fixed in nominal terms is described by equation (39). The money stock should respond not only to the real shock, but also to nominal shocks. Nominal shocks should be just offset so that the aggregate demand curve remains unaffected.

The maintenance of full employment can also be achieved by wage flexibility, which shifts the AS curve appropriately. The ideal indexing formula is given by (16), which shows there should be full indexing to the price level provided there is also indexing to the real shock. The nominal wage rises automatically with the price level and falls with the supply shock. In the face of a supply shock, the ideally indexed wage would shift AS to AS''. Indexing and monetary policy are equally efficient, and either can maintain equilibrium employment. An obvious implication, shown in equation (39'), is that the appropriate monetary policy is not independent of the existence of indexation.

Highlights

One of the highlights of A & F's paper has already been reviewed: the analysis of optimal monetary policy (optimal in the sense of maintaining equilibrium employment) in the face of supply shocks. Another comes in the analysis of suboptimal indexation rules. The result obtained here is that indexation to the price level should be lower, the fewer the contingencies other than nominal shocks taken into account in the indexation formula.

This result can be understood in terms of the general principle that price indexation is optimal for nominal shocks and not for real shocks. In this model indexation to one component of the real shock means, in an expected value sense, partial indexing to the entire shock. Accordingly, the greater the degree of indexing to the real shock, the more indexing can be permitted to the nominal shock (provided, of course, that there is not overindexing to the real shock—and that is ensured by A & F's studying optimal-suboptimal indexation rules).

The results for indexation to the value-added price deflator and to the nominal GNP also deserve attention. The key equation here is:

$$(17') \qquad w = p + \frac{y}{1 + \epsilon},$$

which shows optimal indexation to the price level and real output separately. If there is no elasticity of labor supply, indexation to the nominal GNP is optimal. In general, there is no reason to index to anything beyond the price level and the real GNP. If a choice has to be made between indexation to the nominal GNP and to the domestic value-added deflator, indexation to the latter is optimal only in the unlikely circumstance the elasticity of labor supply is extremely high. I will discuss below the sensitivity of this result to the structure of the model.

Other special indices have also been proposed. One suggestion is to index to the nominal money stock. This is appropriate only if all shocks are money supply shocks. If indexation had been invested by the private sector as a defense against an errant monetary authority, this formula might have something to recommend it.

General Comments and Suggestions

The open economy aspects of the A & F model are not well developed. Indeed, aside from the description of the energy price shock as imported, their analysis of indexation is no different from an analysis of a closed economy. There is no interaction at all between the energy price shock and the balance of payments or the real exchange rate, except to the extent that the price increase affects the price of domestic output. The terms of trade do not enter into the A & F's model.

The basic difficulty here is that neither the current account nor the capital account are analyzed explicitly. The country has free access to foreign capital at the world interest rate. There is no balance-of-payments problem for this country following an oil price shock because it can borrow as much as it wants. But in practice many of the problems facing developing countries in the wake of the oil shock related to the balance of payments, and it is hard indeed to believe that the optimal indexing formula can be independent of that aspect of the problem.

Taking account of the balance of payments would likely increase the attractiveness of indexation to a domestic value-added index rather than to the nominal GNP. This argument is strengthened by the fact that the short-run elasticity of substitution between energy and other inputs is small. Adjustment in the short run to an oil price increase while maintaining full employment would then require a large reduction in the real wage if external balance (defined relative to optimal borrowing in the face of the supply shock) were to be maintained. The absence of a complete model of the balance of payments may thus seriously bias the conclusions of the paper.

The absence of dynamics from the paper certainly also affects the conclusions. Much of the dimness of the view of indexation taken by its critics arises from the possibility that it prolongs rather than speeds up the response of the economy to shocks. Wage indexation works with a lag, and it is therefore in practice always adjusting to yesterday's (or last year's) shocks. In the A & F paper, any lag in the implementation of indexation would make nonindexation the optimal response. That is because all disturbances are serially uncorrelated. A disturbance today says nothing about tomorrow's disturbances, and indexation to yesterday's shocks would merely increase variance in the model.

The serial correlation of disturbances is as crucial a determinant of the optimal indexing formula as the relative variances of shocks. The general rule in the presence of indexing lags would be to index to adjust for effectively long-lived disturbances but not for the short-lived ones. It is not necessarily the disturbances themselves that have to be long-lived, just their effects. For instance, overlapping long-term labor contracts could transform transitory disturbances into longer-lived effects on prices, which would perhaps be adjusted for in the indexing formulas.

The discussion of dynamics raises the question of the accuracy of the conventional view that differences in indexing arrangements are responsible for the differential responses of economies to supply shocks. Labor contracts do not last forever, and a new base wage can be negotiated in new contracts. I am therefore skeptical of the standard view. This skepticism is reinforced by the absence of a strong correlation between the presence of indexation and measures of the rigidity of real wages across countries.[5] For example, Great Britain has rigid real wages but has had only sporadic indexing.

A & F clearly have in mind that inflation, or at least price variability, is undesirable, for they generally present an expression for the variance of the price level. But their theoretical consciences, which have already been violated—for the social good—by predetermining wages and allowing firms to choose the level of output, prevent their writing down a loss function that includes price-level variability. Although their model does not explain why price variability matters, we can assume that it does, and then discuss the choice between indexing and active monetary policy in the light of a criterion that weighs price-level stability against full employment.

Price-level stability requires that monetary policy stabilize against nominal shocks. We saw in figure C3.1 that leaving it to monetary policy to handle real shocks results in greater price-level variability than occurs when indexation undertakes that task. Accordingly, an allocation of tasks in which monetary policy deals with nominal shocks and the labor market deals with real shocks is better than the converse. But when indexation deals with real shocks, there is still some variability in the aggregate price level. The extent to which it is desirable to reduce that variability, by reducing the money stock and causing unemployment in the face of a supply shock that has already resulted in a reduction in the nominal wage, cannot be analyzed without a more detailed model.

By that stage, however, we are in a context in which more difficult questions about monetary policy and inflation arise. For instance, if labor contracts are written in the knowledge that the money stock will be reduced when there is a real shock, and if that monetary policy is followed, perfect price-level stabilization with full employment can be attained. This points to the need for a more complete analysis of the interactions between indexation and monetary policy—which might reveal that when the monetary authority and the private sector have different objective functions, indexation is a defense against, and not a harmonious partner of, monetary policy. That kind of analysis would have to be carried out with an explicitly game-theoretic model. But that would be the topic of another paper.

Notes

1. In A & F's paper, as in several other papers studying indexing, all disturbances can be identified from the level of observables, so that there is no difficulty in moving from formulas that index to disturbances to formulas that index to observables. But it is entirely possible that the disturbances to which there should be indexation are not identifiable: for instance, if there are lags in the implementation of indexing, only the serially correlated part of disturbances should be reflected in the indexing formula. But if disturbances are a mixture of permanent and transitory components, the permanent component cannot be identified and it is necessary to calculate the optimal formula that indexes to observables.

2. Figure C3.1 is not quite in accord with the A & F text in that the analysis in the text sets the expected levels of p, y, $(w - p)$, and u all equal to zero, since these are deviations from means. It is graphically more convenient to show p, y and u all as positive, as in figure C3.1. This causes no errors.

3. See note 2.

4. Precisely these assumptions were made in Fischer (1985).

5. See Branson and Rotemberg (1980), Bruno and Sachs (1985), and Grubb, Jackman, and Layard (1983). In Fischer (1983) I found no correlation between the extent of the inflationary shock suffered by economies after the first oil shock and the presence of wage indexation.

References

Branson, William H., and Rotemberg, J. J. 1980. International adjustment with wage rigidity. *European Economic Review* 13, no. 3: 309–32.

Bruno, Michael, and Sachs, Jeffrey. 1985. *Economics of worldwide stagflation.* Cambridge: Harvard University Press.

Fischer, Stanley. 1983. Indexing and inflation. *Journal of Monetary Economics* 12, (no. 4): 519–42.

———. 1985. Supply shocks, wage stickiness, and accommodation. *Journal of Money, Credit and Banking* 1 (February): 1–15.

Grubb, Dennis; Jackman, Richard; Layard, Richard. 1983. Wage rigidity and unemployment in OECD countries. *European Economic Review* 21, no. 1–2: 11–40.

Comment   Constantino Lluch

This is a very long paper, full of algebra. Practical people must ask themselves where does the algebra lead. What are the results, and how useful are they? I want to answer these questions by summarizing how the results are obtained and by placing them in the context of the real world.

The authors obtain their results by using the following strategy. First, determine the optimal money supply and the rules for the optimal

Constantino Lluch is chief of the Labor Economics Division of the Development Research Department of the World Bank.

indexing of nominal wages in an economy in which nominal wages are sticky; there is some degree of exchange rate flexibility; there are four possible stochastic shocks; and there is equilibrium in three markets: output, money, and labor. Optimality is defined by the adjustment to nominal wages for the quantity of money that would yield the equilibrium real wage in the "shocked" economy.

Second, suppose that indexing is constrained in the sense that the indexation formula does not include real shocks to the economy (either a shock to productivity or a pseudo shock brought about by a change in the relative price of raw materials[1]); or that the degree of flexibility of the exchange rate is not chosen optimally; or that the pseudo shock appears in the adjustment formula but the productivity shock does not. What then are the constrained adjustment coefficients and the associated welfare loss?

Third, examine what all this implies for indexation proposals advanced in practice, such as indexing to nominal incomes or to the value-added price index. Also examine whether there is a link between these proposals and indexing designed to achieve stable employment versus stable real wages.

This strategy produces many results. They can be grouped into two categories: one comprising the results concerning the optimal indexing coefficients; and the other, those concerning the optimal indexing proposals. The first result in the first category says that with a "sophisticated" indexing formula for nominal wages, there is a 100 percent adjustment to a change in prices; either more or less than a 100 percent adjustment to a productivity shock; and less than a hundred percent adjustment to the pseudo shock caused by a change in the relative price of raw materials. The coefficient of the adjustment to the productivity shock is a ratio whose numerator is unity and whose denominator is $\epsilon/\sigma + (1 - \lambda)$, where ϵ is the elasticity of labor supply, σ is the share of capital, and λ is the share of raw materials. If the supply of labor is completely inelastic ($\epsilon = 0$), a productivity shock therefore leads to a more than proportional adjustment in nominal wages of the same sign as that of the shock. The coefficient of adjustment to the pseudo shock (the change in the relative price of raw materials) is always negative and proportional to the productivity-shock coefficient. The factor of proportionality is the share of raw materials.

The equilibrium real wage in the "shocked" economy can be reached through an entirely different device if nominal wages are, and remain, fixed. Obviously enough, there is a new price level that would produce such an equilibrium real wage. The money supply that achieves that new price level is called "optimal."

Two remarks can be made in passing here. First, how nice algebra is! One can determine the desired real wage one way or another, or by any linear combination. Second, only one shock, the productivity shock, is included in the "sophisticated" wage-indexing formula. Two others, though, are recognized as relevant in setting the optimal money supply. Can it be shown that, were those other two shocks included in the wage-indexing formula, their corresponding adjustment coefficient would be zero? The answer is no, because the wage-indexing formula is quite arbitrary, whereas the loss function is not. When prices are fully flexible, this is not a very interesting observation, however. One would substitute out the price change in the wage-indexing formula, using instead the equilibrium condition in the market for money. Adjustment to the price change would still be 100 percent, and this price change would be broken down into changes in the money supply and in all shocks.

I am not advocating to complicate the wage-indexing formula in this fashion. The formulas used in practice do not contain the productivity shock, or any other, because practical people are unable to recognize shocks, alone or in combination, when they see them. It is therefore more relevant to ask what the coefficient of the adjustment to prices is, in the wage-indexing formula, when shocks are not present. This question leads to all the other results in the first category. Of particular interest are those relating to the adjustment in wages and the adjustment in the exchange rate.

I say this advisedly, because the relationship between both adjustments is quite peculiar. The optimal degree of flexibility of the exchange rate is independent of everything else. It is simply equal to the absolute value of the (semi)elasticity of the demand for money with respect to the rate of interest. Substituting this number into the relevant expressions for the loss function yields the basic results about the relative size of the coefficients of the adjustment of wages to prices: they are smaller in magnitude, the more restrictive the indexing formula is.

The fact that there is very little relationship between the optimal exchange rate and the optimal wage is one aspect of how little this economy is actually open—a point made by Fischer in the preceding comment. In general, the ratio of the two variables is an approximation to the real exchange rate; and problems of adjustment to shocks are usually problems of how to shift from excess demand to excess supply of tradables by increasing the real exchange rate, in other words, problems of how elastic the supply of tradable goods is. Wage indexation does affect such elasticity, and of course, it also affects the increase in the real exchange rate. What is the loss function associated with this way of looking at indexation issues?

The results in the second category are very neat and very easily summarized. The elasticity of demand for labor is around 3, considerably higher than the available estimates of the elasticity of labor supply. It then follows that indexation to nominal income is preferable to indexation to the price index of domestic value added, which in turn is equivalent to a preference for indexation rules that stabilize employment rather than the real wage.

So what does all this mean to the practical person who hopes to understand the "real world"? This question may be unfair or ill put. Nevertheless, some attempt to come to grips with it is important, I think, to determine both what research to pursue next and how much enthusiasm one should have for policy proposals that might flow from the paper (such as "adjust wages less than 100 percent" or "index to nominal incomes").

A different way to put this general question is to consider some of the historical experiences with indexation, say in Brazil or Israel, and ask: What does one learn from this paper about mistakes made in those cases? I think the most telling criticism on this point is that made above by Fischer. Indexation has never been instantaneous, but the model employed by Aizenman and Frenkel is instantaneous. How many of their results would apply if there were lags in indexation? My own sense is that none would, because a shock would then be an event that takes place after inflation has already eroded the real wage. By how much depends on the inflation rate and the period of adjustment. The loss function would be quite different in that case.

In any event, practical observers can always make these points. The paper is nonetheless still quite interesting.

Note

1. I call this a pseudo shock because there is no stochastic element to it.

4 Multiple Exchange Rates for Commercial Transactions

Rudiger Dornbusch

4.1 Introduction

This paper reviews exchange rate arrangements that deviate from unrestricted convertibility at uniform fixed or flexible exchange rates. Broadly, these alternatives are called "multiple exchange rate practices," which are formally defined by International Monetary Fund (1981, 23) guidelines as actions that lead to exchange rate spreads in excess of 2 percent between buying and selling rates. They range from multiple rates for commercial transactions and auction markets for designated items to dual rates for capital movements, black markets, and some forms of exchange rate guarantees. The prize no doubt must go to Chile for introducing a "free" market for foreign exchange among nonhabitual, consenting adults. Although these various forms of exchange rate policy defy a simply classification, they do arise out of a common concern, namely, to strike a balance between the allocative efficiency that almost always comes from uniform rates and the macroeconomic advantages that might be gained from a differentiated exchange rate structure.

In the aftermath of the international debt crisis Latin America exhibits once again on a massive scale this diversity of exchange rate arrangements. But Latin America is not alone in instituting multiple

Rudiger Dornbusch is the Ford International Professor of Economics at the Massachusetts Institute of Technology and a research associate of the National Bureau of Economic Research.

This paper is part of a study on exotic exchange rate arrangements prepared for the Trade and Adjustment Policy Division of the World Bank. Companion papers deal with dual rates for capital-account transactions and with collapsing exchange rate regimes. I am indebted to members of the division and my conference discussants for helpful comments and suggestions.

rates. In the early 1980s more than 40 IMF members had at least one multiple currency practice, and in its 1984 review the IMF (p. 37) noted:

> During 1983, as in 1980–82, about one-third of the Fund's members engaged in multiple currency practices, although on a trade-weighted basis the proportion of developing-country members with these practices has risen considerably since 1980 and the importance of the practices in the individual economies has grown. Nevertheless, the recent trend toward increased incidence of multiple currency practices among Fund members levelled off somewhat in 1983.

Multiple exchange rate practices have a long history. In the 1930s, if not earlier, multiple rates and restricted convertibility appeared on a broad front throughout the world economy. In Europe exchange control was widely practiced, and Raúl Prebisch introduced multiple rates in Argentina. Throughout the 1950s and early 1960s exotic arrangements existed in virtually all countries. They were not only common but even in some measure respectable, though never uncontroversial. Triffin (1947, 80) put the case as follows:

> Whenever balance of payment difficulties are due, not to international price disparities but to accidental factors or to cyclical fluctuations in foreign income and demand, compensatory policies should be followed to the fullest possible extent. This requires a high level of reserves. . . . When reserves are unsufficient, foreign or international assistance—such as contemplated under the International Monetary Fund—will be necessary. Failing this, exchange control should be used as a third line of defense, in order to continue compensatory policies and avoid the greater evils inseparable from deflation or devaluation. The disadvantage of the latter policies, as compared to exchange control, is that their corrective effect on the balance of payments is likely to depend on a contraction of income several times as severe as the international deficit to be plugged.

The important research question is whether multiple exchange rates are a perfectly sensible quest for extra policy instruments, both micro and macro, or ill-considered distortions with little payoff in terms of effectiveness but major allocational costs. The answer is interesting from the perspective of the users of the rates, but it is quite separately an issue for international supervisory agencies, specifically the IMF and the World Bank, which are charged with monitoring and inhibiting multiple rate practices. The welfare economics of exotic exchange rate arrangements are complicated not only by the fact of variety that makes this very much a study of special cases. The topic is also complicated because it bridges the uncompromising rigor of microeconomics, issues of income distribution via the price system, and the third-best features of macroeconomics according to which effectiveness comes first and resource allocation questions are asked much later.

4.2 An Overview

This section provides a discussion of exchange rate practices that result in a differentiated exchange rate structure for different commercial transactions. Table 4.1 serves as an introduction to the topic and illustrates a concrete example of a multiple rate structure, the case of Argentina in 1949. The table shows a proliferation of rates at which the authorities buy and sell foreign exchange. The buying rates represent the prices at which exporters are required to surrender foreign exchange, whereas the selling rates are the prices at which the central bank sells foreign exchange for import transactions. In each case the exchange rate (pesos/dollars) is expressed as a percentage of the "basic" export rate. Most of those rates are fixed, but there is also a potentially flexible rate applied in the auction market.

Consider now the details of the multiple rate structure. It is readily apparent that agricultural exports receive the least favorable rate: the index is 100 for these traditional exports. This is a common feature of countries in which the economic structure introduces strong sectoral distinctions between traditional commodity exports and nontraditional manufacturing interests. Argentina is a good case in point. Here the traditional export sector is based on agriculture—wheat, meat, hides and processed agricultural goods. But there is also a manufacturing

Table 4.1   **Categories and Values of Exchange Rates in Argentina, 1949 (Index of the basic buying rate = 100)**

Category	Buying Rate	Selling Rate
Preferential A	144	110
Preferential B	169	158
Special	212	—
Basic	100	179
Auction	—	fluctuating
Free	265	269

Source: Adapted from Schlesinger (1952).

Buying rates:

1. Preferential A: wool, hides, vegetable oil, oilcakes, tallow, meat extract, some prepared meats, poultry, live animals, and minerals (except tungsten).
2. Preferential B: combed wool, cheese, butter, casein, powdered milk, ques-bracho extract, pork, eggs, pulses, shark-liver oil, and glycerine.
3. Special: leather goods, footwear, selected textiles, salted meats, ground bones, fresh fruits, tripe, gelatin, stearin, tung oil, tungsten, and mica.
4. Basic: beef, mutton, wheat, corn, barley, rye, and oilseeds.
5. Free: receipts from all nonmerchandise transactions.

Selling rates:

6. Preferential A: coal, coke, and petroleum and petroleum by-products.
7. Preferential B: raw materials and articles of popular consumption.
8. Basic: articles the import of which is considered less essential than others.
9. Auction: imports of permissible luxury goods.
10. Free: remittances for all nonmerchandise transactions.

sector that competes with imports and appears likewise on the export side.

It is also apparent from table 4.1 that a multiple rate system requires an exchange control mechanism to administer and enforce the differential rates. On the export side, where relatively unfavorable rates apply, the surrender of foreign exchange must be enforced. That is the case even if exporters may sell part of their earnings at a flexible rate. On the import side, where preferential rates apply, the rights to import must be licensed. Where foreign exchange for imports is auctioned, the control authorities must determine the amounts to be allocated. The need for and modalities of the exchange control system are evident in table 4.2, which shows the broad possibilities for multiple rate systems. The two main distinctions are whether for a particular transaction the exchange rate is fixed or market determined and whether foreign exchange supplies are rationed or market determined.

System I in the table would possibly apply to the case in which for each transaction a specified amount of foreign exchange is allocated at a given rate. The distribution among competing users would be based on historical precedent or the discretion of the authority, thus posing the maximum potential for abuse and inefficiency. System II applies similarly to the case in which a given amount of foreign exchange would be auctioned among competing users. This system is frequently used for inessential or luxury imports. System III applies to both imports and exports. The government fixes the rate for different transactions, and importers or exporters choose the amount they wish to buy of foreign exchange or the level of exports, and hence the level of export earnings. A special case of this system is, of course, a uniform rate. Finally, system IV applies when the government allows exporters to sell part of their export earnings from particular categories to importers of some specified classes of goods. A special case is that of unrestricted, flexible rates at which exporters can sell all their earnings to any importer. The splitting of markets and the matching and monitoring of quantities are what require exchange control authorities and give multiple rates a bad name.

But multiple rates are also expected to serve a policy purpose. Multiple exchange rates for commercial transactions are typically introduced for one of four reasons: as a means of raising fiscal revenue; as

Table 4.2   **Possible Multiple Exchange Rate Regimes**

Type of Foreign Exchange Supply	Type of Exchange Rate	
	Fixed	Flexible
Rationed	I	II
Market Determined	III	IV

a form of taxation to affect resource allocation and income distribution; as a macroeconomic shock absorber; and as an instrument of trade-balance adjustment. The remainder of this paper examines each of these uses of multiple exchange rates.

4.3   Fiscal Aspects of Multiple Rates

This section examines two ways in which multiple rates have fiscal aspects. First, to the extent that average buying and selling rates differ from each other, they are a source of aggregate revenue or transfers. Second, differential buying and selling rates across sectors engender an implicit system of protection.

4.3.1   The Implicit Tax-Subsidy Structure

Consider a simple model of the world economy in which our model country, Argentina, is a price taker for all commodities, exportables, and importables alike. Suppose further that all world prices are given and equal to one dollar. In the absence of any taxes, transport costs, or other impediments to exchange, and with a uniform exchange rate, the domestic price of all tradable goods would be equal to the common exchange rate. But, in fact, exchange rates differ among transactions, as will, accordingly, the domestic prices of goods. Foreign exchange for the purchase of some favored import goods can be bought at a favorable rate, and the export proceeds of some categories of goods can be sold at high rates. Other import transactions might be implicitly taxed by a high price of foreign exchange, and likewise some export categories might be taxed by particularly unfavorable rates at which foreign exchange resulting from these transactions must be surrendered. A multiple rate structure thus embeds an implicit tax-subsidy structure.

The implicit tax-subsidy structure can be analyzed by focusing on two of its features. One is the difference between the average selling and buying prices, the difference representing net fiscal revenue to the government from the multiple rate system. The other is the dispersion of rates across transactions and the implicit tax-subsidy allocation across commodities. Let e_i be the exchange rate (pesos/U.S. dollars) applied to the ith import transaction, and let e_j be the exchange rate on the export side. The average import and export exchange rates can be defined simply by taking the weighted average of rates across import and export categories. Let $a_i = M_i/M$ and $b_j = X_j/X$ be the shares of the ith import or jth export transaction, respectively, in the total dollar value of imports (M) or exports (X). The average import and export exchange rates are then defined as:

$$(1) \qquad e_m = \sum_i a_i e_i, \; e_x = \sum_j b_j e_j.$$

Fiscal revenue, in pesos, from the multiple exchange rate structure is equal to the excess of proceeds from foreign exchange sales over the revenue from purchases, such that:

(2) $$R = e_m M - e_x X.$$

If trade is balanced in dollars so that $X = M$, this formula reduces to:[1]

(2') $$R = (e_m - e_x)M$$

The right-hand side of (2') shows that the government derives a net revenue from a multiple rate structure, provided the average selling or import rate exceeds the average buying or export rate. Even though these average rates are not available, a look at table 4.1 immediately indicates that this was obviously not the case in Argentina. For example, the preferential import rates are below the preferential export rates, implying revenue losses unless, as is possibly the case, the large share of "basic" exports that command a very low rate rescues the fiscal balance. More on this point below.

4.3.2 Effective Protection

The multiple rate structure has fiscal aspects not only in the global revenue sense, but also in the allocation of incentives or taxes across activities. Let $e \equiv (e_m + e_x)/2$ be the average exchange rate. Then, the protection or taxation involved for any particular activity is indicated by the relative exchange rate, e_i/e. Activities with a high relative exchange rate on the export side are implicitly subsidized, and activities with a high relative import rate are relatively sheltered from the world markets.

In judging the tax-subsidy features of a multiple rate system, we must, of course, pay attention to the fact that intermediate goods enter into consideration. It is therefore important to define the effective rates of protection implied by the multiple rate structure. The effective rate of protection is defined as the percentage excess of domestic over world value added in a particular activity. Suppose technology is linear with a given input requirement v per unit of output. All goods are internationally traded at the given world prices, and domestic prices are determined by the exchange rate structure. The effective rate of protection for commodity i is then given by:[2]

(3) $k_i = (T_i - \alpha T_j)/(1 - \alpha)$, $\alpha = p_j^* v/p_i^*$, $T_i = (e_i/e - 1)$,

where α denotes the share of the intermediate factor in income; p_i^* and p_j^* are the world prices in dollars of final and intermediate goods, respectively; and T_i and T_j denote the percentage deviation of a particular exchange rate from the economywide average. Equation (3) thus reduces the multiple rate structure to the conventional representation of the effective protection implicit in a tariff structure.

Equation (3) shows that the effective protection rate of an activity depends on the differential rates applied to final goods and inputs and on the differential between final goods and the economywide average. Table 4.1, as an example, indicates a preferential export rate (144) for prepared meats (sausages) and a lower rates (100) for the intermediate good, which in this case is meat. Suppose the income share of meat in the sausage industry is 40 percent and that the economywide exchange rate is 130. Then, the effective protection formula indicates that the sausage industry enjoys a 33.3 percent effective rate of protection. Even though the exchange rate for the final good exceeds the economywide average by only slightly more than 10 percent, there is significant subsidization by the fact that the intermediate good receives an exchange rate that is 23 percent below the average. Of the combined total of 33.3 percent, only about 18 percentage points are the result of the favorable export rate on the final good. The remainder is accounted for by the implicit subsidy stemming from the fact that the intermediate good receives an exchange rate below the economywide average. The Argentine exchange rate structure thus implies an implicit effective protection to processing activities on the export side. Similarly, the low rate for inputs (preferential rates for coal, coke, materials) on the import side compared to that for final goods implies effective protection of domestic manufacturing.

The Argentine example of an effective protection structure makes clear the most basic point about multiple rates for commercial transactions: they are no different from a set of tariffs or taxes. Thus, anything that could be achieved by these multiple rates could, administrative issues aside, be accomplished in precisely the same way by taxes or subsidies, or both.

But what precisely is the equivalence between trade taxes and multiple exchange rates? Suppose we take the basic buying rate as the basis. It does not matter what the basis is, since, as we know from trade theory and Lerner's symmetry theorem in particular, only relative prices and relative rates of taxation matter.

We have seen that the multiple rate structure can be expressed in terms of an equivalent system of effective protection rates. Next, we remember that an import tariff is both a production subsidy and a consumption tax. Similarly, an export subsidy is both a production subsidy and a consumption tax as well. In this interpretation commodity groups with a high tariff equivalent on the import side show protection for producers and taxation of consumers. This is the case, for example, with inessential imports. On the export side we have already noticed the protection granted to processing.

To have a complete idea of the protection structure requires adding together (1) any implicit protection given by the exchange rate structure, (2) protection from quotas and outright taxes or subsidies, and (3) taxes or subsidies implicit in advance deposits, taxes on foreign exchange operations on the import side, or credit subsidies on the export side. These three are the main instruments of commercial policy. Figure 4.1 shows the results of calculations for Argentina showing a broad pattern of sectoral protection through all these instruments combined over the last fifteen years.

The figure shows the peso price of a dollar of traditional exports and of nontraditional exports, respectively, compared to the peso price of a dollar of imports. The calculations are necessarily rough, but the evidence is impressive: Commercial policy through the various instruments placed a massive trade tax on traditional or agricultural exports. Nontraditional exports, by contrast, enjoyed a significant subsidy relative to imports in the mid-1970s, but that differential has since almost disappeared.

4.3.3   Multiple Rates and Efficiency

Multiple exchange rates fit into this protection system as a matter of administrative convenience, not because they can achieve a special effect that cannot be replicated by taxes or subsidies. Because they are so clearly equivalent to taxes and subsidies, there appears no reason to prefer tax-subsidy schemes over multiple exchange rates. A tax-subsidy scheme administered through multiple exchange rates is just as efficient or inefficient as the equivalent system of trade taxes or subsidies. Both as a means of raising general revenue and as an instrument for achieving particular objectives of allocation or distribution, trade taxes are almost always second- or third-best instruments. Their use as a *permanent* system would have to be justified by administrative or political feasibility or convenience rather than by any intrinsic optimality they possess.

Although the use of multiple exchange rates is in all likelihood an inefficient way to achieve long-run revenue, distribution, or allocation objectives, the extent of inefficiency might easily be overestimated. It might appear that a proliferation of multiple rates, as in table 4.1, implies a particularly costly structure. In the revenue case that is true by comparison with, say, a uniform rate e_m that exceeds the export rate e_x and thus generates revenue. But it must also be recognized, as Harberger (1959) has pointed out, that not everyone in an economy can be protected. What matters, by Lerner's symmetry theorem, are relative rates of protection, and thus much of the diversity in table 4.1 cancels out.

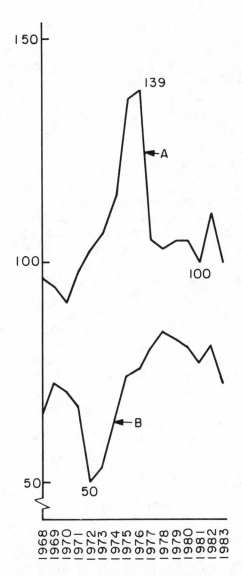

Fig. 4.1　　　　Comparative effective exchange rates in Argentina, 1968–83.
A = Nontraditional exports relative to imports.
B = Traditional exports relative to imports.
Source: El Cronista Comercial, *Carta Económica*, December 1983.

4.4 Macroeconomic Aspects of Multiple Rates

Multiple exchange rates can play a macroeconomic role in two ways. First, they may be an effective instrument of adjustment in cases in which deficit disturbances are transitory and financing is unavailable. Second, they can play the role of a macroeconomic shock absorber, particularly in the case of a transitory improvement in the terms of trade.

4.4.1 Trade-Balance Adjustment

In the absence of reserves or financing, or both, trade deficits require adjustment. Multiple rates *may* be an effective adjustment mechanism in the case of transitory disturbances. I emphasize the case of transitory disturbances because persistent deficits require an adjustment that takes greater account of the inefficiency caused by the lasting trade distortions implicit in multiple rates. In the short run, by contrast, these distortions presumably do not involve significant deadweight losses. If financing, which would be preferable in such a case, is unavailable, multiple rates may be a second-best policy.

There are four possible adjustment policies to correct a deficit: a contraction in aggregate demand, a real depreciation, selective quantitative restrictions, and selective tariffs or equivalent multiple exchange rates. Commercial policy, whichever form it takes, involves a double effect: expenditure *reduction* via the taxation implicit in tariffs, quotas, or multiple rates; and expenditure *switching* as a result of the relative price changes brought about by these policies. To determine which policy intervention is optimal will in general depend on the source of the deficit and the particulars of the short-run macroeconomic flexibility of the economy.

Consider, first, the case in which an increase in aggregate spending causes the deficit. If the economy faces a general increase in spending under conditions of high employment, there will be excess demand for domestic goods and a deficit. A policy combining a reduction in aggregate spending is appropriate, and expenditure-switching policies are not required. But if the disturbances involve a combination of an excess of income over spending and no excess demand for domestic goods, some measure of expenditure switching is also required, since expenditure cutting by itself creates domestic unemployment. The higher domestic unemployment and the more responsive demand and employment, the more appropriate are expenditure-switching policies than expenditure-reducing policies.

The argument against a short-term devaluation as an adjustment policy is well established: In the short run a devaluation may have a net contractionary effect on aggregate demand without at the same time achieving a significant improvement in the external balance. The reason for this is that a real depreciation will cut the purchasing power of wages and hence real aggregate demand for domestic goods. The rise in employment caused by increased competitiveness may be small if demand (foreign and domestic) is not very elastic in the short run and if imported materials account for a significant share of costs and of the consumption basket. Under these plausible conditions a general devaluation is primarily a transfer abroad, not an employment policy or a policy of trade adjustment. Devaluation is precisely the same as a store announcing a sale on *every* item. Such a sale will result in losses if most items have an inelastic demand. The store owner's purposes would be better served by singling out selected items with high elasticities and concentrating on these as the revenue makers, thus avoiding the transfer applying to low-elasticity goods. This consideration is essential because it is implausible to argue that in the time frame appropriate to a short-run trade problem, elasticities of supply and demand are uniformly high. The contrary is well established.

It is easy to imagine a case in which the demand for imports is price inelastic and the domestic production of import substitutes is also unresponsive to price in the short run. A rise in import prices relative to wages would therefore merely cut the purchasing power of labor. But the inelastic import demand implies that a larger fraction of the reduced income will be spent on imports and that demand for domestic goods and hence employment declines. But if foreign demand and the domestic supply of exportables are price responsive, a depreciation on the export side will lead to increased revenues. Why then not simply concentrate the devaluation on the export side via an export subsidy, leaving aside the real wage cut implied by increased import prices?

There is, of course, no reason to expect that the differential elasticities always make particular export goods the target of policy. It is perfectly possible that export goods are in short-run inelastic supply or are particularly sensitive from the point of view of income distribution, whereas imports lend themselves better to adjustment. In any event, the familiar case for selective interventions rather than the exclusive use of expenditure cuts or uniform devaluation has now been restated.

The next question is how to choose between quotas and tariffs or equivalent multiple exchange rates. The use of quotas for short-run balance-of-payments control has been particularly prevalent in Australia, while other countries have favored tariffs or multiple rates. Quotas have the advantage of volume certainty, but there is little else to recommend them. If import demand is inelastic, imposing selling quotas reduces imports but does so primarily as a consequence of the implied budget surplus. The impact on domestic employment would still be adverse just as in the devaluation case. There is once again no substantive difference between selective tariffs or subsidies and equivalent multiple rates, and only administrative expediency comes into consideration.

An auction market for a selected group of imports (inessential or luxury goods), combined with a given uniform exchange rate structure for all other goods, is a particularly effective way of coping with a transitory foreign exchange shortage. The authorities determine at each particular time how much foreign exchange to auction for the particular category of imports, and the exchange rate adjusts to clear the market. The fact that the foreign exchange is auctioned implies that in periods of shortage the equilibrium rate in the auction market will be high relative to other rates, thereby increasing fiscal revenue and exerting a net contractionary fiscal effect. The auction market thus serves as a built-in stabilizer even on a basis of constant foreign exchange sales. If during shortages the amount of foreign exchange (in dollars) available for auction were to be reduced, the fiscal contraction (in pesos) would be reinforced.

The economy reacts to the increased auction price through income and substitution effects. The income effect is the counterpart of increased fiscal revenues and clearly implies a reduction in the demand for all goods, thus helping to contain spending. The substitution effects work to increase the demand for goods not rationed. To some extent this means that spending that is rationed in the market for luxury goods may spill over into other, unrestricted imports or reduce exports. But that spillover may be minimal if most of the substitution is intertemporal. Suppose, specifically, that luxury goods are consumer durables. An increase in the current price relative to other goods and relative to the future price of the same durable (once the transitory foreign exchange shortage has disappeared) leads to intertemporal substitution.

Of course, one might think that a devaluation can achieve exactly the same aggregate effect as an auction price system, and it is therefore natural to ask what is special about multiple exchange rates in this context. The chief difference is that an auction price system combines expenditure-switching and expenditure-reducing features. A look at table 4.1 immediately makes this point. An auction rate applied to luxuries is a very special form of taxation. It applies differentially to high-income groups, and it applies to a commodity group that includes a significant share of consumer durables that are particularly sensitive to intertemporal substitution choices.[3] A devaluation, by contrast, would introduce only expenditure-switching effects and, in the absence of other macroeconomic policies, might not even be made to last in real terms. Once again, of course, an ad hoc tax on luxury imports would achieve exactly the same effect.

4.4.2   Macroeconomic Shock Absorber

A flexible multiple exchange rate system can also play a useful role in coping with external disturbances. The classic example is that of a temporary improvement in the terms of trade. One possible adjustment is to allow a uniform real appreciation as increased real incomes are spent in part on domestic goods. But because the real appreciation is transitory, there might be a preference to avoid that adjustment with its implications for losses of competitiveness in nontraditional export and import industries.

The alternative is to reduce the exchange rate applicable to those exports benefiting from improved terms of trade and thus implicitly tax away part of the windfall profits. Moreover, the increased foreign exchange revenues could be used to achieve transitory liberalization in the auction market, where increased supply would reduce the real exchange rate and promote expenditure switching. An example of such a policy toward transitory terms-of-trade improvements is shown in figure 4.1. In the years 1972–74 the boom in world commodity prices raised export revenues from traditional exports, and the Argentine government responded by taxing away the improvements, thus reducing the relative effective exchange rate to only half of that applicable to imports.

A different possibility arises if there is a transitory terms-of-trade deterioration, say, from an increase in world food prices. To be more concrete, suppose the dollar drastically depreciates in world markets, which in turn leads to an increase in the real prices of commodities, including food. The dollar depreciation is seen as an overshooting that shortly will come to be undone. The question arises whether consumption and production patterns in the economy should be made to adjust to the transitory shock. Specifically, suppose that wages respond to the cost of living. Should a government that has the choice allow the commodity price shock to spread to wages, production costs, and prices throughout the economy and then later face the difficulty that wages might not come down easily? If the import price shock feeds through the economy and wages do rise, some sectors will lose competitiveness and there will be unemployment that may well more than offset the improved resource allocation associated with following world prices. The point here is that any time there is a macroeconomic problem in the form of less than fully flexible wages, adjustment to transitory disturbances is costly. Moreover, it may be more costly than simply running down reserves while a special exchange rate prevents the shock from spilling to the home economy.

The case for multiple rates as stated so far is too favorable. If all it involved were the taxation of rents and the compensation of windfall losses, which otherwise would increase the macroeconomic variance of output, prices, and sectoral allocation, there would be little objection. But the policy may well go beyond that if disturbances in world trade are somewhat persistent. In that case the taxation of transitory terms-of-trade improvements in fact leads to inefficient resource allocation. The failure to pass on the improved terms of trade to producers implies that production will not expand during periods when the real price is high. Production patterns will be frozen regardless of shifting world prices. When that happens the taxation of windfall gains actually becomes a waste of resources. That may still be the preferred policy, but the authority should weigh whatever social benefits accrue from stable or frozen sectoral production patterns or income distribution against the real income gains to be achieved with a resource allocation that leans more in the direction of prices.

4.4.3   Sterilization

We have considered two possibilities in which multiple rates might be used to dampen the impact of disturbances on the economy. First, they function as a fiscal device, producing both expenditure-switching and expenditure-reducing effects. Second, they can be used to limit directly the pass-through to domestic prices and the resource allocation of changes in the world economy. A third possibility presents itself if the multiple rate practice takes the form of the required surrender of foreign exchange earnings from particular transactions in return for a negotiable bond in domestic currency of a specific maturity. This practice represents neither a tax (unless the applicable rate differs from that for other transactions) nor a reallocation of resources. It represents instead a forced loan that helps offset in the short run the monetary effects of export booms.[4]

A policy of postponing the conversion of export earnings into domestic currency by the requirement to surrender earnings in return for an exchange certificate represents a combination of sterilization and taxation. There is implicit taxation because of the delay in payment, the tax being equal to the discount on the exchange certificate. The higher the interest rate and the longer the forced maturity of the exchange certificate, the higher the implicit tax. The delay in payment thus represents a multiple exchange practice with implicit taxation. In addition, of course, there is the possibility of liquidity constraints that make this forced loan have additional adverse effects on absorption.

But the use of exchange certificates also represents an automatic form of sterilization. It is strictly equivalent to the central bank's pegging the rate and expanding the base in the course of a trade surplus and then turning around to offset the expansion by a sale of bonds. In the case of an export boom this forced-loan feature of exchange certificates does not offset the impact of increased real income and real prices on the economy. It merely avoids reinforcing that mechanism by immediate monetary expansion. Since the exchange certificates do come to maturity at some future date, there will ultimately be a monetary expansion or else a need for a sterilization operation whereby the authorities sell securities and use the proceeds to pay off maturing exchange certificates.

On the import side there is a similar practice in the form of advance deposits. Since these deposits do not carry interest, they represent a form of implicit taxation—the more so, the higher the rate of interest or inflation. They also represent a forced loan and an automatic stabilizer in the case of import booms. An import boom leads to an automatic contraction of the money supply ahead of actual import spending and therefore to increased interest rates and hence increased implicit taxation of imports. Both advance import deposits and exchange certificates therefore share the double feature of implicit taxation through forced lending and monetary stabilization.

4.5 Optimal Adjustment

There is no question that the absence of neutral lump-sum taxes and downward rigidity and upward indexation of wages are major shortcomings. They make it impossible to take literally any blow and adjust to it flexibly, without any *excess* burden. If full flexibility did exist, it would be possible at all times to allocate resources optimally and in the background redistribute income to meet social objectives. But once policy makers operate under the constraints that the effects of the price system on income distribution cannot be simply compensated in their income effects and that wages have a life of their own leading often in the wrong direction, there is a need to consider the trade-offs. Now it may be preferable to "misallocate" resources deliberately in order to avoid spillover or distribution effects. That course of action makes sense only when there are no better ways of compensating and only when disturbances are strictly transitory.[5] But when these restrictive conditions are given, multiple exchange rates do make sense. The fact that in practice they are often abused should lead us to identify clearly the limited range of circumstances in which they apply, not to reject them out of hand.

4.5.1 Optimal Intervention

The problem of the optimal intervention can be formulated in the following manner. Assume the authorities minimize a loss function that is linear-quadratic in two arguments: the costs of deviations from an efficient allocation of resources; and the costs of resource reallocation or income redistribution associated with changes in relative prices. The objective function is given in equation (4) below. The terms p_t and p_t^* are the domestic and world real price, respectively, of the commodity on which policy focuses.

$$(4) \qquad V = -\frac{1}{2} E \sum_{i=0}^{\infty} [a(p_{t+i} - p_{t+i}^*)^2 + b(p_{t+i} - p_{t+i-1})^2],$$

where the terms a and b are the weights policy makers attach to the costs of misallocation and reallocation, and E is the expectations operator. The functional form implies an increasing marginal cost to deviations from the world price and to price change. The former reflects the basic results in welfare economics; the latter is a plausible assumption about the costs of price changes. Note also that price changes are assumed to be unambiguously perceived as costs. The opposite, of course, might also be the case, namely, the gainers from a relative price change might carry more weight than the losers and hence policy makers could easily move in the direction of efficient resource allocation. But our concern here is with misallocation, and I shall therefore focus on the case in which a price change is perceived as costly and policy makers thus prefer to "coalesce around the status quo."

The solution to the optimization problem is to find a path of domestic prices, p_{t+i}, for a given expected path p_{t+i}^* that maximizes expected utility. The first-order condition of this problem yields the following difference equation in price:

$$(5) \quad p_t = \gamma p_t^* + \delta p_{t-1} + \delta p_{t+1},$$
$$\gamma = a/(a + 2b), \qquad \delta = b/(a + 2b).$$

Note that the equation admits of a stationary solution, $p = p^*$. That solution prevails, of course, when the costs of price change are zero. Also observe that the current optimal price, p_t, depends both on the international price and on the past and future optimal prices. The appendix outlines the general solution, which involves the entire anticipated path of future prices as well as the initial condition on p_{t-1}. I concentrate here on the special case in which the world price follows a Markov process, such that:

$$(6) \qquad p_t^* = p^* + u_t, \qquad u_t = \rho u_{t-1} + \epsilon_t,$$

where $0 \leq \rho \leq 1$ measures the persistence of disturbances, and u_t is white noise. If ρ is near unity, disturbances are highly persistent and the world price behaves like a random walk. Conversely, with ρ near zero the world price tends to depart only very transitorily from the trend level p^*.

In this special case, and starting from a steady state $p_{t-1}^* = p_{t-1}$, the solution for the optimal price can be written as:

(7) $$p_t = p^* + x\epsilon_t, \qquad x < 1,$$

where x is a fraction that depends both on the persistence of disturbances and on the relative costs of resource misallocation and price changes. This fraction measures the extent to which an innovation in the world price translates into a domestic price adjustment.

Table 4.3 shows the value of the coefficient x for different combinations of the relative cost b/a and the degree of persistence, ρ. The table indicates that with a high persistence of disturbances, adjustment to current prices should be very significant, even if the relative cost of price-change resource allocation is judged to be many times that of efficient resource allocation.

The table brings out that even with a very transitory disturbance and a very high relative cost of reallocating resources, there is some adjustment in the direction of world prices. By contrast, even when disturbances are almost totally persistent and the relative cost of reallocation is virtually negligible, there is still no instantaneous adjustment to world price. That adjustment occurs only over time.

Figure 4.2 shows a simulation for an extreme case in which $\rho = .9$, so that disturbances are highly persistent, and $b/a = 10$, so that there is a large cost assigned to resource reallocation or price changes. Assume a steady-state value of $p^* = 1$, and consider a 50 percent price disturbance. The diagram shows the initial jump in the world price and the gradual tapering off toward the steady-state value. The optimal response is a gradually rising domestic price that meets with the world price after a few years. The initial discrepancy is 25 percent. Note also that the domestic price overshoots and exceeds the world price for some time. The reason for this is that once the domestic price has been pushed up toward the world price, it is costly to take it down again. As the world price falls following the initial jump, the domestic price follows but less rapidly. Even so, the discrepancy is less than 10 percent after only three years and rapidly diminishes to zero.

What does the model imply for multiple rates? If disturbances are relatively short-lived and if policy makers perceive a price change to be costly because of its effects on income distribution, unemployment,

Table 4.3   **The Optimal Degree of Adjustment to Disturbances: x**

	Relative Cost of Resource Reallocation: b/a		
	.2	1	10
$\rho = .1$	.74	.33	.08
$\rho = .5$	.79	.47	.12
$\rho = .98$	.85	.61	.26

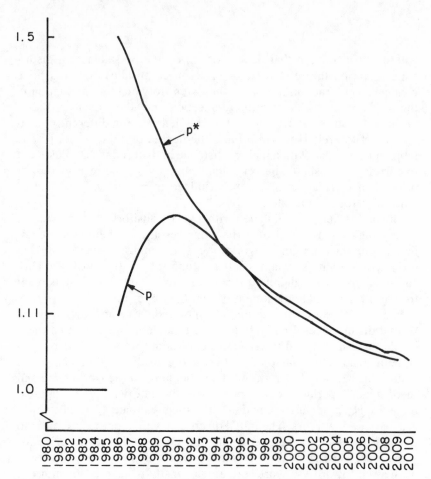

Fig. 4.2   The optimal adjustment to a world price shock.

or inflation indexation, using transitory multiple exchange rate interventions is appropriate. The multiple rate should dampen the impact
of the world price change on the economy, but (almost) never completely offset the price change. It is worth thinking about the optimal
dampening, because doing so reminds us to make a judgment about
the persistence of disturbances and the relative costs of resource
reallocation.

The difficulty with such a formulation is that it assumes from the
outset that inefficient resource allocation is the only way to avoid or
contain the costs of resource reallocation. But clearly it is also conceivable to use fiscal redistribution combined with efficient resource
allocation. If disturbances are highly persistent, it is more efficient to

use fiscal redistribution than trade taxes: the incomes of the gaining producers would be taxed and the proceeds distributed to losers.

4.6 Summary

The use of multiple exchange rates represents a combination of expenditure reducing or fiscal policy and expenditure switching. Multiple rates act in the manner of a differentiated tariff and, except for administrative considerations, amount to exactly the same thing. There are good reasons to use these measures as a policy to cope with transitory disturbances. In the case of trade deficits, and in the absence of financing, it may be efficient to concentrate adjustment on a few sectors. Across sectors there are differential speeds of adjustment, and a policy that focuses exclusively on sectors with high responsiveness may be effective. But there are also costs associated with adjusting the economy to transitory disturbances, and therefore multiple rates can be employed to concentrate adjustment on sectors or activities with relatively low costs.

In the case of transitory surpluses induced by terms-of-trade improvements, multiple rates are particularly effective. They serve a direct fiscal role as a built-in stabilizer, thereby reducing the multiplier impact of a disturbance on the economy. But furthermore, they dampen the effect by reducing the resource reallocation brought about by transitory shocks. The extent to which policy makers should dampen the impact of world prices on the nation's economy depends on the persistence of disturbances and on the political costs of adjustment. The lower these adjustment costs and the more persistent the disturbance, the more complete the optimal adjustment to world prices.

Having made the case for the limited use of multiple exchange rates, I conclude with two warnings. First, it is important to bear in mind that any policy rule that always dampens the domestic repercussions of price increases but does not in a symmetric way offset declining world prices in fact systematically reduces the profitability of the sector that is affected. Argentine traditional exports are a good case in point of a policy that has been overused. Second, multiple rates can easily be abused because they do not represent as overt a tax-subsidy scheme as direct taxes and subsidies. Argentina serves once again as the example (*Carta Económica* 1983, 46):

> One of the clearest examples of the costs in terms of distortions of excessive multiple rates occurred in 1973. In that year the international price of wheat stood at a record level and so did the domestic price: the world price stood at an all time high and the domestic

price at an all time low. At the same time, with the help of a whole battery of measures, exports of automobiles to Cuba were subsidized and were paid for by Cuba with promissory notes that exporters discounted with the central bank. The result is the expected: guided by the low domestic prices farmers did not produce much wheat and thus Argentina missed the opportunity to export a competitive commodity at good prices; instead we exported automobiles in exchange for which we received notes that for many years (perhaps even now?) are part of the international reserves of our central bank. (Translation mine)

Appendix: Optimal Adjustment to World Prices

Policy makers maximize an intertemporal loss function:

$$(A1) \qquad V = \frac{1}{2} E \sum_{i=0}^{\infty} [a(p_{t+i} - p_{t+i}^*)^2 + b(p_{t+i} - p_{t+i-1})^2].$$

The first-order condition, or Euler equation, is:

$$(A2) \quad p_t = \gamma p_t^* + \delta p_{t-1} + \delta p_{t+1},$$

$$\gamma \equiv a/(a + 2b), \qquad \delta \equiv b/(a + 2b).$$

It is immediately apparent from (A2) that with $b = 0$ there is always full and instantaneous adjustment to world prices.

Equation (A2) is a difference equation that can be solved forward.[6] Using the lag operator $Lx_t = x_{t-1}$, we can obtain from (A2):

$$(A2') \qquad\qquad (L^2 - L/p + 1)p_{t+1} = -(\gamma/\delta)p_t^*,$$

which has one stable root. Let λ_1, λ_2 be the roots, of which λ_1 is less than unity in absolute value. Then, rewriting (A2') yields:

$$(A2'') \qquad\qquad p_{t+1}(1 - \lambda_1 L) = -(\gamma/\delta) \frac{p_t^*}{1 - \lambda_2 L}$$

and hence:

$$(A3) \qquad\qquad p_t = \lambda_1 p_{t-1} + (\gamma/\delta)\sum_{i=1}^{\infty} \lambda_1^i p_{t+i}^*,$$

where it is assumed that $\lambda_1, \lambda_2 = 1$.

Suppose now that the world price follows a Markov process, such that:

$$(A4) \qquad\qquad p_t^* = p^* + u_t, \qquad u_t = \rho u_{t-1} + \epsilon_t,$$

where ϵ_t is white noise. Then (A3) reduces to:

(A3') $$p_t = \lambda_1 p_{t-1} + \frac{\lambda_1(\gamma/\delta)}{1 - \lambda_1} p^* + \frac{\lambda_1(\gamma/\delta)}{1 - \lambda_1\rho} \epsilon_t$$

$$= \lambda_1 p_{t-1} + (1 - \lambda_1)p^* + \frac{\lambda_1(\gamma/\delta)}{1 - \lambda_1\rho} \epsilon_t.$$

Notes

1. Equation (2) can be rewritten as $R = e_x(M - X) + (e_m - e_x)M$. The first term represents revenue from depleting foreign exchange reserves and thus cannot properly be thought of as a net revenue.

2. The effective rate of protection of industry i is defined as the percentage excess of domestic value added over world value added, measured in a common currency, or:

$$k_i = [(p_i - vp_j) - e(p_i^* - vp_j^*)]/e(p_i^* - vp_j^*)$$
$$= [(e_ip_i^* - e_jp_j^*v) - e(p_i^* - vp_j^*)]/e(p_i^* - vp_j^*).$$

Dividing by e and p_i^* and defining the exchange rate relative to the average rate, $T_i = (e_i/e - 1)$, reduces the equation to (3).

3. See Dornbusch (1984b) for an analysis of this argument in the context of Chilean currency overvaluation.

4. See Wiesner (1978).

5. It is a silly practice to argue that neutral lump-sum taxes and transfers will address distributional issues, even though we know that these tools simply do not exist. Sticking one's head in the sand, refusing any discussion of second best for societies in which distribution often is more important than efficiency, is poor political economy.

6. See Sargent (1979, 170–200).

References

Baer, W., and Herve, E. 1962. Multiple exchange rates and the attainment of multiple objectives. *Economica*: 176–84.

Bernstein, E. 1950. Some economic aspects of multiple exchange rates. *International Monetary Fund Staff Papers* (September).

Carta Económica. 1983. El Cronista Comercial (December).

de Vries, M. 1965. Multiple exchange rates: Expectations and experiences. *International Monetary Fund Staff Papers*, vol. 12.

Dervis, K., and Robinson, S. 1982. A general equilibrium analysis of a foreign exchange crisis: The case of Turkey. *Weltwirtschaftliches Archiv* 1: 259–80.

Dickie, P., and Noursi, D. 1975. Dual exchange markets: The case of the Syrian Arab Republic. *International Monetary Fund Staff Papers* (July).

Dornbusch, R. 1984a. Argentina since Martinez de Hoz. Cambridge: Department of Economics, Massachusetts Institute of Technology. Photocopy.

―――. 1984b. External debt, budget deficits, and disequilibrium exchange rates. In *International Debt and the Developing Countries*, G. Smith and J. Cuddington, ed. Washington, D.C.: World Bank.

Harberger, A. 1959. Using resources at hand more effectively. *American Economic Review* 49 (May): 134–46.

Harberler, G. 1947. Comments on national central banking and the international economy. In *Postwar economic studies no. 7*, Federal Reserve Board International Monetary Policies. Washington, D.C.: Federal Reserve Board.

International Monetary Fund. 1984. *Annual report on exchange arrangements and exchange restrictions.* Washington, D.C.: IMF.

Kaldor, N. 1964. *Essays in economic policy, vol. 2.* London: Duckworth.

Kanesa-Thasan, S. 1966. Multiple exchange rates: The Indonesian experience. *International Monetary Fund Staff Papers* (July).

Lanyi, A. 1975. Separate exchange markets for capital and current transactions. *International Monetary Fund Staff Papers* (November).

Marshal, J. 1958. Advance deposits on imports. *International Monetary Fund Staff Papers* (April): 239–57.

Moore, O. 1958. The stabilization of the Bolivian peso. *Public Finance*, no. 1: 43–68.

Pechman, C. 1984. *O dolar paralelo no Brasil.* Rio de Janeiro: Paz e Terra.

Sargent, T. 1979. *Macroeconomic theory.* New York: Academic Press.

Schlesinger, E. 1952. Multiple exchange rates and economic development. *Princeton Studies in International Finance*, no. 2. Princeton: International Finance Section, Princeton University.

Schmitt, H. 1981. Economic stabilization and growth in Portugal. *International Monetary Fund, Occasional Papers*, no. 2.

Schott, F. 1959. The evolution of Latin American exchange rate policies since World War II. *Princeton Essays in International Finance*, no. 32, (January). Princeton: International Finance Section, Princeton University.

Sherwood, J. 1956. Revenue features of multiple exchange rate systems: Some case studies. *International Monetary Fund Staff Papers* (February).

Triffin, R. 1947. National central banking and the international economy. In *International Monetary Policies*. Washington, D.C.: Board of Governors of the Federal Reserve.

Wiesner, E. 1978. *Política monetaria y cambiaria en Colombia.* Bogotá: Asociación Bancaria de Colombia.

Williamson, J., ed. 1980. *The crawling peg: Future prospect and past performance.* London: Macmillan.

Woodley, W. J. 1953. The use of special exchange rates for transactions with foreign companies. *International Monetary Fund Staff Papers* (October).

Comment   Manuel Guitián

Over a longer period than I like to acknowledge by now, I have enjoyed reading Rudiger Dornbusch's papers, but this, of course, does not mean that I have always agreed with them. The paper I have been invited to discuss can hardly provide an exception to the rule, particularly since my interest in its subject matter is a strong one. This is not only because multiple exchange rate arrangements are a matter of concern from a theoretical and a policy standpoint, but also because the topic is of direct importance to those of us who work at the International Monetary Fund. As the reader may know, the Fund has to oversee the observance of a code of conduct on the part of member countries in their international economic relations; as such, the Fund (and not the World Bank, as the paper indicates) is the only international agency that exercises control over and regulates the exchange practices of those member countries. As a result the institution has jurisdictional responsibilities to discharge in the general deployment of exchange arrangements, which, needless to say, include multiple exchange rate regimes, or as they are referred to in Fund jargon, "multiple currency practices."

In exercising jurisdiction over multiple exchange rates, the Fund monitors on a continuing basis developments in members' exchange systems. As Dornbusch points out in his quotation of the 1984 IMF *Annual Report,* there has been an increase in the incidence in multiple exchange rates since 1980, with some leveling off taking place on this front during 1983. Broadly speaking, the proportion of Fund members resorting to some form of multiple exchange rate regime remains significant. Partly because of this, when I saw the original title of the paper I wondered whether "exotic" (in the sense of unusual, rare, uncommon) was the most appropriate term to apply to multiple exchange rate arrangements.[1] At the risk of unmasking an occupational disease that afflicts those who are concerned on a regular basis with the safeguard of common norms of behavior, I must say that "deviant" came to my mind as a more appropriate term.

Let me now turn to the paper itself. It deals with multiple exchange rates applicable to commercial transactions, and from a general stand-

Manuel Guitián is deputy director of the Exchange and Trade Relations Department of the International Monetary Fund.

point I found some broad grounds for agreement with what Dornbusch has to say on the subject. I can illustrate a few of those grounds by referring to his statement of the equivalence between multiple exchange rates and tax-subsidy trade schemes, particularly the categorization of both of them as "second- or third-best instruments." I also concur with the assertion that the use of multiple exchange rates can be justified only in terms of "administrative or political feasibility or convenience rather than by any intrinsic optimality they possess." I would underscore even more strongly Dornbusch's recognition that multiple exchange rates are of "limited use" and that any resort to using them should be only "transitory" to deal with "short-lived" disturbances. All of these are points with which I cannot but concur. I would add in this context that I believe these considerations apply to multiple exchange rates in general, that is, to those systems established for commercial transactions, as well as to dual exchange rate regimes used to keep current transactions separate from capital transactions.

With areas of agreement out of the way—which is the easy part of my task—let me now turn to the domains of disagreement. These are varied and I must say they concern both matters of substance and matters of emphasis. Let us consider the reasons that are typically adduced for the introduction of multiple exchange rates. The bulk, if not all, of them fall into two main categories—which, by the way, encompass the four purposes identified in the paper. Multiple exchange rates have been used either as means to repress balance-of-payments pressures—these would include Dornbusch's categories of macroeconomic shock absorption and trade-balance adjustment—or as means to attain certain other objectives that are not directly related to the balance of payments—such as, as noted by Dornbusch, objectives regarding fiscal revenues, resource allocation, and income distribution.

A first area of disagreement—though perhaps only partial—arises in connection with a broad conclusion the paper seems to draw concerning the use of multiple exchange rates for reasons other than the balance of payments. Dornbusch begins by suggesting that multiple exchange rates are an inefficient way of achieving long-run revenue, distribution, and allocation objectives, and this idea seems to me unassailable so far as it goes; but then the author proceeds to suggest that there is a risk that the extent of the inefficiency arising from multiple exchange rates might easily be overestimated. In my experience, it is far more likely for the risk to run in the other direction, in other words, the extent of the inefficiency might be underestimated. I do not think the case for overestimation of the inefficiency caused by multiple exchange rates (whichever that case may be) was made in the paper, and I therefore fail to be persuaded by the statement.

Other areas of disagreement—which are related to the first one—concern the particular tone of some of the arguments presented more than their direction. My comments in this regard reflect the insight I have gathered on this subject in my work at the Fund. From that standpoint, I would stress far more than the paper does the disadvantages of multiple exchange rates that result from the lack of transparency of their effects. In fact, I thought the algebraic derivations and the resulting example provided in the section on effective protection conveyed this point quite effectively. I would contend that the costs of the opaque tax-subsidy schemes that are implicit in multiple exchange rate arrangements typically exceed those that accrue through direct and explicit budgetary means.

Another point I would raise in this context concerns the "transitoriness" that is typically alleged when multiple exchange rate regimes are employed. My impression is that the paper understates an important risk associated with resorting to such regimes: If empirical evidence is to be believed, once they are established, multiple exchange rates typically prove difficult to eliminate and tend to become a permanent feature of the exchange system. In my mind, this is nothing but the corollary of the observation that multiple rates are introduced most frequently for administrative or political convenience. The very process that makes devices like multiple rates more acceptable as a means to suppress an imbalance than the adoption of more direct policy actions is what renders them more difficult to eliminate. In other words, what is convenient to adopt is usually inconvenient to abolish. To the extent that this is the case, the costs of multiple exchange rates in terms of allocative efficiency will outweigh their usefulness as palliatives to existing imbalances and render them less than sensible as policy instruments.

In any discussion of multiple exchange rates, there must be an economic imbalance of some sort somewhere in the background, otherwise there would be no purpose to the discussion. The imbalance may be large or small, and its source may be exogenous or endogenous, transitory or permanent, and so forth. The particular policy response that will be required will depend on some of these characteristics of the imbalance. For example, an exogenous (not policy determined) and transitory (reversible) imbalance will typically call for temporary financing through international reserves or foreign borrowing. This possibility, however, is deliberately left out in the paper, and I cannot but wonder about the reason for this particular assumption. The assumption can only provoke the question whether it is realistic to say that an economy unable to finance a transitory disturbance is not in fact confronting a temporary balance-of-payments problem.

The discussion of the macroeconomic aspects of multiple exchange rates introduced for balance-of-payments purposes (the sections on trade-balance adjustment and macroeconomic shock absorption) seem to me the least persuasive in the paper. If the source of imbalance is determined by domestic policy (endogenous) and leads to an unsustainable level or rate of the growth of aggregate demand or to an inappropriate cost/price relationship with the rest of the world, policy adjustments directly linked to the source of the problem are required. Palliatives like multiple exchange rates, exchange restrictions, or quantitative controls cannot be substitutes for appropriate policy action on any sustained basis. In effect, they tend to compound the imbalance by adding to the distortions in the economy. This is not to say that there may not be specific instances in which multiple exchange rates can offer a potential useful option by providing a respite to allow the necessary policies to be put in place and take hold, but I would contend that these instances are rare.

My observations to this point also apply to a specific sort of multiple exchange rate system often discussed in the literature, namely, a regime of dual exchange rates that are applicable separately to current and capital transactions. As far as I know, there is no presumption that the resource allocation costs that result from multiple exchange rates depend on the particular type of transactions to which those rates are applied. Nevertheless, an argument is frequently made to the effect that an economy should be insulated from the impact of volatile (and massive?) capital flows and that a dual exchange rate system is useful for this purpose. There are problems with this argument, though, since the larger the capital flows, ceteris paribus, the wider the discrepancy between the exchange rates and, with this discrepancy, the deeper the potential distortions (if the markets are successfully separated) or the stronger the leakages between the two markets (if, as is more likely, transactions cannot be kept separate). In this context, it may be worth stressing that capital movements frequently reflect the stance of domestic policies, and when such stance is inappropriate, dual exchange rates again can only serve to repress and compound the underlying imbalance rather than to solve it.

Finally, there are two further observations that are worth making in this context: one is that even though dual exchange rates can contain or temporarily slow the speed of capital flight, they cannot eliminate the prospect of international reserve losses; the other is that when an imbalance is incurred to prevent or postpone adjustments needed in particular sectors of the economy—as is the case with attempts to sustain unrealistic real wage levels—the use of dual exchange rates to suppress the imbalance may make those sectors able to participate in the free exchange market, instead of those sectors for which the scheme was intended, the ultimate net beneficiaries of the scheme.

In conclusion, perhaps one of the stronger arguments that has been made in favor of multiple exchange rates is that they are more efficient than other means of official interference in external transactions, particularly quantitative restrictions, which are administratively cumbersome and relatively easy to circumvent. This point is briefly referred to in the paper, but I think it warrants more elaboration. It is also important to note that in economies in which controls are pervasive, multiple rates can serve to impart some influence to price incentives that otherwise might not be allowed to operate at all. Again, all these arguments, despite their partial validity, lose their relevance if they are used to advocate multiple exchange rates as a regime that can be sustained over extended periods of time; their long-run costs in terms of efficiency will clearly exceed any benefits that may be derived from them in the short run.

Note

1. The original title of Dornbusch's paper was "Exotic Exchange Rate Arrangements," and it was later revised to "Multiple Exchange Rates for Commercial Transactions."

Comment   Richard C. Marston

This paper on exotic exchange rate arrangements is of the high quality we have come to expect from Dornbusch. It features several simple but insightful analytic models, stripped to their bare essentials to highlight the issues under consideration and buttressed with numerous, well-chosen examples. Dornbusch provides an eclectic view of the literature on what the IMF calls "multiple exchange rate practices," which include legally approved systems of multiple commercial exchange rates and "dual exchange markets," as well as "black markets" outside the law.

The subject I would like to focus on here—dual exchange rates—forms the analytical core of Dornbusch's paper. By dual rates, we mean exchange rate arrangements that separate capital-account transactions from most if not all trade transactions, with the former carried out in the so-called free market. Dual exchange markets are often viewed by governments as an effective way to insulate the trade account, and perhaps the real sector, from financial disturbances affecting the exchange rate. The academic literature on dual markets, on the other hand, focuses on those channels of transmission that still remain open under dual rates.

Richard C. Marston is a professor of finance and economics at the University of Pennsylvania and research associate of the National Bureau of Economic Research.

This comment reviews the version of the Dornbusch paper presented at the NBER–World Bank conference. Subsequently, Dornbusch made some changes in that paper.

Before addressing Dornbusch's analysis, I would like to begin by examining those channels that dual markets succeed in cutting off, at least under some dual rate systems. This will help in understanding how these systems work, but also in explaining why it is important to keep the free market rate confined to financial transactions. There are two channels I would like to mention.

The first is the influence of changes in exchange rates on domestic wages and aggregate supply. To the extent that imports consist of consumer goods, a depreciation of the domestic currency exerts upward pressure on wages and hence on the supply prices of domestic goods. To the extent that imports consist of materials used in production, the influence of exchange rate changes on aggregate supply is even more direct. It is immediately obvious why dual exchange rate systems almost invariably channel wage goods and imported materials, often called "essential imports," through the regulated exchange market, thus cutting off this important channel.

The second channel is the influence of exchange rate changes on aggregate demand. A depreciation may lead to changes in relative prices, be they the relative prices of foreign to domestic goods or those of traded to nontraded goods, thus shifting aggregate demand. As long as trade transactions are confined to the regulated market, this channel is also cut off.

Thus, on the positive side, the dual rate system can cut off those price channels by which the exchange rate, and hence financial disturbances, affect the real sector of the economy. If a government wants to shield its nation's economy from temporary financial shocks, for example, then cutting off these channels has much to be said for it. Dornbusch cited in his original conference paper the example of Mexico's dual rate, which was adopted in response to the financial crisis of August 1982. Here is a case where it was clearly advantageous to separate the exchange markets for real and financial transactions, even though the insulation afforded by the dual rate system was both incomplete and temporary in nature.

Dornbusch, as well as earlier writers on dual markets, however, emphasizes the negative features of dual rates, specifically, the failure of dual rates to cut off certain financial channels of transmission. The dual exchange market has an interesting effect on real asset values. The separation of real and financial transactions holds the price level, the deflator of asset values, constant (or at least exogenous with respect to financial disturbances originating abroad). But the nominal value of foreign assets changes. The depreciation of the free rate applying to financial transactions leads to a rise in asset values. And this change in wealth in turn affects aggregate demand. If the depreciation is expected, moreover, interest rates also adjust. So the demand for real balances is affected.

Note that these are channels that do not exist in the simple open economy model without capital mobility, the model familiar from the work of James Meade and others in the 1950s. In such a model, with the exchange market consisting of current-account transactions only, the real sector of the economy is insulated from all foreign disturbances, at least in the simplest versions of the model. In the dual market model, in contrast, the real sector is not insulated, because nominal wealth and interest rates are affected by changes in the financial or "free" exchange rate.

The dynamics of wealth accumulation in the dual market model are also quite different from those found in the purely flexible exchange rate models of Kouri (1976) and Dornbusch and Fischer (1980). In the Kouri or Dornbusch-Fischer model, a current-account surplus is accompanied by an appreciation of the exchange rate, since the accumulation of wealth is in the form of foreign assets and that leads to an excess demand for money. In contrast, in the dual market model, as was pointed out by Flood (1978), a current-account surplus is accompanied by a depreciation rather than an appreciation of the domestic currency because the accumulation is in the form of money balances rather than foreign assets (because the current-account imbalance is satisfied with reserve flows). In any case, we see that the dual exchange rate system cannot cut off the financial channel by which changes in the free exchange rate affect the real sector.

The case against the dual market system is stronger than suggested so far if some real trade transactions take place in the free market. In that instance the dual market system does not succeed in cutting off even the wage and relative price channels by which the exchange rate, and hence financial disturbances, can affect the real sector of the economy. But for that reason, it is no longer adequate for a model of dual markets to focus on wealth and interest-rate effects alone, as most of the literature has done.

In a later section of the paper, Dornbusch introduces a more complex model of a dual market that permits some categories of imports and exports to be traded in the free market. In this model the relative prices of traded goods in the regulated and free markets can change, thereby opening up a new channel of transmission. I would argue that Dornbusch does not go far enough in modifying the earlier model to incorporate relative price effects. First, the model still does not include any relative price of domestic and foreign goods. This is a channel of influence incorporated into the dual market models of both Macedo (1982) and Cumby (1984). Second, there is still no supply sector in the model. We therefore have no idea how the labor force is reacting to changes in all of these relative prices.

But here we reach an important issue concerning research on such dual market models. To accommodate this more complex model of the dual market, Dornbusch has had to grapple with a third dynamic equation. In his model, foreign capital can be accumulated in the free market, since a current-account surplus can occur in that market. He therefore presents an additional accumulation equation. With three dynamic equations, the author now resorts to an analysis of the steady state alone. I would argue that we are much more interested in the short-run dynamics than in the long-run steady state. How do we deal with the short run in a model with three dynamic equations? One answer is to simulate the model dynamically using estimated or nonestimated parameters. Most economists are unenthusiastic about simulation analysis, perhaps because simulations depend so much upon the particular parameters chosen for the model. But I would argue that simulations are preferable to both of the alternatives: focusing on the steady state, as Dornbusch does, or oversimplifying the model by leaving out important channels. Having said that, I should immediately add that the steady-state analysis Dornbusch provides is of considerable interest in itself. No one else, as far as I know, has ever tackled the problem of incorporating real sector transactions into the so-called free market.

I have focused my remarks on the insulation issue because I believe this lies at the heart of dual markets. But in closing, I would like to mention two other issues that are important in evaluating dual exchange rates. The first concerns the distortions to efficient resource allocation that occur when the dual rates, or multiple rates, involve different prices for different goods. Dornbusch does an excellent job of probing the inefficiencies that arise in these dual rate systems, as well as in other "exotic" arrangements. These inefficiencies are a good argument for using dual rates only in speculative crises, although, as with many government policies, the temporary expedient may prove to be permanent. The second issue is one that neither Dornbusch nor the other writers I have mentioned have addressed: the problem of leakages between markets in the dual market system. If the free market premium is large enough, there is obviously an incentive to transfer transactions to the most advantageous market. The possibility of leakages places an effective constraint on the free market premium, if only to prevent resources from being diverted into new ways to cheat the system. We need to see more analysis of this issue to understand better the incentives for cheating and their effects on the workings of the system.

Dornbusch does not cover all of these issues, but his paper provides a firm foundation on which future analysis of the dual market system, as well as other "exotic" arrangements, can be based.

References

Dornbusch, R., and Fischer, S. 1980. Exchange rates and the current account. *American Economic Review* 70 (December): 960–71.

Cumby, R. 1984. Monetary policy under dual exchange rates. NBER Working Paper no. 1424. Cambridge, Mass.: National Bureau of Economic Research.

Flood, R. 1978. Exchange rate expectations in dual exchange markets. *Journal of International Economics* 8 (February): 65–77.

Kouri, P. 1976. The exchange rate and the balance of payments in the short run and in the long run: A monetary approach. *Scandinavian Journal of Economics* 78 (May): 280–304.

Macedo, J. de. 1982. Exchange rate behavior with currency inconvertibility. *Journal of International Economics* 12 (February): 65–81.

II Economic Reform, Foreign Shocks, and Exchange Rates

5 Welfare, Banks, and Capital Mobility in Steady State: The Case of Predetermined Exchange Rates

Guillermo A. Calvo

5.1 Introduction

This paper explores a kind of "minimum framework" with which the role of banks, and particularly their welfare implications, can be examined. This topic of study is of undoubtedly great importance for modern economies, given the worldwide tendency to pursue relatively free banking, a phenomenon that has been unfolding perhaps more in response to the increase in the inflation rate of the leading currencies over the past decade—more by "economic necessity," as it were—than in response to the thoughtful design of influential economists (see, however, McKinnon 1973, Sargent and Wallace 1981).

The need to develop criteria to judge the different responses is particularly salient in countries in which the movement toward a freer banking system has been associated with serious economic disruptions; examples of these are Argentina and Chile in recent years (see Díaz-Alejandro 1985). The relationship here is not necessarily one of cause and effect, but the fact that the two events went together represents for all practical purposes a political indictment of free banking. An unwinding of this road, if at all desirable, will therefore require a deep and persuasive intellectual effort.

The investigation that follows is based on a small-country, overlapping-generations model in which the monetary authority announces a particular path for the exchange rate. Since the analysis concentrates on steady states, the rate of devaluation will be closely related to the rate

Guillermo A. Calvo is a professor of economics at the University of Pennsylvania.

I wish to thank Mario Blejer, Robert Flood, Pentti Kouri, and Maurice Obstfeld for their very helpful comments on a previous draft. I also gratefully acknowledge financial support for this research from the National Science Foundation.

of inflation. Thus, the first research question asked is what is the optimal rate of inflation in the absence of banks, where the criterion of optimality is the population's steady-state expected utility at birth. Contrary to models examining identical individuals, like the ones emphasized in Friedman (1969), the model employed here shows that when there are no distortions in the capital market, the optimal rate of inflation is zero, and, more significantly (because of the greater robustness of the finding), that as a general rule there is no presumption that the optimal nominal interest rate be equal to zero (the condition of "full liquidity"). This latter result is obtained even when the existence of lump-sum taxes and subsidies, as in Friedman (1969), is allowed.

The model presented here is such that if there were no money to speak of, it would be optimal to allow for free international capital mobility. Thus, a natural question is whether the introduction of money implies some optimal intervention in the capital market if the authority could simultaneously control the rate of inflation. The answer is, again, in the negative: the optimum is attained with no control on capital mobility and zero inflation.

The next step in the analysis is to introduce banks as intermediaries that can issue deposits, hold cash, and buy securities. The banks are assumed competitive but may be subject to a minimum cash/deposits ratio. Again, the nonintervention, zero inflation results appear in this case. In addition, the results show that a lowering of the cash/deposits ratio is always welfare improving if capital mobility is perfect and inflation is set at its optimal level. Whether such a movement toward banking liberalization is welfare-enhancing in the presence of distortions is less clear; however, the analysis does indicate that when cash and deposits are perfect substitutes and the government is constrained to collect a given amount of revenue using distortionary taxation, a lower cash/deposit ratio is welfare increasing, despite the fact that as a general rule it will call for a larger, and permanent, rate of inflation.

The discussion so far is covered in more detail in section 5.2 and in the appendix. Section 5.3 examines some extensions of the model, such as imperfect subitutability between cash and bank deposits and the existence of nontradable goods. The "liberal" message is, on the whole, sustained, although it has to be qualified in the presence of government revenue constraints and imperfect cash-deposits substitutability. The section also contains a brief description of the underlying microeconomics of banking.

The above scenarios are very "open" in the sense that trade in both goods and securities is allowed. Up to this point in the paper, however, the implicit assumption is that foreigners have no interest in the small country's "money," and neither does that country in theirs. This assumption is relaxed in section 5.4, where a foreign demand for domestic money is assumed to exist. The reason for emphasizing this aspect of the currencies markets—and not, for instance, the demand for foreign money by domestic residents—is the perception in countries having problems associated with a banking liberalization process that the latter are partly related to the high volatility of "foreign" funds, originally attracted by the relatively high interest rates on domestic bank deposits.

The presence of a foreign demand for domestic money or deposits may call for a drastic departure from the optimum of the currency-isolated economy; this is shown to be particularly the case if, in order to attract foreign funds for this purpose, the central bank is obliged to acquire highly liquid assets as some kind of insurance against, say, a run against the domestic currency. Optimal intervention may require making home deposits much less attractive than under the optimum in the currency-isolated economy. But the analysis presented here also shows that to the extent that cash and deposits are perfect substitutes, it is always welfare improving to lower the cash/reserve ratio and to increase the rate of inflation. In this sense, therefore, the presence of foreigners in the domestic currency market does not necessarily call for a tighter control on the banking system.

Section 5.4 closes with a discussion of alternative ways to reduce the cost of attracting foreign funds. Following the summary in section 5.5, the appendix presents another way of proving the first-best optimality propositions of the text and some discussion of the optimal inflation (rate of devaluation) problem.

5.2 Inflation and Banks in Deterministic Steady State

This section will explore some of the simple economics of optimal inflation and banking in the context of an overlapping-generations model. I will confine my attention to deterministic steady states. Furthermore, to minimize the confounding effects of phenomena that would be extraneous to the discussion, I will assume that net taxes are given back to the public in the form of lump-sum subsidies.

Consider an economy in which the residents live for two periods in a paradisaic steady state with constant population. Assume that, except for their date of birth, all residents are alike. Also assume that this economy is floating along in molecular oblivion, surrounded by a sea of other countries all producing the same output, where the law of large numbers dictates a constant one-period (international) rate of interest, r^*.

As a warm-up exercise let us first examine the nonmonetary equilibrium. The typical consumer's utility function is indicated by $U(c^1, c^2)$, where $c^i (i = 1, 2)$ denotes consumption when young and old, respectively. Marginal utilities are positive, and $U(., .)$ is strictly quasi-concave. Let b denote the output value of bonds held by residents, and let r indicate the domestic real interest rate. Assume that the central authorities are in a position to create a wedge between r and r^*. But since, as indicated above, these authorities are assumed to consume nothing by themselves, we postulate that:

(1) $$(r^* - r)b = g,$$

where g is government lump-sum transfers to the private sector (measured in terms of output.) In words, equation (1) states that the difference between the international and domestic values of the service account (of the balance of payments), is given back to the public in the form of lump-sum transfers.

Let us consider, in particular, the case in which g is given to the old; and to economize on notation, also assume that there is only one individual in each generation. The budget constraints of that individual are defined as follows:

(2) $$y^1 = c^1 + b$$

(3) $$y^2 + b(1 + r) + g = c^2.$$

Equation (2) simply states that income in period 1, y^1, is to be allocated between consumption in period 1 and the bond; equation (2), on the other hand, states that output in period 2, y^2, plus the gross revenue from the bond, $b(1 + r)$, plus government transfers, g, must equal second-period consumption.

Let us now turn to the impact on steady-state utility[1] of a change in r, the domestic interest rate. By equations (2) and (3):

(4) $$c^2 = y^2 + (1 + r)(y^1 - c^1) + g.$$

Thus, if the original solution is interior (an assumption that will be maintained throughout), and if the "envelope theorem" (see Takayama 1974) is applied:

(5) $$dU/dr = (\partial U/\partial c^2)[\partial c^2/\partial r + (\partial c^2/\partial g)(dg/dr)]$$
$$= (\partial U/\partial c^2)(r^* - r)db/dr,$$

where the partial derivatives involving c^2 are supposed to be taken in equation (4); and dg/dr is the total change of g (as defined by equation [1]) when r is increased. More intuitively, the change in U is being evaluated by calculating the increase in welfare that would occur if the entire adjustment fell on c^2. This calculation yields the true variation in U, because the individual is assumed to optimize, taking into account his budget constraint; and the implication is that the marginal utility of the last unit of money spent on any good should be equalized across goods. Notice that db/dr stands for the optimal response of b to both the change in r and the associated change in g.

In the "normal" case in which $db/dr > 0$,[2] maximum steady-state utility is attained, by equation (5), at the point at which $r = r^*$, that is, when there is no control on international capital mobility and, therefore, when the international and domestic interest rates are equalized.

As can easily be shown the above result is not robust to changes in the allocation of g between the young and the old. Nevertheless, the assumption that transfers are given only to the old is interesting, because it implies that in the absence of money and other imperfections, there should not be any interference with international capital mobility. The following discussion will bring money and banks into the picture in an examination of questions about optimal inflation and bank controls and then, in a framework comparable to the above, in an examination of the question about controls on capital mobility.

Assume that (expected) utility at birth is also a function of real monetary balances, m,[3] thus making it possible to write $U(c^1, c^2, m)$. For concreteness, the marginal utility of money is assumed to be positive, and function U is assumed to be strictly quasi-concave in its three arguments. The representative individual's budget constraints are therefore:

(6) $$y^1 = c^1 + b + m$$

(7) $$y^2 + b(1 + r) + m(1 + \pi)^{-1} + g = c^2,$$

where π is the steady-state, one-period rate of inflation. Unlike in equations (2) and (3), the individual is now allowed to hold money in period 1 and to use it in period 2; the output value of m in period 2 is thus $m(1 + \pi)^{-1}$.

Let M_t stand for the nominal stock of money and P_t stand for the price level, both at time t. Seigniorage from money creation in terms of output then equals:[4]

(8) $$(M_{t+1} - M_t)/P_{t+1} = m\pi/(1 + \pi).$$

The budget constraint for the government therefore implies (recall equation [1]):

(9) $$(r^* - r)b + m\pi/(1 + \pi) = g.$$

Again, if we assume interior solutions, the changes in expected utility caused by changes in π and r are, by equations (6) through (9):

(10a) $$dU/dr = (r^* - r)db/dr + \pi(1 + \pi)^{-1}dm/dr$$

(10b) $$dU/d\pi = (r^* - r)db/d\pi + \pi(1 + \pi)^{-1}dm/d\pi,$$

where, without losing generality, $\partial U/\partial c^2$ is set equal to one (this normalization will be used for all the following "dU" exercises). In addition, the following "normality" assumptions are made:

(11a) $db/dr > 0$ (11b) $db/d\pi \geq 0$

(11c) $dm/dr < 0$ (11d) $dm/d\pi < 0$.

It follows from (10) and (11) that if $\pi = 0$, it would be optimal to set $r = r^*$, as in the nonmonetary case. On the other hand, if $r = r^*$, then it is optimal to set π equal to zero. There is therefore a prima facie case for expecting $r = r^*$ and $\pi = 0$ to yield a global maximum. (See the appendix for a formal proof of the latter, $\pi = 0$, that does not even rely on (11).)

A point of considerable theoretical interest is that there is no presumption here that the optimal rate of inflation should, as in Friedman's rule (see Friedman 1969), be related to the market real rate of interest. The example here makes that absolutely clear, since as pointed out before, when there is no interest tax—which Friedman also assumes—optimal inflation is zero.[5] Another important finding of the analysis is that the mere existence of money does not call for controls on capital mobility if the quantity of money is set optimally. If, however, $\pi > 0$, it would not be optimal by (10a), to set r greater than or equal to r^*. As a result, with positive inflation it is optimal to subsidize capital inflows and to tax capital outflows. In other words, in the realistic case in which inflation is a positive number, net borrowing from abroad should be stimulated by subsidizing the rate of interest. This result may be more appealing if the reader notices that positive inflation in this model implies that individuals are receiving the inflation tax in the form of a positive lump-sum transfer during old age. Setting r slightly less than r^* results in a negligible welfare cost because of the change in b (because r is very close to r^*); but since the analysis started at a point at which m was significantly distant from the optimum, the associated increase in m (which was brought about by the lowering of r) has a significant positive effect on welfare. Thus, the subsidy of the interest rate is optimal because of its positive effect on the demand for money; if money demand were totally interest inelastic, for example, the optimal domestic interest rate would equal the international interest rate.

A more difficult question is the optimal policy mix when the government is committed to set g (government transfers) at a given positive level. The answer depends very strongly on the underlying structural parameters; and unfortunately, no generally valid policy rule emerges from the analytical apparatus employed here.

I will now expand the model to analyze the effects of banking. To simplify the exposition, we will assume that there exists only one bank which, however, behaves in a competitive manner (further extensions are discussed in the section 5.3). This bank takes (demand) deposits from individuals and buys bonds yielding the domestic interest rate. Since we assume the costs of operating the bank are nil (or, if you wish, negligible), and since the bank earns zero (pure) profits, we can conclude that if the bank holds a cash/deposits ratio equal to δ, where $0 \leq \delta \leq 1$, the gross return of deposits in terms of output, η, satisfies:

(12) $$\eta = (1 + r)(1 - \delta) + (1 + \pi)^{-1}\delta.$$

The first term on the right-hand side of the equation represents the yield of bonds held per unit of deposit, while the second term is the yield of cash reserves per unit of deposit. Since the bank is a profit maximizer and there is no uncertainty, it will hold all of its assets in only one form, unless the rates of return of the two assets are equal (something that happens only by accident in the present model), or unless it is regulated by, for example, minimum reserve requirements. If we assume the latter here, as long as $(1 + r) > (1 + \pi)^{-1}$—that is, as long as the return on the bond exceeds the return on cash—a profit-maximizing bank will set δ equal to the legal cash/deposits ratio.

Let us now consider the depositors' side. For simplicity of exposition, make the strong assumption that bank deposits are perfect substitutes for cash (extensions to allow for imperfect substitutability are discussed in the section 5.3). Since, by equation (12) and the previous considerations, $\eta \geq (1 + \pi)^{-1}$, individuals will find it to their advantage to hold no cash and to maintain all of their liquidity in the form of bank deposits.[6] Thus, in the utility function m will be identified with (real) bank deposits in the discussion that follows.

The budget constraint for the representative individual is now (recall equations [6], [7], and [12]):

(13) $$y^1 = c^1 + b + m$$

(14) $$y^2 + b(1 + r) + m\eta + g = c^2.$$

Furthermore, recalling equation (8) and that in the present case the bank is the only holder of cash, we find:

(15) $$(r^* - r)[b + (1 - \delta)m] + \delta m\pi/(1 + \pi) = g.$$

A comparison of equations (15) and (9) shows that one innovation is that there are now two types of bond holders: individuals (as before), and the bank. The demand for bonds by the bank just equals the share of total deposits that is not kept in the form of cash balances, that is, $(1 - \delta)m$. Another innovation is that the bank is now the only holder of cash, the demand for which thus equals δm.

Let us again study the welfare implications of changing π and r. By methods similar to those used to specify equation (10), it can be verified that, as in the no-banks situation, optimal inflation is zero if $r = r^*$ (that is, if there is no tax on interest). Furthermore:

(16) $dU/dr = (r^* - r)[(1 - \delta)dm/dr$
$$+ db/dr] + \delta\pi(1 + \pi)^{-1}dm/dr.$$

Hence, if $\pi = 0$ and if:

(17) $(1 - \delta)dm/dr + db/dr > 0,$

then it is optimal to set $r = r^*$. To understand this result better, notice that $(1 - \delta)m$ is the demand for bonds by the bank, and equation (17) therefore requires that the *aggregate* demand for bonds increases with the rate of interest. Moreover, this proposition is the natural extension of the one proved for the no-banks case, since when $\delta = 1$, that is, when the bank holds 100 percent reserves, equation (17) reduces to (11a).[7]

Of even greater interest is to study the impact of changing the minimum cash/deposits ratio at the bank. Suppose that $(1 + \pi)^{-1} < (1 + r)$ so that cash yields a smaller return than bonds. As argued above, δ will therefore be set at the legal minimum. Using similar methods as before, we find that if $\pi = 0$ and $r = r^*$:

(18) $dU/d\delta = - mr,$

which is a negative number if the international real interest rate is positive (which will be assumed in what follows). Under these circumstances a lower cash/deposits ratio is therefore always welfare improving. If there is no technical lower limit on δ, (18) implies that welfare is maximized in a "pure credit" regime according to which high-powered money is eliminated and bank deposits have a 100 percent backing in terms of bonds (or securities).

Suppose now that the government is constrained to raise a given amount of revenue. In this case is there an optimal combination of inflation and a minimum cash/deposits ratio? To answer this question, consider an experiment in which δ and π are changed such that η remains constant; clearly, by equation (12):

(19) $[(1 + \pi)^{-1} - (1 + r)]d\delta - \delta(1 + \pi)^{-2}d\pi = 0.$

Recalling equations (13) and (14), we can see that a change in π and δ that keeps g and η constant—and where, therefore, equation (19) holds—leaves the individual with exactly the same budget constraint. Obviously, this experiment will not result in any change of expected utility.

What about government revenue? By equations (15) and (19):

(20) $dg = - mr^* d\delta.$

Hence, if δ is lowered—and, thus, by (19), π is raised—to keep the return on deposits, η, constant, total government revenue will tend to increase. Since when part of the extra revenue is given back to the public, expected utility will obviously increase, a rather remarkable proposition results, namely, *it is possible to lower the cash/deposits ratio in such a way that expected utility and government revenue are both increased, even when the economy will have to suffer a permanently higher rate of inflation.* Notice that this proposition, contrary to most of the previous ones, does not depend on the sign of any total derivative, and that it holds independent of the initial values of π and r.

This proposition is a local one. We cannot infer from it that δ should be set equal to zero; when $r = r^*$, for example, $δ = 0$ implies, by equation (15), that the revenue would also be zero. In general, there will be a (possibly positive) lower bound on δ, below (and normally also *at*) which the revenue constraint cannot be satisfied.[8] The proposition suggests setting δ as close as possible to that lower bound.

As an important extension of the above result, it is now possible to prove that the above type of experiment may yield even higher welfare when $π ⩾ 0$ if the extra revenue is used to bring r closer to r^*, that is, if the extra revenue is accompanied by a reduction (in absolute value) of the interest-rate tax. To prove the proposition, assume equation (17) holds and examine the region in which the revenue from the tax on interest, $(r^* - r) [b + (1 - δ)m]$, is an increasing function of the tax, $(r^* - r)$, or, equivalently, the region in which:

$$(21) \qquad d\{(r^* - r)[b + (1 - δ)m]\}/dr < 0.$$

This condition would necessarily hold for some neighborhood of r^* if the aggregate demand for bonds is positive—a highly plausible assumption, since bond holdings represent the net financial wealth of this economy outside of high-powered money.

Suppose that associated with the constraint on g, there is an optimal choice of r given π and δ; now, lower δ and increase π as in the previous experiment, momentarily returning the extra revenue to the public. By the previous analysis, this results in larger welfare and government revenue than before; thus, the constraint on g would not be binding. The change in welfare when the constraint on g is not binding is given by equation (16). Hence, if $r > r^*$ we have—recalling equations (16) and (17) and that, by assumption, $π ⩾ 0$—$dU/dr < 0$, so that the optimal r will shift down toward r^*. Suppose now that $r < r^*$; then, by equations (11c), (15), and (21), $dg/dr < 0$. Since the original choice of r is assumed to have been optimal (given r, π, and the constraint on g), it follows that $dU/dr ⩾ 0$; for if contrariwise ($dU/dr < 0$), the expected utility and revenue could be made larger by further lowering r, contradicting optimality. It would therefore be optimal—or more accurately, given the "weak" inequality above, it would not be inoptimal—(once the constraint on g is relaxed) to increase r toward r^*, proving the proposition.

The intuition surrounding this statement is as follows. The local analysis strongly suggests the possibility that the global optimum, when there are no constraints on government revenue, calls for setting $r = r^*$ (the global proof is in the appendix). This equality, of course, would not hold in general when g is subject to a constraint; however, it is quite clear that as the revenue constraint is relaxed, welfare increases and, for some nonnegligible regions, r should move toward r^* (since it has to be equal to r^* when the g constraint is removed.) One way of relaxing the constraint is, as argued before, by a lowering of δ accompanied by an appropriate increase in π. Hence, by the previous reasoning, there should be nonnegligible regions in which the proposition is true. The proposition also gives a set of plausible sufficient conditions for the optimal r necessarily to move toward r^*, although the intuitive justification for those conditions is less obvious.

In sum, this analysis has shown that the presence of a banking system does not, in principle, imply a modification in the optimal values of inflation and interest rate; moreover, when $\pi = 0$ and $r = r^*$, liberalization of the system (a lowering of δ) is always welfare increasing. This is also true if the government is committed to raising a particular amount of revenue, for, as has been shown, within certain bounds a lower δ, accompanied by an appropriately higher π, will result in higher expected utility and government revenue. Furthermore, under plausible conditions even higher welfare would be attained if the tax on interest (in absolute value) were simultaneously reduced. In other words, the present framework strongly suggests that the emergence of a competitive banking system may call for a further *increase* of the degree of free capital mobility.

5.3 Deterministic Steady State: Further Discussion and Extensions

To contribute to the reader's understanding of, and comfort in using, the previous models as analytical tools, it will be useful to check that certain basic relations hold as they should. For instance, by equations (12) through (15) it can be shown that:

$$(22) \qquad y^1 + y^2 + r^*[b + (1 - \delta)m] = c^1 + c^2.$$

The left-hand side of the equation represents the GNP, because it is the sum of total domestic output plus the balance in the service account (in the brackets b denotes private bond holdings, while $(1 - \delta)m$ denotes the bonds demanded by the bank). The right-hand side denotes domestic absorption; equation (22) therefore states that the GNP equals domestic absorption, a relation that necessarily has to hold in a no-growth steady state.

In the earlier, molecular scenario, the speck of land that constituted the country produced only purely tradable goods. An easy extension of that scenario is to introduce nontradables by, for example, letting "leisure" be a factor in the utility function and by assuming that total output is produced by labor alone. Leisure would then stand for the nontradables, and none of the comparative statics formulas is changed, implying, of course, that all the earlier results carry over to this case. The industrious reader may want to pursue the analysis further by studying the impact of the different policies on the "real exchange rate," which could be defined as the inverse of the "real wage," that is, the wage rate in terms tradables.

A blatantly unrealistic assumption of the analysis to this point has been the perfect substitutability between cash and bank deposits. Fortunately, there is easy remedy for that. First, notice that the analysis does not depend on whether b, bond holdings, is an argument in the utility function; the results thus hold whether bonds are "liquid" or not. Now, consider the extreme case in which the legal cash/deposits ratio is zero and it is technically feasible for the bank to hold no cash. As long as cash is a less attractive asset than bonds, the profit-maximizing bank will then set δ equal to zero, and by equation (12), the gross rate of return on deposits, η, will be $(1 + r)$, thus making deposits and bonds equally attractive. Without losing generality, it can then be assumed that individuals hold no bonds, and in the no-banks version of the model (primarily equations [6], [7], and [9]), b can be redefined as deposits, and m as real *high-powered* money. With this reinterpretation, the no-banks model can be applied to examine optimal policy in the context of a perfectly competitive banking system (one with zero cash reserves), but one in which deposits are imperfect substitutes for cash. Recalling the discussion in section 5.2, we can see that if there is no constraint on government revenue, it is possible to make a plausible case for zero inflation and no tax on interest. As a matter of fact, that case can be extended to cases in which δ is exogenous; and in addition, one can show, as in section 5.2, that if $\pi = 0$ and $r = r^*$, welfare improves as δ is lowered.

With imperfect cash-deposits substitutability, it is no longer true that when there is a constraint on government revenue, it is always welfare increasing to lower the cash/deposits ratio at the cost of higher inflation. This is so because, although such an experiment could be done in such a way as not to lower the "quality" of bank money (by the arguments given in the previous section), there is here an additional welfare loss caused by the associated quality loss of cash, which is provoked by higher inflation. It should be pointed out, however, that the degree of substitutability between deposits and currency would normally be a function of government regulations. Thus, a challenging open question is whether it would be optimal to ease the substitutability between these two types of monetary instruments, taking into account the government budget constraint. Such an effort would probably require a more detailed model, one in which the role of money is explicitly stated and liquid assets are not introduced simply as factors in the utility function.

In connection with the last point, it is worth indicating that essentially all of the arguments made so far could be shown in terms of a model that does not include money in the utility function. One can, for instance, assume that money (cash or bank money) is the only savings instrument available in the very short run. A case could be made that individuals do not know their tastes when they make the bond-holding decision (presumably because the bond market is not open at all times), and as a result they carry some purchasing power into the first period of their life without exactly knowing their preferences. When their tastes are revealed (during the first period, say), those who desire to transfer unspent purchasing power to their second period are forced to hold money. Given the return on money, some may prefer to save something extra for next period, thus generating a (precautionary) demand for money. If preferences are "shocked" by identically distributed random variables that are mutually independent across individuals, the result could be a stable demand for money that would be indistinguishable from the one derived in section 5.2 (for details on this model, see Calvo 1984).

An obvious advantage of a more explicit model is that it allows a better understanding of the role of the banking system. In the context of the case just mentioned, for example, banks would be in a position to take advantage of the law of large numbers; by the stochastic assumptions, the bank (again, if we assume there is only one bank) would be in a position to know exactly the sums that will be kept in the form of deposits if it has a very large set of customers. The bank could therefore use those sums (more accurately, what is left of those sums after accounting for the required reserves against deposits) to buy bonds, thus generating a type of money that would dominate cash (in the realistic case in which $[1 + r] > [1 + \pi]^{-1}$).

The model can easily be extended to allow for the existence of more than one bank. In this case the amount of deposits at any given bank will be a random variable, but the interbank loan system may come into play to help replicate the solution that would be attained by one large competitive bank.

In closing this section, I should point out that I have completely abstracted from the stock seigniorage from money creation emphasized by Auernheimer (1974). Nonetheless, the analysis can be extended in that direction with no significant qualitative changes in the results. The next section will take account of the stock seigniorage in connection with the foreign demand for domestic money.

5.4 Foreign Demand for Domestic Money

This section presents a discussion of the possibility that a competitive banking system may not be optimal because it creates a potential for the emergence of a demand for domestic money by foreigners. It will thus be useful to begin by examining some of the mechanics associated with such a demand for money in the simplest case, one with no banks.

Assume that the central bank announces a path of the exchange rate with a constant rate of devaluation and is committed (to the maximum extent of its capabilities) to guaranteeing full currency convertibility at the ruling exchange rate. Let z indicate the demand for real domestic monetary balances by foreigners. Assume now that z was zero up to time zero and $\bar{z}$ thereafter (unless a collapse of the fixed-rates system is expected, as will be explained below). In the kind of scenario discussed in the previous section, with a nonstochastic aggregate demand for domestic money, the central bank would be able to guarantee 100 percent backing for foreign deposits, increase social welfare by buying z units of bonds, and distribute the return on the government's bonds back to the public. There is a potential source of time inconsistency here (see Calvo 1978). Suppose, for instance, that $\bar{z}$ is foreigners' demand for domestic money when the expected rate of devaluation equals π. A way for the government to collect extra revenue would be to announce a surprise devaluation, followed by a renewed promise that the rate of devaluation would henceforth be set equal to π. If the policy was credible, the government would succeed in accumulating more bonds, thus increasing the amount of the transfer to domestic residents. This is not the type of problem I wish to emphasize here, however. To eliminate such "temptations" on the part of the monetary authorities, I will instead assume that the government compensates (taxes) foreigners for any depreciation (appreciation) in the value of their real monetary balances that is caused by a surprise policy change.

Let us now introduce the banking sector, as in section 5.2. There is thus a single domestic bank that is the only holder of domestic currency (or high-powered money).[9] Let Z denote the nominal value of foreign holdings of domestic money (deposits, in this case). The flow of seigniorage based on devaluation that accrues to the government is then given by (recall equation [8]):

(23)
$$\delta(Z_{t+1} - Z_t)/P_{t+1} = \delta z \pi/(1 + \pi),$$

where $z = Z/P$. In addition, the government can collect a return (the rate of which is assumed to be equal to r^*) on the (net) bonds that had to be surrendered by foreigners when they acquired the domestic deposits, that is, δzr^*. Finally, an additional source of revenue is the interest tax on the bonds that the bank acquired with foreigners' deposits, or $(r^* - r)(1 - \delta)z$. Thus, the flow of government revenue (in terms of output) associated with the presence of foreigners in the money market, g^*, satisfies the following:

(24) $$g^* = [(r^* - r)(1 - \delta) + \delta(r^* + \pi/(1 + \pi)]z.$$

It readily follows from equations (12) and (24) that:

(25) $$g^* = (1 + r^* - \eta)z,$$

which states that the government's revenue associated with the presence of foreigners in the money market is just equal to the difference between the return on those deposits if they were entirely invested in the international bond market, $(1 + r^*)z$, and the return that accrues to foreigners as depositors, $z\eta$.

Now make the plausible assumption that (given the rates of return on all the other international assets) foreigners' demand for domestic deposits is an increasing function of the rate of return of domestic deposits, η. That demand can be indicated by:

(26) $$z = f(\eta), \qquad f' > 0.$$

It is interesting to note that the present assumptions (a key one being that reserves at the central bank can be kept in terms of the international bond—see below for further discussion) imply that g^* is a function only the rate of return on deposits, η. Given η, the value of g^* is completely independent of r, π, and δ. This feature will be exploited in the analyses to follow.

Revenue from domestic sources still satisfies equation (15), and the gross return on deposits is given by equation (12). Total government revenue, G, therefore satisfies the following:

(27) $$G = g + g^*.$$

The budget constraints for the representative individual are now given by:

(28) $$y^1 = c^1 + b + m$$

(29) $$y^2 + b(1 + r) + m\eta + G = c^2.$$

In section 5.2 I suggested very strongly (the formal proof is in the appendix) that in the absence of constraints on government revenue, an optimal policy would be to set δ equal to zero and r equal to r^*. By equation (12) this implies $\eta = 1 + r^*$, a consequence of which is, by equation (25), that revenue from foreigners would be zero. But, by (25) and (26), at $\eta = 1 + r^*$:

(30) $$dg^*/d\eta = -f(1 + r^*) < 0.$$

Hence, revenue from foreigners would necessarily increase if η is set at slightly less than the social optimum when there is no foreign demand for domestic deposits. But since taking into account only the domestic variables (everything but g^*), when $\delta = 0$ and $r = r^*$, we have $dU/d\eta = 0$ (the first-order condition for maximum), it follows, by equations (28) through (30), that when there is a positive foreign demand for domestic deposits, it is optimal to set $\eta < 1 + r^*$.

Let $\bar{\eta} < 1 + r^*$ be the optimum level of η. A reasoning similar to the one given in section 5.2 (particularly the discussion around equation [20]) shows that if $\delta > 0$, that is, if there is a nonzero minimum cash/deposits ratio, and if $\pi < \infty$, welfare and government revenue are increased by lowering δ and increasing the rate of devaluation (or rate of inflation, π) in such a way as to keep $\eta = \bar{\eta}$. The previous reasoning can be applied directly because, by equations (26) and (27), the revenue from foreign holdings of domestic deposits is not being changed by this experiment.

Consequently, the presence of a stable foreign demand for domestic deposits offers no new reason against banking liberalization. This is an interesting result because it might appear natural to think that a significantly positive cash/deposits ratio would be the optimal way to collect the seigniorage from foreigners. The analysis has instead shown that the country is always in a better position by collecting the same amount of revenue from foreigners by lowering δ, while at the same time increasing the rate of devaluation (equal to the rate of inflation.) It can easily be shown that the same qualitative result holds even when there is a constraint on government revenue.

Up to this point, the analysis has completely ignored the presence of aggregate random shocks. This assumption will now be relaxed with respect to z, namely, foreigners' demand for domestic money. The main objective here is to gain some insight into situations in which the demand for domestic money that originates abroad is significantly more volatile than that generated by domestic residents. This may be the case, in particular, when foreigners consider the home country's domestic money to be essentially like any other (almost) pure asset, while the country's residents, because they use domestic money for transaction purposes, are more appreciative of the "liquidity services" that domestic money provides. By the law-of-large-numbers argument given in the previous section, one could argue that domestic demand for money is relatively stable and unaffected by random shocks on the rate of return of competing assets.

Consider, first, the case without banks. If the central bank could invest the equivalent of z in the form of international bonds and still maintain the liquidity necessary in case of a random reduction of z, then all that was found in the previous cases applies here as well. But the central bank should normally be subject to transactions constraints. If, as in the scenario in the previous section, individuals have a positive demand for domestic money because, say, the bond market was not open at all times; under these circumstances, it seems quite natural to assume that somewhat similar constraints also apply to the central bank and that it therefore will normally be led to keep some liquid funds (yielding an interest rate less than r^*) as insurance against a random shrinkage of z. I am not interested here in providing a complete theory about the optimal insurance of this type; it is clear, however, that to the extent that the government does not intend to default with a probability of one, it will keep some funds in liquid form. This implies that the rate of return on z realized by the central bank is likely to be smaller than the previous analysis would indicate.

Whether this scenario calls for a higher or lower optimal rate of inflation cannot be answered in general. Thus, to sharpen our intuition, let us assume that no foreign demand for domestic money will arise unless the central bank holds its reserves in the form of assets yielding a zero rate of return, in which case z would become nonrandom, as before. In this case the seigniorage associated with foreign demand is πz and not $(r^* + \pi)z$, as before. If the domestic economy could be isolated from the π that applies to foreigners, and if we examine the region in which the foreign demand for domestic money has an elasticity smaller than one, then the optimal π will tend to be larger than before (that is, when the central bank invested these funds in terms of international bonds, yielding $r^* > 0$[10]). When this fact is combined with domestic considerations, it is likely that the unconstrained optimal rate of devaluation will be larger than before, while the optimal r might be smaller than before. Since a higher π means that smaller amounts of foreign funds will be channeled to the home country, the end result of the policy will tend to be a *smaller inflow of foreign capital in search of domestic money.*

The presence of the banking system may help improve welfare even further if deposits by foreigners can be distinguished from those by residents. In the case in which deposits are perfect substitutes for cash, it can easily be shown that maximum welfare could be achieved by disallowing foreigners to hold domestic deposits and by setting up a perfectly competitive banking system (with a zero cash/deposits ratio).

The rate of devaluation (equal to the rate of inflation) would then be set at the point at which πz is maximized (remember that to be able to attract z the central bank is assumed to be forced to hold assets yielding a zero rate of return).

This separation of domestic residents and foreigners for the purpose of collecting an inflation tax is, however, not very likely to be feasible in practice, given the various ways that individuals can find to hide their identities. Hence, it is interesting to examine the opposite case, one in which foreigners *qua* depositors are indistinguishable from domestic residents. Let us study the case in which the domestic banking system is completely free (that is, $\delta = 0$ and $r = r^*$) and there is therefore no demand for the domestic currency. Suppose, again, that z units of foreign deposits are attracted by the domestic banking system, and that in order to make their deposits at the bank, foreigners first have to exchange foreign currency for domestic currency and second have to make the deposit at the bank. The bank, not having any need or desire to hold domestic currency, takes the domestic currency back to the central bank, exchanges it for foreign currency, and buys bonds yielding a rate of return equal to r^*. The country realizes no gain or loss by this sequence of operations; but the above-mentioned operation is simply infeasible because foreigners are assumed to require that the institution whose liabilities they hold should have equally valued reserves in terms of some zero-interest asset. If the bank makes it perfectly clear that it is not going to acquire any zero-interest assets, no foreigner will want to deposit at the bank, that is, z will be zero. In this case, the banking system would be incompatible with this type of international capital mobility, even when that mobility is unfettered by any form of regulation.

On the other hand, if the central bank would like to attract foreign funds while keeping a perfectly free banking system, it will be forced to offer some kind of deposit insurance. Suppose that deposits are fully insured by the central bank. For z to be positive, the central bank would clearly have to hold an amount z of zero-interest bonds. This would represent a revenue loss of r^*z; and since domestic currency would not be held (directly or indirectly) by foreigners, the result of this operation could not be anything but a welfare loss. An implication of this analysis is that to extract positive seigniorage from foreigners when their identities are totally unknown, the central bank must introduce distortions in the domestic banking system.

In general, when δ is not constrained to be zero, as above, and when $r \neq r^*$ (recall equation [25]):

$$(31) \qquad\qquad g^* = (1 - \eta)z,$$

where r^*z has been subtracted from the right-hand side of equation (25) to account for the revenue lost in order to be able to offer 100 percent backing. It thus follows from (31) that *a necessary condition for foreign deposits to improve welfare is that the (net) real rate of return on deposits* ($\eta - 1$) *be negative.* Notice that in the extreme case in which the banking system is totally free—that is, the case examined in the previous paragraph—$g^* = -r^*z < 0$, as argued before.

An important point to keep in mind is that with no foreign participation in the banking system of the type discussed above, we have found strong indications that the optimal solution would be free banking and no interference with international capital mobility, implying $\eta = 1 + r^*$ (which was assumed to be greater than unity). On the other hand, with deposit insurance and 100 percent backing with zero-interest bonds, foreign holding of deposits will be welfare-increasing only if $\eta - 1 < 0$, *independent of how small z (> 0) happens to be.* It is therefore quite clear that *under these circumstances it could only be optimal to allow foreigners to hold domestic deposits if it were possible to attract sufficiently large sums for this purpose,* that is, if z were sufficiently large. And, in any case, the business of attracting z-type funds would call for a possibly substantial departure from the policy that would be first best if $z = 0$.

It is interesting to note that since, by equations (26) and (31), g^* depends only on η, welfare again is improved by a lowering of δ accompanied by an increase of π that leaves η unchanged (again here, however, the limit at which $\pi = \infty$ is not well defined.) Thus, although the presence of unidentifiable foreign depositors may call for a major interference with the banking system, it is still true that a lower cash/deposits ratio will improve welfare even when it may call for a substantial increase in the rate of inflation.

At a deeper level, it is still necessary to explain the rationale for the 100 percent backing requirement that was assumed in the above discussion. Although it is not my purpose to give a full coverage of this issue here, some pertinent remarks may be in order. In a more realistic situation, z is likely to be stochastic; the backing of foreigners' deposits would therefore be a way of guaranteeing the international value of deposits. We can think of the case discussed above as one in which foreigners are "maximiners" who think only of the worst possible event and one in which all foreign investors would decide to withdraw their funds from the country at the same time, leading to a total loss of value if there were no 100 percent backing. Thus, if there were no "true" stochastic shocks on z, such a backing would remove the foreign investors' anxieties and the economy would be able peacefully to write its own history along a nonstochastic steady state (as in the case examined above).

From the point of view of the foreign investor, it does not really matter who holds the necessary liquid assets in case of an eventual fall of z. We have assumed that someone in the tiny economy should pay for the resulting liquidity cost (if any foreign investor is going to be attracted), but there are other options. A very obvious one is for the central bank to become a member of some international banking system having the power to issue "international" money. Thus, if the small country's currency is pegged to, say, the U.S. dollar, a way to attract foreign investment would be for the central bank (more accurately, the local banking system) to become a member of the Federal Reserve System and the Federal Deposit Insurance Corporation (FDIC). In situations like these, the backing would be automatically provided by the international system. This kind of arrangement is not necessarily costless, however; the local banking system would now be subject to the regulations applying to the international one.

Another way to reduce the cost of backing the currency would be to allow "international" banks to operate in the home country. This would reduce the need for explicit backing if it is well understood by the public that in case of, for example, a bank run, the subsidiaries of "international" banks will be bailed out by their respective headquarters.

5.5 Summary

The basic argument made in this paper has been that the presence of a stable foreign demand for domestic money is not a reason to dismiss efforts to liberalize the banking system. On the other hand, if foreigners' demand for domestic money is either random or a function of the liquidity of, for example, the central bank's assets, the cost of attracting foreign funds into a relatively liberalized banking system may be significant. Thus, an optimal arrangement may call for an important reduction of the rate of return of bank deposits. The analysis presented here has also suggested that a possible way to reduce the costs of foreign demand for domestic money is to have the domestic banking system become a member of some international system or to allow international banks to operate in the home country.

Appendix

This appendix will demonstrate that the first-best global optimality results can be obtained in a rather general and direct way. This alternative proof will also help illuminate the reason for not associating the optimal rate of inflation with a zero nominal interest rate, as in Friedman (1969).

Consider the most general model discussed in the text, in which there is no foreign demand for domestic money, namely, the model described in equations (12) to (15). Let us examine the position of a planner who wishes to maximize expected utility (at birth) subject to the constraints mentioned in the text. After some simple manipulations, the following planner's constraints can be derived:

(A1) $y^2 - c^2 + (y^1 - c^1)(1 + r^*) - \delta m r^* = 0.$

On the other hand, by equations (12) to (14), the budget constraint for the individual can be expressed as follows:

(A2) $y^2 - c^2 + (y^1 - c^1)(1 + r)$
$$+ \delta m[(1 + \pi)^{-1} - (1 + r)] + g = 0.$$

Consequently, given δ, the first-order conditions for the planner and for the representative individual will be the same if $r = r^*$ and $\pi = 0$. In addition, the value of g that is incorporated in the planner's constraint (A1) is given by equation (15), which is exactly the same expression as that which determines g in (A2). A result of that equivalence is that the optimum for the planner is on the budget constraint of the representative individual, and furthermore, when $r = r^*$ and $\pi = 0$, it satisfies the representative individual's first-order conditions. Given the strict quasi-concavity of the utility function, the planner's optimum is therefore unique and decentralizable by choosing $r = r^*$ and $\pi = 0$. In addition, it is quite clear from equation (A1) that expected utility (at birth) increases as δ decreases, that is, as the minimum cash/deposit ratio is being decreased. These are in essence the first-best propositions derived in the text.

To understand more clearly the reason for the novel result for the optimal quantity of money found here, let us examine the simple no-bank case, which is equivalent to setting δ equal to one. It follows from (A1) that the marginal cost in terms of second-period consumption, c^2, of an extra unit of real monetary balances is r^*. Thus, to the extent that $r^* \neq 0$, it will not be optimal to set $\partial U/\partial m$ equal to zero, the "full liquidity" or Friedman's point. This is so because although the representative individual is being compensated for the inflation tax, there are not mechanisms in the model through which he could be compensated for the interest income lost when he accumulates an extra unit of real monetary balances.[11]

One can now readily understand why banks can improve welfare over the level attained without banks: they are a device by which bonds become more "liquid," or more like money, and in addition, *the extra liquidity produced in that way does not have an opportunity cost for the representative individual.*

Obviously, in this simple world the central authorities can generate the same welfare as in the pure credit situation (that is, when $\delta = 0$), for example, by "monetizing" bonds—allowing them to be used as a means of exchange. In more realistic situations, however, ones in which ascertaining the "quality" of bonds requires specialized skills, bond monetization would imply some kind of intermediation. Thus, in the final analysis the central authorities would be operating very much like a regular banking system.

Of greater interest is to examine the implications of paying interest on bank reserves.[12] Imagine the bank scenario of section 5.2, except now the central bank pays a nominal interest i on bank reserves (remember that in such a world all cash is held in banks' vaults.) One can easily verify that equations (12) and (15) are now transformed into:

(A3) $\qquad \eta = (1 + r)(1 - \delta) + \delta(1 + i)/(1 + \pi)$

(A4) $\qquad g = (r^* - r)[b + (1 - \delta)m] + \delta m(\pi - i)/(1 + \pi)$

Hence, by equations (13), (14), (A3), and (A4), the budget constraint faced by the planner is still given by (A1). The global optimum therefore remains the same, implying that there cannot be a welfare gain over the situation, discussed earlier, in which no interest is paid on reserves.

It is, however, of some interest to explore the additional possibilities opened by the existence of i. This can be done, as before, by obtaining the expression corresponding to (A2), when (A3), instead of (12), holds, such that:

(A5) $\quad y^2 - c^2 + (y^1 - c^1)(1 + r)$
$$+ \delta m[(1 + i)/(1 + \pi) - (1 + r)] + g = 0.$$

It is now quite straightforward to argue that the optimum can be decentralized by setting r equal to r^* and i equal to π. Paying interest on banks' reserves could therefore be useful in situations in which, for reasons outside the model, it is not possible to set π equal to zero.

Notes

1. Focusing on steady-state utility, of course, abstracts completely from the transitional aspects of policy. This is one reason why "time inconsistency" will not be a problem here.

2. As a matter of fact, the sign of this derivative is necessarily positive because in the present context it is a pure substitution effect.

3. This is a shortcut; for a more satisfactory way of modeling money that bears the flavor of the present approach, see Calvo (1984).

4. The following expression assumes equilibrium in the money market and that foreigners do not demand domestic money. That they do not is another reason why "time

inconsistency" is not of concern here (see Calvo 1978). Extensions of the model to cover this case are discussed in section 5.4.

5. There is some superficial resemblance between this result and those in, for example, Phelps (1974) and Helpman and Sadka (1979); however, their "anti-Friedman" propositions, unlike the ones here, depend on the assumption that lump-sum taxation is unavailable. See the appendix for a further clarification of this issue.

6. When $\eta = (1 + \pi)^{-1}$, individuals are indifferent to the choice between deposits and cash. To simplify the exposition, assume that they still prefer deposits to cash.

7. See the appendix for a global proof that does not rely on equations (11) and (17).

8. Revenue at the lower bound for δ could very well be smaller than that required by the g constraint, in which case there is, technically speaking, no solution to the maximum welfare problem. Nonetheless, maximum welfare can be approached as closely as desired by setting δ sufficiently close to the lower bound.

9. See Mundell (1972) for an early example along the following lines.

10. For a related result see Auernheimer (1974).

11. Related examples are in Woodford (1983), Abel (1984), and Calvo (1984). A forerunner in this literature was Weiss (1980)—a paper unknown to me until the final stages of this paper—in which the zero-inflation proposition is proved for the case of the utility function being separable in its three arguments. Except for my earlier paper (Calvo 1984), however, no other research seems to have introduced banks into this kind of scenario.

12. The following was inspired by a question posed by Pentti Kouri.

References

Abel, A. B. 1984. Optimal monetary and fiscal policy in overlapping generations models. Revised manuscript. Cambridge: Massachusetts Institute of Technology, December. Photocopy.

Auernheimer, L. 1974. The honest government guide to the revenue from the creation of money. *Journal of Political Economy* 82, (no. 3): 598–606.

Calvo, G. A. 1978. Optimal seigniorage from money creation: An analysis in terms of the optimum balance of payments deficit problem. *Journal of Monetary Economics* 4: 503–17.

———. 1984. Precautionary demand for money, inflation, and banks: Efficiency and optimality in an overlapping-generations model. New York: Department of Economics, Columbia University, July. Photocopy.

Díaz-Alejandro, C. F. 1986. Good-bye financial repression, hello financial crash. *Journal of Development Economics* 19 (September–October): 1–24.

Friedman, M. 1969. *The optimum quantity of money and other essays.* Chicago: Aldine.

Helpman, E., and Sadka, E. 1979. Optimal financing of the government budget: Taxes, bonds or money? *American Economic Review* 69 (March): 152–60.

McKinnon, R. I. 1973. *Money and capital in economic development* Washington, D.C.: Brookings Institution.

Mundell, R. A. 1972. The optimum balance of payments deficit. In *Stabilization policies in interdependent economies*, ed. E. Classen and P. Salin, 69–86. Amsterdam: North-Holland.

Phelps, E. S. 1974. Inflation in the theory of public finance. *Swedish Journal of Economics* 75 (March): 67–82.

Sargent, T. J. and Wallace, N. 1981. The real-bills doctrine versus the quantity theory: A reconsideration. *Journal of Political Economy* 90 (December): 1212–36.

Takayama, A.. 1974. *Mathematical economics*. Hinsdale, Ill. Dryden.

Weiss, L.. 1980. The effects of money supply on economic welfare in the steady state. *Econometrica* 48 (April): 565–76.

Woodford, M. 1983. Transactions costs, liquidity, and optimal inflation. Cambridge: Massachusetts Institute of Technology. Photocopy.

Comment   Mario I. Blejer

I find this paper a valuable addition to the by now quite extensive literature on the macroeconomic effects of predetermined or preannounced exchange rates. The main contribution of the paper is to extend the preannouncement model to consider the role played by financial intermediaries and, more important, to analyze the optimality of a number of policies when some constraints are imposed on the system.

The formal analysis is very carefully elaborated and the conclusions reached are strong, given the assumptions made. I do think, however, that some of the assumptions, as well as the nature of the framework adopted, are rather limiting for the purpose of evaluating the implications of preannouncing the exchange rate path or of liberalizing capital flows. I will mention some of the issues that could be considered to shed light on additional aspects of the topic, although, clearly, they will tend to complicate the structure of the model.

In the first place, I think that a clear limitation of the paper is the absence of any direct consideration of the role of risk in the model. An interesting discussion is provided about the need to hold "liquid reserves" in order to assure that the liabilities of the banks and the home country would indeed be honored, but one misses a direct treatment of risk factors in the determination of the rates of returns. The author, for example, that in the absence of controls on international capital mobility, domestic and foreign interest rates are fully equalized.

Mario I. Blejer is a division chief in the Fiscal Affairs Department at the International Monetary Fund.

But endogenous risk factors clearly tend to introduce a wedge between those rates, a fact that may change some of the subsequent conclusions.

In addition to risk factors, domestic and foreign rates may also differ if, even in the absence of capital controls, foreign banks are not allowed to operate in the domestic markets and if there are technological differences in the operations of financial institutions across countries (a factor observed to prevail in many circumstances). In such cases, the real return to capital in the financial sector will differ, and the absence of capital controls will not necessarily lead to interest rate equalization. Calvo suggests that allowing the entry of foreign banks may reduce the need for "liquidity backing" of foreign depositors. I would think that preventing their entry would actually result in less than perfect capital mobility and that some of the results may not emerge in the same form. In general, the concept of liberalization used is quite narrow, allowing for no capital controls or reserve requirements. Still, many regulatory elements may remain that will tend to prevent full capital market integration.

An additional subject that is not considered is the role of expectations in the specification of some of the central functions of the model. After all, the justification for the use of predetermined exchange rates was not only to attract foreign deposits and gain seignorage, but also to stabilize expectations and help in the process of integrating domestic and foreign markets. In general, the omission of a detailed treatment of risk and expectations, though making the model neat, raises other types of questions, such as what is the mechanism preventing infinite capital flows.

On a rather specific point, I would think that a more symmetrical treatment calls for allowing domestic residents to hold foreign deposits (since foreigners are allowed to hold domestic deposits). Having a richer menu of assets entering the portfolios of domestic residents would result in less restrictive signs for the partial derivative in equations (11a) through (11d). For example, (11b) implies that the demand for real bonds increases with the rate of inflation ($[\partial b/\partial \pi] \geq 0$). That is not a necessary result, since there are many considerations that would lead to the opposite outcome. It all depends on the nature of the bonds and on the other assets available.

These considerations aside, I think the paper is certainly very useful to evaluate the welfare implications of alternative sets of liberalization and exchange rate rules.

6 Capital Flows, the Current Account, and the Real Exchange Rate: Some Consequences of Stabilization and Liberalization

Maurice Obstfeld

6.1 Introduction

This paper develops a dynamic model of inflation and external capital flows that incorporates some key macroeconomic features of the more advanced industrializing economies. Although the model is quite general, it is motivated by recent events in the Southern Cone of Latin America, where wide-ranging economic reforms initiated in the 1970s produced dramatic—and ultimately unsustainable—movements in external accounts and real exchange rates. As observed by Díaz-Alejandro (1981), the measures undertaken in Argentina, Chile, and Uruguay coincided initially with steep increases in the prices of nontraded goods relative to tradables, with weak current-account balances and with massive foreign reserve accumulation. A goal of this study is to analyze the channels through which policy initiatives of the type undertaken in the Southern Cone influence the economy's long-run position and its transitional behavior.[1]

On the price side the economy studied here is characterized by a crawling-peg exchange rate regime and sluggish nominal wages that adjust to labor market disequilibrium and inflation expectations. Nontradable goods use imports as intermediate production inputs, and so there is an immediate pass-through of exchange rate changes to domestic goods prices. On the asset side there may be restrictions on private capital-account transactions, but the model encompasses both

Maurice Obstfeld is a professor of economics at the University of Pennsylvania and a research associate of the National Bureau of Economic Research.

I am grateful for the comments of Sebastian Edwards and the NBER–World Bank conference participants. Financial support from the National Science Foundation and the Alfred P. Sloan Foundation is also acknowledged with thanks.

polar cases—free capital mobility and complete capital immobility—within a single framework.[2] This facilitates study of the macroeconomic effects of capital-account liberalization. Under capital mobility the model traces the dynamic path of the real exchange rate (the price of tradables in terms of nontradables) and the economy's net external assets. Similar paths are traced for cases in which private capital is immobile, but the economy's external assets are then owned entirely by the public sector.[3]

The plan of the paper is as follows. Section 6.2 sets out the basic structure of the model. The real exchange rate occupies a central position, for its level affects both production and consumption decisions while its time path influences the real domestic interest rate.

Section 6.3 works out the model's dynamics under perfect foresight.[4] Asymptotically, the economy approaches a long-run equilibrium characterized by simultaneous internal and external balance. The nature of the path leading there depends, however, on whether a rise in the relative price of tradables improves or worsens the current account. The dynamics of the economy will not generally display the monotonic relationship between external assets and the real exchange rate characterizing the transition paths of most flexible-price, portfolio-balance models. In particular, the approach to long-run equilibrium may be oscillatory.

Liberalization of the capital account is taken up in section 6.4. The key result of this section concerns the short-term effect of liberalization on the real exchange rate. When the prereform domestic interest rate exceeds the depreciation-adjusted world rate, the removal of impediments to private capital movement causes an initial period of real appreciation. A current-account deficit emerges upon removing those impediments, but boom turns into slump as the economy converges to a steady state in which the level of external claims is lower than it was before liberalization. In the long run there is a real depreciation, an example of a more general principle that is also established in section 6.4: Any disturbance that leads to a long-run decline in external assets must also depreciate the long-run real exchange rate (assuming that the domestic capital stock is held constant). A similar result has been noted in other contexts by Bruno (1976) and Obstfeld (1985).

Section 6.5 studies the effects of devaluation and disinflation, with the latter defined as a permanent, credible lowering of the rate of currency depreciation. Devaluation is nonneutral in the long run, leading to an eventual rise in external claims and a long-run real appreciation. In the short run devaluation may occasion a current-account deficit or a domestic contraction, however. When capital is immobile disinflation has effects that are the opposite of those realized under a capital-account liberalization: an initial real depreciation and slump, followed by a long-run real appreciation and increase in net foreign assets. But in the model set out below, a change in the crawl rate is neutral when capital is fully mobile, even though the price of nontraded goods is temporarily fixed. The section concludes by considering possible sources of nonneutrality suggested in the literature.

Section 6.6 summarizes the main results and briefly discusses some limitations of the analysis in the light of actual events in the Southern Cone. An appendix contains technical details concerning the model's dynamics.

6.2   A General Model

This section describes a small, open economy characterized by a crawling-peg exchange rate regime and short-run inflexibility of nominal wages. Two goods are produced: a composite tradable priced exogenously in the world market, and a nontradable good whose price reflects the cost of domestic labor and imported intermediates. The response of the real wage to labor market pressure provides a first component of the economy's intrinsic dynamics. A second source is private saving, which drives the stock of net foreign assets to its long-run level. Detailed discussion of the economy's dynamic behavior is deferred until section 6.3. Here, I merely set out the structure of the economy.

Under a crawling peg the exchange rate follows a path determined by the central bank. To maintain the announced exchange rate when there is free capital mobility, the bank must accommodate any shift in domestic money demand through foreign exchange intervention. When capital controls are in place, however, residents may not purchase foreign currency assets and exporters must sell to the monetary authority any foreign exchange earned. To peg the exchange rate under private capital immobility, therefore, the central bank need intervene only to cover any trade imbalance.

It is not necessary to specify the degree of capital mobility in this section. The model's generality in this respect will prove useful when the liberalization of the capital account is studied in section 6.4 below.

6.2.1   Goods Prices and Production

On the production side the country examined here is a variant of the dependent economy studied by Salter (1959) and many subsequent writers. Let E denote the exchange rate (the domestic money price of foreign money) and P^{T*} the foreign currency price of the composite tradable good. Under the small-country assumption P^{T*} is parametric; arbitrage guarantees that in the absence of trade impediments and transport costs, the corresponding domestic money price of tradables is given by:

(1) $$P^T = EP^{T^*}.$$

A useful generalization of this framework would differentiate between imports and exports and allow for commercial restrictions that separate domestic from world prices. That generalization is forgone here in order to focus on the effects of financial policies. The normalization $P^{T^*} = 1$ is adopted, so that $P^T = E$ according to equation (1).

Tradable commodities are produced using capital and labor. Capital operates only in the tradable sector, but labor is free to move between both sectors of the economy. If W denotes the resulting economywide nominal wage, the supply function for tradables is:

(2) $$y^T = y^T(P^T/W), \qquad y^{T'} > 0.$$

The derived demand for labor, also increasing in its argument, is denoted:

(3) $$n^T = n^T(P^T/W).$$

Output in the nontradables sector is produced using labor (n^H) and imported intermediate materials (m^H) according to a fixed-coefficients technology. The production function for these domestic goods is:

(4) $$y^H = \min\{n^H, am^H\},$$

where intermediate imports are indistinguishable from final tradables. The parameter $1/a$ is the amount of the intermediate material that must be combined with a unit of labor to produce a unit of the domestic good. Constant returns to scale prevail in the nontradables sector according to equation (4), so that output y^H is demand determined. Factor demands are given by:

(5) $$n^H = y^H, \qquad m^H = y^H/a.$$

In equilibrium the price of domestic goods is given by the zero-profit condition:

(6) $$P^H = W + (P^T/a) = W + (E/a).$$

6.2.2   Asset Markets

Residents hold in their portfolios domestic high-powered money, M; domestic bonds paying an interest rate R; and (when private capital mobility is permitted) foreign bonds, B^*, having a face value fixed in foreign currency terms and paying world interest rate R^*. The domestic banking system is not explicitly modeled here. In addition to base money and bonds, there is an exogenous nonmarketable component of domestic wealth that can include, for example, titles to capital operating in the tradables sector. This exogenous component of wealth has a fixed, strictly positive value, k, in terms of tradables (that is, in terms of foreign currency); the determination of k is outside the scope of the model. Under a regime of capital controls, B^* is taken to be equal to zero.[5]

Foreigners do not participate in the domestic bond market. Under free capital mobility, $R = R^* + DE/E$, where D is the time-derivative operator and perfect foresight is assumed. In words, domestic and foreign bonds are assumed to be perfect substitutes, so that interest parity holds when capital is mobile. When capital controls are in place the domestic credit market is essentially a curb market and R generally differs from the depreciation-adjusted world rate (see Bruno 1979; McKinnon and Mathieson 1981; van Wijnbergen 1983b).

Foreigners do not hold domestic money. Because it is assumed that there is no outside domestic government debt, aggregate domestic nominal assets, A, are given by:

(7) $$A = M + EB^* + Ek.$$

The money market equilibrium condition is:

(8) $$M = L(R)A, \qquad L' < 0.$$

Under capital immobility M is a predetermined variable that changes only as a result of current-account imbalances and domestic credit creation by the central bank. (The current account, of course, equals the balance of payments when there is no private international borrowing or lending.) As equation (8) shows, continuous asset market equilibrium is in this case maintained through adjustments in the domestic nominal interest rate, R.

Under capital mobility, however, the domestic interest rate is the sum of the exogenous world interest rate, R^*, and the policy-determined devaluation rate, DE/E. The money stock is now the jumping variable that adjusts instantaneously to preserve asset market equilibrium: for a given rate of currency depreciation, the central bank can peg the level of the exchange rate only if it automatically supplies to the public the money stock dictated by the right-hand side of equation (8). A is predetermined in the model whether capital is immobile or mobile.

6.2.3 Consumers

Let z denote the level of private domestic expenditure measured in nontraded or domestic goods. Define the real exchange rate, q, by:

(9) $$q = E/P^H.$$

By equation (6), the real exchange rate must be smaller than the technological coefficient a in equilibrium if W and P^H are always positive, or in symbols:

$$q < a.$$

A fraction $\sigma(q)$ of expenditure z falls on tradables, where σ is a decreasing function of q. Final consumption of tradables may therefore be written:

(10) $c^T(q, z) = \sigma(q)z/q, \qquad \sigma' < 0;$

and the demand for nontradables takes the form:

(11) $c^H(q, z) = [1 - \sigma(q)]z.$

Let γ be the average share of tradables in the overall consumer price index. (γ can be thought of as a long-run average value of σ [q].) The expected local inflation rate under perfect foresight is then γ (DE/E) $+ (1 - \gamma)$ (DP^H/P^H). (The derivatives are right-hand derivatives, as always.) Private absorption, z, is a function of real domestic wealth and the real interest rate, such that:

(12) $z = z[A/E^\gamma(P^H)^{1-\gamma}, R - \gamma(DE/E) - (1 - \gamma)(DP^H/P^H)].$

As usual, an increase in real assets stimulates absorption, while an increase in the real interest rate depresses it. In symbols, $z_1 > 0$ and $z_2 < 0$. (f_i denotes the partial derivative $\partial f[x_1, \ldots, x_s]/\partial x_i$.)

6.2.4 The Labor Market and Price Adjustment

The nominal wage is taken to be a predetermined, or nonjumping, variable that can adjust only gradually. The determinants of nominal wage inflation are excess labor demand and expected consumer price inflation, as in Obstfeld (1982).

Let n_0 denote the "natural" level of aggregate employment, which is assumed to be constant. If perfect foresight is assumed, the wage evolves according to:

(13) $DW/W = \phi(n^T + n^H - n_0) + \gamma(DE/E) + (1 - \gamma)(DP^H/P^H).$

From equation (6), the wage and the domestic goods price are related by $W = P^H - (E/a)$. Equation (13) may therefore be manipulated to yield:

(14) $DP^H/P^H = \pi(q)(n^T + n^H - n_0) + DE/E,$

where

(15) $\pi(q) = \phi/[a/(a - q) - (1 - \gamma)] > 0.$

Equations (14) and (15) show how currency depreciation and excess labor demand govern price inflation in the nontradables sector.

6.2.5 The Monetary and Fiscal Authorities

It is convenient to consolidate the budget constraints of the monetary and fiscal authorities. All domestic liabilities of the central bank take the form of high-powered money. On the asset side the bank holds domestic credit, C, and foreign bonds, whose foreign currency value is denoted F^*. The balance-sheet identity of the central bank is:

$$(16) \qquad M_t = C_t + E_t F_t^* - \int_{-\infty}^{t} DE_s F_s^* ds.$$

The last term on the right-hand side of equation (16) is the sum of past capital gains on official reserves, which inflate the domestic money value of bank assets without increasing monetary liabilities. As will be seen below in section 6.5, equation (16), which corrects for smooth movements in E, can easily be modified to take account of capital gains resulting from discrete major devaluations.

The fiscal authority levies personal taxes to help finance its consumption of tradables (g^T) and nontradables (g^H). An additional source of revenue is the interest earned on the central bank's reserves, equal to ER^*F^* in terms of domestic money. Any fiscal deficit is financed through domestic credit creation (the government issues no interest-bearing debt). Let T denote nominal taxes and G, nominal government consumption (equal to $Eg^T + P^H g^H$). The monetized deficit is then given by:

$$(17) \qquad DC = G - ER^*F^* - T.$$

The rate of domestic credit creation implied by equation (17) may exceed or fall short of the rate at which domestic money demand increases (the time derivative of the right-hand side of equation [8]). Let M^d denote nominal money demand. According to equation (16), continuous money market equilibrium then requires that:

$$(18) \qquad EDF^* = DM^d - DC.$$

Domestic credit growth in excess of money demand growth leads to a balance-of-payments deficit, so that part of the fiscal deficit is effectively financed through central bank borrowing abroad. After substituting equation (18) into equation (17), integrating forward, and applying the appropriate transversality condition, one obtains the intertemporal budget constraint of the public sector:

(19) $\int_t^\infty [g_s^T + (g_s^H/q_s)]e^{-R'(s-t)}ds$

$$\leq F_t^* + \int_t^\infty [(T_s/E_s) + (DM_s^d/E_s)]e^{-R'(s-t)}ds.$$

Constraint (19) limits the present foreign exchange value of government consumption to that of government revenue from taxes and seigniorage, plus initial foreign reserves. Seigniorage revenue is in turn limited by the public's willingness to add to its nominal balances.

It is assumed that the central bank follows the domestic credit rule:

(20) $$DC = (DE/E)M$$

to avoid protracted payments imbalances. To ensure that credit creation covers the government's cash-flow needs when equation (20) is followed, the government adjusts taxes, T, endogenously according to:

(21) $$T = G - ER^*F^* - (DE/E)M.$$

It can be shown that under the foregoing assumptions, constraint (19) will necessarily hold as an equality, provided the economy is dynamically stable (see Obstfeld 1985).

6.3 Dynamics of the Model

It is now time to pursue the dynamic implications of the structure described in section 6.2. To do so, I reduce the model to a system of two differential equations: one for the real exchange rate, q, and one for the net external asset stock of the economy as a whole, $K^* = F^* + B^*$. Because the nation's foreign assets are given by the history of the current account, K^* is a predetermined variable. Because the nominal wage is predetermined and the exchange rate is pegged, the zero-profit condition of equation (6) implies that q is predetermined as well.

Equation (14) gives the time derivative of q:

(22) $$Dq/q = -\pi(q)(n^T + n^H - n_0).$$

Equations (3), (6), and (9) imply that:

(23) $$n^T = n^T(q), \qquad n^{T'} > 0.$$

The equilibrium condition for the domestic goods market is:

(24) $$y^H = c^H(q, z) + g^H.$$

By equation (5), labor demand in the nontradables sector, n^H, is equal to $c^H + g^H$.

To complete the derivation of the dynamic law for q, I must also show that absorption, z, can be expressed in terms of q and K^*. The definition of the real exchange rate, q, allows an expression of the real interest rate as:

$$R - (DE/E) + (1 - \gamma)(Dq/q).$$

A rise in the expected rate of real depreciation, all else equal, implies a rise in the real interest rate. Equation (7) can be used to write (12) as:

(25) $z = z\{q^{1-\gamma}[(M/E) + B^* + k], R - (DE/E) + (1 - \gamma)(Dq/q)\}.$

Next, note that $D(M/E) = DM/E - (DE/E)(M/E) = DF^*$ (by equations (16) and (20)), and so $(M/E) = F^* + \chi$, where χ is a constant that can be calculated from equation (16).[6] Finally, equation (8) can be solved for the equilibrium domestic interest rate, such that:

(26) $$R = R(K^* + \chi), R' \leq 0.$$

Under perfect capital mobility, $R(K^* + \chi) = R^* + (DE/E)$, and so $R' = 0$. But when private capital is immobile, $K^* = F^*$ and $R' < 0$. In the latter case a rise in K^* is simply a rise in international reserves that increases domestic liquidity, depressing the local rate of interest.

The foregoing observations lead to the equation:

(27) $z = z[q^{1-\gamma}(K^* + \chi + k), R(K^* + \chi)$
$$- (DE/E) + (1 - \gamma)(Dq/q)].$$

With the aid of equations (11), (23), and (27), equation (22) may now be written:

(28) $Dq/q = -\pi(q)\{n^T(q) + [1 - \sigma(q)]z[q^{1-\gamma}(K^* + \chi + k),$
$$R(K^* + \chi) - (DE/E) + (1 - \gamma)(Dq/q)] + g^H - n_0\}.$$

From this equation, one can obtain the reduced-form law of motion:

(29) $$Dq/q = \Gamma(q, K^*).$$

It is assumed that:

(30) $$\Gamma_1 < 0, \qquad \Gamma_2 < 0.$$

Thus, a rise in q raises the demand for labor in both the tradable and the domestic goods sectors, leading in turn to an increasing real wage and, through equation (6), a falling (that is, appreciating) real exchange rate. Similarly, a rise in K^*, by stimulating the demand for nontradables, leads to excess labor demand in the domestic goods sector and, again, an appreciating real exchange rate.[7] The appendix spells out the mathematical conditions under which the inequalities in (30) hold. One condition worth mentioning here is that overall wealth, $K^* + \chi + k$, be positive. This is assumed from now on, although it is stronger than necessary for (30).

Let us now turn to the dynamic equation for K^*. The growth of nominal private assets equals private saving out of disposable income, and so by equation (7):

$$
\begin{aligned}
(31) \quad DA &= DM + DE(B^* + k) + EDB^* \\
&= Ey^T + P^H y^H + ER^* B^* + DE(B^* + k) - T \\
&\quad - Ec^T - P^H c^H - Em^H.
\end{aligned}
$$

Equation (23) implies that y^T can be written as an increasing function of the real exchange rate, q. After the use of equations (5), (10), (11), (16), (20), (21), (24), (27), and (29), equation (31) therefore becomes:

$$
\begin{aligned}
(32) \quad DK^* &= y^T(q) + R^* K^* - g^T \\
&\quad - \sigma(q)z[q^{1-\gamma}(K^* + \chi + k), R(K^* + \chi) \\
&\quad - (DE/E) + (1 - \gamma)\Gamma(q, K^*)]/q \\
&\quad - (1/a)\{[1 - \sigma(q)]z[q^{1-\gamma}(K^* + \chi + k), R(K^* + \chi) \\
&\quad - (DE/E) + (1 - \gamma)\Gamma(q, K^*)] + g^H\} \\
&= \Omega(q, K^*).
\end{aligned}
$$

Equation (32) displays the current-account balance as the difference between the national production of tradables (including services) and the national absorption of tradables. The relative-price effect of a real depreciation tends to improve the current account by increasing the output of traded goods and by discouraging their consumption. But by shifting demand toward nontradables, a rise in q leads directly to increased imports of intermediate materials. The overall relative-price effect is summarized by the Marshall-Lerner condition for the model, which states that with absorption held constant, a real depreciation has a positive effect on the current account, given by:

$$
(33) \quad y^{T\prime} - \{[1 - (q/a)]\sigma' - (\sigma/q)\}(z/q) > 0.
$$

Inequality (33) must hold in equilibrium because q can never exceed a (see the discussion following equation (9) above). But although the expenditure-switching effect of a real depreciation is always positive, it is weakened by the need for imported intermediates in the domestic goods sector.

The absorption effects of a rise in q do tend to worsen the current account: a real depreciation raises the real value of private wealth (under my assumptions) and lowers the expected real interest rate, thereby raising expenditure z. It follows that the sign of Ω_1 is indeterminate. The same is true of the sign of Ω_2, but there are sound theoretical reasons for assuming that a rise in net foreign assets, K^*, causes the current account to deteriorate. Accordingly:

(34) $$\Omega_1 \lessgtr 0, \qquad \Omega_2 < 0.$$

Again, the appendix discusses the precise mathematical conditions underlying the inequalities in (34).

Figures 6.1 and 6.2 show the two possible stable configurations of the dynamic system consisting of equations (29) and (32). The long-run or steady-state levels of the real exchange rate and net foreign asset stock are denoted q_∞ and K_∞^*, respectively. (The existence and uniqueness of these two are assumed.) In the first of these diagrams (corresponding to the case $\Omega_1 > 0$) the economy cycles during its approach to long-run equilibrium. In the second (corresponding to the case $\Omega_1 < 0$) the economy's transition path is either monotonic or a half-cycle. An interesting feature of the dynamics is the possibility that a depreciating (appreciating) real exchange rate will accompany a current-account surplus (deficit) along portions of the transition path. This conjuncture is not typical of flexible-price, portfolio-balance models (for example, Calvo and Rodriguez 1977).

Because $\Gamma_1 < 0$ and $\Omega_2 < 0$, the stability condition for the system's linear approximation near (q_∞, K_∞^*) is:

(35) $$\Gamma_1\Omega_2 - \Gamma_2\Omega_1 > 0,$$

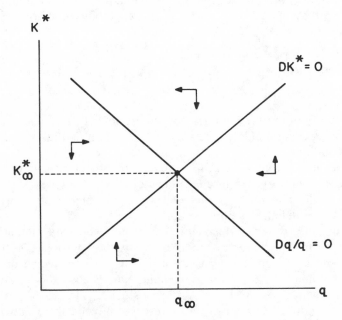

Fig. 6.1   Adjustment to the steady state ($\Omega_1 > 0$).

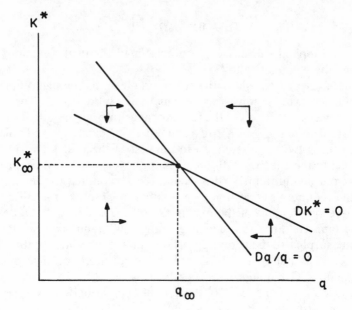

Fig. 6.2   Adjustment to the steady state ($\Omega_1 < 0$).

where all functions are henceforth evaluated at long-run equilibrium. From expressions derived in the appendix, stability condition (35) is equivalent to:

$$(36) \quad 0 < -R^{\cdot}[n^{T'} - \sigma'z + (1 - \sigma)(1 - \gamma)q^{-\gamma}z_1(K^{\cdot} + \chi + k)]$$
$$+ (q^{1-\gamma}z_1 + z_2R')\{(n^{T'} - \sigma'z)[(\sigma/q) + (1 - \sigma)/a]$$
$$+ (1 - \sigma)[y^{T'} - \{[(1 - (q/a)]\sigma' - (\sigma/q)\}(z/q)]\}.$$

The stability of the system does not require that Ω_2 be negative, as is assumed in equation (34). When $\Omega_2 > 0$, equation (35) holds, and the trace condition $q\Gamma_1 + \Omega_2 < 0$ is satisfied, the model has a stable configuration in which the $Dq/q = 0$ and $DK^{\cdot} = 0$ loci have negative slopes but (contrary to figure 6.2) the slope of the latter is greater in absolute value than the slope of the former. In the interest of conserving space, this possibility is pursued no further.

Although the dynamic behavior of the economy appears qualitatively unaffected by the degree of capital mobility, the interpretation of the model and any predictions based on it hinge on the regime one assumes.[8] When there are no private capital movements, $B^{\cdot} = 0$ and $K^{\cdot}$ coincides with the central bank's reserve stock, $F^{\cdot}$. In this case all net external lending takes the form of reserve movements, so that the current-account equation (32) can be interpreted as describing either the balance of payments or the evolution of domestic money holdings measured in tradables. Under capital mobility, however, $K^* = B^* + F^*$, where $B^* + F^*$ equals the consolidated external assets of the private and public sectors. Equation (32) again describes the current account, but it no longer applies to the balance of payments. Even though K^* is predetermined, its components B^* and F^* are not when private capital is mobile. Private portfolio shifts will force foreign exchange intervention by the central bank that is recorded in the balance of payments. That intervention redistributes the ownership of K^* between the private sector and the central bank, but it cannot cause an instantaneous jump in the economy's overall external claims.

6.4   Liberalization of the Capital Account

The first policy action considered is the liberalization of the capital account.[9] Initially, there is no trade in private external assets, and the domestic interest rate is a function of the predetermined money supply. Liberalization takes the form of a complete removal of barriers to financial capital movements. The economy is assumed to be at its long-run equilibrium when the liberalization takes place.

The effect of the liberalization depends on the relationship between the interest rate prevailing before the liberalization and the depreciation-adjusted world rate. It is most natural to assume that the domestic interest rate exceeds $R^* + (DE/E)$ prior to the reform, so that there is a fall in the cost of credit when the reform goes into effect.[10] The initial and long-run effects of the policy change can be visualized with the aid of figures 6.3 and 6.4.

The fall in the domestic interest rate raises absorption for every level of q and K^*. Accordingly, the $Dq = 0$ and $DK^* = 0$ schedules shift downward: for a given real exchange rate, a lower level of wealth is now required for both internal balance (labor market equilibrium) and external balance (current-account equilibrium).[11] The real exchange rate begins to appreciate in the face of excess domestic demand, and a current-account deficit emerges. As wealth and expenditure subsequently fall, the real appreciation ceases and is reversed. The underemployment that appears at this point is gradually eliminated (perhaps with oscillations) as the economy approaches its new long-run equilibrium. What is most noteworthy here is that in spite of its eventually deflationary effects, liberalization of the capital account may cause the economy to undergo a protracted initial phase of currency overvaluation.

On the asset side the fall in the domestic interest rate raises money demand. The private sector reaches portfolio equilibrium by borrowing foreign exchange from abroad and selling it for domestic money. Because the central bank must purchase this foreign exchange to hold the exchange rate fixed, private borrowing leads to an instantaneous rise in the aggregate money supply. The financial capital inflow results in

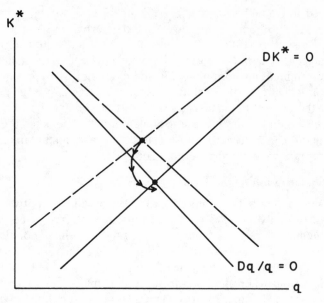

Fig. 6.3   Capital-account liberalization ($\Omega_1 > 0$).

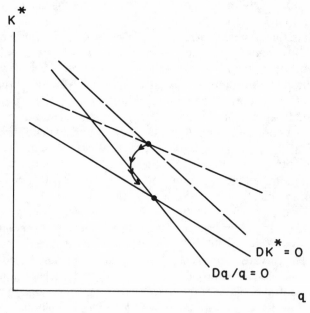

Fig. 6.4   Capital-account liberalization ($\Omega_1 < 0$).

a transfer of external claims from the private sector (which becomes indebted to foreigners) to the central bank (which enjoys an offsetting increase in reserves). K^*, however, cannot jump upon the institution of the reform. As external assets begin to fall in the wake of the liberalization, the balance of payments swings into deficit.

The model suggests that in Argentina, Chile, and Uruguay, the easing of capital controls in the 1970s may have contributed to the real appreciations, external deficits, and capital inflows that accompanied the economic reform programs in those countries. Capital-account liberalization is likely to serve as only part of the explanation, however. In Chile, for example, the beginning of real appreciation certainly predated the relaxation of external financial restrictions (see Edwards 1985).

Figures 6.3 and 6.4 suggest two results that have not yet been demonstrated. First, they suggest that the long-run external debt necessarily increases, a result that is obvious only in the case $\Omega_1 > 0$ shown in figure 6.3. Second, they imply that liberalization necessarily entails a long-run depreciation (in contrast to the real appreciation that clearly emerges in the short run). It is an implication of the system's stability (as will be shown later) that the long-run external asset stock declines. On the assumption that it does, I will now argue that the real exchange rate, q, must rise in the long run. The argument made is of independent interest in that it establishes a rather general proposition: Provided the domestic capital stock does not change, *any* disturbance that causes a decline in steady-state external claims must also cause a rise in the steady-state real exchange rate.

For a given long-run foreign asset stock, figure 6.5 shows the determination of long-run absorption, z, and the long-run relative price of tradables, q. The II, or internal balance, schedule in the figure shows combinations of q and z that clear the labor market (that is, that satisfy (28) with $Dq = 0$). The slope of the schedule is given by:

$$(37) \qquad (dz/dq)|_{II} = - (n^{T'} - \sigma' z)/(1 - \sigma) < 0.$$

Points above II are associated with an excess demand for labor. The XX, or external balance, schedule shows q-z combinations consistent with a zero current account for a fixed value of K^*. Its slope is:

$$(38) \quad (dz/dq)|_{XX} = [y^{T'} - \{[1 - (q/a)]\sigma' \\ - (\sigma/q)\}(z/q)]/[(\sigma/q) + (1 - \sigma)/a] > 0.$$

Points above XX are characterized by external deficits, and XX shifts upward along an unchanging II schedule as K^* rises. Point A, at the intersection of the two schedules, is the sole point consistent with both internal and external balance.

Under the maintained assumption that K^* falls in the long run as a result of liberalization, suppose that long-run absorption returns to its

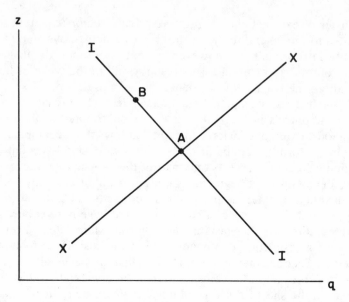

Fig. 6.5   Absorption and the real exchange rate in the long run.

prereform level. Internal balance would then require that long-run q also be at its prereform level, q_∞. But with K^* (and, hence, national income) lower, such a position, shown as point B in figure 6.5, would not be consistent with external balance; in fact, there would be a deficit. To restore full equilibrium with a lower steady-state external asset stock, z must fall and q must rise from q_∞. This downward movement along II brings the economy to point A. It follows that if the external debt rises in the long run, the real exchange rate, after falling in the short run, must ultimately rise above its initial level.

It remains to establish that the stock of foreign claims does indeed fall in the long run. Direct calculation shows that long-run foreign assets move in the same direction as the sign of the expression:

$$(39) \quad z_2[[(n^{T'} - \sigma'z)[(\sigma/q) + (1 - \sigma)/a]$$
$$+ (1 - \sigma)[y^{T'} - \{[1 - (q/a)]\sigma' - (\sigma/q)\}(z/q)]]/(\Gamma_1\Omega_2 - \Gamma_2\Omega_1).$$

Because $z_2 < 0$, stability condition (35) implies that expression (39) is negative.

6.5 Devaluation and Disinflation

This section discusses the effects of abrupt changes in both the level and the rate of change of the exchange rate. An unanticipated discrete devaluation may or may not occasion an initial contraction, but in the long run it appreciates the real exchange rate and increases the foreign asset stock. Disinflation, defined here as a permanent, unanticipated reduction in the rate of currency depreciation, is neutral under perfect capital mobility and rational expectations, price rigidities notwithstanding. But when private capital movements are prohibited, a fall in DE/E causes an initial slump followed by a cumulative balance-of-payments surplus and an eventual real appreciation.

6.5.1   Devaluation

The effects of a sharp rise in E are illustrated in figures 6.6 and 6.7. The monetary authority is assumed to deviate from rule (20) when it devalues, failing to match the exchange rate increase with a compensating increase in domestic credit. Devaluation therefore affects the economy in part by decreasing the foreign exchange value of assets denominated in domestic currency—here, the high-powered money stock. The private sector capital loss, in turn, reduces absorption. In the model this effect takes the form of a change in the relationship linking foreign reserves and the exchange rate–deflated money stock M/E.

Prior to devaluation, $M/E = F^* + \chi$, where, by equation (16):

(40) $$\chi = (1/E_t)(C_t - \int_{-\infty}^{t} DE_s F_s^* ds).$$

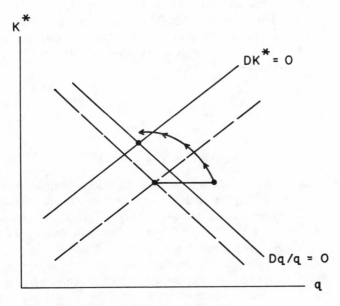

Fig. 6.6   The effects of devaluation ($\Omega_1 > 0$).

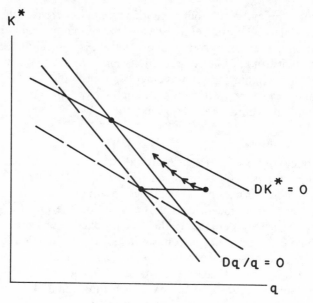

Fig. 6.7   The effects of devaluation ($\Omega_1 < 0$).

Devaluation-induced capital gains on foreign reserves are not automatically reflected in the monetary base but instead lead to the creation of artificial offsetting accounting liabilities on the central bank's balance sheet. Let the exchange rate rise at time t from E_t^- to E_t^+; let $\epsilon = (E_t^+ - E_t^-)/E_t^+$ denote the percentage devaluation; and let M_t^- be the level of the nominal money supply (and F_t^{*-} the level of reserves) just before the devaluation takes place. For all $v \geq t$, the central bank's balance sheet becomes:

$$(41) \quad M_v/E_v = F_v^* + (1/E_t^+)[C_t - \int_{-\infty}^{t} DE_s F_s^* ds - (E_t^+ - E_t^-)F_t^{*-}]$$

or

$$(42) \qquad M_v/E_v = F_v^* + \chi - \epsilon(M_t^-/E_t^-)$$

in the absence of further unanticipated devaluations (compare equation [40]). Equation (42) implies that for any level of external assets, devaluation lowers the foreign exchange value of private wealth by the amount of the concomitant capital loss on domestic money holdings. (See Obstfeld 1986 for further discussion.)

Devaluation lowers private wealth for any value of K^*, so the two loci in figures 6.6 and 6.7 shift upward because, given q, a higher level of foreign claims will be necessary for internal as well as external balance. As in section 6.4 above, dynamic stability implies that the long-run level of foreign claims must increase. (This is obvious in the case illustrated in figure 6.6.) The arguments made in the previous section therefore imply that the real exchange rate falls in the long run. This real appreciation is coupled with a rise in steady-state absorption relative to the initial equilibrium of the economy.

What can be said about the economy's transitional behavior? In addition to shifting the economy's steady state, devaluation also causes an instantaneous initial rise in the real exchange rate. Since the wage is predetermined, equation (6) yields the relative-price effect:

$$(43) \qquad dq/dE = [1 - (q/a)]/P^H > 0.$$

It is clear from this equation (since $P^H = E/q$) that the elasticity of q with respect to devaluation is smaller, the greater the import content of nontradables (that is, the smaller is a); to the extent that devaluation raises costs in the domestic goods sector, its effect on relative final-goods prices is reduced.

In figure 6.6, devaluation shifts the real exchange rate to the right of the new $Dq/q = 0$ locus, so that initially there is an expansion of employment and a current-account surplus. Over time foreign assets rise and the real exchange rate appreciates, with the economy approaching its new resting point in a cyclical fashion. There is no reason in general why the initial postdevaluation position of the economy cannot be to the left of the new $Dq/q = 0$ schedule. This last possibility is the case of a contractionary devaluation, the initial effect of which is a slump in employment and a depreciating real exchange rate. Even in this case, increasing wealth eventually reverses these short-run effects. The probability that devaluation is contractionary is directly related in the present model to the importance of intermediates in the production of nontradables (see also Krugman and Taylor 1978 and Buffie 1986). It is worth reiterating that if a is low, a large *nominal* devaluation may achieve only a minor *real* devaluation because of the substantial and immediate pass-through of import price changes to domestic costs. In this case the short-run expansionary effects of the associated rise in q will be small relative to the contractionary wealth effects that shift the two schedules in figure 6.6 upward.

Under capital immobility there is an initial liquidity squeeze and a rise in the domestic interest rate. But if the capital account has already been liberalized, there is a sharp capital inflow that immediately expands central bank reserves and the monetary base so as to maintain the domestic interest rate at the depreciation-adjusted world level.

Similar dynamics arise in the case shown in figure 6.7, although the economy's approach to its long-run position is direct when $\Omega_1 < 0$. In this case, it is possible that a devaluation will occasion a temporary external deficit that shrinks and is reversed as foreign assets fall and the real exchange rate appreciates. Contractionary devaluation is possible here, too, but only an expansionary devaluation can cause an initial deficit.

The long-run nonneutrality of devaluation contrasts sharply with the asymptotic neutrality results stressed in the monetary approach to the balance of payments (Frenkel and Johnson 1976). The result is in part a consequence of the assumption that central bank reserves earn interest. Under capital immobility individuals save to rebuild their real balances after the sharp initial rise in prices. Steady-state foreign reserves rise as a result, and because these reserves earn interest, national income and private absorption increase in the long run as well. When capital is mobile the liquidity effect of devaluation can be counteracted by capital inflows, but the negative wealth effect induces an initial fall in consumption and a long-run effect on national income similar to that arising when there are capital controls.

It is noteworthy that in models incorporating the Ricardian equivalence of government borrowing and taxation, the wealth effect of devaluation disappears in the mobile-capital case. This is because the increase in private external liabilities associated with the initial capital inflow is exactly offset by a rise in the present discounted value of expected future transfer payments from the government. These additional transfer payments are simply the increased interest earnings on the higher stock of central bank foreign reserves. It is therefore possible for the private sector to rebuild its real balances instantaneously through foreign borrowing without changing its lifetime consumption possibilities. For an analysis of these questions in models based on individual intertemporal maximization, see Obstfeld (1981; 1986) and Stockman (1983).

6.5.2 Exchange Rate Oriented Disinflation

Let us now consider the consequences of a credible, permanent reduction in the rate of devaluation, DE/E. In light of the Southern Cone experiences surveyed by Díaz-Alejandro (1981), it is of particular interest to ask under what circumstances an exchange rate based disinflation scheme causes a real appreciation of the currency. The two cases of internationally immobile and mobile capital are examined in turn.

Under capital immobility the domestic nominal interest rate is predetermined. A fall in DE/E increases the real interest rate (all else equal), leading to underemployment and a current surplus at the initial levels of q and K^*. As (28) and (32) show, both the $Dq/q = 0$ and $DK^* = 0$ schedules therefore shift upward (see figure 6.8). Model stability requires that when $\Omega_1 < 0$, as is the case in figure 6.8, K^* rises in the long run. This is clearly so when $\Omega_1 > 0$, so that the $DK^* = 0$ locus slopes upward. By the results of section 6.4, the steady-state real exchange rate appreciates. Indeed, an *increase* in the devaluation rate has dynamic effects that are qualitatively identical to those of capital-account liberalization.

In figure 6.8 there is an initial period of real depreciation as the increase in the real interest rate leads to underemployment. An external surplus emerges, and spending rises over time while real money holdings are built up and the domestic nominal and real interest rates fall. Excess demand for labor arises as the economy crosses the new $Dq/q = 0$ schedule. The real exchange rate appreciates, and external assets continue rising during the subsequent approach to the steady state. In the alternative configuration of the model (not pictured here), the medium-term dynamics are similar, but the approach to long-run equilibrium is oscillatory.

When capital is mobile the nominal interest rate is given by $R^* + (DE/E)$, and the domestic *real* rate is simply $R^* + (1 - \gamma)(Dq/q)$. A fall in DE/E leaves this real interest rate unchanged, for, as equations (28) and (32) show, it does not affect either of the schedules defining the system's dynamics. With rational expectations, therefore, a permanent and credible reduction in the rate of devaluation is neutral, in spite of the rigidity of domestic prices.

It is instructive to ask why a change in the depreciation rate is neutral with capital mobility. There are two reasons for this. First, the central

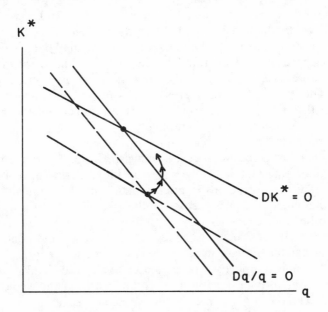

Fig. 6.8   Reducing the rate of devaluation ($\Omega_1 < 0$).

bank's commitment to peg the exchange rate forces it to accommodate fully the private-portfolio shift caused by the change. A fall in DE/E lowers the nominal interest rate and raises money demand. But the public can increase its nominal money holdings immediately by borrowing foreign exchange abroad and selling it to the central bank. This transaction raises official reserves but causes no change in the economy's overall income, wealth, or spending. The second factor ensuring neutrality derives from the assumptions regarding expectations and wage behavior. Because the rate of wage inflation can adjust instantaneously, the fall in DE/E is matched immediately by an equal fall in DW/W, so that no subsequent change in employment need occur. The overall result is a sharp, permanent fall in the domestic inflation rate with no transitional variation in spending or employment.

Neutrality would not hold if the exchange rate were floating and disinflation took the form of a reduction in trend monetary growth. Asset market equilibrium would then require a currency appreciation that would raise real wealth and expenditure. For a discussion of this effect, see Calvo and Rodriguez (1977).

Regardless of the degree of capital mobility, the model as formulated gives little support to the notion that a reduction in the rate of upward crawl is itself a cause of real appreciation. Brief consideration of some mechanisms not included in the present model is therefore worthwhile. (The following list is, of course, not exhaustive.)

Disinflation may lead to real appreciation if expectations of inflation in the nontradables sector are adaptive, as noted by Rodriguez (1982). When uncovered interest parity holds, a widely recognized fall in DE/E lowers the domestic nominal interest rate immediately but leaves DP^H/P^H unchanged in the short run. The associated fall in the real interest rate encourages expenditure and so lowers the relative price of tradables. This fall in the real interest rate is to be contrasted with the increase that occurs in the present model when expectations are rational but capital is internationally immobile.

Dornbusch (1982) suggested that the *rate* of domestic price inflation, like the level of domestic prices, is sluggish. If this is so, a fall in the depreciation rate tautologically forces an initial period of real appreciation. The rate of domestic price inflation must eventually fall to match that in the tradables sector, but the dynamics of this process are likely to be complex.

Buffie (1985) constructed a model in which banks hold nontradable claims to capital that are imperfectly substitutable for foreign bonds and endogenously priced. A reduction in DE/E raises banks' demand for this asset, driving up its price (Tobin's q) and thus investment demand. The result is again a short-run real appreciation.

The present model has assumed for simplicity that disposable income does not influence absorption. In a similar setting, van Wijnbergen (1983a) showed that this neglected channel may lead to real appreciation if disposable income is defined properly so as to reflect the inflation tax on real balances. Because a lowering of the devaluation rate also lowers domestic price inflation, the inflation tax falls and disposable income rises. The resulting increase in consumption falls partially on nontradables, driving their relative price upward. Calvo (1983) also discussed this mechanism.

Yet another channel of nonneutrality is suggested in the optimizing framework of Obstfeld (1981), which incorporated Ricardian equivalence and Metzlerian target-wealth saving behavior. Disinflation causes a rise in desired nominal balances matched by a capital inflow and an increase in interest-bearing official reserves. Because individuals capitalize expected government transfers, there is an increase in the public's perceived consumption possibilities and a rise in expenditure. Although the model does not explicitly encompass nontradables, this rise in expenditure is consistent with a real appreciation.

The foregoing models all consider a permanent, unanticipated fall in DE/E rather than the preannounced, phased decline in the devaluation rate that was a hallmark of the Southern Cone plans. In Obstfeld (1985) I employed an intertemporal maximizing model to study those kinds of schemes. Anticipated disinflation affects the economy by raising the path of an expenditure-based real interest rate reflecting expected changes in the prices of nontradables and liquidity services. If intertemporal substitution is sufficiently low, the immediate result is a rise in spending, an external deficit, and a real appreciation. The temporary real appreciation gives way to a long-run decline in the relative price of nontradables.

A final observation has to do with the question of credibility. As Calvo (1983) and others have emphasized, much depends on the public's belief in official promises to avoid major discrete devaluations. If the public views a discontinuous jump in the exchange rate as a possibility, it will adjust its inflation expectations and subsequent wage settlements accordingly. A persistent belief in a maxi-devaluation that does not materialize will therefore lead to an extended period over which domestic prices rise more quickly than the exchange rate. Even if the initial fear of devaluation was in some sense unjustified, the resulting real appreciation is likely to force the government's hand.[12]

6.6 Conclusion

This paper has constructed a dynamic framework in which liberalization and stabilization measures of the type recently instituted in Latin America's Southern Cone can be studied. The model represents an attempt to capture some salient features of advanced industrializing economies by postulating a crawling-peg form of exchange rate system, slow labor market adjustment, and an important role for imported production inputs. Because the model encompasses economies with closed and open capital accounts as special cases, the impact of capital-account restrictions on the effects of policy decisions is highlighted. A further advantage of this general framework is its ability to delineate the macroeconomic consequences of opening the capital account.

Liberalization of the capital account leads not to an initial period of real exchange rate appreciation but to a real depreciation and an increase in foreign debt over the long run. The economy passes through alternating phases of boom and slump in the transition process. Devaluation is nonneutral even in the long run and may be contractionary in the short run. Even though this measure entails an initial real depreciation effect, it drives the economy to a new stationary position in which the relative price of tradables is lower than it was initially. Finally, attempts to disinflate by manipulating the rate of currency devaluation may have minimal effects under capital mobility. When capital is immobile, however, disinflation has effects qualitatively similar to those of closing the capital account.

Although these results are certainly suggestive regarding the Southern Cone experience, the limits of the model's applicability should be recognized. There is no explicit description of the domestic banking sector, so that the effects of any liberalization there—and of its timing relative to liberalization elsewhere—are not studied. Similarly, the model assumes that the trade account is open and that the fiscal deficit is under control. In reality, the order of liberalization and the degree of consistency of macroeconomic policies differed among the Southern Cone countries. The consequences of these differences have been discussed elsewhere by a number of writers and are surveyed in Edwards (1984).

In this context, an important omitted variable of the model is imperfect credibility: public disbelief in the permanence of reform initiatives and in official promises not to inflict capital losses through devaluation or other measures. There can be little doubt that incredulity played a central role in both the unfolding and the unraveling of the Southern Cone stabilization programs. Our understanding of this phenomenon is incomplete at this time, but it is at the top of the agenda for future research.

Appendix

The purpose of this appendix is to supply a detailed discussion of the assumptions underlying the model's dynamics. Let (q_∞, K_∞^*) denote the steady state of the system described by equations (29) and (32) in the text. The linear approximation to the system near its steady state is:

$$Dq = q_\infty \Gamma_1(q - q_\infty) + q_\infty \Gamma_2(K^* - K^*_\infty),$$

$$DK^* = \Omega_1(q - q_\infty) + \Omega_2(K^* - K^*_\infty),$$

where all functions are evaluated at (q_∞, K^*_∞). Since the two dynamic variables are predetermined, the linearized system is stable if its two characteristic roots are negative. Necessary and sufficient conditions for this are the trace condition $q_\infty \Gamma_1 + \Omega_2 < 0$ and the determinant condition (35).

Direct calculation using (28) and (32) shows that in the neighborhood of the steady state,

$$\Gamma_1 = -\pi[n^{T'} - \sigma'z + (1 - \sigma)(1 - \gamma)z_1 q^{-\gamma} \times (K^* + \chi + k)]/[1 + \pi(1 - \sigma)(1 - \gamma)z_2],$$

$$\Gamma_2 = -\pi(1 - \sigma)(z_1 q^{1-\gamma} + z_2 R')/[1 + \pi(1 - \sigma)(1 - \gamma)z_2],$$

$$\Omega_1 = y^{T'} - \{[1 - (q/a)]\sigma' - (\sigma/q)\}(z/q) - (1 - \gamma)[(\sigma/q) + (1 - \sigma)/a][z_1 q^{-\gamma}(K^* + \chi + k) + z_2\Gamma_1],$$

$$\Omega_2 = R^* - [(\sigma/q) + (1 - \sigma)/a]\{z_1 q^{1-\gamma} + z_2[R' + (1 - \gamma)\Gamma_2]\}.$$

The inequalities (30) and (34) are predicted on the assumption that the economy is near its long-run equilibrium. Those in (30) also rely on the assumption that $1 + \pi(1 - \sigma)(1 - \gamma)z_2 > 0$. For a discussion of this condition, and a theoretical rationale, see Obstfeld and Rogoff (1984). Once it is assumed that $1 + \pi(1 - \sigma)(1 - \gamma)z_2 > 0$, the additional assumption $K^* + \chi + k > 0$ (which is clearly stronger than necessary) yields (30). The inequality $\Omega_2 < 0$ in (34) is simply the standard requirement that an increase in wealth raise absorption by more than it raises income at a constant real exchange rate. As was mentioned in the text, the assumption that $\Omega_2 < 0$ is needed for brevity rather than for stability.

Inequality (36) follows immediately from the partial derivatives listed above and from the assumption that $1 + \pi(1 - \sigma)(1 - \gamma)z_2 > 0$.

Notes

1. For discussions of individual countries, see Foxley (1982), Harberger (1982), Buffie (1985), Calvo (1983; 1986), Dornbusch (1985), and Edwards (1985). See also the papers and discussion collected in Ardito Barletta, Blejer, and Landau (1983). A full account of the collapse of the Southern Cone reform programs is beyond the scope of this paper. Calvo (1986), Díaz-Alejandro (1984), Dornbusch (1985), and Edwards (1985) have addressed that topic. Edwards (1984) surveyed some of the relevant analytical questions.

2. A single exchange rate regime, the pegged rate, is assumed throughout. Bruno (1983) discussed interactions between the degree of capital mobility and the exchange rate regime.

3. Related models have been developed by Blejer and Mathieson (1981), Calvo (1982), and van Wijnbergen (1983a). Blejer and Mathieson (1981) stressed the role of the domestic banking system. The setup in Calvo (1982) is similar to that of the present paper; but whereas a simple Phillips curve governs the wage dynamics described below, Calvo assumed that the domestic price level was an index of firms' predetermined output prices, set at staggered intervals. Another related model, in Buffie (1985), incorporated a banking system and a richer menu of assets but did not pursue the intrinsic dynamics arising from asset accumulation. Khan and Knight (1981) estimated and simulated a fairly detailed macro model of a developing country.

4. By assuming perfect foresight I am pushing aside undoubtedly important questions about the credibility of government policies and the speed with which the public's expectations adjust to new policy regimes. See section 6.5.2 below for a further discussion.

5. The immobile capital model could be modified to allow for a fixed positive level of foreign asset holdings. Unfortunately, this change would lead to considerable additional complexity. Under strict capital controls the market price of domestically held foreign assets is the (dual) financial foreign exchange rate, an endogenous variable determined within the model. It is the wealth effect of financial exchange rate movements that makes the introduction of a parallel financial foreign exchange market a nontrivial task. See Cumby (1984) and the chapter in this volume by Dornbusch for dual exchange rate models of this type, and Obstfeld (1986) for an optimizing analysis. An alternative dual exchange rate regime is one in which the authorities peg the financial rate to allow some target level of private external asset accumulation (Adams and Greenwood 1985).

6. See equation (40) below. The parameter χ can be altered by certain government policies, for example, a discrete devaluation, ΔE, of the currency not matched by a "helicopter" domestic credit increase, ΔC, satisfying equation (20), or by an increase in domestic credit not matched by the appropriate devaluation. Along this model's perfect-foresight paths, however, official transfer payments always compensate the private sector for the depreciation of its money holdings against foreign currency. (Of course, any individual takes these transfers to be parametric and so does not view them as a function of his or her own portfolio decisions.) The effect of an "uncompensated" devaluation on the relationship between M/E and F^* is discussed in section 6.5.

7. It should be kept in mind that under rule (20), the experiment of raising q corresponds to a rise in E (a devaluation) coupled with a compensating increase in domestic credit. (See note 6.) More simply, q can be viewed as rising through a fall in the predetermined nominal wage.

8. Note that both loci are flatter when there is no capital mobility.

9. Khan and Zahler (1983) used a detailed simulation model to evaluate the effects of opening the capital account. The dynamic adjustment produced by their model is quite similar to that found below. Dorlhiac (1984) studied the effect of financial opening on the real exchange rate in an intertemporal maximizing model. Calvo (1982) also studied capital-account liberalization, identifying its effects with those of an increase in domestic wealth. He obtained dynamics similar to those obtained here, but his long-run results were different because he ignored the service account. See Calvo (1983) and Edwards (1984) for alternative, less formal discussions of liberalization.

10. Strictly speaking, the use of the diagrams for this experiment is valid only for small changes. This implies that the difference between the pre- and postreform nominal interest rates cannot be too great.

11. The broken lines in figures 6.3 and 6.4 are, of course, the loci describing prereform internal and external balance. The assumption that $\Omega_2 < 0$ is what permits the assertion that a fall in K^*, all else equal, improves the current account.

12. Under capital mobility, the nominal interest rate will fully and immediately reflect the possibility of devaluation. This may explain why in Argentina, for example, the difference between the local and world nominal rates generally exceeded the preannounced rate of devaluation in the period after January 1979. As Calvo (1983) observed, however, expected devaluation should not affect the expected real interest rate, for it raises the nominal rate and expected inflation by the same amount.

References

Adams, Charles, and Greenwood, Jeremy. 1985. Dual exchange rates and capital controls: An investigation. *Journal of International Economics* 18 (February): 43–63.

Ardito Barletta, Nicolas; Blejer, Mario I.; and Landau, Luis, eds. 1983. *Economic liberalization and stabilization policies in Argentina, Chile, and Uruguay: Applications of the monetary approach to the balance of payments*. Washington, D.C.: World Bank.

Blejer, Mario I., and Mathieson, Donald J. 1981. The preannouncement of exchange rate changes as a stabilization instrument. *International Monetary Fund Staff Papers* 28 (December): 760–92.

Bruno, Michael. 1976. The two-sector open economy and the real exchange rate. *American Economic Review* 66 (September): 566–77.

———. 1979. Stabilization and stagflation in a semi-industrialized economy. In *International Economic Policy: Theory and Evidence,* ed. Rudiger Dornbusch and Jacob A. Frenkel, 270–89. Baltimore: Johns Hopkins University Press.

———. 1983. Real versus financial openness under alternative exchange rate regimes. In *Financial policies and the world capital market: The problem of Latin American countries,* ed. Pedro Aspe Armella, Rudiger Dornbusch, and Maurice Obstfeld, 131–49. Chicago: University of Chicago Press.

Buffie, Edward F. 1985. Price-output dynamics, capital inflows and real appreciation. *Oxford Economic Papers* 37 (December): 529–51.

———. 1986. Devaluation and imported inputs: The large economy case. *International Economic Review* 27 (February): 123–40.

Calvo, Guillermo A. 1982. Real exchange rate dynamics with fixed nominal parities: On the economics of overshooting and interest-rate management with rational price setting. Discussion Paper no. 162. New York: Department of Economics, Columbia University.

———. 1983. Trying to stabilize: Some theoretical reflections based on the case of Argentina. In *Financial policies and the world capital market: The problem of Latin American countries,* ed. Pedro Aspe Armella, Rudiger Dornbusch, and Maurice Obstfeld, 199–216. Chicago: University of Chicago Press.

———. 1986. Fractured liberalism: Argentina under Martinez de Hoz. *Economic Development and Cultural Change* 34 (April): 511–33.

Calvo, Guillermo A., and Rodriguez, Carlos Alfredo. 1977. A model of exchange rate determination under currency substitution and rational expectations. *Journal of Political Economy* 85 (June): 617–25.

Cumby, Robert E. 1984. Monetary policy under dual exchange rates. *Journal of International Money and Finance* 3 (August): 195–208.

Díaz-Alejandro, Carlos F. 1981. Southern Cone stabilization plans. In *Economic stabilization in developing countries,* ed. William R. Cline and Sidney Weintraub, 119–41. Washington, D.C.: Brookings Institution.

———. 1984. Goodbye financial repression, Hello financial crash. New York: Department of Economics, Columbia University. Photocopy.

Dorlhiac, Jorge. 1984. Financial integration and the real exchange rate. New York: Department of Economics, Columbia University. Photocopy.

Dornbusch, Rudiger. 1982. Stabilization policies in developing countries: What have we learned? *World Development* 10 (September): 141–53.

———. 1985. External debt, budget deficits, and disequilibrium exchange rates. In *International debt and the developing countries,* ed. John T. Cuddington and Gordon W. Smith, 213–35. Washington, D.C.: World Bank.

Edwards, Sebastian. 1984. The order of liberalization of the external sector in developing countries. *Princeton Essays in International Finance* no. 156. Princeton: International Finance Section, Princeton University.

———. 1985. Stabilization with liberalization: An evaluation of ten years of Chile's experiment with free market policies, 1973–1983. *Economic Development and Cultural Change* 33 (January): 223–54.

Foxley, Alejandro. 1982. Towards a free market economy: Chile 1974–1979. *Journal of Development Economics* 10 (February): 3–29.

Frenkel, Jacob A., and Johnson, Harry G., eds. 1976. *The monetary approach to the balance of payments.* London: Allen and Unwin.

Harberger, Arnold C. 1982. The Chilean economy in the 1970's: Crisis, stabilization, liberalization, reform. In *Economic policy in a world of change,* ed. Karl Brunner and Allan H. Meltzer, 115–52. Carnegie-Rochester Conference Series on Public Policy vol. 17. Amsterdam: North-Holland.

Khan, Mohsin S., and Knight, Malcolm D. 1981. Stabilization programs in developing countries: A formal framework. *International Monetary Fund Staff Papers* 28 (March): 1–53.

Khan, Mohsin S., and Zahler, Roberto. 1983. The macroeconomic effects of changes in barriers to trade and capital flows: A simulation analysis. *International Monetary Fund Staff Papers* 30 (June): 223–82.

Krugman, Paul, and Taylor, Lance. 1978. Contractionary effects of devaluation. *Journal of International Economics* 8 (August): 445–56.

McKinnon, Ronald I., and Mathieson, Donald J. 1981. How to manage a repressed economy. *Princeton Essays in International Finance* no. 145. Princeton: International Finance Section, Princeton University.

Obstfeld, Maurice. 1981. Capital mobility and devaluation in an optimizing model with rational expectations. *American Economic Review* 71 (May): 217–21.

———. 1982. Relative prices, employment, and the exchange rate in an economy with foresight. *Econometrica* 50 (September): 1219–42.

———. 1985. The capital inflows problem revisited: A stylized model of Southern-Cone disinflation. *Review of Economic Studies* 52 (October): 605–25.

———. 1986. Capital controls, the dual exchange rate, and devaluation. *Journal of International Economics* 20 (February): 1–20.

Obstfeld, Maurice, and Rogoff, Kenneth. 1984. Exchange rate dynamics with sluggish prices under alternative price-adjustment rules. *International Economic Review* 25 (February): 159–74.

Rodriguez, Carlos Alfredo. 1982. The Argentine stabilization plan of December 20th. *World Development* 10 (September): 801–11.

Salter, W. E. G. 1959. Internal and external balance: The role of price and expenditure effects. *Economic Record* 35 (August): 226–38.

Stockman, Alan C. 1983. Real exchange rates under alternative nominal exchange-rate systems. *Journal of International Money and Finance* 2 (August): 147–66.

van Wijnbergen, Sweder. 1983a. The crawling peg, capital flows and the real exchange rate in LDCs. Washington, D.C.: World Bank. Photocopy.

———. 1983b. Credit policy, inflation and growth in a financially repressed economy. *Journal of Development Economics* 13 (August–October): 45–65.

Comment   Marcelo Selowsky

Maurice Obstfeld has developed a well-specified structure, able to trace the dynamics and steady-state values of an economy experiencing a liberalization of its capital account. Given the world's interest rate, a specified rate of crawl in the nominal exchange rate, and an assumption of perfect foresight, the model traces the dynamics of the real exchange rate and the economy's net external assets. The model shows that the removal of impediments to capital movements causes an initial period of real appreciation, followed in the long run by a real depreciation

Marcelo Selowsky is an advisor of the Operations Policy Staff of the World Bank.

and an increase in the country's foreign debt. When capital is fully mobile, a change in the rate of crawl is neutral; it does not affect the steady-state values of the real variables.

The central issue raised by the paper is whether the model can be useful in addressing the typical welfare questions that have arisen from the experiences of Argentina and Chile, where the liberalization of the capital account during the 1970s was a major determinant of the substantial increase in private external debt. (The case of Chile better fits the initial conditions of the model, namely, internal equilibrium made possible by the ability of Chile to control its fiscal deficit.)

Two major questions can be raised in this regard: concerns about the nonoptimality of the size of the debt, that is, whether the private sector overborrowed, even after we have corrected for the influence of unanticipated external factors (movements in dollar interest rates and the terms of trade); and concerns about whether the rate of crawl is truly neutral, that is, to what extent alternative nominal exchange rate regimes during the period of liberalization conveyed different real signals to the capital and current accounts. In other words, what nominal exchange regime institutes the best system of intertemporal signals when the capital account is opened?

These welfare questions do not arise if perfect foresight is assumed. By definition, this assumption rules out the possibility of over- or underborrowing. The assumption implies that private agents are always able to foresee the oscillation and convergence of the *real* interest rate and adjust their external borrowing accordingly. Given dollar interest rates, it also means that agents are able to foresee the oscillation and convergence of the *real* exchange rate. And given the rate of crawl in the nominal exchange rate, it ultimately means that agents are able to foresee the oscillation and convergence of the price level of nontraded goods that will result from the opening of the capital account. These are indeed strong assumptions.

At issue here is what type of nominal exchange rate regime is most successful in helping private agents better predict the oscillation of the real rate—particularly its ultimate depreciation. A failure to foresee the ultimate real depreciation can generate excessive foreign borrowing and excessive reallocation of resources from the traded to the nontraded sector during the period of liberalization. Additional complications arise when alternative nominal regimes induce a differential "nonoptimality" in the movement of the capital and current accounts. In other words, there might be a trade-off in the efficiency with which a particular nominal regime conveys the proper signals to the capital and current accounts. A floating nominal exchange rate, for example, might increase the short-run appreciation of the real rate. This might lead, in turn, to an excessive movement of resources from the traded to the nontraded sector, or it might increase the *expectations* of a future real depreciation, thus restraining external borrowing. A fixed nominal rate, on the other hand, might dampen the short-run real appreciation if there are lags in the upward movement of nontraded goods prices. This fixed rate will dampen the movement of resources from the traded sector; but, it might also lower the expectation of a future real depreciation, thus encouraging an excessive amount of ex ante borrowing. These issues should be incorporated into future extensions of Obstfeld's paper.

III   Case Studies

7   Commodity Export Prices and the Real Exchange Rate in Developing Countries: Coffee in Colombia

Sebastian Edwards

7.1   Introduction

Changes in commodity export prices generally have an important effect on real exchange rate behavior. Under most conditions a commodity export boom results in a real appreciation of the domestic currency, with the extent of this appreciation depending on, among other things, whether the public perceives the change in export prices as being temporary or permanent. Most recent work on the interaction between commodity export prices and real exchange rates has focused on the long-run real effects of changes in export prices, analyzing how resource-based export booms will affect the real exchange rate, wages, employment, and output in the long run.[1] Changes in commodity export prices can also have important short-run monetary effects, however, effects that spill over to the real exchange rate. A resource-based export boom, for example, typically results in a balance-of-payments surplus and an accumulation of international reserves. If this increase in reserves is not fully sterilized, the monetary base will increase, and inflation will likely result. This increase in the price level will in general be one of the mechanisms through which the real appreciation actually takes place. It is possible, however, that the short-run increase in the rate of inflation exceeds what is required to bring about the equilibrium real appreciation generated by the export boom; in this case, the real exchange rate will appreciate in the short run by more than the amount

Sebastian Edwards is an associate professor in the Department of Economics, University of California, Los Angeles, and a faculty research fellow of the National Bureau of Economic Research. He is also a consultant for the World Bank.

I am indebted to A. Choksi, M. Khan, S. Rajapatirana, S. van Wijnbergen, E. Barandiaran, D. Yuravlivker, and M. Carkovic for helpful comments. The opinions expressed here are those of the author and do not represent those of the World Bank.

235

real factors would indicate.[2] These short-run monetary effects of commodity export booms have recently been important in the economies of a number of developing countries, including Indonesia, Kenya, and Colombia.

In spite of the importance of understanding the mechanisms through which changes in commodity export prices are transmitted into real exchange rate changes, very few empirical studies have tackled this subject.[3] This paper develops and tests a model of the interactions among commodity export prices, money creation, inflation, and the real exchange rate. The empirical analysis focuses on the effects of changes in coffee prices on the real exchange rate in Colombia. A number of experts have argued that fluctuations in Colombia's real exchange rate have been mainly determined by world coffee price movements, with most observers emphasizing the consequences of coffee price changes for money creation and inflation. Since 1967 Colombia has had a crawling-peg exchange rate system, in which the rate of devaluation of the peso is determined according to the behavior of a set of indicators that presumably includes the world price of coffee. Moreover, for many years Colombian authorities have tried to implement policies designed to reduce the effects of (temporary) changes in coffee prices on the real exchange rate.[4]

The paper is organized in the following form. Section 7.2 briefly reviews the behavior of the real exchange rate and coffee prices in Colombia. Section 7.3 presents and estimates a model that explicitly takes into account the monetary and inflationary effects of coffee price movements on the real exchange rate. The model also includes an equation for the rate of adjustment of the nominal exchange rate, or rate of crawl. The results reported in that section indicate that changes in (world) coffee prices have been positively associated with money creation and inflation and negatively associated with the rate of devaluation of the nominal exchange rate in Colombia. Finally, the fourth section offers some concluding remarks and argues in particular that the approach taken in this paper is useful for analyzing other cases in which commodity export prices and the real exchange rate have been closely related.

7.2 Coffee and the Real Exchange Rate in Colombia: An Overview

The performance of the Colombian economy has traditionally been linked to the behavior of the world coffee market.[5] A number of authors have argued that changes in the world price of coffee have been transmitted to Colombia mainly through the effect they have on the real exchange rate (Weisner 1978; Urrutia 1981; World Bank 1984). Increases (decreases) in the world price of coffee have generated real appreciations (depreciations) of the Colombian peso. These variations in the real exchange rate, in turn, have altered the competitiveness of the noncoffee tradables sectors, with a real appreciation generating losses of competitiveness or exchange rate "deprotection." For example, the recent coffee bonanza of 1975–79 resulted in a sharp real appreciation, which hampered the ability of the domestic sector to compete in international markets. Earlier episodes of sharp increases in the coffee price (in 1950, 1954, and 1956, for example) also led to steep appreciations of the peso (Weisner 1978; World Bank 1984.) Table 7.1 presents data on real exchange rates, coffee prices, and terms of trade in Colombia between 1952 and 1982, while table 7.2 contains data on money creation, international reserves growth, and devaluation and inflation rates for 1968–82. Figures 7.1 and 7.2 depict two alternative indexes of the real exchange rate and coffee prices.

In principle, changes in the price of coffee should affect the real exchange rate through at least two channels. First, a rise in the price of coffee will result in an increase in disposable income and an increase in the demand for tradable and nontradable goods. To the extent that the price of other (noncoffee) tradables is given by their world price and the exchange rate, this income effect will result in a higher relative price of nontradables and in a real appreciation of the peso. Second, and more important in the Colombian case, an increase in the price of coffee will tend to generate a balance-of-payments surplus and an accumulation of international reserves. If this increase in international reserves is not fully sterilized, the monetary base will also increase, and inflation will tend to result with the consequent further appreciation of the peso.[6] For example, as the data in table 7.2 show, the 1975–79 coffee bonanza generated a steep increase in international reserve holdings and in money creation. Regarding this particular episode, Urrutia (1981, 217) observed, "The increase in coffee prices started to produce increases in money supply which were . . . not neutralized rapidly enough. . . . But by 1976 all conceivable measures were taken to restrict money supply growth and to compensate for the growth in the monetary base caused by the growth in international reserves. . . . All these measures, however, were insufficient, and money supply increased by 34.7 percent."

Since World War II, the Colombian authorities have experimented with several schemes to reduce the impact of changes in coffee prices on the real exchange rate and on the rest of the economy. The main objective of the government during this period has been to reduce the undesirable short-run effects that temporary changes in coffee prices have on the degree of profitability, production, and employment in the rest of the economy.[7] For many years returns from coffee exports have been subject to a lower net rate of exchange than returns from other

Table 7.1   Coffee Prices, Rates of Devaluation, and the Real Exchange Rate
                   in Colombia, 1952–82 (1980 = 100)

Year	Real Price of Coffee (1)	Terms of Trade (2)	Effective Real Exchange Rate (3)	Bilateral Real Exchange Rate with Respect to U.S. Dollar (4)
1952	75.94	—	47.11	62.20
1953	83.08	—	44.21	57.14
1954	110.82	—	40.88	52.70
1955	87.32	—	41.66	53.28
1956	98.53	87.65	39.95	51.65
1957	79.19	84.89	47.74	69.80
1958	71.40	72.18	81.40	104.08
1959	61.21	60.97	76.40	97.27
1960	61.55	63.04	77.23	97.23
1961	59.04	61.63	73.45	90.03
1962	56.91	57.80	75.82	91.50
1963	56.35	52.28	76.81	89.35
1964	70.35	63.21	65.96	76.11
1965	76.39	64.40	73.72	87.28
1966	73.14	51.15	84.97	96.97
1967	62.64	60.21	86.46	96.56
1968	64.34	62.01	94.17	104.99
1969	66.89	61.57	95.09	105.29
1970	83.40	75.02	100.84	108.79
1971	71.00	70.11	106.50	111.34
1972	75.72	73.71	111.81	112.48
1973	83.51	78.49	113.18	113.88
1974	69.60	81.92	111.10	120.10
1975	68.41	75.76	119.85	126.65
1976	126.49	106.29	116.11	123.63
1977	181.95	147.45	101.04	104.52
1978	125.29	110.06	102.85	101.67
1979	112.47	98.38	101.29	99.89
1980	100.00	100.00	100.00	100.00
1981	67.52	84.36	91.62	95.16
1982	72.34	81.87	87.56	98.99

Source: International Financial Statistics (IFS).

Notes: The real price of coffee is defined as the U.S.$ coffee price deflated by the U.S.$ import price index. The effective exchange rate was computed using trade weights and taking into account Colombia's ten major trade partners. The partners (and weights) are: U.S. (0.507); U.K. (0.047); France (0.037); Germany (0.163); Italy (0.033); Netherlands (0.044); Japan (0.058); Sweden (0.032); Spain (0.035); and Venezuela (0.045). According to the definitions of the real exchange rate used in this paper, an increase in the index reflects a real depreciation, whereas a decline in the index represents a real appreciation.

Table 7.2   **Coffee Prices and Rates of Devaluation, Money Growth, International Reserves Growth, and Inflation in Colombia, 1968–82**

Year	Rate of Devaluation (%) (1)	Rate of Growth of High-Powered Money (%) (2)	Rate of Growth of International Reserves (U.S. $) (%) (3)	Rate of Inflation (%) (4)	Real Price of Coffee (1980 = 100) (5)
1968	12.3	23.9	—	5.7	64.3
1969	6.3	25.7	37.3	9.6	66.9
1970	6.5	19.1	−3.1	6.5	83.4
1971	8.1	12.9	−0.5	7.8	71.0
1972	9.7	16.5	64.0	12.6	75.7
1973	8.1	24.3	67.0	18.9	83.5
1974	10.3	22.8	−16.5	21.6	69.6
1975	18.7	21.2	10.2	20.7	68.4
1976	12.2	29.6	131.8	18.4	126.5
1977	6.0	34.2	58.7	28.6	182.0
1978	6.3	39.7	35.4	16.3	123.5
1979	8.8	33.0	62.5	22.1	112.5
1980	11.1	25.5	25.7	23.5	100.0
1981	15.3	23.5	−0.6	24.3	67.5
1982	17.6	18.4	−19.6	24.5	72.3

Sources: Columns (1) through (4), International Financial Statistics (*IFS*); column (5), table 7.1.

exports. Further, in the past the degree of import protection was altered depending on the behavior of coffee prices: it was reduced when the world price of coffee increased and was raised when the price of coffee declined. In addition, several monetary measures, including steep increases in the banking system reserves requirements, have been implemented when the price of coffee has risen. During the 1975–79 coffee bonanza, for example, a novel mechanism was implemented to reduce the monetary impact of the higher coffee price. Specifically, in 1977 the maturity of certificates of exchange—which are government certificates received by exporters when they surrender their foreign exchange—was significantly lengthened. In that way, the monetary effect of the coffee boom was postponed, but not avoided (Weisner 1978).[8]

Many experts have indicated that Colombia's adoption of a crawling-peg system in 1967 was in response to the need to reduce the dependence of the country's real exchange rate on coffee price fluctuations (Weisner 1978; Urrutia 1981; Ocampo 1983). Nonetheless, since the inception of the crawling-peg system, the decision on the rate at which the peso should be devalued has been highly influenced by coffee prices.

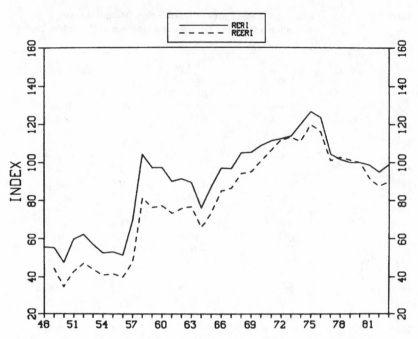

Fig. 7.1   Real (*RERI*) and real effective (*REERI*) exchange rate indexes in Colombia, 1948–83.

For example, according to Weisner (1978, 203), once the crawling peg was adopted, one of the main problems was to decide "at what pace to devalue when coffee prices rise." This problem has been compounded by a trade-off between the rate of nominal devaluation and inflation. In practice there has been an inverse relationship between the rate of devaluation of the peg and coffee prices. This relationship can be seen in table 7.2. The high coffee prices of 1976–79, for example, were accompanied by a significant slowdown in the rate of devaluation; when the price of coffee began to fall in 1980–82, the rate of the crawl was rapidly accelerated. This inverse relationship between world coffee prices and the nominal rate of devaluation in Colombia constitutes another mechanism—in addition to the effect of money creation on inflation—through which higher (lower) coffee prices have been translated into a lower (higher) real exchange rate.

Even though these measures, such as changes in the level of protection and variations in the maturity of exchange certificates, have helped reduce the degree of volatility of the real exchange rate, they have not eliminated its close dependence on the price of coffee. Nevertheless, since coffee prices are not the only determinants of the real exchange rate, during some periods its movement has mainly been in

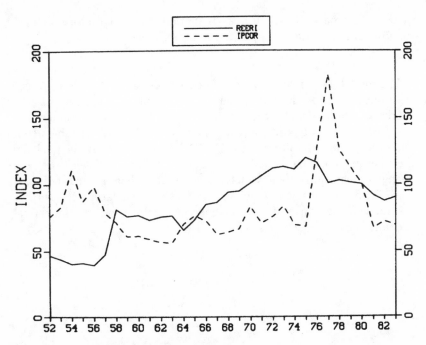

Fig. 7.2   Real exchange rates (*REERI*) and real prices (*IPCOR*) of coffee in Colombia, 1952–83.

response to other variables. Between 1968 and 1973, for example, changes in the real exchange rate were to a large extent the result of the lower degree of import protection and of the imposition of an export promotion scheme (Díaz-Alejandro 1976). The opening up of the Colombian economy carried out during this period resulted in a smooth real depreciation of the peso.

7.3 Coffee, Money, Inflation, and the Real Exchange Rate in Colombia

This section develops and estimates a model of the way in which coffee prices, money creation, inflation, and the real exchange rate interact. A central purpose of the model is to test formally whether, as a number of authors have casually observed, changes in coffee prices have indeed been related to money creation and inflation in Colombia. Also investigated is the extent to which manipulations of the rate of devaluation of the exchange rate have responded to coffee price changes. The model is quite simple, and its structure allows us to concentrate on the problem at hand without being sidetracked by other issues. An obvious drawback of this strategy is that the simple structure requires the imposition of some simplifying assumptions.

7.3.1 The Model

The model focuses on the effects of changes in (world) coffee prices on money creation, inflation, and exchange rate adjustment. As presented in equations (1) through (11) below, the model assumes that there are three goods in the economy: coffee (c), nontradables (N), and other (noncoffee) tradables (T). It also assumes that, as has been the case in Colombia since 1967, the economy has a crawling-peg exchange rate system, one in which the nominal exchange rate is adjusted periodically according to the behavior of a set of indicators. It is further assumed that because of the existence of capital controls, the capital account is exogenously given.

(1) $$\hat{M}_t = \omega \hat{R}_t + (1 - \omega)\,\hat{C}_t;$$

(2) $$\hat{C}_t = c_0 + \phi\,DEH_t + z_t;$$

(3) $$\hat{R}_t = \theta\,(\hat{M}_t^d - \hat{M}_{t-1}) + \psi\,\hat{P}_t^c;$$

(4) $$\hat{M}_t^d = \hat{P}_t + \eta\,\hat{y}_t;$$

(5) $$\hat{P}_t = (1 - \delta)\,\hat{P}_{Nt} + \delta\,\hat{P}_{Tt};$$

(6) $$\hat{P}_{Tt} = \hat{E}_t + \hat{P}_{Tt}^*;$$

(7) $$\hat{P}_t^c = \hat{E}_t + \hat{P}_t^{c*};$$

(8) $$\hat{P}_{Nt} = \hat{P}_{Tt} + \lambda(\hat{M}_t - \hat{M}_t^d) + \rho\,\hat{y}_t;$$

(9) $$\hat{E}_t = \gamma_0\hat{P}_t - \gamma_1\hat{P}_t^{c*} - \gamma_2\hat{y}_t - \gamma_3\hat{P}_{Tt}^* + \gamma_4 x_t;$$

(10) $$\hat{y}_t = g_t + \tau(\hat{P}_t^{c*} - \hat{P}_{Tt}^*);$$

(11) $$e_t = (E_t\,P_{Tt}^*)/P_t.$$

As is customary the "hat" operator ($\hat{\ }$) denotes a percentage change. The following notation is used:

$\hat{M}_t$ = the rate of growth of nominal money in period t;

$\hat{R}$ = the rate of change of international reserves (in pesos);

$\hat{C}$ = the rate of change of domestic credit;

DEH_t = the fiscal deficit in period t as a proportion of the stock of high-powered money in period $t - 1$;

P^c = the domestic price of coffee;

E = the nominal exchange rate, defined as units of domestic currency per unit of foreign currency;

y_t = real income in period t;

P = the domestic price level;
P_T = the domestic price of tradables;
P_N = the domestic price of nontradables;
P_T^* = the world price of tradables;
P_t^{c*} = the world price of coffee;
$\hat{P}_T^*$ = the world rate of inflation;
z_t = other variables influencing domestic credit policy;
x_t = other variables influencing the rate of devaluation of the crawling peg; and
e = the real exchange rate.

The letters ω, ϕ, θ, ψ, η, δ, λ, ρ, τ, and γ represent parameters.

Equations (1) through (4) represent the monetary side of this simple model. Equation (1) states that the percentage change in the nominal quantity of money is a weighted average of the growth rate of domestic credit and of international reserves. Equation (2) gives the growth rate of domestic credit. It is assumed that, as has been the case in Colombia since World War II, domestic credit creation is closely linked to the fiscal deficit (Weisner 1978, Edwards 1983; World Bank 1983 and 1984). In this version of the model it is assumed that the deficit is exogenously determined. This, however, is not the most appropriate assumption for the case of Colombia, where there is some evidence that the deficit and the price of coffee have been negatively related. Lower coffee prices have usually resulted in larger deficits, stemming (partially) from an increase in the government's financial assistance to coffee growers.[9] It is also assumed that domestic monetary policy can be influenced by other factors besides the fiscal deficit. These factors are summarized by the term z_t. Equation (3) depicts the behavior of international reserves over time. According to this expression, reserves respond to two elements. First, an excess (flow) demand for or supply of money will be (partially) reflected in the accumulation or decumulation of reserves. Second, changes in the (domestic) price of coffee in period t will be translated, in the same period, into corresponding changes in reserves.[10] The novelty of this formulation is that, contrary to most monetary models of open economies, it explicitly allows for international reserves shocks to be a source of money creation in the *short run*. In the long run, however, $\hat{P}_t^c = 0$ and $\hat{M}_t^d = \hat{M}_t = \hat{M}_{t-1}$, and reserves will not change (that is, $\hat{R}_t = 0$). Equation (4) presents the rate of change of the nominal quantity of money demanded, where for simplicity it is assumed that the real demand for money is a function only of real income. This assumption, however, is relaxed below, where the expected rate of inflation is also included as an argument in the demand-for-money equation.[11] The parameter η is the elasticity of the (real) demand for money with respect to real income. Combining equations (1) through (4), the following equation for the rate of growth of money in period t is obtained:

$$(12) \quad \hat{M}_t = -\omega\theta \, \hat{M}_{t-1} + \omega\theta \, \hat{P}_t + \omega\theta\eta \, \hat{y}_t + \omega\psi \, \hat{P}_t^c + (1 - \omega) \, \hat{C}_t.$$

Since ω and θ are smaller than one but positive, the convergence of (12) will be oscillatory. According to equation (12), then, a positive coffee price shock (that is, $\hat{P}_t^c > 0$) will result in a short-run increase in the rate of growth of money. But it is easy to verify from this equation that in the steady state (when $\hat{M}_t = \hat{M}_{t-1}$ and $\hat{P}_t^c = 0$) this economy will reach monetary equilibrium: $\hat{M}_t = (1 - \omega) \, \hat{C}_t = \hat{M}_t^d$.

Equations (5), (6), and (8) form the inflation side of the model. According to (5), the domestic rate of inflation is a weighted average of the rate of change in the domestic prices of tradables and nontradables; this equation assumes that the price of coffee is not included in the price level. According to equation (6), the rate of change in the domestic price of noncoffee tradables is equal to the rate of devaluation plus the world rate of inflation in the price of tradables. Equation (8), on the other hand, states that the rate of change in the price of nontradables will depend on the rate of change in the price of tradables, on changes in real income, and in the short run on the excess flow supply of nominal money in period t.[12] Combining equations (4), (5), (6), and (8) yields the following expression for the rate of inflation:

$$(13) \quad \hat{P}_t = \frac{(1 - \delta)\lambda}{1 + \lambda(1 - \delta)} \, \hat{M}_t + \frac{1}{1 + \lambda(1 - \delta)} \, (\hat{E}_t + \hat{P}_{Tt}^*)$$
$$- \frac{(1 - \delta)(\lambda\eta - \rho)}{1 + \lambda(1 - \delta)} \, \hat{y}_t.$$

Notice that in this equation the coefficients of nominal money creation and peso-denominated world inflation ($\hat{E}_t + \hat{P}_{Tt}^*$) add up to one. On the other hand, the coefficient of real income growth can be either negative or positive, depending on whether $\lambda\eta \gtrless \delta$.

Equation (9) is the rule of adjustment of the nominal exchange rate, or rule of crawl. It is assumed that the rate of devaluation in period t will depend on the rates of domestic and foreign inflation, on the rate of growth of real income, on the world price of coffee, and on other variables, such as commercial policies, captured by x_t. The values of the γ parameters will determine the type of crawl rule chosen by the authorities. If $\gamma_0 = 1$, $\gamma_3 = -1$, and $\gamma_2 = \gamma_1 = \gamma_4 = 0$, equation (9) becomes a strict Purchasing Power Parity (PPP) rule of crawl. It will be assumed in this paper that $0 \leq \gamma_0 \leq 1$. If $\gamma_1 = 0$, the authorities do not take into account the behavior of world coffee prices to determine the rate of the crawl. On the contrary, a positive γ_1 means that the authorities recognize the effect of changes in coffee prices on the real exchange rate and therefore try to accommodate them (partially) through adjustments in the nominal exchange rate. Since growth in real income will generate (through equation [8]) a positive pressure on the price of nontradables, $\hat{y}_t$ has been incorporated in equation (9) as a possible determinant of the rate of the crawl. In this way the government is allowed to accommodate the real appreciation resulting from higher growth by manipulating the rate of devaluation. Equation (10) is the rate of growth of real income, and it is formed of two components: a term that is independent from world coffee price behavior (g_t), and a term that depends on coffee prices— $\tau(\hat{P}_t^{c^*} - \hat{P}_{Tt}^*)$. An increase in the world real price of coffee generates a higher real income. Finally, equation (11) is the definition of the real exchange rate. This particular definition of e has been chosen because it has a close empirical counterpart. Alternatively, the real exchange rate could be defined as $E_t P_{Tt}^*/P_{Nt}$. All the qualitative effects discussed in this section will also hold for this definition of the real exchange rate.

The model works in the following way. An increase in the (real) world price of coffee results in higher real income (through equation [10]) and in an increased demand for nontradables. This higher demand, in its turn, affects, through equation (8), the relative price of nontradables. This is the *spending* effect of a commodity export boom (Corden 1982; Edwards and Aoki 1983). Independently of monetary or nominal exchange rate behavior, the higher price of coffee generates a real appreciation.

Let us turn now to the money side. The higher price of coffee, with its resulting higher real income and price of nontradables, affects both the demand for and the supply of money. From equation (4), a higher demand for nominal (and real) money will result. According to equations (3) and (1), however, after the export boom the rate of growth of money creation will also be higher. Depending on the value of the parameters involved, a higher price of coffee can result in either an excess flow supply of money or an excess flow demand for money. The more plausible case of a resulting excess supply of money will be considered here. Through equation (8) this excess supply of money will influence the nominal price of nontradables, further appreciating the real exchange rate.[13] What is the role of the rule of crawl in this story? Two things will happen according to equation (9). First, as a result of the higher coffee price, the rate of the crawl will be slowed down in period t, helping to accommodate the real appreciation generated by the spending effect. This will happen through two channels: $-\gamma_1 \hat{P}_t^{c^*}$ and $-\gamma_2 \tau \hat{P}_t^{c^*}$. Second, there will be a tendency (partially) to compensate the nominal exchange rate for the higher rate of inflation, through $\gamma_0 \hat{P}_t$. The final effect will be a real appreciation, resulting partially from the slowing down of the rate of the crawl and partially from higher inflation. If the liquidity or money creation effect generated by the higher price of coffee is large enough, the real appreciation may be larger in the short run than in the long run.

Equations (9), (12), and (13) can be solved for $\hat{M}_t$, $\hat{P}_t$, and $\hat{E}_t$ in terms of exogenous variables only. These solutions can then be combined with $\hat{P}_{Tt}^*$ to find the formal reduced form for the actual rate of change in the real exchange rate. An interesting property of this model is that under an appropriate parameterization, it can generate time paths of the different variables that closely resemble what is observed. Under the simplifying assumptions that $\hat{P}_{Tt}^* = 0$, $z_t = 0$, and $\gamma_4 = 0$, the following expression for the actual change in the real exchange rate in period t is obtained:[14] (the reduced forms for $\hat{M}_t$, $\hat{P}_t$, and $\hat{E}_t$ are provided in appendix A):

$$(14) \quad \hat{e}_t = -\beta_0\pi_1(\gamma_0 - 1)\Delta^{-1}\,\hat{M}_{t-1} + \beta_0\pi_6(\gamma_0 - 1)\Delta^{-1}\,DEH_t$$
$$-A_1g_t - (A_1 + A_2)\hat{P}_t^{c^*}$$

where

$$A_1 = [\gamma_2(1 - \beta_0(\pi_2 + \pi_4) - \beta_1) + \beta_2(\gamma_0 - 1) + \beta_0\pi_3(1 - \gamma_0)]\Delta^{-1}$$

$$A_2 = [\gamma_1(1 - \beta_0\pi_2) + \beta_0\pi_4(1 - \gamma_0) - \gamma_1(\beta_1 + \beta_0\pi_5)]\Delta^{-1}$$

and

$$\beta_0 = \frac{(1 - \delta)\lambda}{1 + \lambda(1 - \delta)}\,; \quad \beta_1 = \frac{1}{1 + \lambda(1 - \delta)}\,;$$

$$\beta_2 = \frac{(1 - \delta)(\lambda\eta - \rho)}{1 + \lambda(1 - \delta)}\,; \quad \pi_1 = \omega\theta;$$

$$\pi_2 = \omega\theta; \quad\quad\quad\quad\quad \pi_3 = \omega\theta\eta;$$

$$\pi_4 = \omega\psi; \quad\quad\quad\quad\quad \pi_5 = \omega\psi;$$

$$\pi_6 = (1 - \omega)\phi; \quad\quad\quad \Delta = 1 - [\beta_0\pi_2 + \gamma_0(\beta_0\pi_5 + \beta_1)].$$

From equation (14) it is possible to find out, among other things, how an increase in the world price of coffee will affect the actual real exchange rate in period t. Let us first look at the term A_1. This term captures the spending effect of a change in the price of coffee on the real exchange rate. Since stability requires that $\Delta > 0$, the spending effect will, as expected, generate a real appreciation.[15] Next, the term A_2 captures the inflation and exchange rate effects of the higher price of coffee on the real exchange rate in t. As can be seen from this expression, there are three different channels, in addition to the spending effect, through which changes in coffee prices will affect e. Two of these channels indicate that a higher price of coffee will generate a real appreciation.[16] The third channel, however, suggests that $\hat{e}$ and $\hat{p}^{c*}$ are positively related.

There are two main forces exerting a negative effect of $\hat{p}^{c*}$ on $\hat{e}$. First, a higher world price of coffee causes an increase in international reserves and money growth in the same period (see appendix A). Assuming that an excess flow supply of money results, inflation and, other things equal, a real appreciation will be the consequence. Second, according to equation (13), an increase in the world price of coffee slows down the rate of the crawl. The price increase also tends to bring about a real appreciation, other things equal. The forces that tend to generate a real depreciation as a consequence of the increase in the world price of coffee are of a second order of magnitude and work through the following channel. The higher world price of coffee reduces the rate of the crawl and consequently, through equation (13), the domestic price of tradables and inflation. These lower rates of inflation and devaluation, in turn, will tend to result in a lower rate of domestic money creation, through equation (12), and even lower inflation. This lower inflation, of course, will generate, with other things equal, a real depreciation. Given the second-order nature of this effect, however, the strong presumption is that under normal circumstances (that is, if the values of the parameters involved are plausible) the appreciation effects will dominate. But this is an empirical issue, one that will be resolved with the estimation of the model.[17]

It should be noticed that the model presented here employs some simplifying assumptions, including the exogeneity of DEH_t. It also assumes that the exchange rates applied to coffee and to other external transactions change at the same rate. In Colombia, however, a dual exchange rate system has been in effect during some years, with the net exchange rate for coffee changing at a rate somewhat different from the exchange rate prevailing in the rest of the economy (Weisner 1978).

The model presented above does not allow a distinction between the effect of coffee price changes perceived to be permanent and the effect of those perceived to be temporary. The model can be altered in several possible ways to allow for this distinction. The simplest way is to incorporate expected inflation as a factor in the demand-for-money equation:[18]

$$(15) \qquad \left(\frac{M}{P}\right)_t = y_t^\mu \, e^{-a\hat{P}_t^e},$$

where $\hat{P}_t^e$ is the rate of expected inflation, defined as $E_t (\log P_{t+1} - \log P_t)$, and E_t is the expectations operator. It is assumed that expectations are rational and formed conditional on all the information available up to period t. When equation (15) is used to represent the demand-for-money function, equation (14) for the change in the real exchange rate becomes:

$$(16) \quad \hat{e}_t = -b_0\pi_1(\delta_0 - 1) D^{-1} \hat{M}_{t-1} + \beta_0\pi_6 (\gamma_0 - 1) D^{-1}DEH_t$$
$$-B_1g_t - (B_1 + B_2) \hat{P}_t^{c^*} + (\gamma_0 - 1) b_3 \hat{P}_{t+1}^e,$$

where the expected inflation term, $\hat{P}_{t+1}^e$, is:

$$(17) \qquad \hat{P}_{t+1}^e = d \sum_{k=0}^{\infty} b^k E_t(\hat{P}_{t+1+k}^{c^*}) + \ldots ,$$

and where the Bs are:

$$B_1 = \{\gamma_2[1 - b_0(\pi_2 + \pi_4) - b_1] + b_2(\gamma_0 - 1) + b_0\pi_3(1 - \gamma_0)\}D^{-1}$$

$$B_2 = [\gamma_1(1 - b_0\pi_2) + b_0\pi_4(1 - \gamma_0) - \gamma_1(b_1 + b_0\pi_5)]D^{-1}$$

and d, D, and the bs are:

$$d = [b_0(\pi_4 + \pi_3) - (\pi_5 b_0 + b_1)(\gamma_1 + \gamma_2) - b_2];$$

$$D = 1 - [b_0\pi_2 + \delta_0(b_0\pi_5 + b_1)];$$

$$b = \frac{(1 - \delta)\lambda a}{1 + (1 - \delta)\lambda (1 + a)} ; \quad b_0 = \frac{(1 - \delta)\lambda}{1 + (1 - \delta)\lambda (1 + a)} ;$$

$$b_1 = \frac{1}{1 + (1 - \delta)\lambda (1 + a)} ; \quad b_2 = \frac{(1 - \delta)(\lambda\eta - \rho)}{1 + (1 - \delta)\lambda (1 + a)} .$$

The main difference between the new equation (16) for the real exchange rate and equation (14) is that an expected inflation term, $\hat{P}_{t+1}^e$, appears in equation (16). This is a crucial difference, since as shown in equation (17) $\hat{P}_{t+1}^e$ is a function, among other things, of all future expected changes in the price of coffee. That is, once the role of expectations is incorporated into the model, the change in the real exchange rate will depend on all the expected future values of the price of coffee and on the other exogenous variables. Now, for example, if the change in the price of coffee is expected to be permanent, the change in the real exchange rate will correspond to that already discussed above (equation [14]). But if the higher price of coffee is expected to last for one period only, $E_t (\hat{P}_{t+1}^{c^*}) = -\hat{P}_t^{c^*}$, and as equations (16) and (17) show, the real appreciation in period t will be smaller than it would be in the case of a permanent increase in the price of coffee. Another important characteristic of equation (16) is that it is not necessary for the price of coffee to increase to generate a real appreciation. If world coffee prices are only expected to increase in the future, a real appreciation will now take place.

7.3.2 Estimation

This section presents the results obtained from an estimation of a slight variant of the model given by equations (9), (12), and (13). Since from an empirical perspective it is difficult to make a distinction between temporary and permanent changes in the price of coffee, the results reported here do not take this distinction into account.[19] The estimation was performed using annual data for the years 1952–80, with an explicit distinction made between the pre-1967 and the post-1967 periods. The following variant of the money creation equation (12) was estimated (where the v_i terms are error terms):

$$(18) \quad \hat{M}_t = \alpha_0 + \alpha_1 \hat{M}_{t-1} + \alpha_2 \hat{M}_{t-2} + \alpha_3 \hat{M}_{t-3}$$
$$+ \alpha_4 DEH_t + \alpha_5 (\hat{E}_t + \hat{P}_t^{c*}) + v_{1t}.$$

The following version of the inflation equation (12) was estimated, where DUM is a dummy variable that takes a value of zero up to 1967 and a value of one thereafter.

$$(19) \quad \hat{P}_t = \delta_0 + \delta_1 \hat{M}_t + \delta_2 \hat{y}_t + \delta_3 (\hat{E}_t + \hat{P}_{Tt}^*) + \delta_4 DUM_t + v_{2t}.$$

Finally, the exchange rate devaluation equation was the following:

$$(20) \quad \hat{E}_t = \mu_0 + \mu_1 \hat{P}_t + \mu_2 (\hat{P}_t DUM_t) + \mu_3 \hat{P}_{Tt}^*$$
$$+ \mu_4 \hat{P}_t^{c*} + \mu_5 DUM_t + v_{3t}.$$

The system given by equations (18), (19), and (20) was estimated using two- and three-stage least-squares for the years 1952–80. The results obtained are presented in tables 7.3 and 7.4. The data sources are given in Appendix B. As may be seen, these results are very satisfactory. Most of the coefficients have the expected signs and are significant at the conventional levels.

The most interesting result from the estimation of the money creation equations is that they confirm the hypothesis that higher (domestic) prices of coffee resulted in *short-run* increases in the rate of money creation. As discussed above, the mechanism through which this takes place is the accumulation of international reserves that are monetized by the central bank. Moreover, the estimates of the coefficients of the lagged $\hat{M}$ terms suggest that the effect of changes in coffee prices on money growth has some persistence over time. The estimation of the money growth equation (18), then, provides statistical support to the claim made by numerous authors (for example, Weisner 1978; Urrutia 1981) that Colombia's ability to carry out a successful monetary policy has been hampered by the dependence of money creation on the behavior of coffee prices. These results also support the hypothesis that the process of money creation in Colombia has been critically influenced by the behavior of the fiscal side of the economy (equations

Table 7.3   **Two-Stage Least-Squares Estimation of the Model, for the Years 1952–80**

Equation No.	Estimation	S.E.E.	D.W.
(18.1)	$\hat{M}_t = \underset{(-0.177)}{-0.006} + \underset{(3.596)}{0.634}\,\hat{M}_{t-1} + \underset{(0.691)}{0.123}\,\hat{M}_{t-2} + \underset{(2.293)}{0.140}\,\hat{M}_{t-3} + \underset{(3.354)}{0.222}\,DEH_t + \underset{(2.023)}{0.079}\,(\hat{P}_t^* + \hat{E}_t)$	0.037	2.238
(19.1)	$\hat{P}_t = \underset{(-0.729)}{-0.006} + \underset{(2.669)}{0.705}\,\hat{M}_t - \underset{(-0.363)}{0.040}\,\hat{y}_t + \underset{(2.182)}{0.311}\,(\hat{E}_t + \hat{P}_{Tt}^*) + \underset{(0.314)}{0.010}\,DUM_t$	0.060	2.231
(20.1)	$\hat{E}_t = \underset{(-0.119)}{-0.006} + \underset{(2.569)}{1.333}\,\hat{P}_t - \underset{(-1.678)}{0.850}\,(\hat{P}_t\,DUM_t) - \underset{(-0.063)}{0.060}\,\hat{P}_{Tt}^* - \underset{(-1.604)}{0.198}\,\hat{P}_t^* + \underset{(0.469)}{0.043}\,DUM_t$	0.108	1.728

Notes: The numbers in parentheses are t-statistics. S.E.E. is the standard error of the regression. D.W. is the Durbin-Watson statistic. The following instruments were used: lagged, twice lagged and three periods lagged, $\hat{M}$, contemporaneous, and lagged *DEH*, the world price of coffee, world inflation, lagged inflation, the change in the world price of coffee, the dummy variable, and a constant.

Table 7.4   **Three-Stage Least-Squares Estimation of the Model, for the Years 1952–80**

Equation No.	Estimation	S.E.E.	D.W.
(18.2)	$\hat{M}_t = \underset{(0.130)}{0.004} + \underset{(4.115)}{0.602}\,\hat{M}_{t-1} + \underset{(1.014)}{0.145}\,\hat{M}_{t-2} + \underset{(2.165)}{0.109}\,\hat{M}_{t-3} + \underset{(3.218)}{0.180}\,DEH_t + \underset{(2.882)}{0.096}\,(\hat{P}_t^* + \hat{E}_t)$	0.034	2.280
(19.2)	$\hat{P}_t = \underset{(-1.303)}{-0.077} + \underset{(3.331)}{0.723}\,\hat{M}_t + \underset{(0.609)}{0.005}\,\hat{y}_t + \underset{(3.596)}{0.411}\,(\hat{E}_t + \hat{P}_{Tt}^*) + \underset{(0.487)}{0.013}\,DUM_t$	0.057	2.175
(20.2)	$\hat{E}_t = \underset{(-0.637)}{-0.027} + \underset{(4.057)}{1.574}\,\hat{P}_t - \underset{(-1.208)}{0.732}\,(\hat{P}_t\,DUM_t) - \underset{(-0.645)}{0.463}\,\hat{P}_t^* - \underset{(-1.349)}{0.124}\,\hat{P}_{ct}^* + \underset{(0.419)}{0.031}\,DUM_t$	0.102	1.709

Note: The specifications and abbreviations are as described in the note to table 7.3.

[18.1] and [18.2] in the tables). An increase in the fiscal deficit, measured as a proportion of lagged base money, of 10 percentage points resulted, on average, in an increase in the rate of growth of money of approximately 1.8 to 2.2 percentage points. This finding illustrates that the separation of the fiscal and monetary sides of the economy in traditional macroeconomic analysis may not be fully appropriate in studying less developed countries. In developing countries—and especially in Latin America—fiscal deficits are usually financed by printing money; the LM and IS curves are not fully independent.

The estimation of the inflation equation (19) also yields interesting results. With the exception of income growth and the dummy variable, the coefficients are significant and have the expected signs. The coefficient of $\hat{M}_t$ indicates that, with other things equal, an increase in the rate of money creation of 10 percentage points resulted in an increase in inflation of approximately 7 percentage points. On the other hand, according to the coefficient of $(\hat{E}_t + \hat{P}^*_{Tt})$ a higher rate of devaluation or higher world inflation, or both, was passed on in almost one third to price increases.[20] As the model indicates, the sum of the coefficients of the prices of $\hat{M}_t$ and $(\hat{E}_t + \hat{P}^*_{Tt})$ were not significantly different from one. The coefficient of real income growth was, however, insignificant in all the regressions.

The exchange rate adjustment equation (20) yielded, in some sense, less satisfactory results. The estimation indicates that for the post-1967 period—after the crawling peg was adopted—and with other things equal, the exchange rate tended to be adjusted by less than the ongoing domestic rate of inflation. Nonetheless, these results confirm the hypothesis that the Colombian authorities took into account the behavior of world coffee prices when deciding by how much to devalue the nominal exchange rate. Lower (higher) world coffee prices resulted in higher (lower) rates of the devaluation of the crawl. Given the relatively poor results obtained from the estimation of equation (20), several alternative specifications of the exchange rate adjustment equation were also tried. Some of the results obtained are presented in table 7.5, where $\hat{R}^r_t$ is the percentage change in the real value of international reserves, measured in dollar terms. The nonsignificance of the coefficient of this reserves change variable confirms Urrutia's (1981) contention that the Colombian authorities did not directly take into account the level of international liquidity when deciding by how much to devalue the nominal exchange rate. The negative and insignificant coefficient of $\hat{M}_t$ is somewhat surprising, however, because it has been argued that changes in the nominal stock of money have been an important indicator when deciding the rate of devaluation of the peso (Urrutia 1981). Even though these regressions do not represent a significant improvement over those reported in tables 7.3 and 7.4, they do confirm the fact that the rate of devaluation has been positively related to the domestic rate of inflation—with an average coefficient of around one—and negatively related to the behavior of the world price of coffee.

The point estimates obtained from the regression analysis of equations (18) through (20) can be combined to get an approximate idea of the way in which coffee price changes will affect the real exchange rate. For example, from the estimates reported in table 7.3, the effects of changes in world coffee prices on inflation, nominal devaluation, and the real exchange rate, assuming all other exogenous variables as given, are:

$$\hat{P}_t = \frac{\alpha_5 \delta_1 + \delta_3 + \delta_1 \alpha_6}{(\mu_1 + \mu_2 DUM)(\delta_3 + \alpha_5 \delta_1)} \hat{P}_t^{c^*} = 0.513 \, \hat{P}_t^{c^*};$$

$$\hat{E}_t = \frac{(\mu_1 + \mu_2 DUM) \, \delta_1 \alpha_6 + \mu_4}{(\mu_1 + \mu_2 DUM)(\delta_3 + \alpha_5 \delta_1)} \hat{P}_t^{c^*} = -0.208 \, \hat{P}_t^{c^*};$$

$$\hat{e}_t = \frac{(\mu_1 + \mu_2 DUM)\delta_1 \alpha_6 + \mu_4 - (\alpha_5 \delta_1 + \delta_3 + \delta_1 \alpha_6)}{(\mu_1 + \mu_2 DUM)(\delta_3 + \alpha_5 \delta_1)} \hat{P}_t^{c^*}$$

$$= -0.721 \, \hat{P}_t^{c^*}.$$

These numbers are obviously quite large, suggesting that, other things equal, a change in coffee prices will result in substantial changes in inflation, the rate of devaluation, and the real exchange rate. In fact, these results suggest that immediately following an increase in world coffee prices most of the resulting real appreciation will materialize through the money creation and inflation channels. A possible problem with this exercise, however, is the assumption that other things are equal. As discussed above, coffee price movements are likely to be related to some of the variables I have considered exogenous here. In particular, coffee price movements will result in changes in real income, the fiscal deficit, and world inflation. In addition, since no distinction between temporary and permanent changes has been made in the estimation, the results from this exercise should be interpreted with caution.

To summarize, I have developed and estimated in this section a model of the interaction between commodity export prices and the real exchange rate in Colombia. The model focused on three basic elements: the money creation process ($\hat{M}_t$); domestic inflation ($\hat{P}_t$); and the rate of adjustment of the nominal exchange rate ($\hat{E}_t$). These last two elements, plus the rate of foreign inflation, $\hat{P}_{Tt}^*$, constitute, by definition, the elements that determine the behavior of the real exchange rate over time (that is, $\hat{e}_t = \hat{E}_t - \hat{P}_t + \hat{P}_{Tt}^*$). The model

Table 7.5   Two-Stage Least-Squares Estimation of the Exchange Rate Adjustment Equation, for the Years 1952–80

Equation No.	Estimation	S.E.E.	D.W.
(20.3)	$\hat{E}_t = \underset{(0.539)}{0.029} + \underset{(2.452)}{1.273}\,\hat{P}_t - \underset{(-1.050)}{0.961}\,\hat{P}^*_{Tt} - \underset{(-1.168)}{0.424}\,\hat{P}_{t-1} + \underset{(1.251)}{0.967}\,\hat{P}^*_{Tt-1} - \underset{(-2.243)}{0.295}\,\hat{P}^*_t + \underset{(0.854)}{0.052}\,\hat{R}^r_t - \underset{(-0.833)}{0.054}\,DUM_t$	0.115	1.856
(20.4)	$\hat{E} = \underset{(1.812)}{0.223} + \underset{(2.458)}{1.258}\,\hat{P}_t + \underset{(0.081)}{0.089}\,\hat{P}^*_{Tt} - \underset{(-0.603)}{0.225}\,\hat{P}_{t-1} - \underset{(-0.914)}{0.071}\,\hat{P}^*_{Tt-1} - \underset{(-1.769)}{1.364}\,\hat{M}_t - \underset{(-1.617)}{0.172}\,\hat{P}^c_t + \underset{(0.669)}{0.039}\,\hat{R}^r - \underset{(-0.632)}{0.041}\,DUM_t$	0.113	2.220

Note: See table 7.3 for all specifications and abbreviations.

incorporated the traditional spending effect of a commodity export boom and explicitly took into account the monetary effects of changes in commodity prices. In particular, and contrary to most Dutch disease models, the model developed here explicitly allowed for changes in the price of coffee to affect, in the short run, the rate of money growth. The results obtained from the regression analysis were, in some sense, surprisingly robust, and they confirmed the basic hypothesis that higher (lower) coffee prices lead to higher (lower) rates of money growth and consequently in higher (lower) inflation rates. The regressions also showed that the rate at which the Colombian authorities have adjusted the exchange rate has been negatively related to coffee prices: higher (lower) coffee prices have resulted in slower (faster) rates of devaluation.

7.4 Concluding Remarks

With increasing regularity, the exchange rate is being singled out as one of the most important economic variables in developing countries. In fact, it is almost impossible these days to discuss macroeconomic policy problems in the less developed countries without addressing exchange rate issues. From a policy perspective one of the most important problems is determining whether the real exchange rate in a particular country is out of line with respect to its equilibrium value.[21] To the extent that the real exchange rate is misaligned, policy actions designed to reestablish equilibrium will be called for.[22] From a policy viewpoint, then, a crucial aspect of any analysis of real exchange rates is to distinguish between equilibrium and disequilibrium movements of these rates. Only in this way will it be possible to develop appropriate policy measures.

In spite of the obvious policy importance of analyzing the mechanism through which real exchange rate movements take place, very few empirical studies have tackled this problem. In this paper the more specific problem of the effect of commodity export price changes on the real exchange rate has been investigated empirically. The third section of the paper developed and estimated a model of the effects of coffee price changes on money creation, inflation, and the rate of devaluation in Colombia. A virtue of this model is that it highlights two of the channels that have been traditionally mentioned in casual discussions of the effect of commodity price changes on the real exchange rate: money creation and inflation, and the rate of adjustment of the nominal exchange rate (the rate of devaluation of the crawling peg).

The model showed that commodity export booms will generally lead to short-run increases in money creation and inflation and to a real appreciation. In fact, it is possible that the real appreciation generated through this channel exceeds the "equilibrium" real appreciation resulting from the boom. If this boom is perceived as temporary, the real appreciation will be smaller but still potentially significant. An important question that arises in this context is whether there are mechanisms that would allow the authorities to reduce the impact of the changes in commodity export prices on the real exchange rate. Although the model presented here suggests that some mechanisms could actually be made available, none of them is easy to implement or free of problems. First, open market operations could be used to sterilize the monetary impact of changes in coffee prices. A problem with this type of solution in developing countries, however, is that local capital markets have not reached the stage of development required to perform massive open market operations. A second alternative would be to manipulate commercial policy to reduce the fluctuation in the real exchange rate. If commodity export prices are highly volatile, however, this option will be to a large extent impractical. Finally, another alternative is to open the capital account, allowing the short-run excess liquidity generated by the export boom to be curbed by outflows of capital. One problem with this measure, however, is that by fully opening the capital account, other sources of instability could arise.[23]

The model presented in this paper was empirically tested for the case of coffee in Colombia. The results obtained indicate that coffee price changes have indeed been closely related to money creation and inflation. Furthermore, coffee price changes have been negatively related to the rate of devaluation. These results suggest that in Colombia the real appreciation resulting from coffee price increases has been accommodated partially by money creation and inflation and partially by an adjustment in the nominal exchange rate.

The model employed here was deliberately designed to be simple and limited in its scope. As such, it has been useful in clearly pinpointing the role of coffee in the inflation and devaluation process. A drawback of that approach, however, was that it required making some simplifying assumptions.[24]

Appendix A: Solution of the Model in 7.3

Equations (10), (11), and (12) can be combined to find the reduced-form solutions for $\hat{M}_t$, $\hat{P}_t$, and $\hat{E}_t$. Under the simplifying assumption that $\hat{P}_{Tt}^* = 0$ these solutions are:

(A1) $\hat{M}_t = -\pi_1(1 - \gamma_0\beta_1) \Delta^{-1} \hat{M}_{t-1} + \pi_6(1 - \gamma_0\beta_1) \Delta^{-1} DEH_t$
$+ [\pi_4(1 - \gamma_0\beta_1) - \gamma_1(\pi_2\beta_1 + \pi_5)] \Delta^{-1} \hat{P}_t^{c*}$
$- [\beta_2(\pi_2 + \gamma_0\pi_5) + \gamma_2 (\pi_2\beta_1 + \pi_5)$
$- \pi_3(1 - \gamma_0\beta_1)] \Delta^{-1} \hat{y}_t;$

(A2) $\hat{P}_t = - \beta_0\pi_1\Delta^{-1} \hat{M}_{t-1} + \beta_0\pi_6\Delta^{-1} DEH_t$
$- [\beta_2 + (\pi_5\beta_0 + \beta_1)\gamma_2 - \beta_0\pi_3]\Delta^{-1} \hat{y}_t$
$+ [\beta_0\pi_4 - \gamma_1(\pi_5\beta_0 + \beta_1)]\Delta^{-1} \hat{P}_t^{c*};$

(A3) $\hat{E}_t = - \beta_0\gamma_0\pi_1\Delta^{-1} \hat{M}_{t-1} - [\gamma_1(1 - \beta_0\pi_2) - \beta_0\gamma_0\pi_4]\Delta^{-1} \hat{P}_t^{c*}$
$- [(1 - \beta_0\pi_0)\gamma_2 + \beta_2\gamma_0 - \beta_0\gamma_0\pi_3]\Delta^{-1} \hat{y}_t$
$+ \beta_0\gamma_0\pi_6 \Delta^{-1} DEH_t,$

where:

$$\beta_0 = \frac{(1 - \delta)\lambda}{1 + \lambda(1 - \delta)} \; ; \beta_1 = \frac{1}{1 + \lambda(1 - \delta)} \; ;$$

$$\beta_2 = \frac{(1 - \delta)(\lambda\eta - \rho)}{1 + \lambda(1 - \delta)} \; ; \pi_1 = \omega\theta;$$

$$\pi_2 = \omega\theta; \pi_3 = \omega\theta\eta;$$

$$\pi_4 = \omega\psi; \pi_5 = \omega\psi;$$

$$\pi_6 = (1 - \omega)\phi; \Delta = 1 - [\beta_0\pi_2 + \gamma_0(\beta_0\pi_5 + \beta_1)].$$

Stability requires that $|\pi_1(1 - \gamma_0\beta_1)\Delta^{-1}| < 1$. Notice that in this Appendix, in order to simplify the presentation, the rate of growth of real output $\hat{y}_t$ has not been decomposed into its exogenous term g_t and its coffee price–induced term $\tau\hat{P}_t^{c*}$.

Appendix B: Data Sources

All data refer to annual averages.

E	= Pesos per U.S.\$ nominal exchange rate, taken from International Financial Statistics (*IFS*).
M	= M_2 definition of money taken from *IFS*.
P	= Consumer price index taken from *IFS*.
y	= Real gross domestic product taken from *IFS*.

P_T = Price of tradables in pesos. Constructed as the product of the U.S. wholesale price index and the Colombian exchange rate.

P^{c^*} = Price of coffee in dollar terms. Constructed from data in the *IFS*.

DEH = Fiscal deficit, in nominal terms, scaled by the lagged quantity of high-powered money. For the years 1970–80, data that correct for the *cuenta especial de cambio* are used. These data were supplied by Colombia's Departamento Nacional de Planeación.

Notes

1. Much of this work has been done in the context of Dutch disease models. See, for example, the survey of these models by Corden (1982).

2. On the monetary effects of commodity export booms, see, for example, Harberger (1983), Edwards and Aoki (1983), Neary (1984), and Neary and van Wijnbergen (1984). Notice that an export boom will also generate an increase in the demand for money. Inflation will result only if the liquidity effect of the commodity boom exceeds the increase in the quantity of money demanded (see Edwards and Aoki 1983).

3. Moreover, very few papers have discussed the mechanism through which real exchange rate changes actually take place following changes in commodity export prices. Under floating exchange rates, fluctuations in the nominal exchange rate are the main mechanism. Under fixed exchange rates, however, the real exchange rate adjustment will require a change in the price level (more exactly, a change in the nominal price of nontradables) and in the stock of money. In a more general case, the adjustment could be distributed between inflation and nominal exchange rate changes. An important question, and one that has not yet been addressed, is to define the most efficient mechanism for bringing about the real exchange rate adjustment. Another important problem, which also has not been analyzed in detail, is the desirability of allowing the real exchange rate to appreciate when the commodity export boom stems from a *temporary* hike in export prices.

4. On the Colombian economy see, for example, Díaz-Alejandro (1976), Ocampo (1983), Weisner (1978), Kamas (1983), World Bank (1983, 1984). Some recent studies, however, have empirically analyzed the relationship between the terms of trade and the real exchange rate. See, for example, Díaz-Alejandro (1984) and Edwards (1984a).

5. Coffee represents approximately 55 percent of Colombia's foreign earnings from legal exports. It is important to notice that the importance of illegal exports in the Colombian economy makes the empirical analysis of the external sector quite difficult. For obvious reasons there are no reliable data on the magnitude of these illegal transactions. On the importance of illegal exports in Colombia, see Junguito and Caballero (1978).

6. The increase in the world price of coffee will result in a higher real income and consequently in a higher demand for money. Inflation will result only if the accumulation of reserves exceeds the increase in the demand for money (Edwards and Aoki 1983). A number of authors have argued that over the years 1975–79 the resulting inflation largely exceeded what was required to accommodate the equilibrium real appreciation (Weisner 1978; World Bank 1984).

7. To the extent that there are adjustment costs, rigidities, and inflexibilities, short-run real exchange rate movement generated by temporary swings in commodity export

prices can indeed result in adverse (that is, welfare-reducing) effects. See Edwards and Aoki (1983).

8. On the institutional arrangements used for coffee marketing and exporting in Colombia, see the detailed description in World Bank (1984).

9. On credits to coffee growers and fiscal deficits, see Weisner (1978, p. 186). Another simplification in equation (4) is that it does not explicitly allow for sterilization by linking reserves changes to credit creation. Nonetheless, to the extent that DEH_t is negatively related to coffee prices, an indirect channel to trigger (partial) sterilization is allowed. On sterilization in Colombia, see Kamas (1983).

10. Notice that another simplifying assumption of this model is that it ignores the demand for international reserves. For the important role played by reserves demand in Colombia, see Weisner (1978, chap. 1). See also Diaz-Alejandro (1976). For a discussion on the integration of the demand-for-reserves theory and monetary equilibrium, see Edwards (1984b).

11. A reason to ignore interest rates in the demand-for-money function is that there are no reliable data on interest rates in Colombia for the entire period considered in this study. See, however, the discussion below. On interest-rate behavior in Colombia since 1968, see Edwards (1985).

12. This equation can be derived from the equilibrium condition in the nontradable goods sector. See Edwards (1984c).

13. Notice that the assumption of an exogenously given capital account plays an important role here. If, on the contrary, there is perfect capital mobility, the incipient excess supply of money resulting from the higher coffee price would be rapidly eliminated through the capital account, without affecting the price of nontradables.

14. Equation (14) gives the actual short-run, and not necessarily the equilibrium long-run, change in the real exchange rate resulting from a change in coffee prices. To determine the long-run effect, we would have to solve equations (10), (8), (7), and (11) under the conditions of monetary equilibrium.

15. See appendix A. Notice that the real appreciation will take place if the following (plausible) conditions hold: $\omega(\theta + \psi) < 1$; $\gamma_0 \leq 1$; and $\rho > \lambda\eta$. These are sufficient conditions.

16. Díaz-Alejandro (1984) reported results from regressions of the level of the (log of the) real exchange rate and a set of explanatory variables for Colombia and other Latin American countries. For Colombia the coefficient of the (log of the) terms of trade was significantly negative (-0.56), as expected. See also Edwards (1984a).

17. From equation (13) it is also possible to find how changes in the other exogenous variables, such as the fiscal deficit, affect the real exchange rate.

18. There are two other ways to introduce the difference between permanent and temporary changes in coffee prices: changes in permanent income, instead of actual real income, can be used in equation (8); and in the crawling-peg equation the term for coffee price changes can be split in two parts, one corresponding to changes perceived to be temporary, and the other to changes perceived to be permanent.

19. See, however, Cumby and van Wijnbergen (1984).

20. These results are consistent with those obtained by Hanson (1982). See also Edwards (1984c). The money growth equations were also estimated for shorter periods of time. The results obtained confirm those reported in this paper. See World Bank (1984).

21. Cline (1983), for example, has recently pointed out that in many LDCs real exchange rate misalignments contributed to the international debt crisis.

22. On real exchange rate disequilibria and policies to realign them see, for example, Williamson (1983), Artus and Knight (1984), and Edwards (1984a).

23. This is not necessarily the case. On the effect of opening the capital account on the balance of payments in developing countries, see Edwards (1984d) and Obstfeld (1984).

24. A possible interesting extension of this model would be to incorporate an explicit equation for the current account, deriving from it the equilibrium real exchange rate. Even though this is not a difficult thing to do theoretically, the empirical implementation would be much more difficult.

References

Artus, Jacques, and Knight, Malcolm. 1984. Issues in the assessment of the exchange rates in industrial countries, International Monetary Fund Occasional Paper no. 29. Washington, D.C.: IMF.

Cline, William C. 1983. *International debt and stability of the world economy.* Washington, D.C.: Institute for International Economics.

Corden, Max. 1982. Booming sector and Dutch-disease economics: A survey. Working Paper no. 079. Canberra: Australian National University.

Cumby, Robert, and van Wijnbergen, Sweder. 1984. Fiscal policy and speculative runs on the central bank under a crawling peg exchange rate regime: Argentina 1979–1981. Washington, D.C.: World Bank. Photocopy.

Díaz-Alejandro, Carlos. 1976. *Colombia.* Cambridge, Mass.: Ballinger.

———. 1984. In toto, I don't think we are in Kansas any more. Paper presented at the Brookings Panel on Economic Activity, Washington, D.C., September.

Edwards, Sebastian. 1983. The short-run relation between growth and inflation in Latin America: Comment. *American Economic Review* 73 (June): 477–88.

———. 1984a. Exchange rates in developing countries. Working paper. Los Angeles: University of California.

———. 1984b. The demand for international reserves and monetary equilibrium: Some evidence from developing countries. *Review of Economics and Statistics* 66 (August): 500–05.

———. 1984c. Coffee, money, and inflation in Colombia. *World Development* 12 (November/December): 1107–17.

———. 1984d. The order of liberalization of the external sector in developing countries. *Princeton Essays in International Finance* no. 156. Princeton: International Finance Section, Princeton University.

———. 1985. Money, the rate of Devaluation and nominal interest rates in a semi-open economy: Colombia, 1968–1982. *Journal of Money, Credit and Banking* 17 (February): 59–68.

Edwards, Sebastian, and Aoki, Masanao. 1983. Oil export boom and Dutch disease: A dynamic analysis. *Resources and Energy* 5 (September): 219–42.

Hanson, James. 1982. Short-run macroeconomic development and policy in Colombia, 1967–1982. Washington, D.C.: World Bank. Photocopy.

Harberger, Arnold C. 1983. Dutch disease: How much sickness, How much boon? *Resources and Energy* 5:1–22.

Junguito, Roberto, and Caballero, Carlos. 1978. La Otra Economía. *Coyuntura Económica* 8:101–41.

Kamas, Linda. 1983. External disturbances and the independence of monetary policy under the crawling peg. Working paper no. 74. Wellesley, Mass.: Department of Economics, Wellesley College.

Neary, J. Peter. 1984. Real and monetary aspects of the Dutch disease. In *Structural adjustment in developed open economies,* eds. K. Jungenfeld and D. C. Hague. London: Macmillan.

Neary, J. Peter, and van Wijnbergen, Sweder. 1984. Can an oil discovery lead to a recession? A comment on Eastwood and Venables. *Economic Journal* 94 (June): 390–95.

Obstfeld, Maurice. 1984. Capital flows, the current account and the real exchange rate: Consequences of liberalization and stabilization. Paper presented at the NBER–World Bank Conference on Structural Adjustment and Real Exchange Rates in Developing Countries, Washington, D.C., 30 November–1 December.

Ocampo, Juan A. 1983. En defensa de la continuidad del regimen cambiario. *Coyuntura Económica* 13:198–214.

Urrutia, Miguel. 1981. Experience with the crawling peg in Colombia. In *Exchange rate rules,* ed. John Williamson. New York: St. Martin's.

Williamson, John. 1983. *The exchange rate system.* Washington D.C.: Institute for International Economics.

Weisner, Eduardo. 1978. *Politica monetaria y cambiaria en Colombia.* Bogota: Asociación Bancaria de Colombia.

World Bank. 1983. *Colombia: Economic development and policy under changing conditions.* Washington, D.C.: World Bank.

———. 1984. *Macroeconomic and agricultural policy linkages for adjustment and growth: The Colombian experience.* Washington, D.C.: World Bank.

Comment   Armeane Choksi

Sebastian Edwards has written a very interesting paper. He has not gone on a fishing expedition in search of statistically significant coefficients, and, at least on the face of it, his effort is not a case of measurement without theory. He has developed a simple model that attempts to explain the interaction among coffee prices, money crea-

Armeane Choksi is division chief of the Trade and Adjustment Policy Division in the Country Policy Department of the World Bank.

This comment centers on the version of Edwards's paper presented at the NBER–World Bank conference. Subsequently, Edwards made some minor changes.

tion, inflation, and the real exchange rate. I particularly like his clear exposition of how he sees his model working through an increase in the price of coffee, and he has used that structure to derive a set of equations used in the estimating procedure. Edwards makes a number of assumptions, however, that may have a bearing on the results. I would like to talk about five of these assumptions. Some have been explicitly recognized by Edwards in his paper or in the conference presentation, whereas others have not.

First, Edwards explicitly recognized in his original conference paper that the demand for money is a function only of income and not of the interest rate. The reason given is that there are no data on the interest rate, and consequently it is dropped from the model. The second assumption is related to the question that always arises in the context of Colombia: Where is the white stuff? The price of noncoffee tradables is explicit in the structural model, but a significant proportion of such tradables is cocaine, and this, for obvious reasons, is not easily measurable. There is a footnote in the paper that alludes to cocaine, but it does not address the implications of excluding it from the analysis and the estimation process. Excluding it in this manner would suggest that cocaine does not affect the exchange rate, and that is very hard to believe. Third, there is no mention in the paper of the institutional structure by which coffee is sold on the world market; if, for example, there is a form of a marketing board, this may well lead to the smuggling of coffee. Depending on the world price and the price paid to farmers, this omission may or may not be a significant one. If it is, the exchange rate would be influenced accordingly.

These three assumptions could well lead to biases in the estimation procedure. The first misspecifies the model by omitting a variable. The second and third would result in errors in measurement and also lead to a bias. Whether these biases are important or not is not obvious from the presentation, and there is no discussion in the paper to shed any light on this issue. I would suspect, however, that the estimates given are not asymptotically unbiased, as suggested by the theory behind Edwards's two- and three-stage least-squares estimation procedure. I also suspect that this potential bias is at least part of the explanation of the seemingly large size of the estimated coefficients, as pointed by Rajapatirana (see below).

A fourth assumption appears in equation (9), which specifies the rule of crawl as a function of the rates of domestic and foreign inflation, the rate and growth of real income, and the world price of coffee. But as stated earlier in the paper, between 1968 and 1973 changes in the real exchange rate were to a large extent the result of the reduction of the degree of import protection and export promotion schemes. These other variables are not specified here, and again this could lead to biases in estimating the coefficients. Finally, a fifth assumption, which initially struck me as very odd, appears in equation (3), which specifies the behavior of international reserves. The excess demand for money is specified in intertemporal terms, and I cannot see an economic rationale for doing so. Edwards has demonstrated, however, that specifying this excess demand in *contemporaneous* terms makes no substantive difference, except for the fact that the estimated value of θ, the determinant of the speed of adjustment, would be different in the two specifications. Since there is no major difference, I would suggest the use of a specification for which there is an obvious economic rationale, namely, to specify this function in contemporaneous terms.

Turning to the links between the structure and the reduced-form equations, I would have liked to see the latter set of estimation equations more closely related to the structure of the model. As I mentioned before, Edwards does not take a shotgun approach to estimation. I nevertheless believe that the links between the structure and this reduced set should be more direct and obvious than they are in the paper. This is particularly true for the money creation equation (15) which adds on—in the reduced form—additional lags and omits the rate of growth of real income.

As far as the policy implications are concerned, after having read this paper, I came away mainly with the sentiment "interesting, but so what." Edwards has shown that changes in the price of coffee affect, in the short run, the rate of money growth, and he confirms the hypothesis (one I believe very few would question) that higher coffee prices result in higher rates of money growth and higher rates of inflation. Thus, Edwards has formalized and quantified the obvious. This is not necessarily useless; but clearly, by not drawing out the policy implications, Edwards has not done justice to his work. He shows through his estimation procedure (and one must keep in mind the estimation biases mentioned earlier) that there could be some useful and interesting policy conclusions, but he does not follow through by delineating them. For example, one conclusion from which some broad policy suggestions on sterilization may be drawn is that monetary policy in Colombia has been hampered by the dependence of money creation on the behavior of coffee prices. This conclusion may also be used to suggest some changes in the institutional mechanism by which coffee is exported: If state control of export marketing were relinquished to individual economic agents and repatriation of foreign exchange to Colombia were not mandatory, would the formulation of monetary policy be easier? That is, would the private economic agents sterilize foreign exchange earnings in a manner superior to that of the state, or would there be capital flight? Another set of conclusions could be drawn from the quantitative relationships between the fiscal deficit and the rate of growth of money supply, and between money supply and inflation. Both of these relationships have policy implications, as does the relationship between the rate of crawl and the increase in the world price of coffee. Of course, some of these policy conclusions would assume optimizing behavior on the part of the government, and this assumption may not be the case. Furthermore, all of the quantitative conclusions would depend upon the specification of the model and the quality of the estimation procedures. But this is a fruitful area that Edwards must pursue if this paper is not to be dismissed as another article that formalizes and proves the obvious.

Comment   Sarath Rajapatirana

Sebastian Edwards poses a general question: What is the short-term impact of changes in export prices on the real exchange rate? To answer this question, he traces the relationship between these two variables for the case of Colombia over the years 1952–80. The question is, of course, a relevant and important one for countries that rely on only a few exports and have to respond to changes in export prices while pursuing their other national objectives.

My comments on this paper are organized under three headings: the specification of the model, the econometric findings, and the implications of the findings for policy formulation.

The Specification of the Model

In formulating his model to study the relationship between export prices and the real exchange rate, Edwards borrows a page each from the Dutch disease literature, the classical specie flow mechanism, and the Colombian experience, in which the rate of crawl of the peso is thought to be adjusted to changes in the export price of coffee. The effects of changes in coffee prices thus operate through three channels by which an increase in the coffee price causes an appreciation of the real exchange rate: (1) The "spending effect" described by Corden and Neary (see Edwards's references) in the Dutch disease literature; (2) the money creation effect, which takes place when the increase in foreign reserves resulting from increased export revenues are monetized; and (3) the reaction of the government whereby it reduces the rate of crawl or the rate of nominal devaluation in response to an increase in the price of coffee.

Sarath Rajapatirana is a senior economist at the World Bank.

Edwards's model concentrates on the monetary rather than the real side, however, taking international inflation and the size of the fiscal deficit as exogenous.[1] Basically, it is a very simple and clearly defined simultaneous-equations system that allows the author to test three hypotheses: first, that higher prices of coffee result in an increase in the rate of money creation; second, that there is a relationship between the rate of inflation and the exchange rate; and third, that the rate of devaluation of the peso is negatively correlated with the price of coffee.

Although the model specification allows the author to capture the relationships described, one can think of a number of extensions of the model to interject more realism into the model and thereby be able to interpret the econometric results more clearly. Two such extensions are suggested here.

First, as the author himself recognizes, one needs to treat the fiscal deficit as an endogenous variable in order to trace the behavior of public expenditures in response to changes in coffee prices. This requirement is all the more relevant in light of the fact that the Colombian government must rely heavily on coffee for public revenue and in light of its attempts to stabilize the income of coffee growers.

Second, the influence on the real exchange rate of the spending effect and the money creation effect will be very much influenced by the patterns of expenditures in the public and private sectors. If, for example, a larger proportion of the increase in the export price accrues to the government than to the private sector, it is conceivable that the government expenditure on balance will be spent more on nontraded than on traded goods. It may therefore be necessary, especially in the general case, to consider how export revenues are distributed between the public sector and the private sector. This will be an important issue in discussing the policy implications of these findings.

In the general case, with no sterilization of the additional foreign exchange, there is no avoiding an increase in export prices leading to an appreciation of the exchange rate. Under a fixed exchange rate system this happens through domestic inflation when the increase in foreign reserves is monetized. Under a floating rate system the appreciation will operate through the nominal exchange rate. And it is through this appreciation that the resource increase is absorbed. The interesting question here is whether the government should deliberately change the rate of crawl when export prices increase or instead use expenditure policies to handle the disturbance.

The Econometric Results

The econometric results derived through the reduced-form equations generally confirm the hypotheses advanced. Nonetheless, the estimates are surprisingly large. Among the point estimates, a change in the price of coffee by 10 percentage points leads to a 5 percent increase in the rate of inflation, a 2 percent appreciation in the nominal exchange rate, and an appreciation in the real exchange rate of over 7 percent.

As Edwards recognizes the size of the estimates may be the result of taking real income and the fiscal deficit as exogenous and the result of some important export that has a positive covariance with coffee influencing the real exchange rate. The fiscal issue is very important and lies at the heart of the mechanism that transmits export price increases to the real exchange rate. Furthermore, because real income is assumed exogenous in the estimated model, the powerful real effects of a coffee price boom may be being picked up by the monetary variables.

Policy Implications

What then are the implications of these relationships for policy formulation? The question here is what is best policy to pursue when a commodity boom takes place. Should a country fine-tune its response to such external price changes in the short run by manipulating the exchange rate?

I think not. If the export boom is temporary, the government would use fiscal policy through budget surpluses during the boom and through deficits during the slump to stabilize the economy. This response is all the more important if export revenues accrue to the government and if monetary policy is ineffective. With aggregate expenditure policies, the government can aim directly at the source of the disturbance. On the other hand, if the export price rise is permanent, the exchange rate should rightly reflect the new relative price structure.

There is another reason to eschew the use of the rate of the crawl. Policy formulation is difficult if policy makers cannot clearly distinguish between price changes that are transitory and those that are permanent. Adjustment costs can be minimized only by managing the economy in such a way as to avoid unemployment and forgone output costs arising from responses to transitory phenomena (such as a crop failure abroad that will raise export prices and lead to an appreciation).

The Colombian authorities have tried an implicit dual exchange rate system, changing levels of protection inversely with changes in coffee prices, raising the reserves requirement for commercial banks, and paying exporters with certificates of longer maturity. These attempts to accommodate the effects of export prices are second-best to an overall policy, such as public expenditure reduction in the boom and expansion during the slump so as to avoid policy-induced distortions.

Note

1. Although the structural equations (1) through (11) of Edwards's paper include real income as an endogenous variable (the "spending effect"), the estimated model considers real income as exogenous (see the paragraph before Edwards's summary of section 7.3).

8   Stabilization, Stagflation, and Investment Incentives: The Case of Kenya, 1979–1980

William H. Branson

8.1   Introduction and Summary

Stabilization programs in developing countries generally have three components: a reduction in government spending, devaluation, and a slowdown in money growth. If prices and wages are not perfectly flexible, the cut in government spending will produce a recession in the short run. With imported intermediate goods in the picture, the devaluation will generate stagflation; the price level will rise and value added will be squeezed. Both of these components of the program will squeeze profits, and the increase in the price of imported capital goods will raise the cost of capital. These additive effects will reduce investment and future growth. The purposes of this paper are to specify and analyze a model that describes these effects; to provide an illustration of the model by using data on Kenya; and to suggest how the stabilization program can be designed to minimize the effects on investment.

In section 8.2 the basic model is specified and analyzed. I focus on a stylized structure of an economy with two sectors. One produces an agricultural output that is exported and not consumed domestically. This is essentially the case in Kenya, where nearly all of the major export crops—coffee, tea, and sisal—and polyurethane are exported. I assume that output elasticity in this sector is low. The other sector produces a nontraded domestic good using domestic factors and an

William H. Branson is a professor of economics and international affairs at Princeton University and director of the Research Program in International Studies of the National Bureau of Economic Research.

The research reported here was financed in part by a grant from the Division of Policy Research and Analysis of the National Science Foundation.

imported intermediate input, all of which have a low elasticity of substitution among them. A large fraction of capital goods are also imported, again consistent with the case of Kenya. The country is small in its export and import markets. The degree of wage indexation to the consumer price index (CPI) is introduced as a parameter. Section 8.2 goes on to show the effects of a stabilization program on prices, output, inputs, and profits in the nontraded sector and on the trade balance in terms of foreign exchange. Numerical results using Kenyan data are presented in table 8.3. The potential stagflationary effects of a devaluation are an extension of arguments presented in Branson (1983) and Katseli (1983), which in turn were extensions of the earlier results of Cooper (1971) and Krugman and Taylor (1978).

The effects of a stabilization program on investment incentives are discussed in section 8.3. The analysis focuses on the effect on Tobin's q-ratio, the ratio of the market value of assets to their replacement cost. These effects are summarized with numerical estimates from the Kenyan data. This section also compares the effects of a devaluation and a cut in government spending that yield the same result for the trade balance. The results are shown in table 8.4. The spending cut reduces employment somewhat more than the devaluation does, but has a significantly smaller effect on real profits and the relative price of capital goods and thus on investment incentives. The differences between the two alternatives decrease with an increase in the degree of wage indexation. The devaluation is, of course, inflationary, whereas the spending cut is deflationary.

The results in table 8.4 strongly suggest that a country in a situation comparable to Kenya's in 1979–80 should meet an external shock to the terms of trade by directly reducing absorption rather than by devaluation. With low levels of wage indexation, the spending cut will have a much smaller effect on investment incentives and avoid the inflationary consequences of devaluation, which in turn will allow the country to maintain nonindexed of wages. The cost of this program will be a small additional reduction in employment in the domestic goods sector.

In section 8.4 I turn briefly to a more general discussion of the role of devaluation. In an economy with this structure, which may still be typical of the African countries, a devaluation may increase the current deficit in terms of domestic prices, even if it improves the deficit in terms of foreign exchange. Thus, a combination of devaluation and a cut in government spending can be doubly recessionary, and devaluation may not be an appropriate component of a policy program designed to meet an external shock such as the terms-of-trade deterioration in Kenya in 1979–80. On the other hand, devaluation is an appropriate, even necessary, component of a *liberalization* program that follows a protracted disequilibrium characterized by domestic inflation with a fixed exchange rate and rising import controls. It therefore may be important to distinguish between devaluation as an undesirable component of a *stabilization* program and devaluation as a necessary part of *liberalization*.

8.2   A Model of a Stabilization Program

The standard monetary model of a stabilization program comprises one good, flexible wages and prices, and no imported inputs. The model is outlined in Branson (1983). An estimated version with considerable empirical detail is presented in Khan and Knight (1981). The usual stabilization program consists of a reduction in government spending, devaluation, and a reduction in the rate of growth of the money supply. The last is generally tied to the cut in the budget deficit. As discussed in Branson, the devaluation can be thought of as validating the existing money stock as an equilibrium one. The short-run impact of the program comes from the cut in government spending and the devaluation. The longer-run effects also depend on the reduction in money growth. This reduction, too, could have short-run effects if it influences inflationary expectations, but that is unlikely if the stabilization package is aimed at ending a long period of disequilibrium.

In almost any model the very short-run effects of such a stabilization package will be stagflationary. The cut in government spending will tend to reduce output, and the devaluation will push up the price level. In the standard monetary model these effects are very short-lived. Flexible real wages adjust to restore output to its full-employment level. The combination of reduced government spending and devaluation reduces domestic absorption and eliminates the current-account deficit. The anti-crowding-out effect of reduced government spending actually stimulates investment. In the Khan-Knight model the short-run period of stagflation lasts two to three years.

Many developing countries, however, have an economic structure that differs in important ways from the assumptions of the monetary model. Wages and prices may not be flexible in the short run. This can be the result of a Lewis-type structure in which labor is supplied to the modern sector at a wage, real or nominal, that is determined by conditions in the subsistence sector. It can also result from extensive government involvement in the modern sector through the financial sector or through "parastatal" companies. In this case wage determination may be part of the political process, and also be a political problem.

In this situation, a reduction in demand caused by the cut in government spending can result in a significant and persistent drop in output due to wage or price rigidity. In addition, many developing countries import intermediate goods and capital goods as inputs into the production process. This means that a devaluation can raise the costs of imported inputs. The result can be a recession and profit squeeze, reducing saving and investment. Thus, the implications of the stabilization program for output, investment, and growth can depend on wage and price rigidities and the structure of trade. I will show below that the *interaction* of the wage-setting regime with the presence of imported goods can be particularly important for the success of the program.

In many developing countries a useful disaggregation of output is into two sectors: one producing agricultural output that is traded internationally with little domestic consumption, and the other producing a nonagricultural output that is at best an imperfect substitute for imports. The nonagricultural sector uses imported intermediate inputs, and both sectors use imported capital goods.

This framework allows an analysis of the effects of a stabilization package on the two sectors separately, as a first approximation. In this section I lay out the model of the nonagricultural (N) sector. As a first approximation, I assume no domestic consumption of agricultural (A) sector output, and so effects on its output and exports will be determined simply by the movement of the A-sector price along its supply curve. The remaining subsections of this section first describe the model of the N sector with explicit solutions for price, output, profits, unemployment, and intermediate imports. Rough parameter estimates are then introduced for an example based on Kenya. Finally, the numerical results are given under varying assumptions concerning wage determination and the elasticity of substitution between imported intermediates and value added in the N sector.

8.2.1 A Model of the Nontraded Sector

This subsection sets out a model for analyzing the short-run effects of a stabilization program in the N sector. The analytical point of the exercise is to see how the separate components of the program—a cut in government purchases and devaluation—affect output, the price level, and profits. I also want to show how the answers to this question are influenced by the type and degree of wage rigidity, which are to some extent under government control. I want to specify the model in a way that the parameters can be interpreted using readily available data, so that I can later provide the Kenyan example.

The simplest model that meets these requirements is the following. The N sector produces output Q_n using capital K, labor N, and an imported input I. The capital stock is fixed in the short run. The input is supplied elastically at the world market price P_i^*, so that the domestic price is given by $P_i = eP_i^*$. Labor is supplied to the N sector at a wage rate that will be specified as following a parameterized indexation system, so that we can study the consequences of variation in the indexation parameter. Since nearly all the output of the exportable sector is exported, the CPI is also P_n.

An important feature of the production structure the model should capture is the low degree of substitutability between the domestic inputs K and N, and the imported input I in producing gross output Q. To describe this structure as simply as possible, I assume that the production function is separable with a constant elasticity of substitution (*CES*) between value added, $V = F(K, N)$, and I, and that F is Cobb-Douglas. The analysis follows the line taken by Marston and Turnovsky (1983). The demand side will be simpler. I assume that private nominal demand for output Q_n is determined by the money stock and that government demand is exogenous.

The Demand Side

The focus of the analysis in this paper is the complication introduced into the stabilization model when aspects of supply-side structure are taken into account, particularly the presence of imported intermediates and wage indexation. Since I have nothing new to introduce on demand side, I will strip it down to one equation. With all of the output of the A sector exported, and only intermediate imports, all private final expenditure is on the N good. I assume that private sector expenditure for the N-sector output Q_n is proportional to the money stock and that in addition the government purchases N-sector output. The nominal demand for N-sector output can then be written as:

$$P_n Q_n = kM + P_n G = E + P_n G,$$

where M is the money stock, E is private expenditure on Q_n, and G is government purchases in real terms. A demand relationship of this kind can be derived from the usual *IS-LM* analysis; it is also consistent with the structure of rational expectations models. The relationship could also be obtained in a more general two-sector demand structure with consumption of both the traded export and the domestic good and with a unitary elasticity of substitution between the two goods in demand.

Changes in demand are then given as:

$$(1) \qquad \hat{Q}_n + (1 - G/Q_n)\hat{P}_n = (E/P_n Q_n)\hat{M} + (G/Q_n)\hat{G},$$

where a hat (^) denotes a percentage change, e.g. $\hat{M} \equiv dM/M$. In equation (1) the policy variables are $\hat{M}$ and $\hat{G}$. Note that M is nominal and G is real. If the relevant budget variable were nominal government expenditure, $P_n G$, equation (1) would be:

$$(1') \qquad \hat{Q}_n + \hat{P}_n = (E/P_n Q_n)\hat{M} + (G/Q_n) (\widehat{P_n G}).$$

The analysis will use equation (1), with the assumption that government purchases of N-sector output are fixed in real terms. It is easy to rework the results using equation (1'). The elasticity of the demand curve is the ratio $\hat{Q}_n/\hat{P}_n = -(1 - G/Q_n)$ from equation (1), with $\hat{M} = \hat{G} = 0$. This ratio is clearly less than unity in absolute value as long as G/Q_n is positive, that is, as long as there is some government consumption of N-sector output.

The Supply Side

The prices of agricultural output P_a and imported inputs P_i will be taken as given, determined by the exchange rate e multiplied by the world price P^*. Both are traded, and the country in question is assumed to be a "small country." The analysis of the supply side will proceed as follows. First, wages are specified as partially indexed to the price of the nontraded good, which is also the CPI with no consumption of the export and all imports being intermediate goods. Next will come discussion of the production function and first-order conditions for profit maximization in the N sector. From these are derived the demands for labor and intermediates as functions of relative price changes. Then the supply curve of output Q_n as a function of relative prices can be obtained. This will then be combined with the demand side to obtain solutions for $\hat{Q}_n$ and $\hat{P}_n$ as functions of $\hat{P}_i$, representing exchange rate changes, and $\hat{G}$, representing the government budget component of the stabilization program.

The nominal wage in the N sector is assumed to be partially indexed to the CPI, which is P_n, such that:

(2) $$\hat{W} = \gamma \hat{P}_n; \quad 0 < \gamma < 1.$$

Here γ is the indexation parameter; $\gamma = 0$ denotes a fixed nominal wage; and $\gamma = 1$ denotes a fixed real wage. Below I will present results for the range of γ.

The production function for Q_n is assumed to be separable in value added, V, and intermediate inputs, I. I follow Marston and Turnovsky in assuming that value added is a Cobb-Douglas function of capital and labor inputs and that gross output in the N sector is a CES function of value added and intermediate inputs, such that:

(3) $$V = K^{1-\theta_n} N^{\theta_n}$$

(4) $$Q_n = [bI^{-\rho} + (1 - b)V^{-\rho}]^{-1/\rho}.$$

In the second-stage CES function, the elasticity of substitution between I and V is given by $\sigma = 1/(1 + \rho)$. To represent low substitutability between domestic factors and imported intermediates, I assume that $\sigma < 1$; in particular, I will present results for the case in which $\sigma =$

0.2 and for the limiting case of $\sigma = 0$. The 0.2 estimate is based on the previous work of Bruno and Sachs (1979).

In the neighborhood of an initial equilibrium, with the capital stock fixed in the short run, percentage changes in V and Q_n can be given by the following linear approximations:

(5) $$\hat{V} = \theta_n \hat{N}$$

(6) $$\hat{Q}_n = \theta_i \hat{I} + \theta_v \hat{V} = \theta_i \hat{I} + \theta_v \theta_n \hat{N}.$$

Here θ_n is the share of employment in value added, and θ_i and θ_v are the shares of intermediate inputs and value added, respectively, in gross output. The profit function π is given by:

(7) $$\pi = P_n Q_n - WN - P_i I.$$

Producers are assumed to choose N and I to maximize π, given K.

The first-order conditions for profit maximization can be written as:

(8) $$\hat{P}_i - \hat{P}_n = \frac{1}{\sigma}(\hat{Q}_n - \hat{I})$$

(9) $$\hat{W} - \hat{P}_n = \frac{1}{\sigma}\hat{Q}_n - \left[1 + \frac{1 - \sigma}{\sigma}\theta_n\right]\hat{N}.$$

The indexation equation (2) can be used to eliminate $\hat{W}$ from equation (9). Then (8), (9), and the production relation (6) can be solved to obtain the supply equation for $\hat{Q}_n$:

(10) $$\hat{Q}_n = -\frac{\theta_i[\theta_n + \sigma(1 - \theta_n)]}{\theta_v(1 - \theta_n)}\hat{P}_i$$
$$+ \left\{\frac{\theta_n(1 - \gamma)}{1 - \theta_n} + \frac{\theta_i[\theta_n + \sigma(1 - \theta_n)]}{\theta_v(1 - \theta_n)}\right\}\hat{P}_n.$$

This is the equivalent of equation (6) in the Aizenman-Frenkel paper in this volume. From (6), (8), and (9) we can also obtain the reduced-form equations for $\hat{I}$ and $\hat{N}$. Alternatively, once we obtain $\hat{Q}_n$ from (10), we can solve recursively for $\hat{I}$ and $\hat{N}$ in (8) and (9). If indexation is complete, so that $\gamma = 1$, the supply equation (10) is homogeneous. Since the coefficient of $\hat{P}_n$ is positive, an increase in P_n increases Q_n; this is the slope of the supply curve. An increase in P_i reduces Q_n by squeezing value added and profits. This represents a shift of the supply curve.

The parameters of the supply equation (10) can be interpreted as output elasticities with respect to relative price changes. Using the notation that $s_n = \hat{Q}_n/\hat{P}_n$ with $\hat{P}_i$ equal to zero, and so on, we can rewrite equation (10) in the form:

(11) $$\hat{Q}_n = s_n\hat{P}_n + s_i\hat{P}_i,$$

where the s output elasticities are given by the parameter combinations from equation (10), with s_n positive and s_i negative. With equations (11) for N-sector supply and (1) for demand, we can now proceed to obtain explicit solutions for changes in Q_n and P_n as functions of the exogenous prices P_i and P_a.

Explicit Solutions for Price and Output in the N Sector

The demand and supply equations are shown in figure 8.1. The slope of the demand curve from equation (1) is given by $-1/(1 - G/Q_n)$, which is greater than unity. This means that the demand curve for the entire competitive industry is inelastic. An upward or leftward shift of the industry supply curve will therefore raise the value of output in the industry. As we will see in detail in section 8.2.2, this opens the potential for ambiguity in the response of profits to supply disturbances. The share coefficients of $\hat{M}$ and $\hat{G}$ in equation (1) give measures of the horizontal shift of the demand curve when M or G changes.

The slope of the supply curve, from equations (10) and (11) is given by $\hat{P}_n/\hat{Q}_n = 1/s_n$. Since θ_n and γ are both less than unity, this slope is positive. An increase in the indexation parameter γ increases the slope, making the supply curve steeper. The s_i coefficient in equations (10) and (11) gives the horizontal shift of the curve as P_i changes. An in-

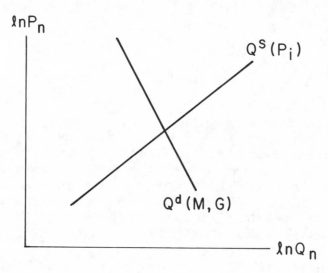

Fig. 8.1   Demand and supply in the N sector.

crease in the elasticity of substitution, σ, increases the coefficient of $\hat{P}_i$, yielding an increase in the supply shift when P_i increases.

This result, combined with the inelasticity of the demand curve, means that as the indexation parameter γ increases, the rise in the value of final output following a devaluation, which increases P_i, also itself increases. This is the source of the result, described below in section 8.2.2, that an increase in γ reduces the squeeze on nominal profits that follows from a devaluation with imported intermediates.

Let us now proceed to the solutions for changes in price and output. Equations (1) and (11) can be combined in matrix form, such that:

$$
\begin{align}
(11')&\\
(1'')&
\end{align}
\quad
\begin{bmatrix} 1 & -s_n \\ 1 & 1 - G/Q_n \end{bmatrix}
\begin{pmatrix} \hat{Q}_n \\ \hat{P}_n \end{pmatrix}
=
\begin{bmatrix} s_i & 0 & 0 \\ 0 & E/P_nQ_n & G/Q_n \end{bmatrix}
\begin{pmatrix} \hat{P}_i \\ \hat{M} \\ \hat{G} \end{pmatrix}.
$$

The solution is:

$$
(12) \quad
\begin{pmatrix} \hat{Q}_n \\ \hat{P}_n \end{pmatrix}
= \frac{1}{|C|}
\begin{bmatrix} 1 - G/Q_n & s_n \\ -1 & 1 \end{bmatrix}
\begin{bmatrix} s_i & 0 & 0 \\ 0 & E/P_nQ_n & G/Q_n \end{bmatrix}
\begin{pmatrix} \hat{P}_i \\ \hat{M} \\ \hat{G} \end{pmatrix}.
$$

The determinant $|C| = 1 - G/Q_n + s_n > 0$. The solutions for $\hat{Q}_n$ and $\hat{P}_n$ can be written as:

$$
(13) \quad \hat{Q}_n = \frac{1}{|C|}\left[\left(1 - \frac{G}{Q_n}\right)s_i\hat{P}_i + s_n\left(\frac{E}{P_nQ_n}\hat{M} + \frac{G}{Q_n}\hat{G}\right)\right]
$$

$$
(14) \quad \hat{P}_n = \frac{1}{|C|}\left[-s_i\hat{P}_i + \frac{E}{P_nQ_n}\hat{M} + \frac{G}{Q_n}\hat{G}\right].
$$

From these solutions and the assumed exogenous changes in prices and government purchases, we can calculate the effects on the rest of the variables in the model. Equation (8) gives $\hat{I}$. It also gives the percentage change in imports in foreign exchange terms, since the world price is exogenous. Equation (9) gives the change in employment $\hat{N}$. The change in the wage rate comes from the wage equation (2). The change in profits can then be computed as a residual, since we already have solutions for the change in output, $\hat{P}_n + \hat{Q}_n$, in the wage bill, $\hat{N} + \hat{W}$, and in the bill for imported intermediates, $\hat{P}_i + \hat{I}$. Profits, π, can be computed from the identity:

$$
(15) \quad \pi \equiv P_nQ_n - WN - P_nI.
$$

Percentage changes in π are given by:

$$
(16) \quad \hat{\pi} = \frac{P_nQ_n}{\pi}(\hat{P}_n + \hat{Q}_n) - \frac{WN}{\pi}(\hat{W} + \hat{N}) - \frac{P_iI}{\pi}(\hat{P}_i + \hat{I}).
$$

The underlying share data of 0.3, 0.3, 0.4 for inputs, profits, and labor, respectively, make the profit equation in the Kenya example:

(17) $\hat{\pi} = 3.33(\hat{P}_n + \hat{Q}_n) - 1.33(\hat{W} + \hat{N}) - 1.0(\hat{P}_i + \hat{I})$.

The powerful effect of an increase in $P_n Q_n$ along an inelastic industry demand curve can be seen in the first term on the right-hand side of equation (17).

Finally, the effects on the trade balance can be computed as follows. The percentage change in intermediate imports is given by $\hat{I}$; the arithmetic change is therefore $dI = \hat{I}I$. The percentage change in exports of the A sector is given by $\hat{X} = s_a \hat{P}_a$, where s_a is the elasticity of supply in the A sector. Thus, the arithmetic change in exports is $dX = s_a \hat{P}_a X$. The change in the trade balance, B, in foreign exchange terms is then simply:

$$dB = s_a \hat{P}_a X - \hat{I}I.$$

It will be convenient to state the change as a fraction of the initial level of exports, such that:

(18) $$dB/X_a = s_a \hat{P}_a - (I/X)\hat{I}.$$

In 1981 I/X in Kenya was about 2.0, as shown in table 8.1 below.

8.2.2   Illustrative Results Using Estimates of Kenyan Data

In this section I will present illustrative estimates of data from the Kenyan economy. These are meant to give an impression of the quantitive magnitude of the stagflation that follows a stabilization program, and the sensitivity of that stagflation to the presence of imported intermediates and to the degree of wage indexation. Here I will show effects per unit devaluation or change in government spending. In section 8.3 I will compare these results to those for an equal change in the trade balance.

The stabilization program is assumed in the short run to include a reduction in government spending and a devaluation. The spending cut is a negative $\hat{G}$ in equations (13) and (14). Under the small-country assumptions, the devaluation raises both P_i and P_a by the proportion of the devaluation. As is apparent from equations (12) through (14), the effects of the components of the program are additive. I will therefore present the multipliers of each component—the coefficients in equations (13) and (14)—separately and then in various combinations to analyze the results.

The analysis will proceed as follows. First, table 8.1 presents the underlying data for the Kenyan economy. These are then combined to give the output response elasticities s_n and s_i and the system determinant C in equations (12) through (14) for the range of γ from 0 to 1 and for the alternative values of the elasticity of substitution of 0 and

0.2. This will represent the full range of wage stickiness from nominal rigidity to real rigidity, as well as a realistic range of substitutability between value added and imported intermediates. The effects for the dependent variables are then given in tables 8.3a and 8.3b.

The Kenyan Data and the Parameters

The relevant data from the Kenyan economy are assembled in table 8.1. The data are from the World Bank and the International Monetary Fund (IMF). N-sector output is the gross domestic product (GDP) at factor cost less output in the traditional, agricultural, and fishing and forestry sectors. Government expenditure on N-sector output G is taken to be general government consumption plus capital expenditures. This overstates G because of the consumption of agricultural sector output and the import of capital goods. The result is a seemingly high G/Q estimate of 0.6. Since the slope of the demand curve is given by $\hat{P}_n/\hat{Q}_n = 1/(1 - G/Q)$, the result is an exaggeration of the inelasticity of the demand curve.

The only quantitatively significant nonagricultural export of Kenya is petroleum products, which account for about 30 percent of total exports. Petroleum product exports are also about 40 percent of all

Table 8.1   Parameter Estimates for Kenya

Variable	Method of Calculation	Value	Source
G	1981 general government consumption plus capital expenditure (K£ millions)	952.7	Standard Tables, 1, 5.1
Q	GDP at factor cost less traditional, agricultural, forestry and fishing (K£ millions)	1,613.6	Standard Tables, 2.1
G/Q		0.6	
I	Imports less reexports of petroleum products (billion 1981 SDRs)	1.5	IMF
X	Exports less reexports of petroleum products (billion 1981 SDRs)	0.7	IMF
I/X		2.0	
θ_n	Share of labor in value added in N sector	0.57	Ahamed (1983)
θ_i	Share of imported inputs in total output in N sector	0.3	Ahamed (1983)
s_a	Elasticity of agricultural output with respect to its own price P_a	0.1	Ahamed (1983)

mineral fuel imports, with the rest of the imports being used in domestic production. To make the data aggregation consistent with the assumptions of the model, I subtract the reexport of petroleum products from both imports and exports to obtain the trade data in table 8.1. In doing so, I implicitly assume that the processing industry is not significantly affected by the stabilization program considered here.

The underlying shares of labor, capital, and imported inputs in gross output in the N sector are approximately 0.4, 0.3, and 0.3, respectively (see Ahamed 1983 and the references therein). The labor share of value added, θ_n, is therefore $0.4/0.7 = 0.57$. The elasticity of export supply is estimated to be approximately 0.1 in Ahamed.

The data in table 8.1 can be combined to give the parameter estimates in tables 8.2a and 8.2b under the range of assumptions for γ and σ. As the indexation parameter γ increases, the supply curve becomes steeper and s_n decreases. The output elasticity of P_i does not depend on γ, since imported inputs do not enter the CPI directly. The determinant C is equal to $1 - G/Q + s_n$, so that it therefore decreases as γ increases. An increase in σ increases s_n, flattening the supply curve. It also increases s_i, the shift parameter.

The Effects on Output, Prices, Inputs, Profits, and the Trade Balance

The effects of changes in P_i, P_a, and G, the components of the stabilization program, on output and the price level in the N sector and on the wage rate, employment, profits, and the trade balance are shown in table 8.3a for $\sigma = 0$ and in table 8.3b for $\sigma = 0.2$. I will henceforth refer to these pairs of tables as one unit, that is, "table 8.3" means

Table 8.2a   Parameter Values in the N-Sector Model, $\sigma = 0$

		Value of γ	
Parameter	0	0.5	1.0
s_n: The Slope of the Supply Curve	1.89	1.23	0.57
s_i: The Output Elasticity of P_i	−0.57	−0.57	−0.57
$\lvert C \rvert$: The Determinant of Supply	2.30	1.64	0.98

Table 8.2b   Parameter Values in the N-Sector Model, $\sigma = 0.2$

		Value of γ	
Parameter	0	0.5	1.0
s_n	1.98	1.32	0.65
s_i	−0.65	−0.65	−0.65
$\lvert C \rvert$	2.39	1.73	0.06

"tables 8.3a and 8.3b." Since the equations for $\hat{Q}_n$ and $\hat{P}_n$ are linear, the effects of independent changes in each variable can be combined to study any particular combination of disturbances. An across-the-board devaluation will increase P_i and P_a by the same proportion; a spending cut will reduce G. The numbers in table 8.3 give the percentage change in each endogenous variable per percentage change in the exogenous variable. For example, in the first row of table 8.3a, with $\gamma = 1.0$ (full indexation), a 10 percent increase in P_i would reduce Q_n by 2.4 percent.

The results in panel A of table 8.3 can be most easily understood by reference to figure 8.2. An increase in P_i caused by a devaluation shifts the supply curve left. An increase in γ steepens the supply curve, and the steeper the supply curve, the greater the effect on both P_n and Q_n as we move up the fixed demand curve. $\hat{Q}_n/\hat{P}_i$ and $\hat{P}_n/\hat{P}_i$ both increase with γ.

An increase in G shifts the demand curve in figure 8.2 out. The steeper the supply curve, the smaller the effect on Q_n and the larger the effect on P_n. $\hat{Q}_n/\hat{G}$ falls and $\hat{P}_n/\hat{G}$ rises as γ increases. An increase in σ both flattens the supply curve and increases its shift with an increase in P_i. The result when G changes is less change in P_n and more change in

Table 8.3a   **Effects on Output, Prices, and Inputs, $\sigma = 0$**

Effects on Endogenous Variables		Value of γ		
		0	0.5	1.0
A.	$\hat{Q}_n/\hat{P}_i$	−0.10	−0.14	−0.24
	$\hat{Q}_n/\hat{G}$	0.48	0.44	0.34
	$\hat{P}_n/\hat{P}_i$	0.25	0.35	0.58
	$\hat{P}_n/\hat{G}$	0.26	0.36	0.60
B. $\hat{P}_i = \hat{P}_a$	$\hat{W}/\hat{P}_i$	0	0.17	0.58
$\hat{G} = 0$	$\hat{N}/\hat{P}_i$	−0.18	−0.25	−0.42
	$\hat{I}/\hat{P}_i$	−0.10	−0.14	−0.24
	$\hat{\pi}/\hat{P}_i$	−0.18	−0.08	0.16
	$(\hat{\pi} - \hat{P}_n)/\hat{P}_i$	−0.42	−0.42	−0.42
	$\dfrac{(dX - dI)}{X}/\hat{P}_i$	0.30	0.38	0.58
C. $\hat{P}_i = \hat{P}_a = 0$	$\hat{W}/\hat{G}$	0	0.18	0.60
	$\hat{N}/\hat{G}$	0.85	0.72	0.60
	$\hat{I}/\hat{G}$	0.48	0.44	0.34
	$\hat{\pi}/\hat{G}$	0.85	0.96	1.20
	$(\hat{\pi} - \hat{P}_n)/\hat{G}$	0.60	0.60	0.60
	$\dfrac{(dX - dI)}{X}/\hat{G}$	−0.97	−0.89	−0.69

Table 8.3b   **Effects on Output, Prices, and Inputs, $\sigma = 0.2$**

Effects on Endogenous Variables		Value of γ		
		0	0.5	1.0
A.	$\hat{Q}_n/\hat{P}_i$	-0.11	-0.15	-0.25
	$\hat{Q}_n/\hat{G}$	0.49	0.45	0.36
	$\hat{P}_n/\hat{P}_i$	0.27	0.37	0.61
	$\hat{P}_n/\hat{G}$	0.25	0.34	0.55
B. $\hat{P}_i = \hat{P}_n$	$\hat{W}/\hat{P}_i$	0	0.19	0.61
$\hat{G} = 0$	$\hat{N}/\hat{P}_i$	-0.09	-0.18	-0.38
	$\hat{I}/\hat{P}_i$	-0.26	-0.28	-0.33
	$\hat{\pi}/\hat{P}_i$	-0.09	0.01	0.23
	$(\hat{\pi} - \hat{P}_n)/\hat{P}_i$	-0.36	-0.37	-0.38
	$\dfrac{(dX - dI)}{X}/\hat{P}_i$	0.61	0.66	0.76
C. $\hat{P}_i = \hat{P}_n = 0$	$\hat{W}/\hat{G}$	0	0.17	0.55
	$\hat{N}/\hat{G}$	0.82	0.74	0.55
	$\hat{I}/\hat{G}$	0.54	0.52	0.47
	$\hat{\pi}/\hat{G}$	0.82	0.91	1.11
	$(\hat{\pi} - \hat{P}_n)/\hat{G}$	0.57	0.57	0.55
	$\dfrac{(dX - dI)}{X}/\hat{G}$	-1.07	-1.04	-0.95

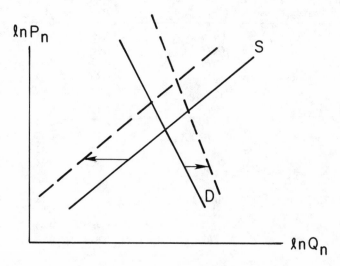

Fig. 8.2   Effect of a stabilization program on Q_n, P_n.

Q_n as σ increases. The net result when P_i changes is not very sensitive to σ in the range of 0 to 0.2.

The effects of a devaluation only with $\hat{P}_i = \hat{P}_a$ on wages, employment, profits, and the trade balance are shown in panel B of table 8.3. There we see that an increase in indexation increases the effect of a devaluation on the nominal wage and on employment, as expected. An increase in γ, however, by steepening the supply curve in figure 8.2, makes the increase in $P_n Q_n$ larger as long as the demand curve is inelastic. This means that the drop in profits is greatest with $\gamma = 0$ and that profits actually rise with a devaluation with $\gamma = 1.0$! In the fourth row of panel B the CPI increase is subtracted from the percentage change in nominal profits. The percentage decrease in real profits is nearly invariant to the degree of indexation, but it falls as the elasticity of substitution increases.

The last row of panel B gives the effect on the trade balance in foreign exchange terms. Paradoxically, this effect increases with the degree of wage indexation! Why? When all imports are intermediate goods with a low elasticity of substitution against domestic factors in the short run, the effect of the devaluation on imports comes mainly from its depressive effect on output. In the extreme case of zero substitution there is no relative price effect. Since the reduction in output increases with the degree of wage indexation, so does the effect on intermediate inputs. This provides a striking illustration of the importance of the role of economic structure in determining policy outcomes, as emphasized in Branson (1983). The basic result was already established in Katseli and Marion (1982). The effect of devaluation on imports in Kenya does not come through substitution among final goods in consumption; it comes mainly through the reduction of imported inputs into production.

The effects of a cut in spending on wages, employment, profits, and the trade balance are shown in panel C of table 8.3 (with signs changed). A reduction in G reduces the wage rate more, the larger the indexation parameter γ, since a cut in G reduces P_i. A reduction in G results in a smaller loss of employment, the larger the value of γ, for the same reason. A cut in G reduces nominal and real profits by an amount that is nearly invariant to the value of γ or σ.

The last row of panel C shows the effects of a spending cut on the trade balance. Since there is no effect on the price of exports (fixed at $P_a = eP^*$), there is no export supply effect. The numbers in this row are twice the $\hat{Q}_n/\hat{G}$ numbers in panel A, with signs reversed. As wage indexation increases, the effect on intermediate imports decreases with the output effect. As σ increases, however, the effect of a change in G on the trade balance increases.

8.3   Investment Incentives in a Stabilization Program

The effects of a stabilization program (or any other exogenous disturbance) on investment can generally be analyzed in two steps. The first step is to determine the effect on the incentive to invest, the net real rate of return in the affected sector. Once the incentive effect is calculated, it can then be multiplied by an estimate of the elasticity of investment relative to that effect to determine the investment effect. This procedure presumably summarizes the effects on growth, at least within the existing economic structure and in the short run, of the given stabilization program.

The elasticity of investment with respect to the net real rate of return must be determined empirically in individual cases. These numbers can be culled from existing studies and assembled into an educated guesstimate, or an econometric study could be attempted if data are available. I focus here on the procedures for determining the effect on investment incentives, building on the model of section 8.2.

The basic approach taken in subsection 8.3.1 is to concentrate on the effects on Tobin's q (see Tobin 1969), the ratio of the market value of new capital stock to its production cost. This gives the addition made to the present value of the firm by a new investment, which in turn is an increase in the capital stock, dK. The capital stock should be an increasing function of q; $dK = f(q)$, with $f(1) = 0$. This is a useful measure partly because it combines the major influences on investment—the real productivity of capital, financial costs, and the real cost of production—into one number. It also permits consideration of disequilibria, where $q \neq 1$ for a significant length of time. In subsection 8.3.1 I show how effects of a stabilization program on q can be calculated in terms of the multipliers of table 8.3. Then in subsection 8.3.2 I calculate the effects on investment incentives of a devaluation versus a spending reduction as alternatives to achieve a given improvement in the trade balance.

8.3.1   Effects on Tobin's q

The q-ratio is defined as the ratio of the market value of an asset (implicit or explicit) to its production cost. If this ratio exceeds unity, a profit-maximizing firm will invest. The task here is to see how a stabilization program is likely to affect q in the N sector.

The q-ratio can be defined as:

$$(19) \qquad q \equiv (R/r)(P_k/P_n),$$

where R is the real rate of return on new investment, and r is the discount factor used to convert that return into an asset value. Thus, R/r is the real market value of the asset; P_k is the cost (or price) of the new investment; and P_n is the output price from section 8.2. P_k/P_n is therefore the real cost of the asset in terms of units of output. For a given value of the discount rate, r, the effect of the stabilization program is given by:

$$(20) \qquad \hat{q} = \hat{R} - (\hat{P}_k - \hat{P}_n).$$

The effect on the real rate of return, R, is given by the effects on real profits from panels B and C of table 8.3 divided by the existing capital stock K. The expression for $\hat{R}$ is thus:

$$(21) \qquad \hat{R} \equiv \left\{ \left[\frac{(\hat{\pi} - C\hat{P}I)}{\hat{P}_i} \right] \hat{P}_i + \left[\frac{(\hat{\pi} - C\hat{P}I)}{\hat{G}} \right] \hat{G} \right\} / K.$$

The expression in parentheses is the effect on real profits from table 8.3. The two terms in brackets are the multipliers from the fourth rows of panels B and C, respectively, in that table. These are multiplied by the assumed percentage devaluation, $\hat{P}_i$, and the assumed cut in government spending, $\hat{G}$, to calculate the effect on real profits. Since the $\hat{P}_i$ multiplier in table 8.3 is negative, the $\hat{G}$ multiplier is positive, $\hat{P}_i$ is positive (devaluation), and $\hat{G}$ is negative (spending cut), $\hat{R}$ will be negative in a stabilization program.

What happens to the cost of capital goods? Let us assume that capital goods are both produced by the N sector and imported, in shares β and $(1 - \beta)$. The percentage change in the real price of capital goods is then given by:

$$\hat{P}_k - \hat{P}_n = [\beta \hat{P}_n + (1 - \beta) \hat{P}_i] - \hat{P}_n,$$

or

$$(22) \qquad \hat{P}_k - \hat{P}_n = (1 - \beta)(\hat{P}_i - \hat{P}_n).$$

Here $(1 - \beta)$ is the share of imports in capital goods supply; and devaluation raises its cost. Table 8.3 gives the changes in P_n per unit change in P_i and G. These can be inserted into equation (22) to give the effect of a stabilization program on the cost of capital goods, such that:

$$(23) \qquad \hat{P}_k - \hat{P}_n = (1 - \beta)\left(1 - \frac{\hat{P}_n}{\hat{P}_i}\right)\hat{P}_i - (1 - \beta)\frac{\hat{P}_n}{\hat{G}} \hat{G}.$$

If $(1 - \beta)$ is 0.8 and $(\hat{P}_n/P_i)$ is 0.37 (from table 8.3a in the case in which $\gamma = 0.5$), a 10 percent devaluation would increase the relative cost of capital goods by 5.04 percent. With $\hat{P}_n/\hat{G}$ equal to 0.34 (in the same case), a 10 percent cut in government spending would raise the relative cost of capital goods by 2.72 percent by reducing P_n for a given P_i. Both parts of the stabilization program thus tend to increase the relative price of capital goods if a significant fraction of these are imported, that is, if $(1 - \beta) \gg 0$. As long as $\hat{P}_i > 0$ and $\hat{G} < 0$, the cost of capital goods in equation (23) increases.

The expressions for $\hat{R}$ from equation (21) and $(\hat{P}_k - \hat{P}_n)$ from (23) can be substituted into equation (20) for $\hat{q}$ to obtain the net effect on investment incentives for the stabilization package. Both parts of the package reduce the real rate of return, R, and increase the relative cost of capital goods $(P_k - P_n)$. In the next section I compare these effects for a given effect on the trade balance.

8.3.2 A Comparison of Devaluation and Spending Reduction

The data in table 8.3 can now be used to compare the effects of a devaluation and a cut in spending as alternative ways to achieve a given improvement in the trade or current-account balance. I will compare the effects on employment and investment incentives and, for completeness, the price of N-sector output as a proxy for inflation. The object here is to investigate the possibilities for minimizing the effects on employment or investment incentives of a stabilization program that is designed to achieve a given improvement in the external position.

The comparison is shown in table 8.4a for $\sigma = 0$ and in table 8.4b for $\sigma = 0.2$. The first row shows the ratio of a devaluation to a spending cut that is aimed at achieving the same reduction in the trade deficit. This is the ratio of the last rows of panels C and B in table 8.3, with the sign changed for $\hat{G}$. As the degree of wage indexation rises, it takes a bigger cut in spending to achieve a given reduction in output and in imports of intermediates. This effect is reduced as the elasticity of substitution increases.

The effects of a cut in spending are shown in panel B of table 8.4. The first three rows repeat the data of table 8.3, showing the reductions in P_n, Q_n and real profits per percentage-point reduction in government spending. The last row of panel B gives the increase in the relative price of capital goods, calculated from equation (23) with $1 - \beta$, the share of imports in capital supply, equal to 0.8. As the price of output falls, the relative price of capital goods increases.

As the degree of wage indexation rises, the employment effect of a cut in spending falls and the effect on investment incentives rises. The latter result comes from an increasing effect on the relative price of capital goods with a rise in wage indexation.

The effects of an equivalent devaluation are shown in panel C of table 8.4. The first three rows are obtained by multiplying the $\hat{P}_i$ effects in table 8.3 by the ratios in panel A of table 8.4. The devaluation is assumed to raise both P_i and P_a. The entries in the last row for $\hat{P}_k - \hat{P}_n$ are calculated from equation (23), with the term for $\hat{P}_n/\hat{P}_i$ taken from table 8.3 and the $\hat{P}_i$ multiplier taken from the ratio in panel A of table 8.4.

Table 8.4a   **A Comparison of the Effects of a Devaluation and an Equivalent Spending Cut, $\sigma = 0$**

	Value of γ		
	0	0.5	1.0
A. Ratio of a Percentage Devaluation to a Percentage Cut in Spending for the Same Reduction in the Trade Deficit	3.23	2.34	1.19
B. Effects per Percentage Cut in G			
Price of Output, $\hat{P}_n$	−0.26	−0.36	−0.60
Employment, $\hat{N}$	−0.85	−0.78	−0.60
Real Profits, $\hat{\pi} - \hat{P}_n$	−0.60	−0.60	−0.60
Price of Capital, $\hat{P}_k - \hat{P}_n$	0.21	0.29	0.48
C. Effects per Equivalent Devaluation			
Price of Output, $\hat{P}_n$	0.81	0.82	0.69
Employment, $\hat{N}$	−0.58	−0.59	−0.50
Real Profits, $\hat{\pi} - \hat{P}_n$	−1.36	−0.98	−0.50
Price of Capital, $\hat{P}_k - \hat{P}_n$	1.94	1.22	0.40

Source: Table 8.3a.

Table 8.4b   **A Comparison of the Effects of a Devaluation and an Equivalent Spending Cut, $\sigma = 0.2$**

	Value of γ		
	0	0.5	1.0
A. Ratio of a Percentage Devaluation to a Percentage Cut in Spending for the Same Reduction in the Trade Deficit	1.75	1.58	1.25
B. Effects per Percentage Cut in G			
Price of Output, $\hat{P}_n$	−0.25	−0.34	−0.55
Employment, $\hat{N}$	−0.82	−0.74	−0.55
Real Profits, $\hat{\pi} - \hat{P}_n$	−0.57	−0.57	−0.55
Price of Capital, $\hat{P}_k - \hat{P}_n$	0.20	0.27	0.44
C. Effects per Equivalent Devaluation			
Price of Output, $\hat{P}_n$	0.47	0.51	0.76
Employment, $\hat{N}$	−0.16	−0.28	−0.48
Real Profits, $\hat{\pi} - \hat{P}_n$	−0.63	−0.58	−0.48
Price of Capital, $\hat{P}_k - \hat{P}_n$	1.02	0.79	0.39

Source: Table 8.3b.

The first two rows of panel C show again the stagflationary effect of devaluation. The third and fourth rows show the effects on real profits and the relative price of capital goods. With the elasticity of substitution equal to zero, both effects are significantly larger than the effects of a spending cut for the same effect on the trade balance, except with

nearly complete indexation. With the elasticity of substitution equal to
0.2, the real profits effects are about the same (-0.57 versus -0.58)
with $\gamma = 0.5$, but the effect on the cost of capital is much larger for
the devaluation than for the spending cut.

With no wage indexation, a spending reduction has a much smaller
negative effect on investment incentives and a slightly higher effect on
employment in the N sector than a devaluation has, and it is of course
deflationary rather than inflationary. With high indexation the effects
of the two alternatives on investment incentives and employment are
about the same; the big difference is in the movement of the price level.

These results suggest that if the source of the problem is a shock to
the terms of trade in an essentially noninflationary initial situation, the
best policy is a reduction in absorption with no devaluation and no
wage indexation. An absence of wage indexation will be easiest to
maintain if the initial situation is one of price stability. It would be hard
to sustain in the face of devaluation-induced inflation, however. Thus,
in the situation facing Kenya in 1979–80, the best program may well
have been a spending reduction as needed to reduce absorption, but
no devaluation and the maintenance of nonindexation of nominal wages.

8.4   The Role of Devaluation: Liberalization vs. Stabilization

Stabilization programs generally include devaluation as part of the
policy package. In a simple monetary model of the balance of payments,
with only one good, the devaluation validates the existing money stock
as an equilibrium by raising the domestic price level. Indeed, the model
of section 8.2 shows the effect of devaluation on the price of nontraded
output, P_n. It seems unlikely that devaluation would be proposed solely
for this purpose, however. If the only problem is a disequilibrium money
stock, the supply of money can be reduced to restore equilibrium.

More commonly, devaluation is proposed to eliminate, or at least to
reduce, a current-account deficit. This benefit must be balanced against
the concomitant depressive effect on output, profits, and investment
in the nontraded sector, as shown in section 8.3. The results there
suggest that devaluation may not be an appropriate component of a
stabilization program in countries with an inelastic supply of exports
and with intermediate imports. These include many of the developing
countries of Africa, which still rely on one or two agricultural products
as their principal exports. In the light of this argument, one might ask
what is the appropriate role for devaluation in these countries. In answer to this question, it is useful to distinguish between stabilization
and liberalization.

A case of pure stabilization arises when a country that is roughly in
internal equilibrium is hit by an external shock that necessitates a

reduction in absorption. The terms-of-trade deterioration in 1979–80 in Kenya is an example. In this case domestic absorption has to be reduced unless there is clear evidence that the disturbance is temporary and the means to finance the deficit are at hand. If the disturbance appears likely to last indefinitely, for example, if the terms-of-trade follow something like a random walk over time, or if financing is not available, spending must be reduced. But a devaluation may only import inflation and depress profits, with little effect on the current-account deficit in the short run. The problem is that absorption is too high, not that the country is insufficiently competitive in trade.

Alternatively, consider a country with a protracted disequilibrium generated by budget deficits and monetary expansion. If the exchange rate is not allowed to move, perhaps following a crawling peg, then import controls and export subsidies are likely to appear to contain the current-account deficit. As the disequilibrium continues, the real exchange rate will appreciate, and increasing stringency of controls will be required. In this case *liberalization* would be appropriate. This would be a package of a decontrol of imports, an elimination of export subsidies, and devaluation to restore an equilibrium real exchange rate. The liberalization could be independent of stabilization. A country could, for example, liberalize in trade and move to a crawling peg after the initial discrete devaluation. Liberalization programs can also produce stagflationary results, however, as shown by Buffie (1984). But devaluation is an appropriate component of a liberalization package.

Stabilization and liberalization can be combined if the objective is twofold: stabilization after a protracted period of disequilibrium, and liberalization to rationalize production and make efficiency gains. The argument here, though, is that it should be clear whether the devaluation is aimed at carrying out the stabilization or the liberalization goal. The former might not be useful, and mixing the two together can result in devaluation being included in a pure stabilization package where it is not needed.

Kenya in 1980 may have been an example of a country in need of pure stabilization. The external shock was a terms-of-trade deterioration caused by a temporarily strong position after the coffee boom. There was no clear history of domestic inflation or overvaluation of the currency in real terms. The 1983 *World Development Report* cites Kenya as a country with a relatively low degree of trade controls. Because Kenya needed to reduce absorption, the devaluation may have been counterproductive. The case of Tanzania may be more complicated. This is probably a situation of a country's maintaining a long disequilibrium by using real exchange rate and trade controls. There the need for *stabilization* versus the need for *liberalization* is a basic choice facing policy makers. The two can be kept separate, however, and devaluation should probably be considered part of a liberalization program, independent of the decision on stabilization.

References

Ahamed, L. 1983. An aggregate model of the Kenyan economy. Washington, D.C.: World Bank, April 14. Photocopy.

Branson, W. H. 1983. Economic structure and policy for external balance. *International Monetary Fund Staff Papers* 30, no. 1 (March): 39–66.

Branson, W. H., and Katseli-Papaefstratiou, L. T. 1981. Exchange rate policy for developing countries. In *The world economic order: Past and prospects,* ed. S. Grassman and E. Lundberg, 392–419. London: Macmillan.

Bruno, M. and Sachs, J. 1979. Supply vs. demand approaches to the problem of stagflation. In *Macroeconomic policies for growth and stability: A European perspective,* symposium, Tübingen, ed. H. Giersch, 15–60.

Buffie, E. F. 1984. The macroeconomics of trade liberalization. *Journal of International Economics* 17, nos. 1–2 (August): 212–38.

Cooper, R. M. 1971. Currency devaluation in developing countries. *Princeton Essays in International Finance* no. 80 (June).

Katseli, L. T. 1983. Devaluation: A critical appraisal of the IMF's policy prescriptions. *American Economic Review* 73, no. 2 (May): 359–64.

Katseli-Papaefstratiou, L. T., and Marion, N. P. 1982. Adjustment variations in prices of imported inputs: The role of economic structure. *Weltwirtschaftliches Archiv* 118 (no. 1): 131–47.

Khan, M. S., and Knight, M. D. 1981. Stabilization programs in developing countries: A formal framework. *International Monetary Fund Staff Papers* 28 (March): 1–53.

Krugman, P., and Taylor, L. 1978. Contractionary effects of devaluation. *Journal of International Economics* 8 (August): 445–56.

Marston, R. C., and Turnovsky, S. J. 1983. Imported materials prices, wage policy, and macroeconomic stabilization. NBER Working Paper no. 1254 (December). Cambridge, Mass.: National Bureau of Economic Research.

Tobin, J. P. 1969. A general equilibrium approach to monetary theory. *Journal of Money, Credit, and Banking* 1, no. 1 (February): 15–29.

World Development Report. 1983. Washington, D. C.: International Bank for Reconstruction and Development.

Comment   Jacques R. Artus

Branson's paper is an important contribution to the literature on the design of stabilization programs. In a research area in which dogmatic views are so common, it is a refreshing attempt to rely on the analytical and empirical evidence. Moreover, it focuses on a very timely issue, namely, whether adjustment to a lasting deterioration in the external terms of trade can be achieved better through devaluation than through a cut in government spending.

Although I like Branson's basic analytical approach because it is well rooted in economic theory, I have serious reservations about the specific empirical application and the policy conclusions derived from it. Taking first the model and the parameter estimates as given, I believe that Branson is going too far when he states that his results strongly suggest that a country with an economic structure such as the one of Kenya should adjust through a cut in government spending rather than through a devaluation. The results warrant a much more subtle conclusion. If we look at the key estimate corresponding to an elasticity of substitution between value added and imported inputs (σ) of 0.2[1] and an indexation coefficient (γ) of 0.5, the decline in employment is nearly *three times larger* when the adjustment is sought through a cut in government spending rather than through a devaluation (see table 8.1). This is a very high price to pay to avoid the two disadvantages of devaluation: the increase in the price of output, and the marked rise in the relative price of imported capital goods.

Furthermore, the disadvantages of devaluation are overstated. In particular, the rise in the price of imported capital goods could be a benefit in disguise. Since the elasticity of the domestic supply of saving with respect to the yield on saving is probably small, the amount of investment may be unaffected. The effect is instead likely to be a substitution of domestically produced capital goods for imported capital goods, through changes both in production techniques and in the structure of production. There could also be a change in the pattern of development toward more labor-intensive techniques of production and economic activities. Given the existence of a large pool of unemployed labor, the ultimate effect could be a significant rise in economic growth.

In contrast, Branson understates the disadvantages of a cut in government spending. The resulting reduction in economic activity would likely have a negative effect on private investment. Entrepreneurs do not add to their capital stock when a large part of it is idle. Moreover, a cut in government spending would probably

Jacques R. Artus is an advisor in the Research Department of the International Monetary Fund.

mean a decline in public investment and social expenditures. Ultimately, there is no doubt that in Branson's model the "size of the pie" is smaller with the cut in government spending than with the devaluation, since output is less and the current-account balance remains unchanged. Unless it leads to lower investment, the cut in government spending could imply a much lower private consumption than the devaluation would. Thus, it is not obvious that the cut in government spending would be more socially and politically acceptable than the devaluation.

Even more important, I believe that some of the specific values assigned to key parameters of the model should be modified. Once this is done, the model would lead to the conclusion that devaluation is clearly the better policy. In particular, the value of 0.1 assigned to the supply elasticity of exports with respect to their own price (s_a), is much too low.[2] There is considerable empirical evidence on the agricultural response to prices in Sub-Saharan African countries. Most studies find that the supply elasticity for the cash crops exported by those countries are in the ranges 0.3 to 0.5 in the first year and 0.5 to 1.5 after three to five years.[3] Of course, the response will be influenced by the initial situation and the overall policy strategy of the authorities; the response will tend to be relatively small if the initial price is already sufficient to ensure that the plantations will be well maintained and well harvested, or if there is a severe shortage of credit, fertilizer, and other inputs. This was not the case in Kenya in 1980. Moreover, Kenya's exports of manufactures account for about 20 percent of its total nonoil exports. The supply elasticity for those manufactures is probably sizable.[4]

It is also likely that the value Branson assigns to the elasticity of substitution between value added and imported inputs in the nontraded sector (σ) is too low. He indicates that the 0.2 estimate is based on the work of Bruno and Sachs. The problem is that the estimate of Bruno and Sachs referred to the substitution between value added and intermediate inputs in industrial countries. Basically, those authors were looking at the effect of changes in the prices of fuels and raw materials on their uses in production. This price effect tends to be small because it is difficult to substitute labor and capital for either fuels or raw materials, say, in the production of steel. The issue is quite different in Kenya. A large part of the imported inputs used in the Kenyan nontraded sector is accounted for by semifinished products. A change in the exchange rate can affect the demand for these products even if there is no change in the techniques of production. First, some products may be manufactured in Kenya rather than imported. Second, some of the relatively few specific sectors that import much of the semifinished products and contribute little domestic value added may have to scale down their production.

The use of more realistic values for the supply elasticity of exports (s_a) and the elasticity of substitution between domestic value added and imported inputs (σ) would be enough to tilt the scale in favor of devaluation in Branson's model. The results appear to be particularly sensitive to the value of the σ parameter. For example, in the central case in which $\gamma = 0.5$, the increase in the value of σ from zero to 0.2 reduces by half the negative effects of devaluation on employment and real profit (see table 8.1). In contrast, the unfavorable effects of the cut in government spending are not reduced when the value of σ increases.

Although devaluation would emerge as the better policy in Branson's model once more realistic values were chosen for the important parameters, it is easy to conceive of an extended model in which this might not be true. A cut in spending could be a good alternative if it were limited to categories of expenditures that have a relatively high import content and a relatively low marginal utility. It could also be a good alternative if the model were extended to include other countries exporting the same primary commodities. If all those countries shared the same external adjustment problem, devaluation by all of them could lead to a deterioration in their terms of trade.

Finally, and on a different level, the situation of Kenya in 1980 was far more complex than Branson indicates. In particular, import controls were extremely pervasive. Indeed, the 1983 *World Development Report* cited by Branson classifies Kenya as one of the developing countries with the highest degrees of protection of domestic manufacturing (see p. 62 of that report).[5] Moreover, by 1980 budget deficits and monetary expansion had been a problem for several years. Monetary expansion (broad money) averaged 23 percent per annum over the years, 1975–79, during which time the inflation rate averaged 14 percent per annum. Since the exchange rate had not been allowed to move, the international competitiveness of Kenya had deteriorated substantially. These considerations largely explain why Kenya did choose to devalue in 1981. Nonetheless, this observation should be viewed as an aside. Branson's paper is mainly concerned with the case for devaluation when a country with the economic structure of Kenya is experiencing a lasting decline in its terms of trade, rather than the specific policy options of Kenya in 1980. With respect to this broad analytical issue, Branson's analytical framework is moving us in the right direction. But more work, especially on the empirical side, has to be done. At the present state of knowledge on the subject, Branson's policy conclusions are thus rather premature.

Notes

1. Branson indicates that he took the estimate $\sigma = 0.2$ from Bruno and Sachs (1979). Since this is a point estimate, it is unclear why he presents stimulations for $\sigma = 0.2$ and $\sigma = 0$ and speaks of a range from 0.2 to 0. The range should extend on both sides of the 0.2 estimate.
2. Branson refers to this elasticity as the "elasticity of agricultural output with respect to its own price" because of his assumption that all agricultural output is exported and nothing else is exported.
3. See, for example, Marion E. Bond, "Agricultural responses to prices in Sub-Saharan African countries," *International Monetary Fund Staff Papers* 30, no. 4 (December 1983).
4. Logically, one should consider exports of both goods and services rather than exports of goods only. International tourism, for example, is an important source of foreign exchange for Kenya, and there is little doubt that it is influenced by exchange rates.
5. The report classified Kenya as a country with a relatively low *overall* degree of price distortion mainly because Kenya did not have major price distortions in agriculture or in the energy sector.

Comment   Ravi Gulhati

The main conclusions of the Branson paper are as follows. First, in 1979–80 Kenya experienced an external shock, a deterioration in its terms of trade. Internally, the situation was "roughly in internal equilibrium." Second, the appropriate policy response by the Kenyan government would have been to reduce absorption and not to devalue. Third, the Kenyan case is typical of many African countries, which rely on few primary exports whose supply tends to be inelastic. Those countries also use imported intermediate goods that constitute a large share of their total imports. In all those African countries devaluation is the wrong policy. Finally, by contrast, the Tanzanian case was characterized by a long disequilibrium accompanied by a proliferation of monetary controls. Branson advocates instead the use of devaluation when reforms are aimed at liberalization.

My own assessment of Kenya in 1979–80 is quite different from Branson's. The country faced a major structural adjustment problem at that time, and the deterioration in the terms of trade was merely aggravating the situation. That structural problem was reflected in a number of more specific problems. First, the rate of growth of agricultural production had slowed down because of the exhaustion of land with high agricultural potential; the lack of technological programs suitable for the cultivation of arid and semiarid areas; an overvaluation of the Kenyan shilling and a policy of protection against imports of

Ravi Gulhati is chief economist of the Eastern and Southern Africa Region of the World Bank.

manufactures produced in the domestic economy, which made the internal terms of trade disadvantageous for agriculture; and the adverse effects of government intervention in the pricing and marketing of several agricultural goods. Second, the growth of manufacturing production had also decelerated because of a reduction in the growth of the internal market and a breakdown of the East African Common Market. Third, an acceleration in the population growth rate was exerting pressure on arable land, accentuating already serious underemployment and adding to budgetary problems by expanding fiscal outlays for education and other government services.

In those circumstances the economic policy recommended by Branson, which would merely have reduced effective demand in order to adjust to the deterioration in the terms of trade, would have been grossly insufficient. What was required was a policy package that combined reduced outlays, devaluation, trade liberalization, improved budget controls, and measures to reduce fertility.

To assess the role of exchange rate policies in securing economic recovery in Africa, we need an analytical framework that addresses not only short-term stabilization issues, but also questions bearing on diversification in the commodity and market structure of exports; reduction in the import component of consumption, production, and investment without violating the canons of dynamic comparative advantage; and mobilization of domestic savings and external resources. The Branson model does not provide such a framework. The author's position is instead characterized by a great deal of unnecessary pessimism regarding the response of export production and import requirements to price adjustments. Elsewhere I have argued that although structural rigidities are present in many African countries, there are no grounds for unqualified pessimism about elasticity (Gulhati, Bose, and Atukorala 1985). But it is true that the short-run response is unlikely to be large unless excess capacity exists and can be activated quickly. What is essential in most African countries is a set of policies (of which the exchange rate is a critical part) that will bring about diversification in the structure of production and corresponding changes in the supply of tradables—both exports and import substitutes.

Reference

Gulhati, R., Bose, S., and Atukorala, V. 1985. Exchange rate policies in eastern and southern Africa, 1965–83. Washington, D. C.: World Bank Staff Working Paper.

9 Discrete Devaluation as a Signal to Price Setters: Suggested Evidence from Greece

Louka T. Katseli

9.1 Introduction

The origin of this paper can be traced back to early February 1983, following my visit to a small shoe repair shop in a suburb of Athens. The owner of the shop had angrily protested the decision of the firm that supplied him shoe polish to issue a new price list, which effectively raised the prices of almost all of its main products by 20 to 34 percent. His anger was focused not so much on the extent of the price change but on the fact that, contrary to his expectations, the new price list was issued so soon after the last list in October. He maintained that this was a clear violation of the client-supplier relationship, since in the past the implicit price contract set between them left prices unchanged for a period of six to nine months. The justification provided by the firm for this "breach" of contract was the "unprecedented" devaluation of the drachma during the preceding month. To this the shoemaker replied that the price-surveillance department of the Ministry of Commerce should intervene because the polish firm used only domestically produced goods and thus had used the pretext of the devaluation to raise profits. In Okun's terms, "customers appear willing to accept as fair an increase in price based on a permanent increase in cost" (Okun 1975). To the Athenian shoemaker the January devaluation did not entail a permanent increase in cost to the shoe polish firm. This attitude was obviously not shared by the firm itself.

Louka T. Katseli is director general of the Center for Planning and Economic Research (KEPE), Athens, Greece.

I would like to thank J. Anastassakou, E. Anagnostopoulou, N. Papandreou, and P. McGuire for helpful assistance. Financial support from the German Marshal Fund is gratefully acknowledged.

On 9 January 1983 the Greek drachma was devalued against the U.S. dollar by 15.5 percent, raising the price of the dollar from 71 to 84 drachmas. On a monthly average, the devaluation of the drachma between December 1982 and January 1983 was 14.14 percent against the dollar and 14.77 percent in effective terms. As can be seen in figures 9.1 and 9.2, this was the largest discrete change both in the bilateral Dr/$ rate (*BIE*) and in the effective exchange rate (*EFE*) since the Greek government's introduction of a crawling-peg system in March 1975. It was at that time that the drachma ceased to be pegged to the U.S. dollar and that a basket of 12 currencies became the basis for the conduct of the country's exchange rate policy. Thus, over a ten-year period of managed float, the January 1983 devaluation of the drachma was one of the few incidents of a discrete and large adjustment of the exchange rate as opposed to a daily smooth crawling.

The object of this paper is to investigate the effects of exchange rate management on price behavior and thus on the real exchange rate in a small, semi-industrialized country like Greece.

Traditionally, the main policy objective behind a nominal devaluation is to promote competitiveness in third markets and to improve the

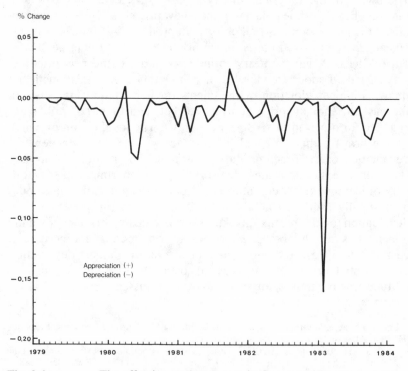

Fig. 9.1   The effective exchange rate in Greece, 1979–84.

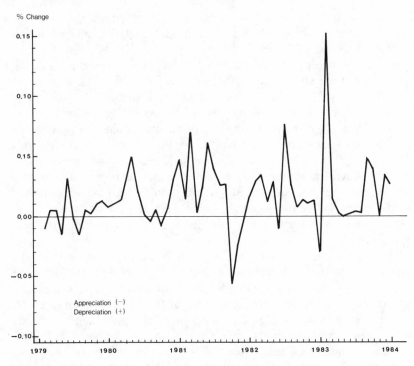

Fig. 9.2   The drachma/dollar exchange rate, 1979–84.

balance of payments. J-curve considerations aside, the balance-of-payments effects following a nominal devaluation depend on the extent to which the real exchange rate is depreciated and on the effects of the real exchange rate adjustment on net export receipts. Regarding the first factor there is already an extensive literature on the subject that focuses on the potential adjustment of the relative price of domestic to traded goods following a devaluation.[1] An increase in the price of traded goods relative to nontraded goods as a result of a devaluation shifts demand toward the nontraded goods sector, giving rise to a current-account surplus that increases reserves and the money supply. The degree of balance-of-payments improvement depends on elasticities, income and absorption effects, conditions in asset markets, and, finally, expectations. Eventually, the price of nontraded goods will rise to its steady-state level. In the meantime employment and output in the non-traded goods sector will increase (Katseli 1980).

As I have shown elsewhere (Katseli 1980) these results are sensitive to the underlying assumptions regarding the structural characteristics of the economy and, more specifically, to the degree of wage indexation and the presence of imported intermediate goods. In both these cases the demand shift is coupled with a cost shift, making the effects on the real exchange rate, the output response, and the balance of payments at best ambiguous.

In the absence of an adjustment of the real exchange rate, a devaluation can work solely through a real balance effect. The increase in the price of foreign exchange then reduces real balances. If the demand for money is exogenously determined,[2] the excess demand for money is translated into a reduction in absorption and a balance-of-payments surplus that is the vehicle by which money balances are replenished (Katseli 1983). In this case, as absorption is reduced the improvement in the balance of payments is achieved at the expense of real consumption in the economy and output and employment in the nontraded goods sector. Given these considerations, it is important to look at the implications of exchange rate management for real exchange rate developments.

The central hypothesis of this paper is that both the extent and the speed of adjustment of the real exchange rate are influenced by the way in which the central bank manages the nominal exchange rate. Specifically, a large discrete adjustment of the nominal exchange rate is more likely to result in a rapid adjustment of prices than is a policy of a smooth and continuous crawling peg. To use Cooper's (1973) terminology, whether exchange rate policy occupies the "high-" or "low-politics realm" does in fact matter in a country's international competitiveness and in the output and employment effects during the adjustment period.

If domestic prices instantaneously adjust to their steady-state level, the improvement in the balance of payments can come about only through a natural or policy-induced squeeze in absorption. In both cases the effects of the devaluation will tend to be stagflationary, at least in the nontraded goods sector.

The channel through which management of the nominal exchange rate influences real exchange rate developments is the process of price adjustment. As will be shown in section 9.2, this process has at least two important features, namely, the magnitude and the frequency of price changes. The existing finance literature on exchange rate policy has in general focused on the first aspect only, that is, on the responsiveness of domestic prices to a nominal devaluation. The industrial organization and macroeconomics literature, on the other hand, has increasingly focused on sluggishness. As Barro (1972, 17) has noticed,

> The firm's elastic demand curve must be discarded in disequilibrium if the firm is ever to change price. In this sense the response of prices to disequilibrium is essentially a monopolistic phenomenon even if the individual units perform as perfect competitors in equilibrium.

Therefore, it seems clear that a theory of monopolistic price adjustment is a prerequisite to a general theory of price adjustment.

Monopolistic price adjustment implies joint determination of two pricing features on the part of the firm: the length of the implicit or explicit "price contract," and the magnitude of the adjustment at the end of the contract period. As Gray (1976) has shown, analogous modeling can be applied to the workings of a labor market characterized by the existence of a strong union. In that case the contract length and the indexing parameter are the important contract characteristics.

In merging these two strands of the literature, this paper argues that exchange rate management can affect both the length of the price contract between firms and clients and the magnitude of the price adjustment. This hypothesis can be tested directly only through the use of micro or firm-level data, since the path of price adjustment varies across firms. These data are in fact available for Greek firms. As will be shown in section 9.3, the prices set by Greek firms for specific products exhibit properties of a step function. The contract length and the magnitude of the price adjustment can thus be investigated in relation to exchange rate management.

The econometric analysis of price behavior by firms is complicated, however, by the existence of special institutional characteristics of trading. More specifically, most developing countries are apt to employ some institutional mechanism for price surveillance or direct price controls.

In the case of Greece, price controls have existed since the mid 1930s. After World War II they covered only a small number of products and were intended to curb excessive profits earned from the sale of goods in short supply. Over time, those controls were extended to cover numerous other products by specifying price ceilings or maximum allowable markups over costs. The type of control that has been used has varied across goods and business operations and has been applicable to the industry, the wholesaler, or the retailer, that is, to any stage within the production and distribution systems (Lalonde and Papandreou 1984).

The complexity of the system thus seriously hinders an extensive analysis of price behavior by firms unless one investigates thoroughly the underlying institutional arrangements that affect each specific product or enterprise. In the presence of differentiated product controls, profit-maximizing behavior on the part of firms implies that the pricing of noncontrolled goods also departs from the expected pricing under free-market conditions. It has been observed, for example, that firms tend to price overall production in such a way as to ensure large enough profits in some lines of production and thus cover losses generated in the production of price-controlled products. It follows that an increase in expected or actual costs affects not only the overall price level but also the relative prices of different commodities.

In view of these complexities, the central hypotheses of this paper can be formulated as follows. Section 9.2 argues that discrete adjustment of the exchange rate tends to shorten the implicit price contract between sellers and buyers and to augment the rate of price adjustment. This is so because firms tend to strengthen their expectations about an overall increase in costs and about an aggregate shift in the demand curve for the firms' output. A discrete change in the exchange rate thus acts as an "information signal" in the market that leads to a relatively rapid overall price adjustment of traded and nontraded goods alike. Given the presence of controls, the prices of noncontrolled goods should tend to adjust faster than those of controlled goods, even though sooner or later the regulatory agency itself is apt to allow price increases in the controlled part of the market. The output response to these effects depends not only on the expected increase in demand for the firm's output relative to its costs, but also on the ability of each firm to diversify production with commodities that are exempt from price controls.

The econometric analysis provided in section 9.3 should be interpreted with caution. Given the existing institutional complexities, it has to be conducted at the macro, sectoral, and product levels. Even though the existing evidence is not conclusive, the data do not reject the central hypotheses of section 9.2, making this line of research both interesting and promising.

9.2 The Magnitude and Frequency of Price Adjustment Following a Discrete Adjustment of the Exchange Rate

In the international finance literature exchange rate management has been analyzed in the context of the benefits and costs of alternative exchange rate regimes. As early as 1970, Cooper and other authors argued for greater exchange rate flexibility on three separate grounds: to provide smoother adjustment to changing fundamentals; to avoid speculative runs on the national currency; and to reestablish the effectiveness of monetary policy (Cooper 1973).

As consensus on the advisability of flexible exchange rates grew, the focus of attention shifted to the manner in which the "gliding parity" should be managed. It was demonstrated, for example, that exchange rate adjustment could be unstable if the rate of change in the nominal exchange rate followed the rate of change in foreign exchange reserves, as opposed to following developments in the current-account or the basic balance (Rodriguez 1981). The so-called shock treatment, namely, an unexpected sudden devaluation or revaluation of the nominal exchange rate, was judged inferior to the "gradualist solution" because it was considered highly unlikely that central authorities would possess the necessary information to arrive at an equilibrium real exchange rate through discrete action (Rodriguez 1981).

Despite the advantages of continuous exchange rate adjustment to correct underlying fundamental disequilibria, a number of countries during recent years have chosen to pursue a discrete adjustment policy. Sweden, Spain, and Greece are the most recent examples.

Discrete adjustment of the nominal exchange rate has usually been associated with either political transitions or interruptions in the normal conduct of exchange rate policy. It is thus undertaken at the beginning of a new government's term in office in an attempt to slow the necessary rate of devaluation in the following year and to attribute the need for the adjustment to earlier government policy. This scenario probably applies to both Sweden and Spain. Discrete adjustment is also initiated during periods when, for various economic or institutional reasons, the real exchange rate becomes overvalued, giving rise to speculative runs on the currency. In both cases the discrete adjustment of the nominal exchange rate is a response to growing disequilibria in the economy. Finally, discrete adjustment is also used by policy makers to influence expectations about the future rate of devaluation and thus the rate of inflation. It is often a signal for a reversal in policy stance and is usually accompanied by other changes in fiscal or monetary policies. This is the most likely explanation for the Greek case. Such adjustment, if credible, could in fact have negative real effects on output and employment.

As Calvo (1981) has shown, an unanticipated devaluation always improves the balance of payments of a small, open economy, whereas below a certain critical deficit level, an increase in the rate of devaluation could bring about a deterioration. In the presence of nontraded goods, these results will continue to hold, especially if the relative price of traded to nontraded goods is altered. A devaluation of the real exchange rate[3] thus strengthens the case for a balance-of-payments improvement (Katseli 1983). If, as a response to an unanticipated devaluation, the prices of nontraded goods jump to their steady-state value, then even the transitory improvement in the balance of payments could be questioned. This is especially true in developing countries, where the decrease in absorption might be limited by inflationary expectations that lead to an increase in consumption and imports of durables or to an accumulation of inventories. Furthermore, inflationary expectations and a decrease in output might reduce money demand, offsetting the excess demand for money that is necessary for a balance-of-payments improvement. It could therefore be argued that a devaluation of the real exchange rate is more necessary for a balance-of-payments improvement when the conditions for a smooth working of the real balance effect are unfavorable.

Can the process of price adjustment differ depending on the way the exchange rate is managed? The answer would be positive if one analyzes price behavior in price-setting markets instead of in simple auction markets. As Gordon (1981) has noted, the assumption of "pervasive heterogeneity" in the types and quality of products and in the location and timing of transactions is crucial for such a theory of price adjustment. This approach thus undermines "the new classical macroeconomic models based on a one-good economy postulated by identical price-taking yeoman farmers" (Gordon 1981), or Calvo's world of a one-family, one-good economy, in which "the price level is the exchange rate [that is, the relative price] of domestic currency in terms of some other given currency" (Calvo 1981).

There is already a fairly substantial literature on the microeconomic foundations of price adjustment. Apart from issues related to the existence of a "non-Walrasian" or "conjectural" equilibrium, as early as the 1960s another set of contributions attributed partial price adjustment to adjustment costs and incomplete information. In that tradition one could cite the works of Alchian (1969), Phelps and Winter (1970), Okun (1975), and more recently Blinder (1982) and others.[4]

From that viewpoint and in sharp contrast to the prototypical firm in traditional short-run market analysis, pervasive heterogeneity and the cost of information make each firm behave in the short and the medium run as a monopolist. In that role the firm acts as a quantity taker and price maker. As Okun has remarked, "Even firms with minuscule market shares put price tags on their commodities; in the short run, they are never surprised by the price, and always subject to surprise about the quantities they sell" (Okun 1975, 360).

Following this line of thought, Gordon has argued that the fundamental reason for gradual price adjustment is the "large local component of actual changes in demand and costs, together with the independence of those costs and demand changes" (Gordon 1981, 522). Combining price-setting behavior by a typical monopolist with Lucas's analysis of expectation formation Gordon has reached the following conclusions: that price adjustment will be complete if the perceived marginal cost responds fully to an aggregate shock but not if otherwise; that the expected cost mimics expected aggregate demand if the aggregate variance of a shock dominates the local variance; and that only in the extreme case when the aggregate component of the variance of both demand and cost shifts is very large relative to the local component, as during wartime or a hyperinflation, does price adjustment capture fully the aggregate demand shift.

In this view, therefore, heterogeneity of products makes firms behave as monopolists that purchase their inputs from and sell their output to other firms. The extent to which a particular shock that affects cost and demand is perceived as "local" or "global" critically affects pricing decisions. The adjustment of the price will be larger if a shock in demand is expected to affect other firms as well and thus in the end give rise to an increase in the firm's input costs.

How can this framework be applied to exchange rate management? In the case of a discrete devaluation that is typically large, there is an "announcement effect." A high-level official usually announces to all market participants that effective immediately the prices of all traded goods will be increased. That announcement thus stimulates or confirms expectations, even in the nontraded goods sector, that demand for output and the cost of inputs will increase. The increase in production cost is expected to take the form not only of an increase in the cost of imported inputs, but also in the cost of intermediate or capital goods purchased from other domestic firms. In the non-union sector labor costs are expected to rise concomitantly, while in the unionized sector, wages are expected to be adjusted at the end of the contract period or when contracts are renegotiated. Discrete adjustment of the exchange rate thus induces an expected increase in the overall cost of production, that is, in both its local and its aggregate components. On the demand side, the larger the discrete devaluation, the greater the likelihood of an overall demand shift in the economy and thus the smaller the perceived cost to each firm of raising its own price. A discrete adjustment of the exchange rate therefore strengthens expectations regarding inflationary pressures in the economy that will produce an increase in both demand and marginal costs.

The trade-off between price and output adjustment depends on firm specifics. The expected increase in marginal costs, however, is more likely to mirror the expected increase in demand in the case of a discrete change in the exchange rate than in the case of a crawling peg. Hence, in comparing these two regimes one would expect price rather than output adjustment to be dominant in the former case.

Discrete adjustment of the exchange rate induces not only an increase in the average expected cost of production, but also in the variance of the aggregate component as opposed to the local component. As the local component of actual changes in demand and costs becomes small, price adjustment in the specific firm tends to approximate the rate of devaluation.

With a simple cost-push model similar to that developed by Gordon (1981), it is easy to show that the percentage change in price (P_{it}) will be positively related to a discrete change in the exchange rate, defined as the ratio of the unexpected change in the exchange rate relative to its variance, or $\dfrac{R_t - E_{-1}R_t}{\text{Var } R}$.

For the monopolist, P_i is a weighted average of the actual change in nominal revenue (α_{it}) and of expected changes at time t in the marginal costs at time $t + 1$, or $E_t(C_{it+1})$. Thus:

(1) $$P_{it} = \psi\alpha_{it} + (1 - \psi)E_t(C_{it+1}),$$

where i refers to the specific firm, and E is the expectations operator.

The expected change in marginal costs for the individual firm i is a weighted average of the actual cost increase of imported inputs and of the expected costs of other inputs that are determined by a different set of agents, including labor and other firms (W). If the change in the price of imported inputs at time t is assumed to equal R_t, and the mean of the local component of W is assumed to equal zero, it follows that:

(2) $$E_t(C_{it+1}) = zR_t + (1 - z)(1 - \phi)E_t(W_{t+1}),$$

where ϕ is the ratio of the variance of the local component of the cost shift to the sum of the variances of the local and aggregate components.

Apart from a known component ($\overline{W}$) that captures information about existing contracts, past pricing behavior, and known institutional factors, expectations about non–firm-specific costs, $E_t(W_{t+1})$, are assumed to be positively related to the unexpected component of the exchange rate change, this being defined as the difference between the actual change at time t and that expected during the previous period, $E_{-1}(R_t)$, divided by the historical variance of exchange rate changes. Thus:

(3) $$E_t(W_{t+1}) = \overline{W}_{t+1} + \beta\left[\frac{R_t - E_{-1}(R_t)}{\text{Var } R}\right],$$

Making all appropriate substitutions, we find that:

(4) $$P_{it} = \psi\alpha_{it} + (1 - \psi) zR_t$$
$$+ (1 - \psi)(1 - z)(1 - \phi)\left\{\overline{W}_{t+1} + \beta\left[\frac{R_t - E_{-1}(R_T)}{\text{Var } R}\right]\right\}.$$

Given equation (4) it is easy to see that P_{it} is positively related to $\dfrac{R_t - E_{-1}(R_t)}{\text{Var } R}$. More specifically if we assume that $E_{-1}(R_t) = 0$, then:

(5) $$\partial P_{it}/\partial(R_t/\text{Var } R) = (1 - \psi)z\text{Var}R$$
$$+ (1 - \psi)(1 - z)(1 - \phi)\beta > 0.$$

From equation (5) it follows that for any given unexpected change in the exchange rate, P_i becomes larger as the aggregate component of the variance of costs becomes larger in relation to the local component, or $\phi \to 0$. This is probably the case when there is a switch in regimes from a smooth crawling peg to that of a discrete exchange rate adjustment. If this is so, then both $E(W_{t+1})$ and $(1 - \phi)$ are positively related to $\dfrac{R_t - E_{-1}(R_t)}{\text{Var } R}$.

Finally, it should be noted that the increase in price will be even larger if $E(W_{t+1})$ is made to represent the expected aggregate change in income. In that case, as in Gordon (1981), equation (3) could be replaced by:

$$(3') \quad E(W_{t+1}) = \theta \left\{ \bar{W}_{t+1} + \beta \left[\frac{R_t - E_{-1}(R_t)}{\text{Var } R} \right] \right\} + (1 - \theta) \, \alpha_{it},$$

where the demand shift is assumed to consist of a local component and an aggregate component. In (3'), θ, like ϕ, is the ratio of the local component of the demand shift to the sum of the local and aggregate variances. The replacement of (3) by (3') does not change the qualitative nature of the results.

The analysis so far is limited to the magnitude of the price response to a discrete devaluation. One would expect, however, that implicit price contracts will also be arbitrarily shortened or renegotiated.

In analyzing labor market contracts, Gray argued that the "optimal contract length is inversely related to the variance of the industry-specific shock" (Gray 1978, 11). Firms are assumed to determine the degree of indexation and the length of the labor contract by minimizing a loss function (z) of the form:

$$(6) \qquad z = 1/l \, (\lambda \int_0^l E \, [(\ln Y_t - \ln Y_t^0)^2] \, dt + C),$$

where l is the contract length, and λ is a relative price that converts losses expressed as squared output deviations into losses expressed in the units of the contracting cost (C).

Intuitively, the optimal contract length in Gray's analysis is determined by a condition that at the margin "balances the per period savings on transactions costs that could be achieved by lengthening the contract against the concomitant increased losses in the form of larger expected output and employment deviations." Thus, whereas "increased uncertainty brings about a shortening of contract length, increased contracting costs lead to a lengthening of contracts" (Gray 1978, 7).

In the case of the monopolistic firm that determines both price and output, it is the cost of information that includes the costs of prediction and of establishing reliability and permanence that leads to implicitly long-term contractual relationships. These considerations have to be weighed against the profit losses that would be incurred if underpricing were to continue for too long. A large discrete adjustment of the ex-change rate both reduces the cost of information as defined above and establishes, as we have seen, firms' expectations about the prospective increase in costs. Since cost-oriented pricing with a markup offers the "most typical standard of fairness in buyer-seller relationships" (Okun 1975) a discrete devaluation allows sellers to pursue cost-oriented price increases. Thus, a discrete devaluation, as opposed to a crawling peg, reduces the cost the firm bears in explaining to its customers the reason for the price increase leading to a renegotiation of existing contracts with those customers.

The length of the new contracts is probably indeterminate as firms attempt to guess the intentions of the central bank. This is especially true if the discrete adjustment is a break from past exchange rate management practices. If after some initial period firms believe that the policy marks a switch in regimes from a crawling peg toward a regime of discretely adjustable exchange rates and that the established rate is in fact tenable, implicit price contracts will again be renegotiated for corresponding periods of time.

Uncertainty as to the central bank's intentions, on the other hand, calls for short-period adjustment lags. Finally, the length of the rene-gotiated contracts will probably be the same as before if after the discrete adjustment the exchange rate continues to crawl. In all cases the contract length will also be affected by expectations about economic fundamentals and the ability of policy to correct existing disequilibria.

In summary what can be said unambiguously is that a discrete ex-change rate adjustment will give rise to recontracting and also, in the absence of a clear signal by the government as to its intentions, to an increased tendency for contracts of shorter duration. This conclusion is similar to that of Aizenmann (1982), who in a different context argued that "the optimal frequency of wage recontracting depends on mea-sures of aggregate volatility."

9.3   The Econometric Analysis

The purpose of this section is to investigate empirically whether the responsiveness of nontraded goods prices to exchange rates was more rapid in the period following the January 1983 Greek devaluation than in the previous periods. The analysis is therefore conducted at the aggregate, sectoral, and product levels, using monthly data for two distinct periods: the period January 1979 to December 1983 (the long period), and the period January 1979 to December 1982 (the short period).

Table 9.1 presents a summary of Greek exchange rate statistics. The definitions of the notations for all the variables therein are given in table 9.2. It can readily be seen that both the standard deviations and the coefficients of variation of the effective and bilateral exchange rates were greater in the long period than in the short period. This can largely be attributed to the January 1983 devaluation (see again figures 9.1 and 9.2), which was the largest discrete adjustment of the exchange rate since the beginning of the crawling-peg period.

As shown in table 9.3, the nominal devaluation of the exchange rate in January 1983 produced a real exchange rate devaluation during the first quarter of the year on the order of 7 to 12 percent, depending on the index used to calculate the real effective exchange rate. By the second quarter of 1983, however, the real effective exchange rate returned to roughly its 1980 level as relative prices deteriorated, thereby dissipating some of the effects of the nominal adjustment.

Looking more closely at the time-series properties of exchange rates before and after the discrete adjustment of January 1983, tables 9.4 and 9.5 present the autoregressive structure of the relevant series for

Table 9.1   **Greek Exchange Rate Statistics**

	Level of the Exchange Rate	
	1979.1–1982.12	1979.1–1983.12
EFE		
Mean	52.875	49.415
STD	7.501	9.687
CVAR	0.142	0.196
	1978.6–1982.12	1978.6–1983.12
BIE		
Mean	48.702	55.754
STD	12.227	18.949
CVAR	0.251	0.340
	Percentage Change in the Exchange Rate	
	1979.2–1982.12	1979.2–1983.12
EFE		
Mean	−0.009	−0.011
STD	0.013	0.023
CVAR	−1.444	−2.091
	1978.7–1982.12	1978.7–1983.12
BIE		
Mean	0.012	0.015
STD	0.025	0.030
CVAR	2.083	2.000

Note: For definitions of notations used, see table 9.2. 1979.1 denotes January 1979; 1982.12 denotes December 1982, for example.

Table 9.2   **Definitions of Notations Used in the Tables**

Notation	Definition
EFE	The effective exchange rate: the 12-currency basket as defined by the Bank of Greece. An increase in the index represents a nominal appreciation of the exchange rate. *Source:* Bank of Greece.
BIE	The bilateral Dr./U.S.$ exchange rate. An increase in the index represents a nominal depreciation of the exchange rate. *Source:* Bank of Greece, *Monthly Statistical Bulletin,* various issues.
STD	Standard deviation.
CVAR	Coefficient of variation.
RCPI	The consumer price index (CPI) of Greece relative to the weighed CPI of twelve trading partners, adjusted for exchange rate changes. Both indexes are expressed in dollars. 1970 = 1.000. *Source:* Bank of Greece.
RWPI	The wholesale price index (WPI) of Greece relative to the weighted WPI of 21 competitor countries. Both indexes are expressed in dollars. 1980 = 1.000. *Source:* Bank of Greece.
L	The natural logarithm of a variable.
ΔL	The differenced natural logarithm of a variable.
D	A change in the variable.
ER	Exchange rate.
C	The contracting cost.
D.W.	Durbin-Watson statistic.
SEE	Standard error of the estimation.
P	Price level.
PM	The wholesale price index of finished products of foreign origin. 1970 = 1.000. *Source:* National Statistical Service of Greece, *Statistical yearbook of Greece,* various issues.
PE	The wholesale price index (WPI) of exported products of domestic primary and industrial production. 1970 = 1.000. *Source:* ibid.
NT	The WPI of finished products of domestic industrial production for domestic consumption. 1970 = 1.000. *Source:* ibid.
GI	The WPI of finished products of domestic and foreign origin for domestic consumption. 1970 = 1.000. *Source:* ibid.
K20	The WPI of domestically produced foodstuffs for domestic consumption. 1970 = 1.000. *Source:* ibid.
CPI	The consumer price index. 1970 = 1.000. *Source:* ibid.

Table 9.3   **Quarterly Data on Nominal and Real Effective Exchange Rates in Greece, 1980–84**

(1980 = 100)

Year/ Quarter	EFE	% ΔEFE	RCPI[†]	%ΔRCPI	RWPI[†]	%ΔRWPI
1980						
1.	107.54		103.13			
2.	99.11	− 7.84	98.77	− 4.2	100.0	
3.	96.95	− 2.18	96.45	− 2.4		
4.	96.40	− 0.57	101.03	4.8		
1981						
1.	92.16	− 4.40	101.06	0.0	104.2	
2.	88.63	− 3.83	99.85	− 1.2	102.6	− 1.5
3.	86.70	− 2.18	97.33	− 2.5	102.6	0.0
4.	87.87	1.35	103.86	6.7	105.8	3.1
1982						
1.	85.06	− 3.20	103.02	− 0.8	105.0	− 0.8
2.	81.46	− 4.23	103.48	0.5	104.5	− 0.5
3.	77.95	− 4.31	98.79	− 4.5	103.1	− 1.3
4.	77.32	− 0.81	102.16	3.4	104.4	1.3
1983						
1.	65.50	− 15.29	90.30	− 11.6	96.7	− 7.4
2.	66.56	1.61	96.56	6.9	100.6	4.0
3.	65.54	− 1.53	94.52	− 2.1	99.9	− 0.7
4.	61.33	− 6.42	92.33	− 2.3	98.1	− 1.8
1984						
1.	58.08	− 5.30	89.80	− 2.7	98.2	0.1

[†]A positive value denotes an appreciation; a negative value denotes a depreciation.

both periods. Each variable is regressed against past values of itself, going back roughly two quarters. As was expected, the exchange rate series can be described as an AR1 or random-walk process in which the first lagged coefficient is close to unity in both periods. This implies that only the constant term is significant in the autoregressive structure of first differences. The identification of the Greek exchange rate with an AR1 process is consistent with similar results obtained for most other European countries. In almost all cases the exchange rate in the current period proves to be the best predictor of the rate in the next period (Katseli 1984). As was expected, the coefficient of the constant term was higher in the long period than in the short period when the change in the exchange rate was more sluggish (table 9.5).

Contrary to the experience of most European countries, wholesale prices in Greece also tended to exhibit properties of an AR1 process, as shown in tables 9.6 and 9.7. In Katseli (1984) this finding also characterized price adjustment in Italy, another high-inflation country during the period under consideration. Only the price index of exported

Table 9.4   **Time-Series Properties of the Level of the Exchange Rate**

DEP	C	LER_{-1}	LER_{-2}	R^2	$\bar{R}^2$	D.W.	SEE
1. *LEFE*	−.0246	.9411	−.0072	.99	.98	2.06	.02
1979.8–1983.12	(0.05)	(5.65)	(0.03)				
2. *LBIE*	.0660	.7971	.0898	.99	.99	1.98	.04
1979.1–1983.12	(0.85)	(5.25)	(0.46)				
3. *LEFE*	1.5944	1.0188	−.4536	.99	.99	1.87	.003
1979.8–1982.12	(1.49)	(4.84)	(1.52)				
4. *LBIE*	.1735	.9575	−.0217				
1979.1–1982.12	(1.67)	(4.88)	(0.08)				

Note: The estimated equation is of the form $LEFE = C + \alpha_1 LEFE_{-1} + \ldots \alpha_6 LEFE_{-6} + Lt +$ dummy variables. Only the estimated coefficients C, α_1, and α_2 are reported here. The numbers in parentheses are t-statistics.

products (*PE*) exhibited higher-order autoregressive properties, probably as the result of a conscious pricing policy. The coefficient of the first-month lag of nontraded goods (*LNT*) was typically smaller than that of traded goods but rose considerably between the two periods under consideration. The same is true for all the other price indices, implying that the adjustment of prices is on average faster when 1983 is included in the sample period. This is also reflected in the fact that the coefficients of the constant terms in table 9.7 are higher in all cases in the long period than in the short period. In the case of the *NT* index, the average monthly rate of change increased from 1.7 to 1.9 percent across periods, implying an even larger rate of increase in 1983 alone. In both the *DLPM* and the *DLPE* autoregressions, the inclusion of 1983 raises the coefficients of the constant terms and reduces the coefficients of the significant lagged terms.

These results support the hypothesis that the adjustment of the prices of both traded and nontraded goods was faster in 1983 than in the previous years. The relationship of this development to exchange rate behavior thus provides further evidence that the discrete devaluation of 1983 produced an almost instantaneous reaction in the prices of traded and nontraded goods alike.

When *DLGI* is regressed against lagged values of itself and against current and lagged values of the exchange rate (effective and bilateral), the coefficient of the current exchange rate change term becomes large and significant only in the period that includes 1983, as shown in table 9.8. The same is true in the case of *DLNT*, where the current effective exchange rate change (*DLEFE*) seems to influence the current change in nontraded goods prices only in the long period. The results are more mixed when the bilateral exchange rate is used instead, as shown in table 9.9a. What these results suggest is that the adjustments of non-

Table 9.5   **Time-Series Properties of Changes in the Exchange Rate**

DEP	C	$DLER_{-1}$	$DLER_{-2}$	R^2	$\bar{R}^2$	D.W.	SEE
1. *DLEFE*	-.0226	-.0405	-.1574	.13	.01	1.97	.03
1979.8-1983.12	(3.78)	(0.28)	(1.10)				
2. *DLBIE*	.0185	-.0113	.0368	.03	-.08	2.00	.05
1979.1-1983.12	(2.86)	(0.08)	(0.27)				
3. *DLEFE*	-.0109	.3033	-.1636	.14	-.01	1.99	.01
1979.8-1982.12	(2.44)	(1.76)	(0.91)				
4. *DLBIE*	.0102	.1749	.1568	.11	-.02	1.85	.02
1979.1-1982.12	(1.85)	(1.10)	(0.98)				

Note: The estimated equation is of the form $DLEFE = C + \alpha_1 DLEFE_{-1} + \ldots + \alpha_6 DLEFE_{-6} + v_t$. Only the coefficients C, α_1, and α_2 are reported here. The numbers in parentheses are t-statistics.

Table 9.6   Time-Series Properties of the Level of Prices

Dependent Variable	Constant	LP_{t-1}	LP_{t-2}	LP_{t-3}	R^2	$\bar{R}^2$	D.W.	SEE
1. *LPM* 1979.7–1983.12	.0671 (3.24)	1.2855 (6.93)	−.3965 (−1.35)	.1190 (0.40)	.997	.996	1.80	.017
2. *LPE* 1979.7–1983.12	.0374 (1.13)	1.3886 (7.70)	−.5953 (−2.05)	.4937 (1.67)	.995	.993	1.64	.019
3. *LNT* 1979.7–1983.12	.0837 (4.93)	.8250 (5.24)	.0232 (0.11)	−.1166 (−0.56)	.999	.998	1.80	.012
4. *LGI* 1979.7–1983.12	.0675 (4.05)	1.1260 (6.39)	−.2557 (−0.99)	−.0527 (−0.20)	.999	.998	1.89	.011
5. *LPM* 1979.7–1982.12	.0727 (3.06)	1.2691 (5.70)	.4113 (−1.25)	.1942 (0.64)	.999	.997	2.06	.012
6. *LPE* 1979.7–1982.12	.1448 (3.16)	.9453 (4.64)	−.2001 (−0.72)	.4393 (1.63)	.996	.993	1.54	.015
7. *LNT* 1979.7–1982.12	.1210 (3.81)	.6704 (3.48)	−.0065 (−0.03)	−.0710 (−0.31)	.998	.997	1.83	.012
8. *LGI* 1979.7–1982.12	.0912 (3.46)	.8765 (4.47)	−.1218 (−0.48)	.1182 (0.47)	.999	.998	2.05	.008

Note: The estimated equation is of the form $LP = C + \alpha_1 LP_{-1} + \ldots + \alpha_6 LP_{-6} + Lt +$ dummy variables. Only the estimated coefficients of C, α_1, α_2, and α_3 are reported here. The numbers in parentheses are t-statistics.

Table 9.7   Time-Series Properties of Price Changes

DEP	C	DLP_{-1}	DLP_{-2}	DLP_{-3}	R^2	$\bar{R}^2$	D.W.	SEE
1. DLPM 1979.8–1983.12	.0183 (3.09)	.3883 (2.56)	−.1645 (1.03)	.0274 (0.17)	.22	.11	1.91	.018
2. DLPE 1979.8–1983.12	.0149 (2.83)	.2568 (1.81)	−.1306 (0.94)	.2251 (1.61)	.14	.03	1.83	.015
3. DLNT 1979.8–1983.12	.0187 (2.62)	.0542 (0.39)	−.0879 (0.63)	−.2492 (1.76)	.10	−.02	1.91	.009
4. DLGI 1979.8–1983.12	.0200 (3.39)	.1940 (1.31)	−.0624 (0.42)	−.1320 (0.87)	.09	−.03	1.91	.008
5. DLPM 1979.8–1982.12	.0115 (2.12)	.6364 (3.65)	−.1823 (0.91)	.1315 (0.70)	.36	.25	1.93	.014
6. DLPE 1979.8–1982.12	.0085 (1.73)	.2446 (1.56)	.0668 (0.45)	.4022 (2.69)	.25	.12	1.82	.008
7. DLNT 1979.8–1982.12	.0166 (1.96)	.0480 (0.30)	−.0990 (0.61)	−.1890 (1.15)	.10	−.06	1.94	.007
8. DLGI 1979.8–1982.12	.012 (1.80)	.2237 (1.29)	−.0201 (0.11)	−.0354 (0.20)	.06	−.11	1.91	.005

Note: The estimated equation is of the form $DLP = C + \alpha_1 DLP_{-1} + \ldots \alpha_6 DLP_{-6} + u_t$. Only the estimated coefficients, C, α_1, α_2, and α_3 are reported here. The numbers in parentheses are t-statistics.

traded goods prices and exchange rates become contemporaneous when 1983 is included in the estimation. This can be seen clearly in figures 9.3 and 9.4, in which the exchange rate and price adjustments in January 1983 are completely synchronized.

Two additional points concerning the price adjustment of nontraded goods are also worth noting. The evidence presented in figures 9.3 and 9.4 is also confirmed by the relatively low explanatory power of equations 1 and 2 in table 9.9. Over the entire period in question, the exchange rate was only partially responsible for the observed variation in nontraded goods prices, as other factors, such as imported inflation, wage rate adjustment, monetary developments, and the position of the economy over the business cycle, became more important. It was only in January 1983 that the devaluation of the currency became the dominant factor explaining most of the variation in LNT. Unfortunately, the lack of consistent monthly data prevents a disaggregated analysis along these lines. With quarterly data, however, it can be shown that for the entire period 1979.II–1983.IV, the price of imported goods in the domestic currency is the most important explanatory variable for $DLNT$. This variable reflects changes in both foreign prices and exchange rates and thus picks up the significant terms-of-trade shocks undergone during the period, such as the second oil price increase. As one would expect, the explanatory power of the estimated equation (equation 5 in table 9.9b) is raised considerably when this variable is included.

The lack of sufficient disaggregation in data available also prevents an effective analysis of the relationship between pricing behavior and expectations regarding exchange rate adjustment. According to the evidence presented in table 9.9, a 10 percent devaluation of the effective exchange rate was expected to raise the prices of nontraded goods by 1.4 percent during the same month. The unexpected component of the price change between two consecutive months is picked up by the residual in the estimated equation. The vector of estimated residuals from the estimated price equation can thus be correlated or regressed against the current and lagged values of the residuals obtained from an exchange rate adjustment equation. This exercise allows an analysis of the responsiveness of prices to news of an impending change in the exchange rate. When monthly and quarterly data are used, however, the results are completely uninformative. For example, although the correlation coefficient of the residuals was positive, it was low, never exceeding 0.12. Similarly, the coefficients of the current and lagged unexpected changes in the exchange rate never proved to be significantly different from zero.

These results probably reflect the structure of expectations regarding exchange rate developments. Since exchange rates are announced daily,

Table 9.8   Monthly Data on Aggregate Price Adjustment and Exchange Rate Adjustment

DEP	C	$DLGI_{-1}$	$DLGI_{-2}$	DLBIE	$DLBIE_{-1}$	DLEFE	$DLEFE_{-1}$	R^2	$\bar{R}^2$	D.W.	SEE
1. DLGI 1979.4–1983.12	.0103 (3.64)	.0748 (0.55)	.0314 (0.27)			−.2622 (4.76)	−.1368 (2.06)	.39	.34	2.0	.010
2. DLGI 1979.4–1983.12	.0107 (3.41)	.1546 (1.10)	−.0274 (0.22)	.1792 (3.57)	.0433 (0.78)			.24	.18	2.0	.011
3. DLGI 1979.4–1982.12	.0117 (3.33)	.0870 (0.59)	−.0573 (0.40)			−.1421 (1.2)	−.3141 (2.56)	.24	.17	2.0	.010
4. DLGI 1979.4–1982.12	.0128 (3.38)	.1684 (1.05)	−.0631 (0.40)	.0665 (0.95)	.0622 (0.86)			.09	.00	1.97	.011

Table 9.9a Monthly Data on Nontraded Goods Price Adjustment and Exchange Rate Adjustment

DEP	C	$DLNT_{-1}$	$DLNT_{-2}$	$DLNT_{-3}$	DLBIE	$DLBIE_{-1}$	$DLBIE_{-2}$	DLEFE	$DLEFE_{-1}$	$DLEFE_{-2}$	R^2	$\bar{R}^2$	D.W.	SEE
1. DLNT 1979.5–1983.12	.0169 (3.54)	.0311 (0.22)	−.1043 (0.75)	−.1635 (1.21)				−.1427 (1.88)	−.0814 (1.04)	−.1157 (1.47)	.19	.09	1.95	.013
2. DLNT 1979.5–1983.12	.0206 (3.90)	.0541 (0.39)	−.1266 (0.92)	−.2263 (1.60)	.0096 (0.52)	−.0096 (0.15)	.0788 (1.24)				.10	.01	1.93	.014
3. DLNT 1979.5–1982.12	.0163 (2.91)	−.0210 (0.13)	−.0647 (0.44)	−.1127 (0.74)				.1255 (0.77)	−.3326 (1.96)	−.2427 (1.4)	.24	.12	1.90	.014
4. DLNT 1979.5–1982.12	.0163 (3.45)	.0704 (0.43)	−.0924 (0.57)	−.2005 (1.27)	−.1457 (1.64)	.0237 (0.24)	.1339 (1.41)				.15	.02	1.86	.014

Table 9.9b Quarterly Data on Nontraded Goods Price Adjustment and Exchange Rate Adjustment

DEP	C	$DLNT_{-1}$	DLW	DLPM	$DLEFE_{-1}$	R_2	$\bar{R}^2$	D-W	SEE
5. DLNT 1979II–1983IV	.0497 (2.67)	−.3354 (1.29)	−.0544 (0.35)	.3465 (2.40)	−.1176 (0.83)	.34	.13	1.5	.0207

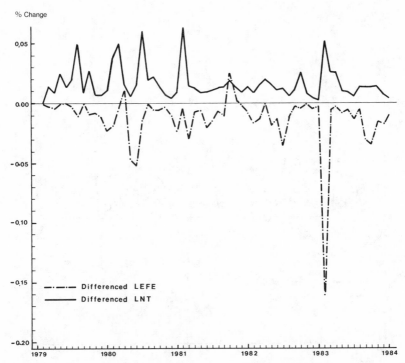

Fig. 9.3   The effective exchange rate and nontraded goods prices.

expectations are formed or revised in a daily basis as well. It therefore would be interesting to proceed with the above analysis using daily data; unfortunately, only anecdotal evidence of price adjustment following the January 9th devaluation exists, precluding an econometric analysis of the second-order autoregressive system. Furthermore, since most of the price adjustment was completed within a few days following the devaluation, the adjustment of prices can be adequately explained by the expected component of the exchange rate change when monthly data are used.

The wholesale price index for nontraded goods is a weighted average of sectoral indices. The food industry sector (*K20*), excluding beverages, possesses the largest weighting coefficient, 18.1 percent. In 1980 only 6.6 percent of the total consumption of processed food was imported, whereas 90 percent of the total production originating in 51 domestic firms was directed toward the domestic market. Moreover, the ratio of imported intermediate and capital goods to total production costs was 19.2 percent, one of the lowest ratios in all of Greece's industrial sectors.[5] The food industry can therefore be classified on all grounds as in the nontraded goods sector.

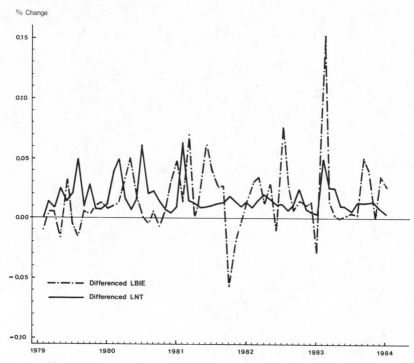

% Change

Fig. 9.4   The drachma-dollar exchange rate and nontraded goods
prices.

Figures 9.5 and 9.6 present the monthly variation of the price index
(*DLK20*) against that of the effective and bilateral exchange rate. It is
relatively easy to see that the change in the exchange rate almost
systematically preceded price adjustment by two months. This observation is confirmed by the econometric evidence presented in table
9.10, where *DLK20* is regressed against previous values of itself and
against current and lagged values of the exchange rate. In both time
periods (1979.5–1982.12 and 1979.5–1983.12) price adjustment was relatively sluggish, with the own first- and second-month lag generally
significant and the second lag on the drachma-dollar exchange rate
significant in both periods.

There is no clear evidence, however, that the responsiveness of the
price to an exchange rate change is significantly altered in the long
period, even though the coefficient of the constant term and the overall
explanatory power of the regression increase when 1983 is included.

The ambiguity in the results as one moves from the aggregate to the
sectoral data has to do with the composition of the index and with the
institutional factors affecting price behavior. The sectoral index is a

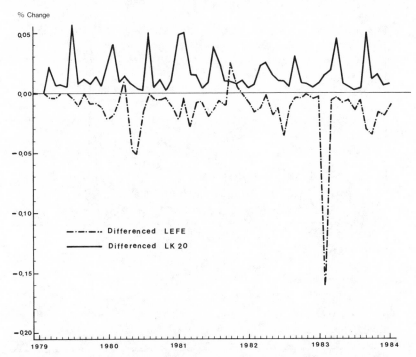

Fig. 9.5   The effective exchange rate and the food industry price index.

weighted average of the price of products that might or might not be exempt from price controls. The legal basis for price controls in Greece is the Market-Law Code, which essentially classifies products into three categories: essential and in short supply; essential and not in short supply; and nonessential. The first category includes basic consumer goods for which, in most cases, a maximum price is set. For some goods in this category, and for all goods in the second category that are considered essential but not key consumer goods, the Greek Ministry of Commerce sets a maximum allowable markup over average unit costs. The third category includes goods that are essentially exempt from controls (Lalonde and Papandreou 1984).

The behavior of product prices and hence of the aggregate sectoral index is thus affected by the ministry's actions in adjusting the price ceiling as a result of pressure from firms. This is especially true in the food sector, a large number of whose products fall in the first category.

Figure 9.7 illustrates the rate of change in flour prices over the period 1973–84. Since flour is considered an essential commodity a price ceiling for it is set by the ministry. Effective prices are almost always set at the price ceiling. As shown in the figure, the price has been typically adjusted once a year during the summer months. The 1983

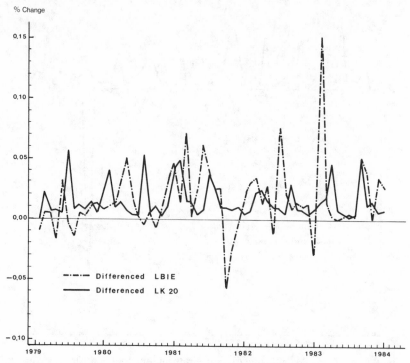

% Change

—·—·— Differenced LBIE

——— Differenced LK 20

Fig. 9.6   The bilateral exchange rate and the food industry price index.

price adjustment in August was the largest one in three years—18.7 percent. Since firms producing flour have limited possibilities to diversify their production,[6] the increase in perceived costs implied by the devaluation gave rise to a fall in profits and a reduction in output or quality. As shown in table 9.11 the average production of grain mill products during the first six months of 1983 was 4.5 percent lower than the corresponding average in 1982.

A different type of response is evidenced by firms that can diversify their production across control categories, such as dairy product firms. Dairy firms usually produce milk, butter, cheese, and yogurt—all items under price controls—as well as ice cream, which is not subject to controls. Although these firms still exercise pressure to adjust the price ceiling, any losses they suffer in profits and output are mitigated by rapid price adjustment in the noncontrolled items. As indicated in table 9.12, while the prices of all controlled dairy products increased between 12 and 14 percent within the first quarter of 1983, ice-cream prices rose by almost 10 percent between December 1982 and January 1983 and by almost 33 percent between December 1982 and March 1983 (also see figure 9.8). As there is no reason to attribute the increase in the

Table 9.10   Food Price and Exchange Rate Adjustment

DEP	C	DLK_{-1}	DLK_{-2}	DLK_{-3}	DLBIE	$DLBIE_{-1}$	$DLBIE_{-2}$	DLEFE	$DLEFE_{-1}$	$DLEFE_{-2}$	R^2	$\bar{R}^2$	D.W.	SEE
1. DLK20 1979.5–1983.12	.0254 (4.24)	−.3455 (2.54)	−.2604 (1.86)	−.2041 (1.49)				−.0083 (0.72)	−.0315 (0.28)	−.1987 (1.74)	.19	.06	2.2	.021
2. DLK20 1979.5–1983.12	.0247 (4.29)	−.3463 (2.67)	−.2696 (2.02)	−.2469 (1.89)	−.0154 (0.17)	.0231 (0.26)	.2510 (2.80)				.25	.16	2.1	.020
3. DLK20 1979.5–1982.12	.0244 (3.28)	−.3646 (2.27)	−.2520 (1.53)	−.1725 (1.08)				.0045 (0.02)	−.1164 (0.42)	−.2423 (0.90)	.16	.03	2.1	.023
4. DLK20 1979.5–1982.12	.0244 (3.64)	−.3533 (2.29)	−.2434 (1.54)	−.2227 (1.44)	−.0375 (0.27)	−.0168 (0.12)	.3007 (2.14)				.22	.10	2.1	.022

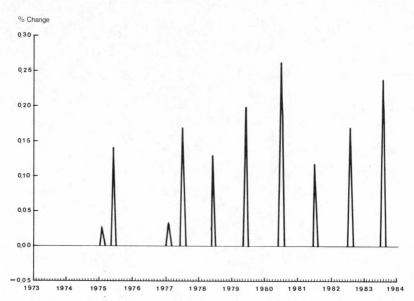

% Change

Fig. 9.7   The differenced log of flour prices, 1973–84.

relative costs of ice-cream production during that period to any other factor, it is reasonable to argue that the perceived increase in costs resulting from the devaluation was met by price overshooting of the noncontrolled goods. The output of dairy products stayed roughly constant in the two periods.

Finally, within the same sector some firms produce commodities in the second and third categories of the Market Code, for example, tomato juice, tomato pulp, canned fruits, and fruit juices. In that case, price adjustment is distributed more evenly across goods. As indicated in table 9.12 between February and March of 1983 the prices of tomato juice and tomato pulp rose by 8.70 percent and 2.90 percent, respectively, whereas the prices of canned fruits rose sharply in January and February and fell in March, that is, when the prices of the controlled items were allowed to increase. As shown in Table 9.11 the production of canned fruits and vegetables was 30 percent higher in the first half of 1983 than in the first half of 1982 as domestic firms were able to capture a larger share of the domestic market from foreign firms.

The analysis so far suggests that firms responded to the discrete devaluation in a predictable fashion. If institutional or other factors prevent prices from changing, the expected increase in costs implied by a devaluation brings about a decrease in profits and a decrease in output. The drop in output could be mitigated by the expected increase in demand, depending on the cross-elasticity of substitution of domestic and imported final goods. In diversified firms, on the other hand, the

Table 9.11   **Monthly Indices of the Industrial Production of Specific Products**

	Grain Mill Products	Dairy Products	Fruit Juices	Canned and Preserved Fruits and Vegetables
1982.1	148.8	154.7	176.3	11.2
2	142.3	198.2	247.4	14.6
3	154.0	233.1	207.2	15.6
4	149.2	238.6	50.3	29.9
5	141.0	288.8	22.1	30.4
6	145.6	325.0	5.1	75.7
7	142.6	314.1	17.0	119.8
8	85.5	248.3	0.0	1118.5
9	115.2	202.4	45.9	1043.8
10	103.9	158.7	46.2	403.3
11	113.0	155.3	40.4	54.8
12	106.5	145.2	106.0	32.2
1983.1	114.9	158.2	255.6	22.3
2	143.8	199.9	258.4	21.4
3	159.0	220.3	115.7	21.9
4	152.5	274.3	37.6	29.2
5	130.6	286.5	156.7	54.4
6	140.6	288.6	11.3	81.0
7	132.2	257.8	24.0	452.5
8	138.7	235.3	56.9	1494.3
9	142.1	193.4	109.8	515.3
10	126.6	171.5	0.0	68.6
11	126.7	162.4	9.5	30.3
12	117.8	151.4	30.4	23.5

Table 9.12   **The Price Adjustment of Specific Products in the Food Sector**

Food Stuffs	1982.12–1983.1	1982.12–1983.2	1982.12–1983.3
Price Controlled			
Yogurt	0.00	0.0	14.3
Milk	0.00	1.7	13.0
Soft Cheese	0.07	3.5	13.8
Butter, Creams	0.13	3.6	12.7
Flour	0.00	0.0	0.00
Farina	0.00	0.0	0.00
Markup Regulated			
Chicken	−0.74	0.24	0.59
Tomato Juice	0.00	0.00	8.70
Tomato Pulp	0.00	2.90	2.90
Noncontrolled			
Ice Cream	9.82	28.21	32.41
Fruit Juices	0.00	1.31	7.36
Canned Fruits	5.09	6.10	2.00

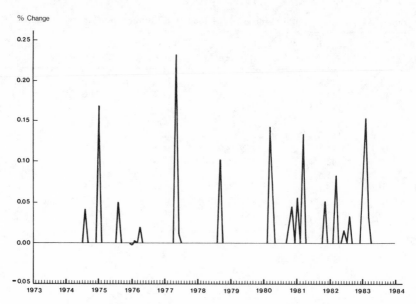

Fig. 9.8   Differenced log of ice-cream prices.

loss in profits is cushioned by selective increases in the prices of non-controlled goods and in output expansion of those goods for which the demand has increased.

The analysis also confirms the hypothesis that, regardless of the category of price control, price adjustment is generally sluggish, so that a monopolistic price adjustment model is a suitable one for the pricing behavior of firms. "Price contracts" are evidenced in all the product cases examined here. Even though their length depends on institutional factors, a cursory look at pricing behavior suggests that at least in the noncontrolled sector contracts were in fact shortened as aggregate exchange rate variability rose, as shown in figures 9.8 and 9.9. The evidence also suggests that recontracting occurred almost instantly in the noncontrolled sector, and organized pressure by firms to relax price ceilings was successful within a few months, especially in the second product category (essential and not in short supply).

Overall, the arbitrary control of prices by central authorities in Greece did not seem to mitigate in the medium term the inflationary consequences of the 1983 devaluation. After a large and discrete adjustment of the exchange rate, the price level was adjusted earlier than expected, thereby lessening the increase in the demand for nontraded goods and exacerbating the stagflationary effects of the devaluation.

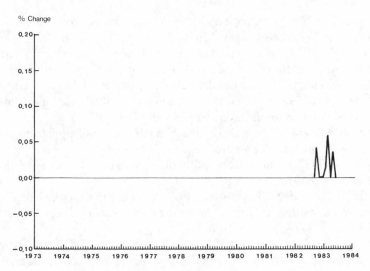

Fig. 9.9   Differenced log of fruit juice prices.

Notes

1. For a review of this literature, see Katseli (1983).
2. This is usually guaranteed by the perfect substitutability of all goods and assets in a small, open economy and by the perfect flexibility of wages and prices.
3. Defined as the ratio of the prices of traded to nontraded goods.
4. For an excellent review of those works, see Gordon (1981).
5. The data on those 51 firms were obtained from a sample of 423 firms gathered annually by the Bank of Greece.
6. Flour mills usually produce flour and farina, which is also included in the first category of products.

References

Aizenmann, J. 1982. Optimal wage renegotiation in a closed and an open economy. NBER Working Paper no. 1279. Cambridge, Mass.: National Bureau of Economic Research.

Alchian, A. A. 1969. Information costs, pricing and resource unemployment. *Western Economic Journal* (June): 109–28.

Barro, R. J. 1972. A theory of monopolistic price adjustment. *Review of Economic Studies* (January): 17–26.

Blinder, A. 1982. Inventories and sticky prices: More on the microeconomic foundations of macroeconomics. *American Economic Review* (June): 334–48.

Calvo, G. 1981. Devaluation: Levels versus rates. *Journal of International Economics* (May): 165–72.

Cooper, R. 1973. Flexing the international monetary system: The case for gliding parities. In *The economics of common currencies,* ed. H. Johnson and A. Swoboda, 229–43. London: Allen and Unwin.

Gordon, R. J. 1981. Output fluctuations and gradual price adjustment. *Journal of Economic Literature* (June): 493–530.

Gray, J. A. 1976. Wage indexation: A macroeconomic approach. *Journal of Monetary Economics* (April): 221–35.

———. 1978. On indexation and contract length. *Journal of Political Economy* 86 (no. 1): 1–18.

Katseli, L. T. 1980. Transmission of external price disturbances and the composition of trade. *Journal of International Economics* 10 (August): 357–75.

———. 1983. Devaluation: A critical appraisal of IMF's policy prescriptions. *American Economic Review: Papers and Proceedings* (May): 359–63.

———. 1984. Real exchange rates in the 1970's. In *Exchange rate theory and practices,* ed. J. Bilson and R. Marston. Chicago: University of Chicago Press.

Lalonde, B., and Papandreou, N. 1984. An appraisal of price controls in Greece: Past, present, future. KEPE *Studies,* forthcoming.

Okun, A. M. 1975. Inflation: Its mechanics and welfare cost. *Brookings Papers on Economic Activity* 1: 351–401.

Phelps, E., and Winter, S. E. 1970. Optimal price policy under atomistic competition. In *Microeconomic foundations of employment and inflation theory,* eds. E. S. Phelps et al., 309–37. New York: Norton.

Rodriguez, C. 1981. Managed float: An evaluation of alternative rules in the presence of speculative capital flows. *American Economic Review* (March): 256–60.

Comment   Stanley W. Black

The paper by Louka Katseli offers us a stimulating new idea concerning the effects of exchange rate changes on the economy. Earlier in the NBER–World Bank conference Carlos Díaz-Alejandro told us that "Juan Valdez the coffee picker" knows that changes in coffee prices affect real income and the terms of trade in Colombia. Katseli seems to be telling us that "Zorba the shoemaker" knows that a discrete exchange

Stanley W. Black is the Lurcy Professor Economics at the University of North Carolina at Chapel Hill.

rate adjustment signals that inflation has increased in Greece. Perhaps this tells us that changes in inflation are as significant for Greek shopkeepers as changes in coffee prices are for Colombian coffee pickers.

The basic hypothesis of the paper has two components. First, the *speed of adjustment* of domestic prices to discrete changes in the exchange rate depends on the *size* of the exchange rate change; equivalently, the effect on prices is faster, the larger the changes in costs. Second, the *frequency* of price changes rises with the size of the change in the exchange rate. If this hypothesis is true, a crawling peg would allow exchange rate changes to have larger real effects than would a discretely adjustable peg, ceteris paribus.

There are some other hypotheses, not mentioned by Katseli, that also bear on this question. Discrete adjustment is often thought to reflect "reluctant" adjustment, with the exchange rate lagging behind domestic inflation. It thus distorts the real exchange rate, imposing reallocation costs of the type discussed by Johnson (1966), Hause (1966), and more recently Coes (1981), as resources are first driven away from and then pulled back into the traded goods sectors. There is also the "quantum" effect first discussed in Orcutt's famous (1950) article. Orcutt argued that large, discrete exchange rate changes will have *larger* real effects on trade than smaller changes will because fixed costs of adjustment will prevent any response to small changes.

Katseli derives her hypotheses from contemporary theory. The speed-of-adjustment hypothesis is derived from Gordon's (1981) theory of sluggish adjustment to local versus global changes in demand and costs. Gordon used the (1973) Lucas argument that the response to global demand shocks will take the form of a price increase, whereas local demand shocks will lead primarily to changes in real output. According to Katseli, a large change in the exchange rate signals a global shock, implying a large price response. The frequency-of-adjustment hypothesis is based on Gray's (1978) model of optimal contract length, which shows that the frequency of recontracting increases as the variance of industry-specific or local shocks increases. Katseli argues that a discrete exchange rate adjustment may raise uncertainty about the central bank's future intentions and hence shorten the average life of contracts. Since a discrete, reluctant exchange rate adjustment should imply a higher variance of aggregate shocks, a la Johnson and Hause, it would have been useful if the paper had examined the effect of aggregate shocks on the degree of *indexation* or automatic pass-through of cost increases, as suggested by Gray.

Let us turn to the evidence Katseli brings forward to test the hypotheses on price adjustment. I would have liked to test the speed of response of prices to costs by fitting markup equations. The time-series autoregressions on prices presented in the paper are somewhat less satisfactory, particularly since they are based on only 60 monthly observations. And the results in tables 9.4 and 9.6 for price *levels* involve nonstationary time series. Tables 9.5 and 9.7 for price *changes* show increases in the constant terms relative to the coefficients of lagged price changes and therefore in the speed of adjustment, if the period of the large exchange rate adjustments is included. But the increases in the constant terms are not statistically significant. The constant term in the nontraded goods equation of table 9.7 increases by 0.0021, which is only about 25 percent of the standard error. Thus, the results do not really support the hypothesis in a statistically significant way.

Table 9.8 shows that the change in the exchange rate adds significantly to an autoregressive aggregate price equation in the longer time period that includes the large devaluation. The results for nontraded goods in table 9.9 also show that the lag of prices behind exchange rate changes shortens when 1983 is included. These statistically significant results appear, however, to be due to only one observation, the January 1983 devaluation. Their robustness is therefore open to question.

The subsequent analysis of detailed price changes for flour and dairy products is fascinating and suggests that the *frequency* of price changes rose in 1983, again apparently due to the single observation. It is interesting to observe that a Johnson-Hause reallocation effect begins to appear for flour milling, in which the industry controlled price only reluctantly adjusted to increased costs.

I am quite in sympathy with the paper's overall conclusion that a crawling peg is better than a reluctant adjustment with large discrete changes in the exchange rate. "Exchange rate management matters," one could say. Certainly, the desire to avoid resource allocation costs would argue for a crawling peg. And Katseli has provided some suggestive, if not conclusive, evidence that a crawling peg might minimize a pass-through into prices and strengthen the resulting real adjustment.

References

Coes, D. V. 1981. The crawling peg and exchange rate uncertainty. In *Exchange rate rules: The theory, performance, and prospects of the crawling peg,* ed. J. Williamson, chap. 5. London: Macmillan.

Gordon, R. J. 1981. Output fluctuations and gradual price adjustment. *Journal of Economic Literature* 19: 493–530.

Gray, J. A. 1978. On indexation and contract length. *Journal of Political Economy* 86: 1–18.

Hause, J. 1966. The welfare costs of disequilibrium exchange rates. *Journal of Political Economy* 74: 333–52.

Johnson, H. G. 1966. The welfare costs of exchange rate stabilization. *Journal of Political Economy* 74: 512–18.

Lucas, R. E., Jr. 1973. Some international evidence on output-inflation tradeoffs. *American Economic Review* 63: 326–34.

Orcutt, G. H. 1950. Measurement of price elasticities in international trade. *Review of Economics and Statistics* 32: 117–32. Reprinted in *Readings in International Economics,* ed. R. E. Caves and H. G. Johnson, chap. 31. Homewood: Ill.: Richard D. Irwin, 1968.

Comment   John Williamson

I am always pleased to find a paper that assumes that firms set prices, rather than that prices are set by some mysterious auctioneer who is determined to clear all markets. The former corresponds to the way I think most of the world works. I have to confess that at various times in the last 15 years I have felt intellectually isolated because the bulk of the profession appeared to have abandoned contact with reality on this point.

The main conclusions that Katseli lists at the end of her paper also seem to me eminently reasonable. So is the observation that changes in the exchange rate are (or ought to be) undertaken to influence the real exchange rate, and not just to reduce absorption. There are other, and generally better, instruments to reduce absorption, namely, fiscal and monetary policy. Hence, I like the main features of the paper.

The main subject of the paper is a problem I first concerned myself with 15 years ago when I was fighting a one-man battle in Her Majesty's Treasury to persuade members of the British government that if they wanted to save the Bretton Woods system they had better support the limited flexibility of exchange rates to complement the introduction of the special drawing rights (SDR). One of the devastating charges then made against the crawling peg was that it would be neutralized by induced inflation, since an announcement that a necessary devaluation would be implemented gradually by a crawl would cause all wage adjustments to go up in proportion and would prevent any change in the real exchange rate. I was invited to contrast this with the heroic way the British public was accepting Harold Wilson's assurance that the pound in its pocket had not been devalued in November 1967. The argument did not seem to me very convincing, but my lack of conviction had no empirical evidence to back it up, which doubtless contributed to my loss of the battle for limited flexibility.

I was not, incidentally, impressed at that time by the Orcutt argument mentioned in Black's comment above. I think this was because I re-

John Williamson is a senior fellow at the Institute for International Economics.

called a paper of Harberger's in the 1950s that made the point that though many agents might not respond to a small devaluation, others might be pushed over a threshold. Hence, there is really no very convincing reason to expect a nonlinearity of the type Orcutt was postulating.

In any event the 1969 debate in the British Treasury was not satisfactory. The question continued to trouble me, so that ten years later, when I organized the conference in Rio on the crawling peg, I invited the authors of the country papers to present any relevant evidence on the subject. I was not rewarded for that invitation.

My claim used to be that there is no good reason to expect a greater neutralization of a nominal exchange rate change with a crawl than with a discrete devaluation. Katseli makes a much stronger claim in her paper. She argues that a large change in the exchange rate is actually *more* likely to generate neutralization.

I did not find her evidence in support of this convincing; indeed, she herself describes it as inconclusive. Some evidence in the paper, in fact, seems to point in the opposite direction to her thesis. Table 9.3, for example, seems to say that the change in the nominal exchange rate was offset by about 50 percent within six months after the big devaluation in early 1983. Subsequently, the crawl was accelerated and the real exchange rate went down a bit more. It is not clear that there is any difference in the pass-through coefficient between the two cases. I therefore remain unconvinced that there is any evidence to suggest that the extent of the pass through differs systematically between crawling and discrete changes.

When I first started thinking about this issue, some 20 years ago, the equation that represented a conventional way of describing profit-maximizing behavior in the context of imperfect competition was:

$$P = \alpha\bar{p} + (1 - \alpha)c = \alpha e p^* + (1 - \alpha)c,$$

where $\bar{p}$ represents the average price being charged by competitors, and c represents unit costs. In the context of the impact of a devaluation on the prices of differentiated manufactured products (McKinnon's tradables I), the natural interpretation of the price of competitors is the exchange rate (e) times the foreign price of similar products ($p*$). The question arose as to the value of α. This was answered in the empirical literature on pass-through coefficients. It turns out that α varies from something modest like 0.1 in the case of a large country like the United States to something like 0.9 in a small, open economy like Costa Rica, but typically it is not equal to unity even then. This suggests that the imperfect competition framework is an appropriate and useful one, and that the "law of one price" is not an adequate description of price-setting behavior.

In applying this framework to devaluation, one notes that the prices of competitive goods rise and thus pull up the prices of competing goods, thereby reinforcing the cost-push effects that come via imported intermediate goods and the wage pressures generated as workers try to restore their real incomes when faced with the price increases. One would expect that when applying this type of equation to nontraded goods, the reaction to an exchange rate change would be much less pronounced; and that also seems to be empirically confirmed (Corbo 1983).

But applying this approach today, as opposed to 20 years ago, one would do some things differently. One would no longer include simply the previous values of $\bar{p}$ and c but would also specify the expected future values of those variables over the contract period. One might even analyze whether the contract period would be expected to remain constant. Nonetheless, the basic approach is still valid.

The relevance of these recollections to the Katseli paper is to explain the theoretical basis of my longstanding presumption that there is no systematic difference between discrete and crawling devaluations in effectively changing real exchange rates. If price setting is determined (rationally) by the twin influences of competitive prices and own costs, the manner in which a given change between the two is accomplished should have no effect on the price set. My presumption that it does not has not been overturned by Katseli's paper.

Let me finally remark that there is one interesting case that reinforces my view and is encouraging for those of us with a prejudice in favor of the crawling peg. Three years ago Colombia set out to devalue its currency with the express purpose of restoring the country's competitiveness, not by a discrete devaluation but instead by accelerating the crawl. Unfortunately it set out too late—it is not clear that Colombia will get by without an economic crisis similar to that now facing most of the rest of Latin America. But the crawl *has* achieved a more competitive real exchange rate. That is perhaps the most persuasive evidence so far that a crawl can in fact increase competitiveness.

Reference

Vittorio Corbo. 1983. International prices, wages and inflation in the open economy: A Chilean model. Santiago, Chile: Universidad Católica. Photocopy.

10 Collective Pegging to a Single Currency: The West African Monetary Union

Jorge Braga de Macedo

10.1 Introduction

Under the present international monetary system, a large number of countries peg their exchange rates in some way, and a fair number of small countries peg to a single currency. Few countries, however, are members of exchange rate unions in which the rates are collectively pegged to a single currency or basket of currencies.

Even fewer countries establish a full monetary union, with a union-wide central bank. In fact, until the transformation of the East Caribbean Currency Authority into a central bank in October 1983, the closest examples were the monetary institutions of the Franc Zone. In particular, the West African Monetary Union (known by its French abbreviation UMOA) consists of former French colonies in West Africa that have maintained a fixed bilateral exchange rate against the French franc since October 1948. That they have done so is all the more remarkable in light of the repeated changes in the parity of the French franc relative to the dollar and to other major European currencies.

Actual monetary unions may be few, but nonetheless a considerable analytic literature on the subject exists. It emerged during the 1960s in connection with the celebrated controversy over the desirability of fixed versus flexible exchange rates, and it was revived with the creation of the European Monetary System (EMS) in 1979.[1]

Jorge Braga de Macedo is an assistant professor of economics and international affairs at Princeton University and a faculty research fellow of the National Bureau of Economic Research.

An earlier version of this paper was presented at the NBER–World Bank conference and in a seminar at the University of Pennsylvania. Comments from the participants are gratefully acknowledged. Any errors are my own.

There is a general agreement that the key factors on which the impact of a monetary union depends are, first, the sources and types of economic disturbances giving rise to exchange rate fluctuations; second, the trade patterns of the country joining the union; and third, wage and price behavior at home and abroad. As Marston (1984a) stated, the conditions under which a fixed exchange rate regime is superior to a rate that floats according to some social welfare criterion involve a complicated weighting of these key factors, making any generalizations about the unions difficult.

The model of a monetary union presented in this paper is designed to illuminate monetary and exchange rate policy in the West African Monetary Union. The discussion centers on the interaction of UMOA members with one another, through the common central bank, and on their interaction with France and the rest of the world. As a consequence, the structure of the national economies is highly stylized. Indeed, country size is the major structural characteristic in the model.

The relative size of the partners is of course reflected in the sources and types of disturbances, as well as in the trade pattern. Although the model can also account for real and nominal wage rigidities, the focus is on the two key factors just mentioned. In the model, therefore, large countries (such as France) are not affected by disturbances originating in small countries, but small countries (such as the members of UMOA) are affected by domestic disturbances in the large countries. The collective nature of the pegging is important because the small countries are assumed to be of equal size.

The paper is divided into two parts. Section 10.2 presents a four-country macroeconomic model in which one of two large countries establishes what Corden (1972) would call a pseudo–exchange rate union with two small countries, which together form a full monetary union with their own central bank. The effect of the arrangement on monetary and real disturbances originating inside and outside the union is analyzed.

The pseudo–exchange rate union with the large partner is shown to have no effect on the real exchange rates of the small countries but to affect their price levels, whereas a full monetary union requires in principle a transfer whose allocation between the two small countries may have real effects. This transfer is provided by the large country, as guarantor of the fixed exchange rate arrangement. Because of size differences, the converse is not true. When both small countries are in surplus, there is a reverse transfer to the large country, with no monetary consequences.

The characterization of the UMOA in section 10.3 begins with an overview of African monetary history, contrasting the experience of the Franc Zone with that of the former British colonies along lines suggested by Mundell's (1972) classic contribution to the subject. Using rough indicators of financial development to compare several African countries, the analysis shows that in the 1970s the countries of the Franc Zone increased their propensity to hold near-money at a faster rate than the countries of the Sterling Zone of Africa. This finding is consistent with the emphasis of the model on the requirement of a transfer from France to guarantee the fixed exchange rate agreement. Evidence on the composition of the money stock in the UMOA confirms the importance of the French transfer.

A comparison of nominal and real effective exchange rates in several African countries yields mixed results, but as mentioned in the conclusion, the pattern of relative price adjustment among members of the UMOA does seem to reflect the emphasis on monetary allocations. In effect, surplus countries such as Ivory Coast experienced real appreciations, whereas deficit countries such as Senegal experienced real depreciations.

Finally, it should be kept in mind that although the model is designed to illuminate the workings of the West African Monetary Union, the two parts of the paper are largely self-contained. In particular, the possible real effects of the union cannot be ascertained by the evidence provided in section 10.3.

10.2 A Model of Collective Pegging to a Single Currency

10.2.1 A Two-Tier, Four Country Model

The model consists of standard aggregate demand and aggregate supply relationships, with trade and capital movements linking national economies.[2] Account is taken of the unequal size of the potential partners by modeling two pairs of identical economies, one large and one small. In the two identical large economies the bilateral exchange rate floats freely. In the two identical small economies the authorities decide whether to float their exchange rate or fix it with one of the large countries; in so doing, they also allow the unionwide central bank to decide on monetary allocations.

Because of the difference in size between the partners in the union, only the distribution of money between the two small countries is endogenously determined, but even there it can be modified by the allocation of a monetary transfer from the large partner. There is a pseudo–exchange rate union between one of the large countries and the two small countries but full monetary integration between the two small countries.

Each national economy is highly stylized, and the model focuses on the interaction of the members of the monetary union—the two small countries, labeled country 1 (Senegal) and country 2 (Ivory Coast)—which take as given the member of the pseudo–exchange rate union, labeled country* (France) and the country outside the union, labeled country** (the United States). The model is therefore recursive.

Because of the devaluations of the French franc mentioned earlier, a more accurate procedure would be to specify a three-tier, rather than a two-tier, structure. If the two large countries are the United States and Germany (as a proxy for the EMS) and France is treated as a small country, the recursiveness of the model is preserved. The structure of the monetary union between two (very) small countries would allow them to trade with France and the two large countries, or at least one of them (the United States), but not with each other. This would again preserve the recursiveness of the model, but there would be two exogenous exchange rates: the franc-dollar rate and the franc-Ecu rate shocking the (very) small economies. To illustrate the interaction between France and the UMOA, though, a three-tier structure would be too cumbersome.

The four national economies are described by conventional aggregate relationships. Demand for domestic output (the IS curve) is a function of foreign outputs, relative prices or the real exchange rate, and the real interest rate. It can be changed by an exogenous demand disturbance, which can also be interpreted as the result of fiscal policy. Demand for real balances (the LM curve) is a function of domestic output and the nominal interest rate as a measure of the return differential. Eliminating the nominal interest rate yields an aggregate demand curve that relates domestic output to the real exchange rate, to foreign output, and to the exogenous demand and monetary disturbances. A real depreciation increases the demand for domestic output along conventional foreign trade multiplier lines.

The supply of domestic output is derived from labor market equilibrium, in which the supply of labor by workers responds to the wage deflated by a consumer price index, and the demand for labor by firms responds to the wage deflated by the price of the domestic good. Eliminating the nominal wage yields an aggregate supply curve relating domestic output to the real exchange rate and to an exogenous supply disturbance that can be interpreted as a change in productivity. A real depreciation lowers the supply of domestic output because it raises the product wage. Prices change as a proportion of the difference between demand and supply, so that a Phillips curve allowing for real wage rigidity is featured.

The model is closed by the assumption that domestic and foreign assets are perfect substitutes, so that interest rates are equalized in the stationary state. This recursively determines the real exchange rate and the price of domestic output in terms of the exogenous real and monetary disturbances, respectively. Under flexible exchange rates, the nominal exchange rate is then given by monetary disturbances, whereas under fixed rates, the nominal money stock is determined endogenously.

Size does not affect the interest-rate elasticities of money demand and aggregate demand, which are common to all four countries. It may affect the other parameters, which are, however, identical in each pair of large and small countries. In particular, the steady-state money stocks in the two small countries are the same. These assumptions could be somewhat relaxed, but an analytical solution does require some symmetry between economic structures.[3]

The assumptions of labor market equilibrium and of perfect substitutability between domestic and foreign assets are particularly strong. Nevertheless, the case of an infinitely elastic supply of labor has often been used in the context of developing countries. The exchange rate union, on the other hand, rules out some special risks attached to the assets of small countries, making the perfect substitutability assumption slightly more palatable but the comparison with a perfectly flexible exchange rate regime less appropriate. Indeed, imperfect asset substitutability, as recognized by Marston (1985), would seem to call for the three-tier structure discussed earlier.

The model is used below to assess the effect of fixing the bilateral exchange rates of the two small countries with one of the large countries. Under price flexibility the exchange rate regime has no effect on the real exchange rate, since the effect on the nominal exchange rate and the price level offset each other. Nevertheless, a monetary union between one of the large countries and the two small countries may require a transfer from the large partner to offset internal and external disturbances. To that extent the union allows the central bank of the small countries to enforce an asymmetric monetary allocation rule. Prices then will not be adjusted to the nominal exchange rate, and the real exchange rate will also have to change as a consequence of the price rigidity.

10.2.2   Flexible Exchange Rates

The Two Large Economies

I present the model here in logarithmic deviations from the stationary state and denote rates of change by dots. Assuming perfect foresight about prices and exchange rates, the model of the two large economies consists of the following set of equations:

(1) $y^* = \upsilon y^{**} + a\theta^* - b(i^* - \dot{p}_c^*) + u_A^*$ $\left.\begin{array}{c} \\ \\ \end{array}\right\}$ IS equations

(2) $y^{**} = \upsilon y^* - a\theta^* - b(i^{**} - \dot{p}_c^{**} + u_A^{**}$

(3) $\theta^* = e + p^{**} - p^*$ the real exchange rate

(4) $p_c^* = p^* + \beta\theta^*$

(5) $p_c^{**} = p^{**} - \beta\theta^*$ } consumer price indexes

(6) $u_m^* - p^* = y^* - ci^*$

(7) $u_m^{**} - p^{**} = y^{**} - ci^{**}$ } LM equations

(8) $\dot{p}^* = \gamma(y^* + k\beta\theta^* - u_\pi^*)$

(9) $\dot{p}^{**} = \gamma(y^{**} - k\beta\theta^* - u_\pi^{**})$ } price adjustment rules

(10) $i^* = i^{**} + \dot{e},$ interest parity

where y^j is the real output of country j ($j = {}^*, {}^{**}$);
  p^j is the price of the output of country j;
  e is the price of the double-starred currency in units of the starred currency;
  i^j is the nominal interest rate in country j;
  u_A^j is a demand disturbance in country j;
  u_π^j is a supply disturbance in country j;
  u_m^j is a monetary disturbance in country j;
  v is the (common) foreign output multiplier;
  a is a (common) term involving trade elasticities divided by the multiplier;
  b is the (common) real interest semielasticity of aggregate demand;
  c is the (common) interest semielasticity of money demand;
  β is the (common) share of foreign goods in the consumer price indexes;
  γ is the (common) speed of adjustment of domestic prices; and
  k is the (common) real exchange rate elasticity of aggregate supply.

I will concentrate here on the stationary-state solution of the model.[4] The real exchange rate is obtained from the difference in the cyclical positions of the two countries, whereas the interest rate is obtained by their sum. In other words, relative disturbances are channeled through the exchange rate; and global disturbances, through the interest rate, such that:

(11) $$\theta^* = -\frac{u_*^d}{H_*}$$

(12) $$i^* = i^{**} = \frac{u_*^s}{b},$$

where $H_* = a + k\beta(1 + v)$;

  $u_*^d = {}^*u_A^d - (1 + v)^* u_\pi^d$ is a composite relative real disturbance;

$u_*^s = {}^*u_A^s - (1 - \upsilon)^*u_\pi^s$ is a composite global real disturbance;

$${}^*u_i^d = \frac{u_i^* - u_i^{**}}{2} , i = A, \pi; \text{ and}$$

$${}^*u_i^s = \frac{u_i^* + u_i^{**}}{2} .$$

The size of the multiplier H_* is smaller, the larger the demand and supply elasticities a and k. Now, given θ^*, we can obtain y^* and y^{**} by equating to zero the right-hand sides of equations (8) and (9), and we can obtain the price of domestic output from equations (6) and (7).

Thus, in country**:

(13) $p^{**} = -k\beta\theta^* - u_\pi^{**} + ci^{**} + u_m^{**}$

$$= \frac{1}{H_*} (k\beta^*u_A^d + a^*u_\pi^d) + \frac{1}{\phi} [{}^*u_A^s - (1 + \phi - \upsilon)^*u_\pi^s] + u_m^{**},$$

where $\phi = b/c$. The first term on the right-hand side of the equation is a modified real exchange rate effect; the second term, a modified interest rate effect; and the third term, an own monetary effect. Note that the first term enters negatively in p^*.

Given prices and the real exchange rate, the nominal exchange rate is determined by equation (3). The interest rate effect drops out, so that again only relative disturbances matter, such that:

(14) $e = (1 + 2k\beta)\theta^* + 2^*u_m^d - 2^*u_\pi^d$

$$= \theta^* + 2^*u_m^d - \frac{2}{H_*} (k\beta^*u_A^d + a^*u_\pi^d),$$

where $^*u_m^d = \dfrac{u_m^* - u_m^{**}}{2}$.

Let us now consider the effect of each of the disturbances in turn. Monetary disturbances have no effect on the real exchange rate and offsetting one-to-one effects on the nominal exchange rate and on the own price level. An increase in the demand for the good of country*, $u_A^* > 0$, appreciates the real exchange rate by $\frac{1}{2}H_*$.

According to the first equation in (13), the effect of a change in the real exchange rate on the nominal exchange rate is augmented by $2k\beta$ because of the effect of aggregate demand expansion in country* in raising prices in country**. The real appreciation of the domestic currency is always less than the nominal appreciation.

Demand expansion in country** increases the price level there by one half of $([1/\phi] - [k\beta/H_*])$ so that the nominal exchange rate depreciates by more, with the factor given by the effect of the real on the nominal exchange rate change, $1 + 2k\beta$. The effect of supply or productivity disturbances is also stronger on the nominal exchange rate, the difference being proportional to the trade elasticities.

Equally distributed demand, supply, or monetary disturbances (such that $*u_i^d = 0$ and $*u_i^s = *u_i$, $i = A$, π, m) leave the exchange rates unchanged ($\theta^* = e = 0$). The size of the effect of a supply shock on the price level differs from the size of that of a demand shock by the factor $1 + \phi - \upsilon$, shown in the second term on the right-hand side of (13). Negatively correlated real disturbances (such that $*u_i^s = 0$ and $*u_i^d = u_i^*$) leave interest rates unchanged ($i^* = i^{**} = 0$). Their effect on the price level is given by the first term in equation (13). That effect vanishes when there are no supply effects ($k = u_\pi^i = 0$).

The structure of the large economies can thus be simplified by ruling out supply effects. If, in addition, their monetary policies are perfectly correlated ($*u_m^d = 0$) and there are only relative demand disturbances ($*u_A^s = 0$), the nominal and real exchange rates are the same, and they will be the only channel of external disturbances to the small countries.

The Two Small Economies

The model of the small economies consists of the same relationships as in the model of the large economies. Care is taken, though, to distinguish between trade with each of the two foreign countries, one of which, country*, is a partner in the exchange rate union. I will present the model of what I will call the domestic economy in log-linear form, expressed again as a deviation from steady state. It will be easy to modify the model to consider the other (identical) small country, which will be the partner in the monetary union.

The following set of equations describes the domestic economy:

(15) $\begin{aligned} y &= (a^* + a^{**})\theta - a^*\theta^* + \upsilon^*y^* \\ &\quad + \upsilon^{**}y^{**} - b(i - \dot{p}_c) + u_A \end{aligned}$ IS equation

(16) $\theta = e^{**} + p^{**} - p$ real exchange rate

(17) $p_c = p + (1 - \alpha)\theta - \alpha_*\theta^*$ consumer price index

(18) $u_m - p = y - ci$ LM equation

(19) $\dot{p} = \gamma[y - h\alpha_*\theta^* + h(1 - \alpha)\theta - u_\pi]$ price adjustment rule

(20) $i = i^* + \dot{e}^*$ interest parity

(21) $e^* = e^{**} - e,$ triangular arbitrage,

where $e^*(e^{**})$ is the price of the starred (double starred) currency in units of the domestic currency;

$a^*(a^{**})$ is a term involving trade elasticities with country* (country**) divided by the multiplier;

$\alpha_*(\alpha_{**})$ is the share of goods from country* (country**) in the consumer price index, $\alpha_* + \alpha_{**} + \alpha = 1$;
$v^*(v^{**})$ is the multiplier for trade with country* (country**); and
h is the real exchange rate elasticity of aggregate supply.

Concentrating again on a particular solution to the model (with $\dot{p}_c = \dot{p} = \dot{e}^* = 0$), we can solve for the real exchange rate, θ, as a function of the foreign real exchange rate, θ^*, and the common interest rate, i^*; supply disturbances in the two large countries; and domestic disturbances, such that:

$$(22) \quad H\theta = [\bar{a}^* + (v^* - v^{**})k\beta]\theta^* + bi^* - v^*u_\pi^* - v^{**}u_\pi^{**} - u_A + u_\pi,$$

where $\bar{a}^j = a^j + h\alpha_j, j = {}^*, {}^{**}$; and $H = \bar{a}^* + \bar{a}^{**}$.
    The role of trade patterns is apparent. Indeed, when trade multipliers are the same ($v^* = v^{**} = v/2$), equation (22) simplifies to:

$$(23) \quad H\theta = \bar{a}^*\theta^* + {}^*u_A^s - {}^*u_\pi^s - u_A + u_\pi.$$

Even in this special case, global disturbances abroad affect the real exchange rate of the small countries unless they are the same as domestic disturbances ($u_i = {}^*u_i^s, i = A, \pi$).
    Substituting the right-hand side of (19) into (18) yields an expression for the price of domestic output in the same form as (13) above:

$$(24) \quad p = h[(1 - \alpha)\theta - \alpha_*\theta^*] + \frac{u_*^s}{\phi} - u_\pi + u_m.$$

Substituting for θ yields in the strongly symmetric case of equation (23):

$$(25) \quad p = \chi A^* \theta^* + \frac{u_*^s}{\phi} + \chi({}^*u_A^s - {}^*u_\pi^s) - \chi u_A - (1 - \chi) u_\pi + u_m,$$

where $A^* = (a^*\alpha_{**} - a^{**}\alpha_*)/(1 - \alpha)$ and $\chi = h(1 - \alpha)/H$
    If there is no difference between the relative shares of foreign output in the domestic price index and the relative trade elasticities, then $A^* = 0$. This is the case, emphasized by Marston (1984a), of "balanced" sensitivities. With equal real disturbances at home and abroad, the effect of a supply shock therefore differs from the effect of a demand shock by the same factor, $1 + \phi - v$, as in equation (13) above.
    When foreign real disturbances are perfectly negatively correlated and $A^* = 0$, the price of domestic output is a χ-weighted average of demand and supply disturbances plus the monetary disturbance. From equation (18), then, output is given by:

$$(26) \quad y = \chi u_A + (1 - \chi) u_\pi.$$

Similarly, the real exchange rate can be written as:

$$(27) \qquad \theta = \zeta\theta^* - \frac{1}{H}(u_A - u_\pi),$$

where $\zeta = \tilde{a}^*/H = \alpha_*/(1 - \alpha)$ when $A^* = 0$.

To solve for the nominal exchange rate of the small country with the numeraire currency, use the definition of the real exchange rate, which is obtained by adding θ and p in equations (25) and (27) and subtracting p^{**} in (13). In the absence of supply and interest-rate effects in the large countries, we find:

$$(28) \qquad e^{**} = \zeta e - U + u_m - u_m^{**},$$

where $U = \xi u_A + (1 - \xi) u_\pi$ and $\xi = [1 + h(1 - \alpha)]/H$.

To sum up the results under flexible exchange rates, monetary disturbances have no effect on the real exchange rate, and only domestic monetary disturbances (u_m) have an effect on the price of domestic output (the effect is one-to-one, as before). An increase in the demand for domestic output ($u_A > 0$) appreciates the real exchange rate, and an increase in productivity ($u_\pi > 0$) depreciates it by the same amount, $1/H$.

In the two-country model the effect is not symmetric because account has to be taken of the output repercussion in the foreign country, which is zero for the small, open economy. Thus, in equation (11) the depreciation caused by a supply shock is larger than the appreciation caused by a demand shock by $v/2H_*$.

Another difference is the unambiguously negative effect of demand expansion on the domestic price level. Since the fall in prices induces a real depreciation, the nominal exchange rate has to appreciate by more than the real rate. The effect of the supply shock on prices is also unambiguously negative, but the nominal exchange rate will depreciate only if the trade elasticities are small ($a^* + a^{**} < 1$, or equivalently $\xi > 1$), because in that case the fall in prices is less than the real depreciation.

10.2.3   Fixed Exchange Rates

It is useful to define the effective exchange rate of the domestic economy, a weighted average of the exchange rates of the two partners, by the weights given by the respective shares in the foreign component of the consumer price index, that is, by ζ, such that:

$$(29) \qquad E_e = \zeta e^* + (1 - \zeta) e^{**} = e^{**} - \zeta e.$$

The second equation is obtained by triangular arbitrage. Taking it into account, we can see from equation (28) that in this simplified setting the effective exchange rate is a function only of domestic disturbances. If the home country fixes its exchange rate with country*, then $e^* = 0$ and $e^{**} = e$. We thus have the effective exchange rate under the union, denoted by a tilde, such that:

$$(30) \qquad {}^E\tilde{e} = (1 - \zeta)\, e.$$

The effective exchange rate under the union appears in the expression for the exchange rate with the potential partner, obtained from (28) by triangular arbitrage, such that:

$$(31) \qquad e^* = -(1 - \zeta)e - U + u_m - u_m^*.$$

Under the union, equation (31) becomes an equation for the endogenous money stock of the home country, denoted by m, such that:

$$(32) \qquad m = u_m^* + {}^E\tilde{e} + U.$$

Because of the difference in size between the two partners, however, the money stock of country* continues to be policy determined, and there is no problem of monetary allocation between the two partners. Thus, u_m^* can be interpreted as an exogenous increase in the unionwide money stock. If $*u_m^d = 0$, foreign monetary expansion increases the domestic money stock one-to-one, since there is no induced depreciation of the exchange rate of country*.

Associated with the money stock under the union is a price of domestic output, denoted by a tilde. From equation (25), in the absence of global real disturbances and when sensitivities are balanced, we find:

$$(33) \qquad \tilde{p} = -y + m.$$

Since according to (26) and (27) y and θ are given by real domestic disturbances, the difference between the fixed and flexible exchange rate solutions is matched by the difference in money stocks and prices, such that:

$$(34) \qquad e - e^{**} = \tilde{p} - p = m - u_m.$$

Equation (34) shows that if the fixed exchange rate is lower than the one prevailing before the agreement, the money stock and the price of domestic output will decrease by the same amount. The decrease in the money stock is brought about by a capital outflow that would increase in magnitude if the government attempted to increase the supply of domestic assets to the public. As long as real output does not change, the real money stock remains fixed, and the fall in money balances is transmitted to prices. Only by increasing demand for real output could the government enforce a different nominal income. Alternatively, as we will see, the loss in reserves could be offset by a transfer from abroad.

In general, the price of domestic output has to be different from its equilibrium level for the real exchange rate to be different under the union. For example, domestic prices may be downwardly rigid.

Consider, thus, a price level p_T associated with a real exchange rate θ, which under the union gives a real exchange rate θ^T. The difference in real exchange rates then equals the difference in nominal rates, so that, from equation (34):

$$(35) \qquad \theta^T - \theta = \bar{p} - p_T.$$

The difference between the price prevailing in the neutral situation of equation (33) and that prevailing in the rigid situation can be decomposed further into the difference in real outputs and in money stocks. The latter, in turn, can derive from an increase in the foreign money stock. Assuming that $*u_m^d = 0$, denoting the common increase by $\bar{u}_m$, and that $\theta = 0$ under the "neutral" union (that is, $u_A = u_\pi = 0$), we find:

$$(36) \qquad \bar{p} - p_T = m - m_T - y + y_T$$

$$= -\frac{1}{H} u_A^T - \bar{u}_m,$$

where m_T is given by equation (32) with $U = \xi u_A^T$ and $u_m^* = \bar{u}_m$. A demand expansion, u_A^d, perhaps in the form of a fiscal expansion, appreciates the real exchange rate by $1/H$, whereas a monetary transfer from abroad has a one-to-one effect.

When account is taken of the induced real appreciation, the demand expansion increases output by $\chi < 1$. Given monetary policy, this expansion would reduce prices by the same amount by which it expands output, so that the nominal appreciation would be given by $\chi + 1/H = \xi$. Ruling out the exchange rate change and the fall in prices requires an increase in the money stock by the same factor ξ, which will be less than one if the trade elasticities are high enough. The real appreciation is accompanied by a rise in prices in the amount $1/H$. To keep the nominal exchange rate constant, demand expansion must therefore be consistent with the increase in the money stock, or $u_A = \bar{u}_m/\xi$. Of the equivalent rise in nominal income, a proportion, χ/ξ, goes to real output expansion, and the remainder, $(1 - \chi)/\xi$, goes to the rise in prices and fall in the real exchange rate.

In sum, the effects of a fixed exchange rate regime are confined to nominal variables unless there is a price rigidity, an induced demand for domestic output as a consequence of fiscal expansion, or a transfer from abroad. The last possibility is particularly relevant when there is a monetary union involving the two small countries, henceforth indexed 1 and 2.

10.2.4 Two-Tier Monetary Unions

A Monetary Union of Two Small Countries

If country 1 fixes its exchange rate with country 2, e_1^* will equal e_2^* in equation (31). Unlike in the previous case, we must keep track of the monetary allocation. In fact, any exogenous increase in the union-wide money stock, denoted by t, will be allocated between the two partners in proportion to their steady-state shares (assumed to be equal). Setting $\bar{u}_m = 0$ for simplicity, we find:

$$(37) \qquad m_1 = t + U^d$$

$$(38) \qquad m_2 = t - U^d$$

$$(39) \qquad e^* = t - (1 - \zeta)e - U^s,$$

where t is the increase in the unionwide money stock; $U^d = (U^1 - U^2)/2$; and $U^s = (U^1 + U^2)/2$.

Given the unchanged real exchange rates, equations (37) through (39) are the solution of the exchange rate union between two small countries. If $t = 0$, the money stocks are unchanged when demand and supply disturbances are perfectly correlated ($U^d = 0$). In that case, the exchange rate with country* appreciates by $U^s = U^1$.

A Three-Country Monetary Union

In general, fixing the exchange rate with country* requires an increase in the unionwide money stock given by making $e^* = 0$ in equation (39). If real disturbances are exogenous, the transfer must adjust. Denoting this endogenous monetary transfer from abroad by a tilde, we find:

$$(40) \qquad \tilde{t} = E_{\bar{e}} + U^s.$$

According to equation (40), a depreciation of the franc against the dollar requires an increase in $\tilde{t}$ that is larger, the higher the consumption share of goods from country** relative to goods from country* (the lower the ζ). On the other hand, a unionwide demand expansion requires an increase in $\tilde{t}$ that is larger, the larger the consumption share of nonunion relative to union goods (the lower the α).

The endogenous increase in the unionwide money stock ($\tilde{t} > 0$) can be interpreted as a transfer from the large partner that guarantees the fixed exchange rate agreement. Although t could be zero in equations (37) through (39), $\tilde{t}$ will generally be nonzero in (40).

Conversely, the transfer may remain exogenous if expenditure is adjusted by fiscal policy in both countries, such that (with $u_\pi^i = 0$):

$$(41) \qquad \bar{u}_A^s = (t - {}^E\bar{e})/\xi.$$

I continue to assume that the transfer has no effect on the money stock of country* because of the size difference. It is, nevertheless, required by the union and would be zero only if there were no unionwide demand or supply disturbances and no external real disturbances either, so that $U^i = e = 0$.

I will analyze next how the allocation of the transfer can have real effects.

A Monetary Allocation Rule

If the unionwide central bank allocates the transfer in equation (40) according to (37) and (38), the full monetary union will have no real effects. This is easy to verify by eliminating $t = \tilde{t}$.

Consider now a monetary allocation rule whereby money increases in each country, denoted as u^i_T, are based on a share ω of the sum of the equilibrium money stock increases. The percentage change in each money stock is given by $2\omega\tilde{t}$ when the two small countries are identical in steady state, so that:

$$(42) \qquad u^1_T = 2\omega\tilde{t}$$

$$(43) \qquad u^2_T = 2(1 - \omega)\tilde{t}.$$

Using equations (40), and (42), and (43) in (35), we find:

$$(44) \qquad \theta^T_1 = \theta_1 + (1 - 2\omega) \, ^E\bar{e} + (1 - \omega)U^1 - \omega U^2$$

$$(45) \qquad \theta^T_2 = \theta_2 - (1 - 2\omega) \, ^E\bar{e} - (1 - \omega)U^1 + \omega U^2.$$

The effects of various disturbances on θ^T_1 are displayed in table 10.1. Since the exchange rate gaps are of the same magnitude and of opposite sign (if $\theta^T_1 > \theta_1$, then $\theta^T_2 < \theta_2$), the results for country 2 are easy to obtain. Thus the first column, first row shows that the effect of a depreciation of the franc-dollar rate is ambiguous when $\omega > \frac{1}{2}$. The effect will be a real depreciation in the small countries if trade is sufficiently biased toward France. When $\omega = \frac{1}{2}$, the effect is the same as under flexible exchange rates.

The first column, second row shows that demand expansion in country 1 has an ambiguous effect on the real exchange rate, unless the whole transfer goes to country 2 ($\omega = 0$), in which case the effect will be positive. The condition for a negative effect will be weaker than $\omega > \frac{1}{2}$ if the supply elasticity is high enough, that is, if $h(1 - \alpha) > 1$. When the entire transfer goes to the expanding country ($\omega = 1$), the effect is the same as in equation (27) above.

The effect of demand expansion in country 2 is a real appreciation in country 1, and the same is true of a productivity improvement if trade elasticities are high enough ($\xi < 1$). As shown in the third row, both effects are dampened by ω, so that they vanish when the entire

Table 10.1 **The Effect of Disturbances on the Real Exchange Rate of Country 1 (θ_1^T)**

	Disturbance		
	Demand ($j = A$)	Supply ($j = \pi$)	Both
1. Foreign (e)	$\dfrac{\alpha_* + \alpha_{**}(1 - 2\omega)}{1 - \alpha}$	n.a.	n.a.
2. Domestic (u_j^1)	$\chi - \omega\xi$	$1 - \chi - \omega(1 - \xi)$	$1 - \omega$
3. Partner (u_j^2)	$-\omega\xi$	$-\omega(1 - \xi)$	$-\omega$
4. Unionwide			
4.1 Global ($u_j^1 = u_j^2$)	$\chi - 2\omega\xi$	$1 - \chi - 2\omega(1 - \xi)$	$1 - 2\omega$
4.2 Distribution ($u_j^1 = u_j^2$)	χ	$1 - \chi$	1

transfer goes to country 2 ($\omega = 0$). The effect of a domestic productivity improvement is an unambiguous real depreciation, so that a harvest failure ($u_\pi^1 < 0$), for example, causes the real exchange rate to fall. When the entire transfer goes to country 1 ($\omega = 1$), the effect is again the same as in equation (27).

As shown in the fourth rows, the effects of unionwide global disturbances are the same as in (27) when $\omega = \frac{1}{2}$. On the contrary, inversely correlated disturbances are independent of ω and always have an effect given by χ. In general, the real exchange rate gap can be avoided by the choice of a suitable ω. For example, if $U^1 > U^2$, then $\omega > \frac{1}{2}$ for $\theta_i^T = \theta_i$.

The model described above shows how a monetary allocation rule induces a change in the real exchange rates of the members of a monetary union. This description implies that there is also a pseudo–exchange rate union that includes, aside from the members of the monetary union, a large country ready to ensure the fixed exchange rate agreement by transferring real resources to the union.

Because of the size difference between the partners, an increase in the large partner's money stock could also imply a change in the real exchange rate of the small partner, to the extent that the price level was different from the one to which the exchange rate was pegged. Similarly, the real effects of demand expansion could be interpreted in terms of a fiscal expansion induced by the union, as long as the large partner is willing to transfer real resources and therefore increase real money balances.

Nevertheless, the focus of the analysis was on the allocation of a given transfer between the two small countries, because this is an important feature in the recent experience of the West African Monetary Union. The major implication of the model was therefore that changes in the real exchange rate of the small partners are to be expected when the allocation of a given transfer is different from the one implied by the assumed equality of the steady-state monetary shares of the two small countries.

10.3   The West African Monetary Union

10.3.1   The Franc Zone

Established in the mid-1940s between France and its colonies, the Franc Zone survived the independence of the colonies in the early 1960s and the move to generalized floating exchange rates in the early 1970s.

Summing up the African monetary experience of the Bretton Woods era, Mundell (1972, 93) wrote:

> The French and the English economic traditions in monetary theory and history are different. At the risk of gross oversimplification . . . the French tradition has stressed the passive nature of monetary policy and the importance of exchange stability with convertibility (within the franc area); stability was achieved at the expense of institutional development and monetary experience. The British countries by opting for monetary independence have sacrificed stability, but gained experience and better developed monetary institutions. The simplest test of this is the extent of development of money substitutes.

Mundell went on to present indicators of financial intermediation for eleven "rich countries" and 33 African countries, classified into "Franc Africa," "Sterling Africa," "North Africa," and "Central East Africa." His figures showed that in 1968 the median propensity to hold cash was 21 percent in OECD countries, 33 percent in Sterling Africa, 47 percent in Franc Africa, and 45 percent in the other two regions of Africa.

Table 10.2 provides evidence along the same lines for the United States and France, as rich countries; Kenya, a Sterling Africa country; several countries of Franc Africa; Barbados, a member of the East Caribbean Currency Area; and Sudan.[5] The figures for 1962 and 1972 confirm the lower development of money substitutes in Franc Africa.

The Franc Zone has changed considerably over the last 40 years. Upon independence, it was adapted through the creation of common central banks for the former French colonies of West, Central, and East Africa. In particular, Benin, Ivory Coast, Mauritania, Niger, Senegal, Togo, and Upper Volta created UMOA, managed by the Central

Table 10.2   **Indicators of Financial Intermediation in Various Countries, in Percentages**

Country	Propensity to Hold Near-Money			Propensity to Hold Cash		
	1962	1972	1982	1962	1972	1982
Rich Countries						
United States	60	71	80	8	6	6
France	36	60	70	25	11	6
Sterling Africa						
Kenya	29[a]	30	37	21[a]	21	18
Franc Africa						
Cameroon	7	18	36	52	38	27
Ivory Coast	8	17	30	56	42	33
Senegal	3	9	28	51	39	32
Mauritania	3	8	26	49	40	31
Madagascar	2	19	21[b]	55	39	31[b]
Mali	3	3	6	61	59	62
Other						
Barbados	57[a]	71	70	13[a]	10	13
Sudan	6	13	18	50	45	32

Source: International Monetary Fund, *International Financial Statistics* (IFS)

(1) Line 35 } divided by lines 34 plus 35 (M2) unless otherwise noted
(2) Line 14a }

France (1) Lines 35 plus 65a } divided by lines 54 plus 56a (M3)
       (2) Line 14a. }

U.S.
       (1) Lines 59mcb minus 59 mab } divided by line 59 mcb (M3)
       (2) Line 14a. }

[a]1966.
[b]1979.

Bank of the West African States (known by its French abbreviation BCEAO), whereas Cameroon, Central Africa, Chad, Congo, and Gabon established the union of the members of the Bank of Central African States. The members of those two monetary unions signed an agreement of monetary cooperation with France whereby the exchange rate between the French franc and the franc of African Financial Cooperation (CFA) was fixed, foreign exchange reserves were pooled, and exchange controls were common to the whole zone. Most importantly, an "operations account" at the French Treasury guaranteed the convertibility of the CFA and provided a channel for monetary transfers between France and UMOA.

Although Mali participated in the UMOA negotiations, it refused to sign the agreement and left the Franc Zone in 1962. Its justification was consistent with Mundell's view of the British tradition: Monetary sovereignty, Mali argued, was an essential instrument of development. Monetary stability ws a less pressing consideration.

Mali's criticism of the Franc Zone as a neocolonial obstacle to "self-centered" development is only one example of a fairly widespread view that the arrangement has served to benefit France.[6] Since the repeated devaluation of the French franc after 1981 and the implementation of tighter areawide exchange controls, the desirable trend toward trade diversification away from France seems to have been reversed. As a consequence, the British tradition might now provide an argument for leaving the Franc Zone: There will be no monetary stability in the UMOA if there is none in France.

This controversy about the costs and benefits of the Franc Zone arrangements merely illustrates how the volatility of major exchange rates over the last ten years has changed the terms of the Mundellian trade-off between monetary stability and development. Stability relative to one currency means instability relative to other floating currencies, so that fixing "the" exchange rate is no longer an option. The figures for 1982 reported in table 10.2 also suggest a blurring of the difference between the French and the English monetary traditions. Certainly, the propensity to hold cash remains higher in the former French colonies than in Kenya, but except for Madagascar, the propensity to hold near-money increased much faster in the countries of Franc Africa than it did in Kenya or Sudan.

To the extent that both groups were subject to the global shocks of the 1970s, the acceleration of financial development casts the agreements of monetary cooperation with France in a new light. The originality of their design has been emphasized in the work of the Guillaumonts (1984). Rather than being a historic relic, the Franc Zone represents in their view a conscious choice of monetary and exchange rate policy by sovereign states. Similarly, for Vinay (1980, 3), it is a "unique organization in which the traditional legalism of French institutions was replaced by a fertile pragmatism." The fact that some former French colonies, such as Madagascar and Mauritania, left the union in 1972 is, of course, consistent with the idea of choice.[7]

Pragmatism can also be found in the posture of Mali. Three years after choosing monetary sovereignty, Mali began negotiations for a return to the Franc Zone, and a special arrangement was agreed upon in 1967 whereby the Malian franc was devalued by 50 percent relative to the CFA. In addition, France was to lobby for the accession of Mali to the UMOA. The agreement involved two preliminary phases. A one-year fiscal adjustment-cum-liberalization was followed by bilateral cooperation with France along BCEAO lines. The duration of this phase was not specified, since full membership for Mali might not in the end be welcome by the other members. This is not surprising in light of the country's singular monetary underdevelopment, apparent from table 10.2, and its persistently negative operations account with France. Political considerations also played a role, as emphasized by Crum (1984).

Nevertheless, Malian membership in the UMOA was agreed upon in Niamey, Niger in October 1983. The third phase was thus completed in 1984. Because of the increasing transfer of resources from France to the UMOA, the reversal of Mali's position might be explained by a desire to receive the transfer through the UMOA rather than directly from France.

If fixing is impossible in a world of floating rates and a pure float is not a viable—let alone desirable—option for a developing country, an alternative to the institutions of the Franc Zone would be for the UMOA collectively to peg to a basket of currencies. This was proposed by Nascimento (1984) on the basis of his econometric analysis of the costs and benefits of various exchange rate regimes for the union as a whole. He measured the trade-off between monetary sovereignty and the "liquidity" by, respectively, the loss in reserves associated with an excess supply of money (the offset coefficient) and the variances of departures from purchasing power parity. According to this operationalization of the Mundellian trade-off, offset coefficients and real exchange rate variability in the UMOA are smallest under a basket peg and largest under a crawling peg relative to the French franc.

Both the neglect of the French transfer—which allows the continued sterilization of the loss in reserves—and the assumption of purchasing power parity cast doubt on the applicability of Nascimento's analysis to the UMOA, let alone to its members with persistent deficits, such as Senegal. All the same, for a given transfer, pegging to a basket allows for the choice of optimal weights. Since it is unlikely for the optimal weight of a particular currency to be one, such a regime would dominate the present arrangement. Similarly, it is unlikely that the rate of crawl would be zero, so that a regime by which indicators are optimally chosen will also dominate the basket peg.[8] This arrangement would make the UMOA look like the EMS rather than part of the Franc Zone. The problem for a deficit country in the UMOA would then be how to ensure a continued transfer from its surplus partners, if there are any.

10.3.2 Monetary Allocations in the UMOA

During its first decade the UMOA followed the prudent course cited earlier as being characteristic of the French monetary tradition. From its Paris headquarters, BCEAO managed to keep the composition of the union's money stock (M2) virtually constant. The net foreign assets of the banking system grew almost without interruption and remained at about one third of the money stock, so that domestic assets accounted for the other two thirds, as shown in table 10.3, column 3. The propensity to hold near-money increased from 4 percent in 1962 to 13 percent ten years later (column 4). Finally, as a share of the French money stock, the UMOA's money showed a slight increase over that period (column 5).

The situation changed in the 1970s, but the reversal was obscured by the drastic increases in the reserves of Ivory Coast in 1974 and 1977, largely as the result of higher world prices for coffee (19 percent and 20 percent, respectively) and cocoa (56 percent and 69 percent, respectively). The reserves of Togo also jumped in 1974 as the result of a rise in the price of phosphates (by 483 percent); and as a share of the union money stock they went from 14 percent to 27 percent. At the same time the institutional reforms allowed the BCEAO greater freedom to conduct monetary policy from its newly established African headquarters.[9]

Table 10.3   The Composition of Money Stock in the UMOA, 1962–82

Year	Net Foreign Assets (CFAF billion)	Money (M2) (CFAF billion)	Ratio (1)/(2)	Ratio Time Deposits/(2) (%)	Share of France
	(1)	(2)	(3)	(4)	(5)
1962	31.0	88.3	35	4.3	1.2
1963	31.0	90.2	34	4.1	1.1
1964	32.2	103.1	31	10.0	1.1
1965	43.5	103.6	40	7.8	1.0
1966	43.5	108.0	40	8.2	1.0
1967	38.8	112.1	35	10.3	.9
1968	43.8	133.6	33	12.7	.9
1969	53.7	159.6	34	16.9	1.1
1970	79.5	185.7	43	16.1	1.1
1971	81.3	204.1	40	16.4	1.0
1972	63.7	217.0	29	13.3	.9
1973	52.9	261.0	20	18.3	.9
1974	81.0	387.2	21	21.1	1.2
1975	30.2	437.4	7	20.9	1.2
1976	37.1	596.0	6	21.8	1.4
1977	62.8	811.7	8	23.5	1.7
1978	38.5	941.2	4	25.4	1.7
1979	−73.0	945.1	−8	22.4	1.5
1980	−282.0	1,024.7	−28	23.5	1.5
1981	−431.1	1,186.2	−36	25.1	1.6
1982	−547.5	1,273.9	−43	27.0	1.5

Sources: (1) IFS line 31n summed over country pages; it excludes long-term borrowing (line 36cl) and SDR allocations (included in other items, line 37r).
(2) IFS lines 34 and 35 summed over country pages.
(4) IFS line 35 divided by (2).
(5) (2) plus (3) divided by IFS lines 34 plus 35 for France.

As shown in table 10.4, the negative foreign asset position of the commercial banks overtook the claims of the central bank in 1979, and the operations account of the central bank moved from a claim of CFAF 54.6 million on France in December 1979 to a liability of CFAF 13.2 million in March 1980. The steep increases in the reserves of Togo in 1981 and 1982 were no longer sufficient to offset the declines of the two major partners, Ivory Coast and Senegal. The external liabilities of the banking system increased from 10 percent of the money stock in December 1979 to 36 percent in June 1982 and reached 56 percent in June 1983.

Put in another way, domestic assets increased from 96 percent of the union money stock in 1978 to 143 percent in 1982. In the meantime the domestic assets of France fell from 82 percent to 69 percent of the money stock in 1980 and increased to 77 percent in 1981 and 1982. This change reflected the loss of foreign exchange reserves associated with the expected devaluations of the franc during those two years (and thus offset the revaluation of existing resources).

The evolution of the shares of UMOA members in the union's money stock (M2) is summarized in table 10.5. Measured by the coefficient of variation, the Senegalese share was the second most stable, but it was the most unstable over the entire period 1962–82. Of the two largest shares, the share of Ivory Coast has been positively correlated with the UMOA share in the French money stock, whereas the corresponding correlation for Senegal has been negative. During the 1960s the

Table 10.4   **The Net Foreign Assets of the UMOA, 1975–83 (CFAF billion)**

	Assets of the Central Bank (1)	Liabilities of the Commercial Banks (2)	[(1) − (2)] (3)
December			
1975	66.4	44.8	19.7
1976	70.2	44.0	26.2
1977	94.6	41.3	53.3
1978	125.2	90.4	34.9
1979	32.5	131.5	− 99.0
1980	− 120.2	189.5	− 309.7
1981	− 237.8	190.1	− 427.9
1982	− 356.8	203.6	− 560.5
June			
1982	− 260.4	174.1	− 434.5
1983	− 533.0	180.3	− 713.3

Source: BCEAO (includes long-term borrowing and SDR allocations that are excluded in the IFS presentation of table 10.3).

Notes: The totals in column (3) may not add due to rounding. The figures in (2) represent new series since 1979. The June 1983 figure in (3) excludes Benin (data not available).

converse was true (− .55 for Ivory Coast and .62 for Senegal, as reported in Macedo 1985a). For the last few years Senegal's allocation was therefore insulated from the decline of the total.

That the insulation was on average at the expense of Ivory Coast is suggested by the negative correlation of .8 between the two monetary allocations, shown in table 10.6. The strength of the inverse link between the two economies was even higher in the 1960s (over the years 1962–72 the correlation reached − .99), largely because of the deterioration of the Ivorian external position after 1980.[10] If the French transfer decreases, however, the negative shares correlation will increase again.

The increase in UMOA money relative to French money has reversed in the last few years, as France has grown reluctant to replenish the operations account on a continuing basis. This implies that in the future the monetary allocation of the transfer will become a central policy issue for the members of the UMOA. The membership of Mali, another country with a structural deficit, is also likely to tighten the constraint on the shares.

Table 10.5   **Summary Statistics of Members' Shares in the UMOA Money Stock, 1973–82, in Percentages**

Country	Mean		Coefficient of Variation		Correlation	
Ivory Coast	58	(54)	6	(12)	.33	(.37)
Senegal	19	(22)	8	(29)	− .72	(− .37)
Togo	7	(7)	14	(19)	.24	(.43)
Niger	6	(6)	18	(14)	.26	(.06)
Benin	5	(6)	18	(14)	− .42	(− .46)
Upper Volta	5	(5)	9	(12)	− .44	(− .47)
Total/France	1	(1)	17	(22)	1.00	

Source: IFS, lines 34 and 35.

Notes: The numbers in parentheses refer to data for 1962–82. The coefficient of variation is the standard deviation divided by the mean (times 100).

Table 10.6   **Correlations of Monetary Allocations, 1973–82**

	Ivory Coast	Senegal	Togo	Niger	Benin
Senegal	− .76(− .96)				
Togo	− .71(.60)	.41(− .76)			
Niger	− .52(− .24)	− .10(.02)	.52(.20)		
Benin	− .78(− .65)	.60(.51)	.24(− .27)	.24(.21)	
Upper Volta	− .82(− .88)	.65(.81)	.27(− .58)	.34(.31)	.84(.66)

Source: Same data as in table 10.5.

Note: The numbers in parentheses refer to 1962–82.

10.3.3 Nominal Stability and Real Volatility

Table 10.7 lists the 1980 trade shares of France, Senegal, and the other African countries covered in table 10.2 by loosely defined Ecu and dollar areas. The shares of the Franc Zone (including France) and of the United States are also indicated. The non–U.S. members of the dollar area are obtained residually.

Ivory Coast, Madagascar, and Mali show a lower share for imports from the dollar area than Senegal. Their share of imports from the United States is similar to that of Mauritania, Cameroon, and Madagascar. The Franc Zone export share is highest in Senegal, followed by Mauritania, Mali, and Ivory Coast. On the import side, however, Senegal has the lowest share among Franc Zone countries. Thus, trade diversification increased the dollar-area share in the trade of the Franc Zone countries, but, as mentioned earlier, the trend has probably been reversed in recent years.[11]

Because of the different trade patterns, there are sizable differences between the nominal effective exchange rate of France and

Table 10.7   Trade Shares by Currency Area, 1980, in Percentages

	Ecu	Of which Franc Zone	Dollar	Of Which Unified States
Imports				
Senegal (1)	53	37	47	4
France (1)	47	0	53	8
Ivory Coast (2)	52	42	48	7
Cameroon (3)	51	43	49	5
Mali (3)	79	67	21	0
Mauritania (5)	37	29	70	5
Madagascar (3)	62	41	38	4
Kenya (1)	31	0	69	17
Sudan (5)	29	5	71	8
Exports				
Senegal	56	46	44	0
France	48	0	52	5
Ivory Coast	63	29	37	9
Cameroon	53	21	47	29
Mali	59	26	41	0
Mauritania	48	29	52	0
Madagascar	40	23	60	19
Kenya	34	0	66	4
Sudan	16	5	84	0

Source: International Monetary Fund, *Direction of Trade* (Washington, D.C.).

Notes: The numbers in parentheses indicate the minimum share; for example, for Senegal all partners with a one percent share or larger were included in the computation. Except for the United States, the dollar area is obtained residually. The data on French shares are for 1981.

those of the Franc Zone countries. In the 1970s changes in the effective exchange rate of the U.S. dollar have also become an important source of divergence. Thus, the mean annual rate of depreciation over the 1973–82 period was 2.5 percent for France, 1 percent for Ivory Coast, and zero for Senegal, using 1980 import weights. With export weights, there was no change for the UMOA countries and a 2 percent per annum change for France. The standard deviation was also lower for the UMOA countries, but relative to the mean their nominal effective rates were more volatile than France's, as shown in table 10.8.

After a decade of experience with flexible exchange rates, the notion that real exchange rates would be stabilized by the offsetting of nominal variations by inflation differentials, very popular in the mid-1970s has been abandoned even by its most ardent defenders. The failure of purchasing power parity is evident in the substantial variability of most measures of real effective exchange rates in the industrialized countries.[12] Data availability precluded the computation of effective exchange rates using more narrowly based indexes than the so-called African consumer price index or even correcting prices for exchange rate changes.[13]

Table 10.8   **Nominal and Real Exchange Rates, 1973–82**

	Mean (% p.a.)		Coefficient of Variation		Correlations Between Nominal and Real
	Nominal	Real	Nominal	Real	
Export Weights					
Ivory Coast	.32	−1.92	15.53	3.18	.63
Cameroon	1.95	−.24	2.93	26.04	.82
Madagascar	2.84	−.96	2.41	5.78	.10
Mauritania	−1.61	−.64	4.14	14.95	.96
Sudan	11.19	3.28	1.51	4.39	.82
Kenya	−2.08	−2.41	4.97	5.36	.90
Senegal	.36	.84	6.66	7.83	.70
France	1.70	.83	2.92	5.12	.96
Import Weights					
Ivory Coast	1.11	−1.51	2.85	4.16	.62
Cameroon	1.37	−.41	1.72	7.41	.57
Madagascar	1.91	−1.32	2.14	4.08	−.19
Mauritania	−1.76	−1.13	3.66	8.52	.98
Sudan	11.43	3.44	1.60	4.33	.87
Kenya	4.26	.87	.90	5.24	.33
Senegal	.16	1.69	28.13	5.60	.77
France	2.54	1.44	2.28	5.53	.86

Source: IFS, with weights as described in Macedo (1985a).

The evolution of real effective exchange rates in table 10.8 shows Senegal and France as the only French-speaking countries to have depreciated in real terms. In terms of real variability, Senegal was also close to France (6), with Mauritania the highest (8), and Ivory Coast the lowest (4). The mean changes are close in absolute values, but the correlation between nominal and real changes is lower in Ivory Coast. Furthermore, the correlation between the real rates in the two countries increased to .45 in the 1970s.

Figure 10.1 shows a real depreciation of the franc since 1968 and pronounced swings around the upward trend, which are most pronounced when the 1981 weights are used. It is also evident from the figure that after 1976 Senegal moved opposite to France, whereas Ivory Coast magnified the French movement. There was a substantial gap between the real rates of the two partners until 1980, as would be expected from the automatic adjustment mechanism of the balance of payments. This suggests that the monetary allocation rule did respond to the external performance of the economies, particularly when the total share of the UMOA ceased to increase in relation to the French money stock.[14]

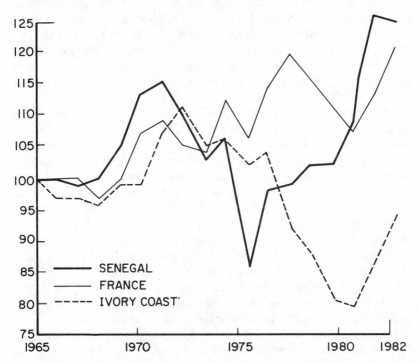

Fig. 10.1   Real effective exchange rate indices (1980 import weights). Source: Same as table 10.8.

10.4   Conclusion

Although there are few monetary unions, there are many models thereof. Most of those models are concerned with the choice of a single country to peg to a single currency. The case analyzed in this paper is even more unusual because it involves a collection of countries pegging to a single currency. Nevertheless, an effort was made to analyze the workings of a full monetary union that has been in existence for about four decades.

The theoretical model presented in section 10.2 focused on the interaction of two small and two large countries and showed under what conditions the monetary union would imply changes in the real exchange rates of its members. A transfer of real resources from the large partner was an especially relevant case, since this is what has happened in the last few years with the UMOA and France.

Building on the available studies of the institutional structure of the UMOA, section 10.3 described the process of monetary allocation. The drastic deterioration of the net foreign asset position of the UMOA over the last five years shows the importance of the French transfer. Over the last 20 years, however, monetary allocation within the union was associated with a very high negative correlation between the two major partners, Senegal and Ivory Coast. To the extent that the transfer from France disappears, a fixed exchange rate with the French franc will require a restoration of this pattern rather than the growing union-wide deficit that has been observed since 1979.

The comparison of the interaction between exchange rate and relative price changes in Senegal, Ivory Coast, and France confirmed the expected failure of purchasing power parity to stabilize the real exchange rate. More surprising—despite the presence in the price index used of nontraded goods and goods whose prices are controlled—was the insulation of (African) consumer price inflation in the UMOA from French consumer price inflation. The stability of the nominal effective rates in the UMOA was therefore accompanied by unstable real effective exchange rates. Since this relative price is only weakly positively correlated with the terms of trade, it can be said that the monetary union achieved nominal stability at the expense of real volatility. The unfortunate consequences of this pattern for resource allocation led Nascimento (1983) to propose a basket peg for the UMOA. But his argument ignores the increasing French transfer of the last four years.

The comparison of the real effective exchange rates of Senegal and Ivory Coast with several other African countries confirms the singularity of the Senegalese experience. All the rates depreciated in nominal terms, but Senegal achieved a real depreciation during the floating rate period, whereas the other former French colonies appreciated in real terms. Real exchange rate variability over the sample period was less pronounced in Madagascar, Mauritania, and Sudan.

This comparison suggests that if the loss of monetary autonomy did not induce a gold-standard type of adjustment to external inflation in Senegal (as it did in Ivory Coast before 1980), the reason is to be found in the increase of the unionwide money stock relative to the exogenously determined French money stock in the 1970s. More important, from 1975 to 1980, if the monetary allocation rule allowed Ivory Coast to drain money from Senegal through the balance of payments, it would have induced real appreciation in the former country and real depreciation in the latter, as was indeed observed.

Needless to say, this paper merely scratches the surface of the problem of choosing an exchange rate regime for the members of the UMOA and for developing countries in general. The model does not capture enough stylized features of the small African economies, and much more work needs to be done on characterizing them empirically. Some features of the large industrialized economies were also left out, especially the effect of the changes in the franc-Ecu rate.

Finally, the model suggested an exogenous administrative procedure to determine the crucial monetary allocation parameter. The effect of the recent threat of a reduction in the transfer from France is therefore likely to be increasing conflicts about the monetary allocation rule, making it endogenous. A model like the one presented in section 10.2 can, of course, be extended to incorporate some of these conflicts.

Notes

1. Since the survey by Tower and Willet (1976), there have been contributions by Allen and Kenen (1980), Aoki (1983), Marston (1984a; 1985), Melitz (1984), and Huizinga (1984), among others. On exchange rate policy in developing countries, see Lewis (1977) and Kenen (1978).

2. See Macedo (1983) for a two-country model along the same lines and Marston (1984b) for a discussion of supply effects. The model used here is a simplified version of that in Macedo (1985b).

3. It is possible to introduce further asymmetries by marginal changes in the parameters, using the methodology developed by Aoki (1981).

4. The homogeneous solution is in Macedo (1985b).

5. The relationship between monetary and real integration in Africa is emphasized in Letiche (1972). On the West African experience, see McLenaghan, Nsouli, and Riechel (1982) and Robson (1983). Helleiner (1983) assessed the prospects for Africa's relations with the International Monetary Fund. Note that since Sudan is in the Middle Eastern Department at the IMF, it is not included in IMF (1968–77).

6. Raffinot (1982) is one of the most systematic attempts at defending this view. It surfaces, however, in Mulumba (1976), cited almost approvingly by Connolly (1983).

7. Indeed, Allen (1983) reviewed the institutional structure of the UMOA as part of the preparation for setting up the East Caribbean Central Bank.

8. See the analysis of Branson and Katseli (1982) and, on the choice of indicators, Branson and Macedo (1982).

9. Bhattia (1982) emphasized the importance of the 1974 reform in his study of the UMOA up to that date. The need for a more active interest rate policy is clear from Leite (1982).

10. Discreetly, the 1980 report of the BCEAO assigned the responsibility for the decline to "un État membre de l'Union" (p. 45).

11. The use of export and import shares to measure the relative importance of trading partners' currencies neglects the growing weight of services and interest. In the case of Senegal the current-account shares are not very different from the ones reported in table 10.7. See Macedo (1985a).

12. Nascimento (1984) and Connolly (1983) assumed that purchasing power parity holds between the UMOA and the EMS (or France).

13. Plane (1983) compared the African index and the national output deflator. He also computed "synthetic indices of competitiveness" based on ratios of unit values as well as on average market shares. Those indexes behave quite differently from the real exchange rates. No real rates are reported here for Mali because the IFS lists no price index. Plane (1983) presented such an index and singled it out as showing a clear overvaluation, unlike the other nine African currencies he studied.

14. The correlation of the relative shares of the two countries in the UMOA and the ratio of their real effective exchange rates was rather weak during the period 1965–82 ($-.25$ using 1980 import shares) and basically disappeared in the 1970s ($-.05$). This was also the case, but to a lesser extent, of the correlation between money shares and relative consumer prices, which dropped from $-.35$ to $-.15$ between the two sample periods.

References

Allen, E. M. 1983. Multi-state central banking, with special reference to the East Caribbean Currency Area. Paper prepared for the International Monetary Fund Institute Seminar in Barbados, August.

Allen, P. R., and Kenen, P. 1980. *Asset markets, exchange rates and economic integration.* Cambridge: Cambridge University Press.

Aoki, M. 1981. *Dynamic analysis of open economies.* New York: Academic.

————. A fundamental inequality to compare dynamic effects of real and asset sector disturbances in a three-country model of the world under alternative exchange rate regimes. *Economics Letters* 11:263–67.

Banque Centrale des Etats de l'Afrique de l'ouest. *Rapport Annuel.*

Bhattia, R. 1982. The West African Monetary Union: Experience with monetary arrangements, 1963–74. IMF departmental memorandum. Washington, D.C.: International Monetary Fund, September.

Branson, W., and Katseli, L. 1982. Currency baskets and real effective exchange rates. In *The theory and experience of economic development (Lewis Festschrift)*, ed. M. Gersovitz et al. London: Allen & Unwin.

Branson, W., and Macedo, J. 1982. The optimal choice of indicators for a crawling peg. *Journal of International Money and Finance* 2:165–78.

Connolly, M. 1983. Le choix de régimes de change pour l'Afrique. Columbia, S.C.: University of South Carolina, July. Photocopy.

Corden, M. 1972. Monetary integration. *Princeton Essays in International Finance* no. 93. Princeton: International Finance Section, Princeton University.

Crum, L. L. 1984. Mali and the U.M.O.A: A case study of economic integration. *Journal of Modern African Studies* (September): 469–86.

Guillaumont, P., and Guillaumont, S. 1984. *Zone Franc et développement Africain*. Paris: Economica.

Helleiner, G. 1983. The IMF and Africa in the 1980s. *Princeton Essays in International Finance* no. 152. Princeton: International Finance Section, Princeton University.

Huizinga, H. 1984. An analysis of strategic behavior in a two-country monetary union. Senior thesis. Department of Economics, Princeton University.

International Monetary Fund. 1968. *Survey of African economies, vol. 1: Cameroon, Central African Republic, Chad, Congo (Brazzaville), and Gabon*. Washington, D.C.: IMF.

———. 1969. *Survey of African economies*, vol. 2: *Kenya, Tanzania, Uganda, and Somalia*. Washington, D.C.: IMF.

———. 1970. *Survey of African economies*, vol. 3: *Dahomey, Ivory Coast, Mauritania, Niger, Senegal, Togo and Upper Volta*. Washington, D.C.: IMF.

———. 1971. *Survey of African economies*, vol. 4: *Democratic Republic of Congo (Zaire), Malaysi Republic, Malawi, Mauritius, and Zambia*. Washington, D.C.: IMF.

———. 1977. *Survey of African economies*, vol. 7: *Algeria, Mali, Morocco, and Tunisia*. Washington, D.C.: IMF.

Kenen, P. 1978. The role of monetary policy in developing countries in Central Bank of the Gambia. In *The role of monetary policy in developing countries*. Banjul.

Leite, S. 1982. Interest rate policies in West Africa. *International Monetary Fund Papers*, vol. 29, no. 1 (March).

Letiche, J. 1972. Conditions and objectives of African economic development. In *International economics and development (Prebisch Festschrift)*, ed. L. Di Marco. New York: Academic.

Lewis, W. A. 1977. *The LDCs and stable exchange rates*. Washington, D.C.: International Monetary Fund.

Macedo, J. 1983. Policy interdependence under flexible exchange rates. Woodrow Wilson School Discussion Paper in Economics no. 62. Princeton: Princeton University, December.

———. 1985a. Small countries in monetary unions: The choice of Senegal. Research Program in Development Studies Discussion Paper no. 117 (March). Princeton: RPDS, Princeton University.

————. 1985b. Small countries in monetary unions: A two-tier model. Research Program in Development Studies Discussion Paper no. 118 (March). Princeton: RPDS, Princeton University.

Marston, R. 1984a. Exchange-rate unions as an alternative to flexible exchange rates: The effects of real and monetary disturbances. In *Flexible exchange rates in theory and practice*, ed. J. Bilson and R. Marston. Chicago: University of Chicago Press.

————. 1984b. Real wages and the terms of trade: Alternative indexation rules for an open economy. *Journal of Money, Credit and Banking* 16, no. 3 (August): 285–301.

————. 1985. Financial disturbances and the effects of an exchange rate union. In *Exchange rate management under uncertainty*, ed. J. Bhandari. Cambridge, Mass.: MIT Press.

McLenaghan, J., Nsouli, S. and Riechel, K. 1982. Currency convertibility in the economic community of West African States, IMF Occasional Paper no. 13. Washington, D.C.: International Monetary Fund.

Melitz, J. 1984. The welfare case for the European monetary system. City: INSEE, April. Photocopy.

Mulumba, M. 1976. La coopération monétaire en Afrique: Des zones monétaires à l'Union africaine des paiements. Kinshasa: Presses Universitaires du Zaire.

Mundell, R. 1972. African trade, politics and money. In *Africa and monetary integration; Afrique et integration monétaire*, ed. R. Tremblay. New York: Holt, Rinehart & Winston.

Nascimento, J. C. 1983. L'appartenance de l'UMOA à la Zone Franc dans le contexte actual. In *La point economique* (Dakar), October.

————. 1984. The choice of an optimum exchange currency regime for a small economy: An econometric analysis. Dakar, Senegal: Ecole Superieure de gesbon des Entreprises, October. Photocopy.

Plane, P. 1983, Taux de change en économie sous-développee; Essai de détermination pour dix pays de l'Afrique de l'Ouest. Discussion Paper no. 12, Clermont-Ferrand France: Centre d' Etudes et Recherches sur le Developpement Internationel.

Raffinot, M. 1982. Gestion étatique de la monnaie, parités fixes et dépendance: Le cas de la Zone Franc. *Tiers-Monde* 22, no. 91 (July): 549–67.

Robson, P. 1983. *Integration, development and equity: Economic integration in West Africa*. London: Allen & Unwin.

Tower, E., and Willet, T. 1976. *The Theory of optimum currency areas and exchange rate flexibility*. Princeton Special Paper in International Economics no. 11. Princeton: Princeton University.

Vinay, B. 1980. *Zone Franc et coopération monétaire*. Paris, France: Ministry of Cooperation.

Comment   Liaquat Ahamed

Macedo's paper addresses two quite separate conceptual issues associated with the West African Monetary Union (UMOA). The first is the problem of the most appropriate exchange rate regime for a small African economy. The paper focuses specifically on the consequences for a small country of pegging its exchange rate to the currency of a large country, as each of the countries in UMOA have done with respect to the French franc. The second issue is the effect of establishing a monetary union among a number of small countries, whereby they share a common central bank and pool their foreign exchange reserves. Although both of these financial arrangements are found in the UMOA, it is important to keep them conceptually separate. It is perfectly possible, for example, for each country in the UMOA to have singly pegged its exchange rate to the French franc without entering into the monetary union. By the same token, a monetary union among the members of the UMOA would have been perfectly feasible without necessarily setting up a fixed exchange rate between the French franc and the franc of the UMOA.

In a world of generalized floating exchange rates, why does a small country choose to peg its exchange rate to the currency of a single large country rather than to some optimally chosen basket of currencies? The answer, it seems, lies in the credibility of the two different quasi-fixed exchange rate regimes. When a developing country pegs to a basket, the credibility surrounding the maintenance of that peg depends mainly on perceptions about the policies of the government of the developing country. By contrast, in an arrangement such as the UMOA, France is lending its authority to the peg. It is implicitly announcing that it will exert the necessary discipline on its African partners' macroeconomic policies and will also provide to its partners the required credit line to support the convertibility of the UMOA franc at the fixed peg. Although Macedo alludes to these considerations, particularly the effects of the transfer from France, the sort of macroeconomic model that he presents in his paper is not really an adequate framework for formalizing the full range of benefits accruing from the peg to the French franc. The empirical section of the paper does, however, contain a discussion of some of the benefits. For example, the greater propensity to hold near-money in the Franc Zone than in the other African countries is highlighted in the paper. This financial deepening could be the consequence of an enhanced credibility regarding the stability of the exchange rate.

Liaquat Ahamed is a senior investment analyst at the World Bank.

There are two types of costs associated with the peg against the French franc. When a country fixes its exchange rate, it is renouncing the use of the nominal exchange rate as an instrument. This does not pose a problem for macroeconomic policy as long as domestic prices and wages are perfectly flexible. If, however, there is some degree of nominal price rigidity, one of the costs of a fixed exchange rate regime is the possibility of domestic unemployment in the event of an adverse shock, such as a fall in the demand for exports. A further cost arises when a country pegs its exchange rate to the currency of another country. Here, the country is not merely renouncing an instrument. It is, in effect, handing it over to the monetary authorities of another country—in this case France. The macroeconomic model outlined by Macedo does offer some insights into the costs of the fixed peg against the French franc. To complement the theoretical model, it would have been useful to have some empirical comparisons of the macroeconomic performance of the Franc Zone and that of the other African countries, particularly with regard to output growth, unemployment, and inflation.

Let me now turn to the consequences of establishing a monetary union. The first step is to clarify precisely what monetary arrangements and capital market policies bind a union together. At one extreme, for example, is the form of union that prevails between Texas and California, whereby there is a free mobility of capital. As a consequence, the distribution of money stock between Texas and California is demand determined. A monetary allocation rule by the Federal Reserve Board would have no influence on such a monetary union. At the other extreme, one can envisage a monetary union in which there are controls on internal flows of capital so that each individual partner, within certain limits and for short periods of time, can pursue an independent monetary policy. The joint central bank in such a union would serve primarily as an institution for pooling and thus economizing on foreign exchange reserves.

From the information provided in Macedo's paper, I find it difficult to assess where to place the UMOA along this spectrum of possible monetary unions. This not only has implications for the macroeconomic behavior of members of the UMOA but also for the efficiency of resource use by the members. In terms of the formal model outlined in the paper, the question essentially boils down to one of specifying how the money supply is determined for each of the partners of the UMOA. Is the money supply in each of the member countries exogenously determined by the joint central bank, or are capital transactions among the member countries sufficiently fluid that it is endogenously determined? The model the author uses is based on the assumption that the central bank can and does control the money supply in each member country. This assumption needs some justification.

In sum, although the paper and its model do provide some important insights into the workings of the UMOA, a broader conceptual framework is necessary to evaluate fully the costs and benefits of the monetary system embodied in the UMOA.

Comment   Stephen O'Brien

The author's purpose in this paper has been to examine the costs and benefits, within a monetary union, of pegging to a single currency. Macedo demonstrates that, ceteris paribus, pegging to a single currency cannot be an optimal choice for the members of the union, and that, a fortiori, pegging to a fixed rate over the long term, as has been the case for the West African Monetary Union (UMOA), must be suboptimal. Nevertheless, he concludes that on balance the union has been beneficial to its members, when the transfers from France through the "operations account" are taken into account, and probably has been on balance a net benefit to France as well, at least until 1977 when the overall foreign asset position of the UMOA began to deteriorate sharply.

It is precisely these broader issues of the overall costs and benefits of such a monetary system for developing countries that is of particular relevance, I believe, for the theme of this volume: structural adjustment and the real exchange rate. In this brief comment I would like to draw on some of the points raised in the paper to examine further these costs and benefits.

On the cost side the lack of national control over exchange rate policy clearly must be flagged. The author points out that there have been significant changes in the real exchange rates of UMOA member countries; and in recent years those changes have had adverse effects on the development of several of the members' economies. At the same time the members have been constrained in their ability to adjust to these changes. (Nevertheless, it must be acknowledged that the majority of the other African countries that have had the freedom to pursue an active exchange rate policy have not done so.) Along with the loss of freedom to determine exchange rates, the UMOA members have been forced to rely on second-best instruments for balance-of-payments management: subsidies, tariffs, quantitative restrictions, price controls, and so on. In recent years, member countries such as Ivory coast, Senegal, and Togo have intensified their use of those policy instruments in pursuit of stabilization and structural adjustment. It is too early,

Stephen O'Brien is the chief economist of the Western Africa Region of the World Bank.

however, to assess the impact of these policy adjustments, or to compare these examples with countries that have relied primarily on exchange rate movements.

With respect to benefits the author rightly mentions the importance of the French transfer, but any full assessment of the UMOA cannot be based only on the operations account. This account is only the cornerstone of the relationship between France and the African member states, a relationship that also includes trade, investment, technical assistance, and various forms of concessional aid. French underwriting of the deficits of the union, and its assurance of the convertibility of the CFA franc, also facilitates trade and capital flows (but not significantly increased trade among the UMOA members). Another important benefit the union confers is the fiscal and monetary discipline it imposes on its members under the rules of the West African Central Bank. There are indications, however, that this discipline has been weakening since the late 1970s, as all the member countries have faced severe fiscal problems leading to the accumulation of domestic arrears and other manifestations of internal imbalance. This has contributed to the rapid buildup in the operations account. Although the UMOA still represents only a negligible share of the French money stock, there nevertheless exists the possibility, as the author mentions, that France might be compelled to change the rules of the monetary "game" in response to the rising burden placed on the French Treasury by the union.

Finally, in support of the thesis that the union, and the associated linkages with France, confers a net benefit on its African members, one can point to both its durability and its growth prospects. It is truly remarkable, given the rather disappointing record of regional organizations in Africa, that the UMOA has lasted for over 40 years, and for some 25 years since the independence of the member states. And the union is likely to expand rather than contract. Mali reentered the UMOA in 1984. (The author speculates that Mali may have wished to rejoin so as to receive the transfer necessitated by its persistently negative operations account through UMOA rather than directly from France; one could argue instead that France encouraged the Malian reentry on the grounds that the fiscal and monetary discipline mentioned above could be more effectively applied through the union than bilaterally.) Other countries are likely to follow: Guinea, possibly Mauritania in time, and even nonfrancophone countries such as Guinea-Bissau and Gambia, following the example of Equatorial Guinea and the Central African Monetary Union.

This paper has provided us with useful information and analysis on the functioning of the UMOA and its impact on its members. Further research on the union and its developmental significance is clearly warranted. This is so for at least two reasons: first, because the union has demonstrated its staying power and is almost certain to become more important in the economy of West Africa in the future; and second, because at the same time, the members of the union are collectively experiencing the most severe economic crisis they have faced since independence, and this crisis is putting heavy pressure on the union and its financial links with France.

IV Economic Adjustment and the Real Exchange Rate

11   Economic Adjustment and the Real Exchange Rate

Arnold C. Harberger

11.1   Introduction and Summary

At the time of this writing (July 1985) it is hardly necessary to try to motivate a study seeking to clarify the concept of the real exchange rate and to improve our understanding of the reasons for its movements. Among the major currencies, the Deutschmark has moved from a high of around .55 U.S. dollars in 1979 to a low of around $.30 in 1984–85. Over roughly the same period the British pound has fluctuated from more than two dollars down to barely over one. These movements far exceed the differential rates of inflation of the countries concerned. Real rates in both cases have exhibited swings spanning a factor of 1.5 or more.

Even though those variations in the dollar/Deutschmark and the dollar/ pound exchange rates were greeted with widespread surprise and comment, they look minor when compared with the movements experienced by many less developed countries. For these countries, even after double deflation to correct for movements in their general price levels and in that of the United States, the observed range of variation of real exchange rates is nothing short of dramatic. For example, Mexico's real exchange rate vis-à-vis the U.S. dollar increased by around 80 percent between the fourth quarter of 1981 and the third quarter of 1982; Brazil's took a similar swing between the first quarter of 1982 and the third quarter of 1984; Uruguay's about doubled from the third quarter of 1982 to the first quarter of 1984; Chile's did the same from

Arnold C. Harberger is the Gustavus F. and Ann M. Swift Distinguished Service Professor of Economics at the University of Chicago and a professor of economics at the University of California, Los Angeles.

I am indebted to Sebastian Edwards and Michael Mussa for helpful comments.

the first quarter of 1982 to the first quarter of 1985. And Argentina broke recent records with a more than quadrupling of its real exchange rate from the first quarter of 1981 to the third quarter of 1982. Even after substantial adjustment Argentina's real rate remained (at the end of 1983 and the beginning of 1984) at around three times its level of three years earlier.

The exploration of issues regarding the real exchange rate has surely been made more vital and pressing by this recent history, but at the same time it has been made more difficult to expound because of the enrichment our theoretical arsenal has experienced in the past few decades. Whereas the so-called elasticities approach was once king, its hegemony has more recently been challenged by the absorption (income-expenditures approach) and by the monetary approach to the balance of payments. And whereas a supply-demand framework based on flows once ruled supreme, more modern analyses deal with stocks as well as flows. In addition, they treat phenomena such as substitution between and among currencies that were not contemplated in the earlier traditions of international economics. Thus, although real exchange rate analysis may appear quite straightforward and natural in terms of the earlier traditions, it seems less self-evident to those who have worked predominantly within the spheres defined by more recent research currents and trends.

11.1.1 A Model of Real Exchange Rates

To begin, then, I shall try to place the phenomenon of real exchange rates, and the approach to be followed in this paper, in a setting that reveals its full compatibility with both the older and the newer strands of economic thinking.[1] A convenient springboard is provided by the following "generalized" demand equation:

(1) $\quad Q_i^d = a_0 + a_{1i}(P_i/\bar{P}_d) + a_{2i}\, y + a_{3i}\, \Delta D + a_{4i}(M^s - M^d).$

$\quad\quad$ [elasticities $\quad\quad\quad$ [absorption $\quad\quad\quad$ [monetary
$\quad\quad\quad$ approach] $\quad\quad\quad\quad$ approach] $\quad\quad\quad\quad$ approach]

Here Q_i^d is the quantity of the ith good demanded; $(P_i/\bar{P}_d)$ is its relative price (in relation to a general price index $\bar{P}_d$ faced by local demanders); y is a measure of the real income of the demanders; ΔD is the net increment (measured in the same metric as y) to their borrowings from abroad; M^s is the actual money supply in their possession; and M^d is the amount they would demand in a full comparative static equilibrium if all key determining variables were to remain at their present levels.

The exposition presented in this paper is in terms of the flow supply of and demand for foreign exchange. The demand for imports of good

i is equal to the excess of the demand for purchases of good i (Q_i^d in the above equation) over the domestic supply of (Q_i^s) of the same. Since Q_i^s can also be expressed as a function of the relative price $p_i/\bar{p}_d$, we can, for given levels of y, ΔD, and ($M^s - M^d$), together with other variables influencing Q_i^s, determine the demand for imports of i ($Q_i^d - Q_i^s$) as a function of $p_i/\bar{p}_d$. In a similar way, the supply of exports of good j ($Q_j^s - Q_j^d$ can be derived as a function of $P_j/\bar{P}_d$. The demand functions for individual import goods then provide the basis for the (flow) demand curve for foreign currency; likewise, the (flow) supply curve of foreign currency is built up from the supply functions for the individual export items. The equilibrium exchange rate (in the absence of capital movements) is the price that equilibrates the supply and demand for foreign currency thus derived, with appropriate adjustment for capital movements.

In the framework described by equation (1), the absorption approach is represented in part by the term $a_{3i}\Delta D$. This term reflects how additional indebtedness contracted abroad will influence the demand for good i; it is kept separate from the income term because the coefficients a_{2i} and a_{3i} are likely to be different from each other. When foreign borrowing occurs, it is often for a quite specific purpose (such as an investment project) with its own requirements for goods and services. The pattern of these requirements (reflected in a_{3i}) will only by accident be similar to the pattern (reflected in a_{2i}) in which incremental income is typically spent.

In part, too, the absorption approach is reflected in the term a_{4i} ($M^s - M^d$). If "excessive" domestic credit creation occurs, not backed by loans from abroad, it will lead to "excessive" (in the sense of additional) demand for goods and services. In the process "excess" money balances will be created, which over some span of time will be worked off. To the extent, then, that the excess of expenditures over income, dealt with in the absorption approach, is a disequilibrium phenomenon financed by domestic credit expansion, it appears in the fourth term of equation (1).

The term a_{4i} ($M^s - M^d$) also captures essential elements of the monetary approach to the balance of payments and of the idea of currency substitution. When the central bank engages in creating money (for simplicity, say, under a fixed exchange rate regime), the excess of the new money supply over the amount desired by economic agents will tend to be spent. Over time, this excess will tend to be reflected in a loss of reserves, which in turn will normally have the effect of inducing the monetary authorities to put on the brakes. If they do not, a devaluation crisis may be in the making.

Summing the demand functions for imports (derived as indicated above) over all the relevant goods and services yields the main component of the flow demand (F^d) for foreign currency. Doing the same for export goods and services yields the main component of the corresponding flow supply (F^s). Thus, we may write:

(2a) $F^d = b_0 + \sum_i a_{1i}(P_i/\bar{P}_d) + b_2 y + b_3 \Delta D$

$$+ b_4(M^s - M^d) + \ldots$$

[the demand for foreign currency arising from imports]

(2b) $F^s = c_0 - \sum_j a_{1j}(P_j/\bar{P}_d) - c_2 y - c_3 \Delta D - c_4(M^s - M^d) + \ldots$

[the supply of foreign currency arising from exports].

Here b_2 would be equal to $\Sigma_i a_{2i}$, b_3 to $\Sigma_i a_{3i}$, and b_4 to $\Sigma_i a_{4i}$, where the summation runs over the set i of import goods and services; c_2, c_3, and c_4 would have similar connections to the a_{2i}, a_{3i}, and a_{4i}, the summation here being over the set of goods and services j that end up as exports.

Equations (2a) and (2b) do not tell the complete story of the flow demand for and supply of foreign currency. We must recognize that the net new indebtedness of a country (ΔD) is itself a component of the supply of available funds. Thus, when the net increment to debt within a period is fully spent on tradable goods, the increment of debt by itself causes the flow supply of foreign exchange to increase by ΔD. But the spending of the borrowed funds causes the flow supply to contract by $c_3 \Delta D$ (because of increased spending on exportables), while the increased spending on importables causes the flow demand for foreign exchange to expand by $b_3 \Delta D$. Thus, if $b_3 + c_3 = 1$, as it must if the new indebtedness is indeed fully spent on tradables, there is no cause for the equilibrium price of foreign currency to change. The added demand for foreign exchange associated with spending the borrowed funds is just matched by the added supply (as represented by the new debt itself).

In this context ΔD should be defined broadly. An increment in a country's dollar indebtedness, if used to acquire Miami real estate or equities on the New York Stock Exchange, would entail a zero ΔD. The same increment to dollar debt, used for the purchases of imports or of goods and services in the country's domestic market, would entail a positive ΔD, whereas the straight purchase of assets in Miami or New York (without borrowing the dollars) would generate a negative ΔD. In short, we want ΔD to reflect net foreign investment in the standard national accounting sense.

One possible cause of a negative ΔD (in this sense) is a wave of currency substitution. Rather than acquiring capital assets located within the United States, a country's residents might simply buy dollar bills to hold as a store of value or as a medium of exchange. Such an act would be treated, for the purposes of the present analysis, as if it were a capital movement from the country in question to the United States (that is, a negative ΔD). If this movement were fully matched by increases in the supply of exports or reductions in import demand (that is, if for this particular "capital movement" $b_3 + c_3$ were equal to one), the whole operation would entail no pressure on the exchange rate. But if the increment in demand for foreign currency came at the expense of nontradables or simply as a shift of money holdings from local currency to U.S. dollars, the negative ΔD would not be offset and the country's currency would experience a tendency to depreciation.

In the framework of this paper, the exchange rate is the variable that equilibrates the flow demand for and the flow supply of foreign exchange, that is, that brings about:

(3) $$F^d = F^s + \Delta D.$$

In terms of its time dimension or assumed degree of adjustment, one can probably say that the analysis concentrates on the middle to long run rather than on an extremely short one. Changes in a country's commercial policy, reasonably lasting shifts in the size or direction of capital flows, or both, and changes in the relative prices of particular products in world markets—these are the types of disturbances that will be analyzed here.

In conducting the analysis, the focus will accordingly be on those variables that bring about a new "equilibrium" of the economy under the changed circumstances. I therefore will pass over such elements as currency substitution, speculative waves, transitory disequilibria between M^d and M^s, and undesired changes in the levels of a country's international reserves. But this does not at all mean that the analysis presented here is somehow incompatible with these elements. They are left to one side only because I concentrate on the comparison of one equilibrium and another, in each of which the flow supply of and demand for foreign exchange come from exports and imports of goods and services that can be expected to be maintained at a relatively steady pace for some time, and the difference between flow supply and flow demand is compensated by voluntary capital movements that (within either the beginning or the ending equilibrium) likewise are not expected to be dramatically altered in the near term.

11.1.2 An Overview of the Analysis

The purpose of this paper is to take the reader on something of a guided tour of exchange rate analysis. Starting from the most elementary building blocks of international trade theory, I will deal first, in section 11.2, with the determination of the nominal exchange rate under idealized circumstances: a flexible exchange rate system supported by a monetary policy that keeps the general level of prices stable. I will then move on to an equally familiar set of problems: examining the international adjustment mechanism for a small country with a fixed exchange rate. In each of these cases we shall examine the economic adjustments required by six different types of disturbances: (a) the imposition of import restrictions; (b) the imposition of export restrictions; (c) an inflow of capital spent exclusively on tradable goods; (d) an inflow of capital spent exclusively on nontradable goods; (e) a rise in the world price of an export product; and (f) a rise in the world price of an import product.

I will show that the equilibrium nominal exchange rate (the domestic currency price of foreign money) falls as a result of (a), rises as a consequence of (b), remains unchanged under (c), and falls under (d) and (e). The adjustment to disturbances of type (f) is ambiguous; its direction depends critically on the elasticity of the demand for imports of the affected product(s).

Our first meeting with the concept of the *real* exchange rate will come in section 11.3. When the nominal exchange rate is held constant, the same adjustments dealt with in section 11.2 take place through movements of the general price level. Whereas under a flexible exchange rate (with stable monetary policy) the disturbances (a) through (f) result in movements in the nominal exchange rate, E, the same disturbances give rise to movements in the general price level, $\bar{p}_d$, when a fixed exchange rate policy is pursued. When the exchange rate variable to be studied is defined as $(E/\bar{p}_d)$, the identical analysis is capable of answering the problems posed in both sections 11.2 and 11.3.

Section 11.4 explores in some detail the concept of the "dollar's worth" as the unit of measurement of the quantities of imports and exports. This concept implies that the exchange rate depends on the world prices of tradable goods in a fashion analogous to the way in which it depends on import and export restrictions, and on capital flows spent on tradable and nontradable goods. In particular, the exchange rate depends on the world prices of a country's export goods in one way, and on the world prices of that country's import goods in another, quite different way.

This concept argues powerfully against thinking of the real exchange rate as the price index of tradable goods relative to that of nontradables. In the simple analysis of sections 11.2 and 11.3 the nominal exchange rate is always the peso price of the dollar. The real exchange rate in these simple exercises is the peso price of the dollar relative to the general price index (or some other chosen numeraire).

Section 11.5 addresses the problem of following a country's real exchange rate over time. It is argued there that in so doing one should try to replicate insofar as possible the analysis of sections 11.2 and 11.3. The problem is one of dealing with changes in the value of the dollar (or other relevant foreign currency unit) over time. We know that for simple cases like those in sections 11.2 and 11.3 we want to measure imports and exports in units of the "dollar's worth"; we also know that the number (quantity) of such units should change with alterations in the dollar prices of one or more import or export goods. But these conclusions were reached by doing exercises that were "time-less" in the sense that all comparative static theory is timeless. When we postulate changes in the dollar prices of some imports and exports, we are implicitly holding other dollar prices constant. This assumption is not made when we follow a real-world economy over time. In addition to the movements of the dollar prices of each particular country's tradables, there is a general movement of world prices, measured in terms of dollars or any other relevant foreign currency. We would like to be able to correct for general world price movements when we work with data spanning extended periods of time, yet at the same time we want to allow for changes in the relative prices of some or all of a country's imports and of some or all of its exports.

This last objective is accomplished by the choice of some general dollar (or world) price level, $\bar{p}^*$, as the yardstick for measuring over time the "real dollar's worth." Thus, the nominal demand for foreign exchange arising out of imports is Mp_m^*, where M is the quantity and p_m^* the dollar price of imports; the nominal supply of foreign exchange arising out of exports is Xp_x^*, with X being the quantity and p_x^* dollar price. The real quantity of foreign exchange demanded (for imports) is then measured over time t by $M_t p_{mt}^*/\bar{p}_t^*$, and the real quantity supplied (for exports) by $X_t p_{xt}^*/\bar{p}_t^*$. The corresponding real price of foreign exchange is $E_t \bar{p}_t^*/\bar{p}_{dt}$, where p_t^* is the general dollar price index and $\bar{p}_{dt}$ is the general price index of the country in question, all at time t. The product of the real price times multiplied by the quantity would be, for imports, $(M_t p_{mt}^*/\bar{p}_t^*)\,(E_t \bar{p}_t^*/\bar{p}_{dt}) = M_t p_{mt}^* E/\bar{p}_{dt}$, and for exports, $(X_t p_{dt}^*/\bar{p}_t^*)(E_t \bar{p}_t^*/\bar{p}_{dt}) = X_t p_{xt}^* E/\bar{p}_{dt}$. That is, the real price times the real quantity of foreign exchange in either category is equal to its nominal domestic currency value at the border divided by the general index of domestic prices. This is as it should be. The real *value* of the foreign exchange demanded or supplied, as distinct from its real quantity or its real price, is independent of the index chosen to correct for changes in world prices over time. It depends, as it should, only on the current nominal market values of the foreign exchange transacted, and on the current value of the domestic price index used to convert nominal domestic currency values into real values.

In section 11.6 I discuss the issues surrounding the choice of an appropriate index to correct for foreign inflation. Having previously established that the real exchange rate should fall when the dollar prices of exportables rise and should also be influenced by changes in the dollar prices of importables, I rule out the use of these specific prices, separately or in combination (that is, the dollar price level of the country's tradables), as the relevant deflating index. Ruling out a country-specific deflating index automatically suggests that a single dollar-price index be used for determining the real volume of foreign currency demand and supply and for defining the basket of goods whose relative price in each country is that country's real exchange rate. The questions that arise in this context are (a) whether the index should refer to dollar prices or to prices expressed in other currencies as well and (b) whether the index should reflect mainly or wholly the prices of tradables (even though it is not separately calculated for each country's tradables) or instead attempt to achieve a broader coverage of goods and services.

The answers given to these questions are admittedly judgmental rather than deterministic, suggesting useful and convenient conventions rather than solutions that are dictated in some absolute sense by the underlying theory. The answer suggested for (a) is that so long as the relevant trade statistics are presented in terms of U.S. dollars, the deflating index should be a deflator of dollar prices, but this does not prevent it from being an average of U.S. prices along with German prices converted at the dollar price of the Deutschmark, British prices converted at the dollar price of the pound, Japanese prices converted at the dollar price of the yen, and so on.

With respect to question (b), the concept is suggested of a basket of tradable goods somewhere on the high seas. The grounds for using wholesale price indexes are that they are composed predominantly of tradables and that they are available on a monthly basis and in general quite promptly. Simplest would be the use of the U.S. wholesale price index to deflate dollar values of imports and exports and to define over time the "real dollar" for which the real exchange rate of any country's currency is the relative price. More complicated but probably preferable would be a weighted average of the dollar prices of the wholesale price baskets of the major trading nations.

The notion that what is being priced is a bundle of tradables floating on the ocean rules out consumer price baskets and gross domestic (national) product (GDP) baskets. But one could conceive of a weighted average of the tradable components of these baskets. To the extent that separable GDP price deflators are already calculated for the manufacturing and the agricultural sectors, the possibility exists of building national price indexes for tradables on the basis of these components.

11.2 The Equilibrium Exchange Rate Under a Flexible Rate System

The six types of disturbances listed in the previous section are here analyzed for a flexible exchange rate system, under the assumption that monetary policy is managed in such a way as to keep constant the general price level ($\bar{p}_d$) of the country in question. Unless otherwise specified, prices in the rest of the world (expressed in the relevant foreign currency units—in this case dollars) are also assumed to be constant. Thus, the movements in the nominal exchange rate as derived in this section will also be movements in the real exchange rate as defined in the preceding section.

The demand curves for imports and the supply curves for exports presented in figure 11.1 are calibrated so that the quantity axis refers to units that cost one dollar at world market prices. Thus, if the world price of coal is 50 dollars a ton (2,000 pounds), coal will be measured in units of 40 ($=$ 2000/50) pounds. If aluminum has a world price of 80 cents a pound, it will be measured in units of 1.25 pounds. In this way the foreign currency demand curves created by many different import goods can be amalgamated with a single demand curve for foreign currency to pay for imports; and the foreign currency supply curves created by many different export commodities can be aggregated into a single foreign currency supply curve created by exports. The two aggregate curves thus constructed are the demand curve for imports and the supply curve for exports, as these terms are commonly used in the literature of international economics.

When tariffs on imports exist, the demand for foreign currency created by any import good is derived by taking the demand price net of tariff for each successive dollar's worth of the import. This is done in figure 11.1a for the case of a general tariff (T_m) on all imports. The tariff is assumed to be a fixed percentage of the local currency price of the product; this assumption generates a net-of-tariff demand curve that spins out from the same quantity-axis intercept as the gross-of-tariff curve. One can easily see how the equilibrium exchange rate is reduced by the imposition of the tariff: both imports and exports fall (balanced trade is assumed here unless otherwise specified).

In figure 11.1b the case of a uniform export tax is examined. In this case the equilibrium market exchange rate must be sufficient to pay both the fundamental supply price of exports (given by the height, at any quantity, of the solid supply curve of exports) and the tax that is taken by the government. When there is no tax the equilibrium is at $M_0 = X_0$, and the market exchange rate E_0 goes only to pay the suppliers of exports; when there is a tax the equilibrium shifts to $M_1 = X_1$, where the market exchange rate produces enough to pay both what

a) IMPORT TARIFF (T_m) IS IMPOSED

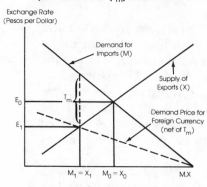

b) EXPORT TAX (T_x) IS IMPOSED

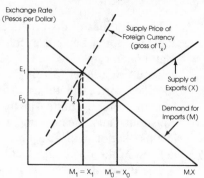

c) CAPITAL INFLOW SPENT ON IMPORTS

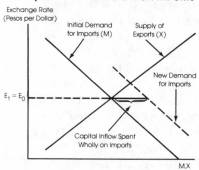

d) CAPITAL INFLOW SPENT ON NONTRADABLES

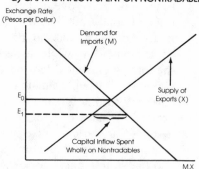

e) WORLD PRICE OF EXPORTS DOUBLES

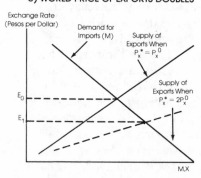

f) WORLD PRICE OF IMPORTS DOUBLES

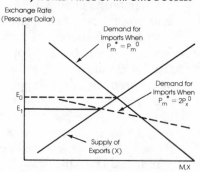

Fig. 11.1 Adjustment to disturbances under a flexible rate system. (The general price level P_d is held constant by monetary policy and imports (M) and exports (X) are measured in units worth one dollar at the world market price)

the suppliers of exports require to provide the quantity X_1 and what the government demands in the form of export taxes.

A comparison of figures 11.1a and 11.1b confirms the familiar proposition that under conditions of balanced trade the identical equilibrium can be produced either by a uniform import tariff (1a) or a uniform export tax (1b). It is worth nothing that although such an equilibrium is identical in terms of the quantities of exports and imports (at $M_1 = X_1$), and in terms of the gross price paid by the demanders of imports and the net price received by the suppliers of exports, it is *not* identical with respect to the exchange rate. In the specific case examined here, the nominal exchange rate falls as the result of an import tariff and rises as a consequence of an (otherwise equivalent) export tax. More generally, we will find that the equilibrium real exchange rate likewise has opposite directions of movement in response to import tariffs, on the one hand, and export taxes, on the other.

Figures 11.1c and 11.1d trace the consequences of inflows of capital. The first case is that in which the proceeds of the borrowing are spent on imports. This means that the demand curve for imports shifts to the right by the amount of the borrowing. Since the equilibrium of the balance of payments will require imports to exceed exports by the amount of foreign borrowing, there is no cause for the exchange rate to change in this case. It would be the same if the proceeds of the borrowing were spent fully on exportables (in which case the supply curve of exports would shift to the left by the amount of the borrowing, while the demand curve for imports would stay put) or if these proceeds were divided, with one part being spent on exportables and the remainder on importables. In the latter case the supply curve of exports would shift to the left by the amount of borrowing spent on exportables, and the demand curve for imports would shift to the right by the amount of the borrowing spent on importables. The combination of these two shifts would create, at the old exchange rate E_0, an excess of import demand over export supply equal to exactly the amount of the borrowing. Hence, when foreign borrowings are spent on tradables, they do not affect the equilibrium exchange rate.

The story is different when foreign borrowings are spent on nontradables. Here an economic adjustment must be made (the so-called transfer problem must be solved) in order to validate in real terms what would otherwise be simply a transfer of monetary purchasing power. The receiving country effectively *uses* a net capital inflow only to the extent that it imports more than it exports. When the capital flow is directly spent on tradables, the required excess of imports over exports is automatically created (see above). But when the capital flow is spent on nontradable goods and services (such as for roads, housing construction, and irrigation projects), the money borrowed from abroad (dollars) must be sold to obtain the domestic currency (pesos) needed to pay wages and cover other domestic costs. In the process, the exchange rate will fall, as depicted in figure 11.1d, so long as monetary stability is maintained.

Of course, any actual capital inflow from abroad is unlikely to be spent exclusively on either tradables or nontradables. It should be clear from figures 11.1c and 11.1d that in such a case the exchange rate will still fall, since the part of the capital flow spent on tradables has no effect while the part spent on nontradables introduces downward pressure on the rate.

Figure 11.1e depicts the by now familiar phenomenon of "Dutch disease." A substantial increase in the world prices of exports—in real-world cases, a rise in the price of an important export product (natural gas, for example, in the case of Holland)—generates a large increase in the amount of foreign currency available in the market, which in turn leads to a reduction in the exchange rate (the price of foreign currency). The rise in the world price of exports causes a shift in the supply curve of foreign currency, even though the supply curve of the export good in terms of its own peso price remains constant. A single point on the peso supply curve, showing 20 million pounds of sugar at a price of one peso per pound, will be reflected in a supply of foreign currency of two million dollars against an exchange rate of 10 pesos per dollar if the world price is ten cents a pound; a supply of foreign currency of four million dollars against an exchange rate of five pesos per dollar if the world price is 20 cents a pound; and a supply of foreign currency of one million dollars against an exchange rate of 20 pesos per dollar if the world price is five cents a pound. Thus, an unchanged supply curve of sugar in terms of its domestic relative price will be translated into different supply curves of foreign exchange,[2] depending on the dollar price of sugar in the world market. Accordingly, as shown in figure 11.1e, the market exchange rate will fall (from E_0 to E_1) under a flexible rate regime in conditions of monetary stability.

Figure 11.1f shows that the foreign exchange demand curve created by imports also undergoes a shift with a changing world market price of the import goods in question. Though the nature of the shift is identical to that applying to the supply curve of exports, the shift in figure 11.1f looks different from that in figure 11.1e. This is only because the demand curve for imports slopes downward, while the supply curve of exports slopes up. The nature of the economic adjustment to a rise in the world price of imports is clear. The initial response is simply a rise in the internal (peso) price of the good(s) in question. This response will be reflected in unchanged peso expenditures if the elasticity of demand for imports of the good is one; in increased peso expenditures if the elasticity is less than one; and in reduced peso outlays if the elasticity of demand for imports of the good is greater than one. From this we can deduce that there will be a range in which the demand for dollars (at a given exchange rate) will be reduced and another range in which that demand will be increased as a consequence of a rise in the world price of imports. In the case depicted, the initial equilibrium (at exchange rate E_0) was in the range in which the demand for imports had an elasticity greater than one; hence, the consequence of the price rise is a reduction in total peso outlays on dollars. Had the initial equilibrium been in a different range, peso outlays might have gone up rather than down, in which case the equilibrium exchange rate would have risen rather than fallen.[3]

11.3   Economic Adjustment Under Fixed Exchange Rates

Figure 11.2 shows how the adjustment process works under a fixed exchange rate system. The key element that distinguishes this system from that of the flexible rate is that now the money supply and the general price level, $\bar{p}_d$, play an active role. Figure 11.2a considers the imposition of a 50 percent uniform import tariff. Since the world prices of importables and exportables are given, the tariff will cause the price of imports to rise, while that of exports (at the fixed exchange rate) stays constant. The reduction in imports resulting from the price increase causes a surplus to emerge in the balance of trade (which initially was in equilibrium). This, in turn, leads to expansion of the money supply as the central bank buys the extra dollars. As the money supply expands, upward pressure is placed on the general level of prices and costs, $\bar{p}_d$. Since the demand for imports and the supply of exports are functions of the relative prices ($p_m/\bar{p}_d$ and $p_x/\bar{p}_d$, respectively) of imports and exports, the upward pressure on $\bar{p}_d$ causes these curves to shift upward.

The new equilibrium consistent with a 50 percent uniform tariff is shown at $M_1 = X_1$ in figure 11.2a. The price paid by demanders of imports is 15 pesos per dollar's worth. Of this, five pesos goes to the government, and ten pesos goes to buy the necessary foreign exchange at the fixed rate of ten pesos per dollar. The amount of foreign exchange demanded is M_1; this is equal to X_1, the amount supplied. The supply of foreign exchange has been reduced in the adjustment process as the pressure of increasing costs shifted the supply curve upward from S_x^0 to S_x^*.

Figure 11.2b shows how the adjustment process works when a uniform export tax of 33 ⅓ percent is imposed. In this case the effect is to reduce the supply of exports relative to the demand for imports. A deficit in the balance of trade emerges, which has as its consequence a loss of international reserves and a reduction in the money supply. There is a downward pressure on $\bar{p}_d$, the general level of prices and

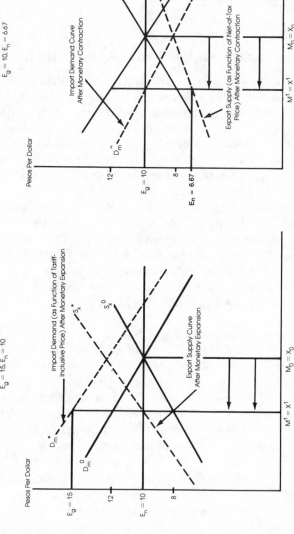

A 50% Uniform Tariff on Imports Causes
Monetary Expansion; New Equilibrium has
$E_g = 15$, $E_n = 10$

Pesos Per Dollar

$E_g = 15$

12

$E_n = 10$

8

D_m^*

Import Demand (as Function of Tariff-Inclusive Price) After Monetary Expansion

S_x^*

S_x^0

D_m^0

Export Supply Curve
After Monetary Expansion

$M^1 = X^1$ $M_0 = X_0$

a) IMPORTS (M) & EXPORTS (X)
(Dollars' Worth)

A 50% Uniform Export Tax Causes
Monetary Contraction; New Equilibrium has
$E_g = 10$, $E_n = 6.67$

Pesos Per Dollar

12

$E_g = 10$

8

$E_n = 6.67$

$\hat{D}_m$

Import Demand Curve
After Monetary Contraction

S_x^0

$\hat{S}_x$

Export Supply (as Function of Net-of-Tax
Price) After Monetary Contraction

$M^1 = X^1$ $M_0 = X_0$

b) IMPORTS (M) & EXPORTS (X)
(Dollars' Worth)

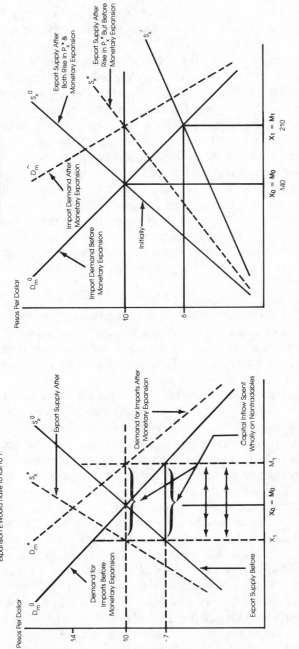

A Capital Inflow Spent on Nontradables is Absorbed via an Import Surplus. Surplus is Brought About at E = 10 via Monetary Expansion. Without Monetary Expansion E Would have to fall to 7.

A Rise in the World Price of Exports (P_x^*) Causes an Increase in the Dollar Volume of Both Imports & Exports. With Fixed Exchange Rate at E = 10, Monetary Expansion Occurs to Bring This About. Otherwise E Would Fall to 6.

d) IMPORTS (M) & EXPORTS (X) (Dollars' Worth)

e) IMPORTS (M) & EXPORTS (X) (Dollars' Worth)

Fig. 11.2 Adjustment to disturbances under fixed exchange rates, with uniform import tariffs and export taxes. (A fixed exchange rate of ten pesos per dollar is assumed)

costs. Equilibrium is reached in a situation like that represented by the broken-line curves $\hat{D}_m$ and $\hat{S}_x$. The quantity of imports demanded (at a price equal to ten pesos per dollar's worth) has fallen from M_0 to M_1 because the general price level ($\bar{p}_d$) has fallen while import prices remained the same. The quantity of exports has fallen because in the presence of the tax, exporters are receiving only 6.67 pesos per dollar's worth. Costs have fallen, and this has caused a shift of the supply curve of exports from S_x^0 to $\hat{S}_x$, but the incentives are still for a reduction in supply from the initial equilibrium at $M_0 = X_0$. This is because the prices received by exporters have fallen more than the general price level, causing a movement back along $\hat{S}_x$ from X_0 to X_1.

This is the appropriate time to compare the results of figures 11.2a and 11.2b with those of 11.1a and 11.1b. The new equilibrium in the latter two cases can be replicated in figure 11.2 by following the solid curves D_m^0 and S_x^0 to the new equilibrium. If the general price level remains constant while the exchange rate falls, the equilibrium in figure 11.2a would be at an exchange rate of eight pesos per dollar; buyers of imports would pay 12 pesos per dollar's worth, because of the 50 percent import tariff.

The adjustment mechanism under fixed exchange rates produces (figure 11.2a) an equilibrium in which demanders pay 15 pesos per dollar's worth of imports, and suppliers receive ten pesos per dollar's worth of exports when the exchange rate is ten pesos per dollar and a 50 percent import tariff is in effect. With the same exchange rate, a 33 1/3 percent export tax would generate (figure 11.2b) an equilibrium in which demanders would pay ten pesos, and suppliers would receive 6.67 pesos per dollar's worth. But in real terms all of these equilibria are the same. In all of them the price paid by demanders for a dollar's worth of imports ends up 50 percent higher than the price received by suppliers for a dollar's worth of exports. The differences in the levels of import and export prices simply mirror what happens to the general price level in each of the three cases. In the flexible exchange rate case (solid-line curves) the general price level, $\bar{p}_d$, remains constant. In the fixed exchange rate case with a 50 percent import tariff the monetary expansion produced by the adjustment causes the general price level to move up from index 100 to index 125. Under a 33 1/3 percent export tax, the deflationary process entailed by the adjustment causes the general price level to fall from index 100 to index 83 1/3. Thus, in each of the final equilibria the price of imports has risen 20 percent and the price of exports has fallen 20 percent, *relative to the general price level*.

Figure 11.2d is comparable to figure 11.1d. A capital inflow equal in amount to $(M_1 - X_1)$ dollars and spent wholly on nontradables would, if the general price level $\bar{p}_d$ were held stable by monetary policy, cause the nominal exchange rate E to fall from ten to about seven pesos per dollar. This is shown by the gap $(M_1 - X_1)$ between the solid-line curves D_m^0 and S_x^0. Obviously, this cannot happen if the country is maintaining a fixed exchange rate. In such a case the initial impact of the capital inflow will come through the sale of the borrowed foreign exchange (dollars) to the central bank so as to obtain the domestic currency (pesos) needed for buying nontradable goods and services in the domestic market. This causes an expansion of the peso money supply—an expansion that continues until the gap between imports and exports becomes equal to the size of the capital inflow (here assumed to be a continuing flow over time, not a one-shot injection of funds). In the case depicted in figure 11.2d equilibrium is reached when the monetary expansion has caused a 40 percent upward shift in the demand curve for imports and in the supply curve for exports. This is consonant with a rise of 40 percent in the general price level, $\bar{p}_d$. Comparability between the fixed rate and the flexible rate cases is maintained. In the fixed rate case the general price level rises from 100 to 140, while the exchange rate stays constant at ten pesos per dollar. In the flexible rate case the general price level is assumed to remain constant; under that assumption the equilibrium exchange rate must fall to $10 \times (1/1.4) = 7.14$, shown on the graph as approximately equal to seven.

Figure 11.2e shows the response of the economy to a rise in the world price of exports when a fixed exchange rate is assumed. The rise in price itself shifts the supply curve of foreign currency to the right (as also occurred in figure 11.1e, and as is explained in greater detail in the discussion of figure 11.3b below). This *would*, with a flexible exchange rate and a stable general price level $\bar{p}_d$, cause the nominal exchange rate to fall from ten to six pesos per dollar. Instead, with a fixed exchange rate of ten pesos, monetary expansion occurs as a result of the inflow of foreign exchange, driving up the general level of prices $\bar{p}_d$. Its new equilibrium level is 166 ⅔ rather than 100. The new equilibrium real exchange rate, $E/\bar{p}_d$, is therefore the same under a fixed exchange rate system as it would be under a flexible one.

11.4   The Concept of the "Dollar's Worth"

It is hardly a new idea that when dealing with problems of international trade for a small country, one should treat world prices as given and should use the concept of composite commodities based on the given world prices when working with aggregates such as the demand for tradables, the supply of tradables, the demand for imports, and the supply of exports. Indeed, far from being new, the idea has become commonplace to the point that a shorthand notation has been developed for it. When a writer wants to key his readers into this well-established line of thinking, he usually begins by saying something like "the following analysis will be based on a small-country hypothesis" and then proceeds to his task.

It is my contention that we have probably become too complacent, too cavalier in working with the small-country hypothesis. Under its convenient shorthand, I believe, we have in effect buried at least two important issues. First, by correctly assuming that nothing a small country can do will change the world prices it faces, we have somehow fallen into the trap of neglecting changes in the world prices of individual commodities as an important class of disturbances to be analyzed. Second, and in part as a consequence of the first, we have been far too uncritical in accepting as a definition of the real exchange rate the ratio of the "price of tradables" to the "price of nontradables."

On the first point, let us recognize that one uses the small-country hypothesis in building the demand curve for imports, the supply curve for exports, and their counterparts for importables, exportables, and tradables generally. Each of these is typically a composite good; in constructing the demand or supply curve of that composite, we assume the individual prices of its separate component items move up and down together, that is, in the same proportion. Many of the problems that are dealt with in this context, particularly at the textbook or the very general analytical level, can be handled using composite goods thus defined.

Let the relative price of each member of the composite be defined as $p_j^* E(1 + t_j)/\bar{p}_d$, where p_j^* is the world price; E, the nominal exchange rate translating the world price from dollars into pesos; and t_j, the distortion (tariff in the case of imports, export subsidy in the case of exports) causing the internal price to be above the world price converted at the market exchange rate. The relative price of all tradables, thus defined, will move up and down if the exchange rate moves up and down, as would naturally happen, other things equal, with a change in the rate of capital inflow under a flexible exchange rate system. The relative price of all tradables would react similarly to capital flows under a fixed exchange rate system, but in this case the common fluctuations in each relative price derive from changes in $\bar{p}_d$ rather than in E.

In dealing with uniform tariffs—standard fare for textbook treatments of this type of material—one must distinguish between importables and exportables. But once that distinction is made one can see how, under the small-country hypothesis, a uniform tariff will cause the relative prices of all importables to move up by an equal amount, and those of all exportables to move down by a given amount. An export tax has a similar effect. A uniform export subsidy works on the relative prices of all exportables in the same way as a uniform import tariff works on the relative prices of all importables.

From the above we can derive such familiar results as the equivalence (under balanced trade) of uniform export taxes, on the one hand, and uniform import duties, on the other, and the fact that (again under balanced trade) a uniform import tariff combined with a uniform export subsidy at the same rate has no ultimate real effect at all, producing instead only a countervailing movement, from one equilibrium to another, in the ratio $E/\bar{p}_d$.

The same framework has also been widely used in discussions of purchasing power parity. It shows, for example, how, when all p_j^* terms (for imports and exports alike) change by a given percentage, equilibrium can be restored under a fixed exchange rate by an equal percentage movement in $\bar{p}_d$. More generally, the necessary adjustment can be achieved through an offsetting movement in the ratio $E/\bar{p}_d$. When the predominant forces at work are monetary ones and they cause all the p_j^* terms to move by a certain percentage while $\bar{p}_d$ moves by a different percentage, the relative price of each tradable $(p_j^*E[1 + t_j]/\bar{p}_d)$ can nonetheless be kept constant by an offsetting movement in E. Such a move is stimulated when a country sets a new nominal exchange rate level by applying a purchasing power parity formula.

The above examples show how much can be done while still maintaining the assumption that the prices of all tradables (or exportables, importables, exports, or imports, as the case may be) move together. But obviously there are many problems that cannot be dealt with under that assumption. It is my impression that on the whole those problems have been dealt with by using more of a partial-equilibrium framework. Examples are the analysis of the effects of a tariff or an export tax on a single commodity; the calculation of rates of effective protection; and the finding of second-best optima, such as the Ramsey problem of choosing tariff rates for a subset of commodities so as to minimize the efficiency costs of raising a given amount of revenue therefrom.

In at least one case—the so-called Dutch disease problem of a dramatic rise in the world price of a country's principal export good—the nature of the problem demanded a macroeconomic framework and precluded the assumption of a composite export commodity. Here, in my opinion, the analysis has on the whole been correct and to the point, but the relationship of this case to the other general-equilibrium problems discussed above was not, in general, made clear.

In my view, we should try wherever possible to imbed our "partial" analysis in a general-equilibrium setting. In the matter at hand this means we should couch our analysis of a tariff on a single commodity in such a way that when imports are viewed as being subjected one after another to a given tariff rate, until finally all are covered, we get the correct answer for a uniform tariff. Similar reasoning applies for export taxes and subsidies and for the various combinations discussed above, of uniform taxes and subsidies on all exports and on all imports.

This means, of course, that we should recognize that each import tariff on each single good produces a downward shift in the demand curve for foreign exchange and a corresponding downward effect on the real exchange rate. Likewise, each export tax on a single good causes a leftward shift in the supply curve for foreign exchange and a corresponding upward effect on the real exchange rate.

These facts cause no apparent difficulties until we realize that p_j^* and $(1 + t_j)$ enter in a similar way in the expression for the relative price $(p_j^* E[1 + t_j]/\bar{p}_d)$ of imports of j. Just as we do not want to confine ourselves to analyzing only uniform tariffs or export taxes, so too do we not want to confine ourselves to cases in which all the p_j^* terms for all tradables move together. We should strive for an analysis that can deal with changes in the price of individual export or import goods, or both, and one that can do so in such a way that the sum total of the individual effects on all such goods is equal to the already well-recognized general-equilibrium result.

Figures 11.3a, 11.3b, and 11.3c illustrate how the demand and supply curves of foreign exchange (created by imports or exports of particular commodities) are altered when the world price of the relevant good changes. In figure 11.3a, the effect of doubling of the price of imports of good j is explored; in figure 11.3b, a doubling of the price of exports of good k is assumed. In each case what is shown is the demand curve for (or supply curve of) foreign exchange created by the market for the good in question.

Each demand and supply curve is built on the assumption that the world price of the commodity in question is given. The units in which the horizontal axis is measured are units of a "dollar's worth"—the amount of the commodity in question which at the given world price sells for a dollar. The units of price are the demand or supply price (relative to the general level of prices, $\bar{p}_d$) corresponding to each separate quantity unit.

Consider the case of a commodity, wheat (w), selling in the world market for $4 a bushel. Its ordinary demand curve will measure bushels on the horizontal axis and the relative price of the bushel ($p_w^* E[1 + t_w]/\bar{p}_d$) on the vertical axis. To express this demand curve in units of dollar's worth, stretch the quantity axis by multiplying by p_w^* ($4 in this case); the quantity units are now in dollar's worth. Since the price of a dollar's worth is $(1/p_w^*)$ times the price of a bushel, the new price axis is measured in units of $E(1 + t_w)/\bar{p}_d$. This expresses what demanders actually pay per dollar's worth and includes the tariff or other tax received by the government. To produce a demand curve in which the demand price represents the actual price for foreign currency, we must shift the ordinate of each point downward, dividing by $(1 + t_w)$. The resulting

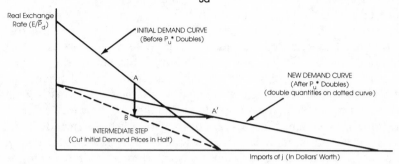

3a

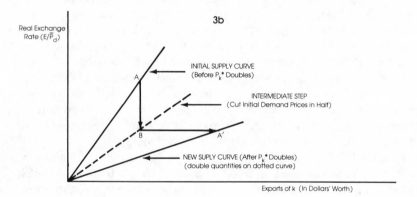

3b

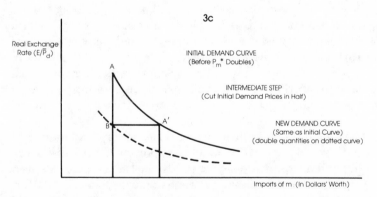

3c

Fig 11.3   Demand and supply curves for foreign exchange.

demand curve has dollars' worth on one axis and $E/\bar{p}_d$, the relative price of a dollar's worth, on the other.

Now when the world price of wheat p_w^* changes, this same transformation must be performed again. Each ordinate of the curve must be multiplied by the old p_w^* ($4) and divided by the new one (say, $8); similarly, the quantity of foreign exchange demanded at each price must be divided by the old p_w^* and multiplied by the new one. This is what is done in figure 11.3, for a postulated doubling of the world price of the good in question. Figure 11.3a deals with a linear demand curve. In effect, it shifts from measuring demand in units of a quarter-bushel to measuring it in units of an eighth-bushel. Here as an initial step the vertical intercept is cut in half; this operation produces the broken-line curve. Then the abscissa of each point must be doubled (reflecting the doubled quantity of dollars that each physical quantity unit, for example, each bushel, now produces). This second step produces the new foreign currency demand curve created by imports of j.

Figure 11.3b does the same thing for an export supply curve. To obtain the (intermediate step) broken-line curve, the height of each point on the old supply curve is cut in half; to obtain the new foreign currency supply curve created by exports of good k, the abscissa of each point on the broken-line curve is then doubled.

Figure 11.3c shows how these transformations map a unit-elastic demand curve onto itself. Starting at point A we cut the height in half to get point B; then we double the quantity to get point A'—a different point on the same unit-elastic demand curve with which we began.

From figure 11.3c it is also easy to visualize how, starting from a demand curve of a constant elasticity less than one, a rise in the world price of the commodity will result in a new demand curve (for foreign currency) that lies everywhere to the right of the original one. Likewise, if we start from a demand curve of a constant elasticity greater than one, a rise in the world price will map that curve into a new demand curve for foreign currency that lies everywhere to the left of the original one.

Thus, the Dutch disease phenomenon is not in any way limited to changes in the world price of the principal export(s) of a country. Even the least important export goods give rise to the same type of disease, only in very small doses. All import goods (except those with a fortuitously unit-elastic demand curve) also generate, when their world prices change, effects on the real exchange rate. In cases in which there is domestic production of the imported good or of close substitutes, the demand is likely to be of greater than unit elasticity, and a rise in world prices will cause a decline in the demand for foreign currency and in the real exchange rate. For imports of essential goods that are not produced domestically (most particularly, raw materials), the demand is likely to be inelastic,[4] with a rise in world price producing an increase in the real exchange rate.

All of this suggests a complex set of connections between the world prices of tradable goods and the real exchange rate. If one were trying to explain variations in the real exchange rate as resulting from changes in the world price of tradables, one would probably want to distinguish at least three separate explanatory variables: the world price level of the country's exports, the world price level of its competitive imports, and the world price level of its noncompetitive imports. But even here the strength of the causal connection would differ from commodity to commodity within each category, depending on its individual elasticity of import demand and export supply. Hence, one has no particular reason to expect to find a particularly good (or "tight") empirical relationship between variations in the real exchange rate and changes in the separate price levels of exports and of the two classes of imports. Even less would one expect to find a good "fit" for equations depicting movements in the real exchange rate on the basis of changes in the terms of trade (the ratio of the world price level of exports to the world price level of all imports) or changes in the world price level of a country's tradable goods (typically a weighted average of the price levels of its exports and all of its imports).

This leads to the second main point of this section: how tricky or precarious it may be to think of the real exchange rate as the ratio of the price level of tradables to that of nontradables. This definition works without any problem when the disturbance in question is a capital movement spent on nontradables, for in this case it follows from the nature of the disturbance that all tradables prices will move together (or remain constant while $\bar{p}_d$ undergoes changes stemming from movements in nontradables prices). But in just about every other interesting case—a world oil boom, looked at either from the standpoint of an oil-exporting or an oil-importing country; a reduction in the real costs of producing a particular tradable good, either locally (as a backward country adopts a technology already known but new to it) or worldwide (as in the "green" revolution or the arrival of the computer age); the introduction or relaxation of trade restrictions, either selectively or across the board—differential movements of tradables prices or different forces influencing production separate one or more tradables from the rest. In none of these cases is the ratio of tradables prices to that of nontradables prices particularly illuminating or useful as an analytical concept or tool. For example, knowing precisely what happens to this ratio does not tell us how the listed disturbances will influence the nominal exchange rate (E) in the event that the general level of prices $(\bar{p}_d)$ is held constant, or what will happen to $\bar{p}_d$ in the event E is held fixed.

More broadly, we should realize that just as we must use the unit of the dollar's worth to measure the demand for imports and the supply of exports in determining the real exchange rate $(E/\bar{p}_d)$ as defined here, so too must we use that unit when talking about the demand for and supply of importables and exportables. After all, the demand for imports (under the small-country hypothesis) is nothing more nor less than the excess-demand curve obtained from juxtaposing the demand and the supply curves for importables; and the supply of exports is nothing but the excess-supply curve obtained when doing the same thing for exportables. Finally, of course, the dollar's worth has to be the unit for measuring the supply and demand for tradables—at least if we want to maintain the magnificently useful identity between the balance of trade and the excess supply of tradables.

Thus, if this line of argument is correct, we should not put p_t/p_n (the price of tradables divided by the price of nontradables) on the vertical axis when we model demand and supply in the market for tradable goods. Rather, the vertical axis (in a timeless, comparative static analysis) should be labeled $E/\bar{p}_d$, just as it is when we directly analyze adjustment in the market for foreign exchange.

Finally, we should also remember that the demand and supply curves of tradables themselves undergo shifts when world prices of particular import and export goods change, as well as when tariffs, domestic excise taxes, export taxes and subsidies, and other types of distortions and restrictions are imposed. I come away from this entire exercise with a new respect for the old way of thinking about exchange rate determination as taking place in the market for foreign exchange. This way of thinking is not just a guide to the day-to-day setting of the nominal exchange rate. It is also a sound guide to help us understand the forces determining the equilibrium real exchange rate $E/\bar{p}_d$.

11.5 The Domestic Deflator, $\bar{p}_d$

The matters treated in this and the next section are more practical than conceptual, having more to do with the actual indexes used in empirical work than with the underlying theory of the subject. At the purely theoretical level, we know that the real side of economics deals with real (as against nominal) quantities and with relative prices. At some point, therefore, one typically has to choose a *numeraire* commodity—one in terms of whose price the remaining prices are expressed. The analysis to date has taken us part of the way down the road, in the sense that we have specifically singled out the world and internal prices of export(able) and import(able) goods, and we have recognized the possibility that the internal demand and supply prices might differ because of excise taxes or subsidies. The problem then is:

Relative to which price or price level do we wish to express these various supply and demand prices of the different tradable goods?

Although one could in theory pick any arbitrary good to serve as a numeraire,[5] this would miss the point; the numeraire would then have no particular economic content or meaning. Our concern is to give specific content and meaning to what we have already identified as $\bar{p}_d$. As far as I can see, there are only two reasonable candidates: (a) a general price index covering, in principle, all goods and services, including the tradables; and (b) a general index (p_n) of nontradable goods. If I had to make the choice only at the theoretical level, I would be inclined to opt for (b), on the grounds that it is cleaner to work with p_m/p_n and p_x/p_n than with $(p_m/[\alpha_1 p_m + \alpha_2 p_x + \alpha_3 p_n])$ and $(p_x/[\alpha_1 p_m + \alpha_2 p_x + \alpha_3 p_n])$, even though any given values of the former pair will imply specified values for the latter pair.

But if I intend to use actual data—even of estimated (or guesstimated) elasticities of demand and supply—my inclination tilts strongly toward option (a). In the first place, well-established indices of nontradable goods, especially ones that are reliable and readily (and speedily) available, are typically not at hand. In the second place, nearly all of the elasticity estimates in the literature express relative prices as ratios of individual goods prices to a general index like the consumer price index or the GDP deflator. Not only are the numerical estimates derived in this way, but our intuitive sense as to the likely orders of magnitude is based, in the final analysis, on such estimates. In the third place, when working through the theory of the international adjustment mechanism under flexible exchange rates, it is much more reasonable to assume a monetary policy that is designed to stabilize (or otherwise take as its target) the general price index than to assume that it is some nontradables price index that is being stabilized (or targeted). Similarly, it is much more natural to think of the adjustment mechanism under fixed exchange rates as taking place through movements of the money supply and the general price level, rather than through movements of money and of the price level of nontradables alone, since it is the general price level that presumably governs people's behavior with respect to their holdings of money and other assets denominated in money terms. This is true even in cases in which, theoretically, only movements in nontradables prices can cause the general price level to change. These are, as it were, the pure textbook cases; there are other textbook cases in which tradables prices would change (either exogenously or as a result of policy changes); and, of course, in the real world the prices of some tradables or others are always changing. The general index of prices $\bar{p}_d$ is under these circumstances the deflating index that one can most rely on in dealing with both theoretical and empirical problems.

Having opted, therefore, for the general index $\bar{p}_d$ rather than an index covering nontradables only, I will deal only briefly with the question of which index to use for $\bar{p}_d$. To my mind, wholesale price indexes are everywhere very heavily weighted with tradables—the mere fact that they are typically based on the prices of tangible and transportable goods practically guarantees that. Obviously, even though the deflating index is not a pure nontradables index, it should at least give them their due weight. Two widely used indexes that do this are the consumer price index (CPI) and the GDP (or GNP) deflator. Of these the latter is the more comprehensive, but the former is (so long as it is formulated following accepted professional standards) conceptually sound, acceptably general, and above all readily and quickly available (in nearly all countries), on a monthly as well as a quarterly and an annual basis. Thus, for most purposes I would choose the CPI as a deflator, probably reserving the GDP deflator mainly for historical time-series work where yearly data are all that is needed.

11.6   The Dollar-Price or World-Price Deflator, $\bar{p}^*$

It is well to recall at the outset of this section that one does not need a dollar-price or world-price deflator for most analytical purposes. The nominal price of an import good at the country's border is $p_m^* E$; its relative price at the border is $p_m^* E/\bar{p}_d$; and the relative price of a dollar's worth of it at the border is simply $E/\bar{p}_d$. This is true of each and every import good, at all times. The same can be said for export goods: their relative price at the border is $p_x^* E/\bar{p}_d$, and the relative price of a dollar's worth is always $E/\bar{p}_d$. With this definition of the real exchange rate we can analyze tariffs, quantitative import restrictions, export taxes and subsidies, domestic taxes, domestic production subsidies, agricultural price supply programs, and changes in the world prices, p_m^* or p_x^*, of particular imports or exports, or of groups of them, or of all of them, recognizing, of course, that some of these introduce distortions by which the relative prices paid for a dollar's worth by domestic demanders, or received by domestic suppliers, or both, are different from the corresponding relative prices at the border.

But when we thus argue the power of $E/\bar{p}_d$ as a measure of the real exchange rate, we should recognize that we are talking in the world of theory. Our analyses of things like tariffs and excise taxes are carried out in the timeless world of comparative statics. We analyze policies or other disturbances one at a time (or in packages of our own choosing), with other potentially complicating factors held constant. Through it all, as explained earlier in this paper, we measure our quantities of tradable goods in units of the dollar's worth.

But what if the value of the dollar changes over time? This question can be answered in three ways. First, there are many problems for which the fact of the dollar changing over time is of no particular moment. Thus, if a 50 percent uniform tariff causes $E/\bar{p}_d$ to be 20 percent lower than it otherwise would be, this disincentive to export activity will presumably be present when the dollar-price level is 100, when it is 200, and when it is 500 as the dollar suffers the throes of inflation. The presence of inflation does not by itself alter or modify the disincentive.

Second, our precise purpose may be to analyze the effects of an inflationary process in the world (dollar) economy. This can be done (analytically) by assuming that all dollar prices of goods and services move up together. Obviously, once this assumption is made any dollar-price numeraire can be used to convert the "dollar's worth" of different time periods into units of constant purchasing power. All will give the same answer. In particular, it does not matter whether we use an index $(\beta_1 p_m^* + \beta_2 p_x^*)$ of the dollar prices p_m^* and p_x^* of the specific imports and exports of the country in question, or whether we use instead a more general dollar-price index $\bar{p}^*$; nor, if we use $\bar{p}^*$, does it matter what its composition is.

Third, we may be concerned with the empirical analysis of real-world data characterized by ample fluctuations in the relative prices of individual goods (and groups of goods) as well as irregular movements in the general dollar price level (however defined). Here we want to find a deflating index that defines a meaningful concept of the real dollar's worth. At this stage I would suggest ruling out goods in the nontradable category. For example, technological advance in the tradables category in the United States and other advanced countries can cause a rise in the dollar prices of nontradable goods and services while the general dollar price level of tradables stays relatively constant. One would not expect such a change to cause an adjustment of the real exchange rate (properly defined) of a developing country. A simple way to ensure that this attribute also applies to our *measure* of the real exchange rate is to keep nontradable goods and services out of the index used to convert nominal dollars' worth into real dollars' worth.

At this point I have limited our search for the relevant deflator to the subset of goods that I call tradable. I believe the most interesting question here is whether (a) we should use one index (based on the country's own exports and imports) of the value of the dollar when we are talking of the real exchange rate of Spain, another when we are dealing with the real exchange rate of India, a third for Colombia, and so on or (b) we should seek a common measure of the value of the dollar to be used in all cases.

The choice between (a) and (b) is not clear-cut or obvious, but my own inclination is strongly toward (b). In the first place, a country by its own trade policy can alter the composition of its tradables: it can drive goods out of the import category by prohibitions or very high tariffs, and it can drive goods out of the export category simply through a policy of generally heavy protectionism (leading to such a strong appreciation of the real exchange rate that many exports are rendered unprofitable). On the whole, it does not seem appropriate for such policy-induced changes in the mix of a country's traded goods to dictate changes in the index used to convert inflated dollars into dollars whose purchasing power is constant over time.

Second, we definitely want to be able to distinguish situations in which the disturbance is a change in the relative dollar price of one or more key commodities from one in which a general world inflation prevails. An extreme example would be a country whose sole export was natural gas and whose principal imports were petroleum products. An energy price boom could then cause the dollar prices of both its exports (p_x^*) and its imports (p_m^*) to rise by the same percentage. Even though this might have the same effect on the particular country as a general world inflation would, that similarity would be picked up in the analysis by working with the relative prices $(p_x^*/\bar{p}^*)$ and $(p_m^*/\bar{p}^*)$ and using $\bar{p}^*$ as the general dollar-price deflator. This procedure seems to me better than ignoring $\bar{p}^*$ and using a country-specific term $(\beta_1 p_m^* + \beta_2 p_x^*)$ as the general dollar deflator.

A third consideration is the fact that a fair amount of empirical work in international economics deals with cross-sections of countries. Here a definition of the real dollar's worth that remains invariant as one moves from country to country (at any given time) has obvious appeal.

Fourth, and in a similar vein, there are occasions a commodity-price rise has an impact on the economies of the countries producing or using that commodity. It would seem reasonable in such circumstances to deal with a rise in the relative dollar price of, say, oil that is the same for all countries. This, of course, would not be the case if the general deflating index differed across countries, weighting the different commodity prices by their relative importance in each country's own trade. Particularly for a commodity like oil, which is practically the sole export in some producing countries and has a more moderate weight in others, differing weights for the commodity in an index of the form $(\beta_1 p_m^* + \beta_2 p_x^*)$ might cause a doubling of oil prices to be reflected as changes of very different percentages in the relative world-market price of oil in different countries. But this does not seem sensible to me. The price of oil, translated into local currency and expressed relative to the domestic general price level $\bar{p}_d$, will very likely differ from country to country, and in ways that reflect how the relative importance of oil in total output, exports, consumption, and so on differs among countries. But here I am not talking of the relative price of oil $(p_j^* E[1 + t_j]/\bar{p}_d)$ within Nigeria, Indonesia, or Venezuela. Instead I am talking about its relative price $(p_j^*/\bar{p}^*)$ in the world market. The former relative price does in reality differ among countries; and our analysis must capture and explain this. I see no reason, however, why the relative price of oil in the world or dollar economy should differ from country to country.

I therefore propose that the index $\bar{p}^*$ for converting nominal dollars' worth into real dollars' worth be an index of the dollar prices of tradable goods and that the weights used for the different goods in this index should not vary as we move from one developing country to another. I allow for the possibility that in a particular developing country the relative prices of both its importables and its exportables could rise (or fall) during a given period; the analysis then would capture the total effect of such a change as being similar, for the country concerned, to that of a general world inflation.

The single index $\bar{p}^*$ can be thought of as an index of the prices of tradable goods "somewhere on the high seas." The analogy is apt because it clearly connotes that there is no principle dictating that it should be an index of U.S. prices, or German prices, or U.K. prices.

Throughout this paper I have talked of the dollar's worth as the unit of measurement of tradables. This is clearly the result of the dominance of the U.S. dollar as the key currency during the past few decades and of its likely continued importance into the next few. As a consequence of this role of the dollar, many international trade statistics are measured in terms of dollars; this creates a pragmatic necessity for a deflator to convert these nominal dollar data into real terms.

The most natural, readily available index for doing this job is the U.S. wholesale price index. But it is not difficult to convert the German, British, or Japanese wholesale price indexes into dollar terms by multiplying by the dollar price of the mark, the pound, or the yen. On this basis we could then create a dollar wholesale price index based, say, on the relative weights of the different major currencies in the SDR (that is, Special Drawings Rights, the unit, a basket of major currencies, in which credit from the International Monetary Fund is measured). The index would then be not a U.S.–price index but a *dollar*-price index, one that could appropriately be used to deflate trade statistics expressed in dollars and to trace over time the real exchange rates reflecting the price of the dollar in different countries' domestic currencies.

One alternative to the use of wholesale price indexes is to work with those components of GDP deflators that are most readily identifiable as relating to tradables. These are clearly those for the manufacturing, agricultural (including forestry and cattle raising), and mining sectors. With these components it would be easy to construct for any country a national index of tradables prices.

Once again one could here think of using the U.S. "tradables GDP deflator" as the relevant index, or alternatively a weighted average of several countries' "tradables GDP deflators," each converted into dollar terms by the relevant dollar exchange rate of the respective country's currency. The appeal of this index is its conceptual clarity, with respect to both the definition of tradable goods (here, manufactures plus agricultural and mineral products) and the weights with which their prices are combined in each country (that is, the relative weights they have in the corresponding GDP). The disadvantages of this index are that it is never available on a monthly basis (and not always even quarterly) and that it often appears with a long lag and in relatively obscure sources.

My vote for work to be done in the near future would be to use the U.S. wholesale price index as the deflator for the dollar values of trade. If consensus regarding the conceptual framework is approached, one can hope that the International Monetary Fund might begin to publish (in *International Financial Statistics*) monthly indexes of the wholesale prices in a number of major countries (say, those whose currencies compose the SDR), converted into dollars by the relevant exchange rate and also, if possible, averaged together (presumably with SDR weights). Once such an index was regularly calculated and readily available, I believe it could claim superiority over the U.S. wholesale price index for the purpose at hand.

It is also my belief that indexes based on components of the GDP deflator, either of the United States alone or of a combination of countries, will be useful in the future, but for rather more restricted purposes than those based on wholesale price series. Nonetheless, I believe the time is ripe for researchers to make imaginative use of price indexes of tradables baskets that are built up from corresponding components of GDP deflators.

11.7 Reflections and Conclusions

The writing of this paper has been much more difficult than I had initially anticipated. The process has been sobering, too; among other things I have come to appreciate how a concept of the real exchange rate that is simple and obvious in one context can lead one seriously astray in others.

Among the contending concepts are (a) the price level of a country's tradables deflated by that of its nontradables, (b) the nominal exchange rate deflated by a general price index, (c) the nominal exchange rate (for example, the peso price of the dollar) double deflated by a peso-price index and a dollar-price index of a similar concept, and (d) the nominal exchange rate deflated by an index of nominal wages and salaries.

Of these, concept (a) is very naturally suitable in examining problems of international capital movements and the transfer problem generally; concept (b) is quite appropriate for dealing with internal inflation in the country in question, as well as for handling other policies, such as tariffs, taxes, and subsidies; (c) has been sanctified for the better part of a century in the literature on purchasing power parity, and it is appropriate when monetary movements take place at different rates in the country in question and in the rest of the world; and (d) is powerful medicine, forcefully bringing home the fact that a required devaluation of the real exchange rate often necessarily entails a fall in real wages and salaries.

Being a firm believer that language (and communication in general) must always be understood in the context in which it is imbedded, I am not too uncomfortable with the thought that these and other competing notions of the real exchange rate will probably swirl through economic discourse for years to come. But I am quite a bit more uncomfortable with that idea now than I was before I undertook writing this paper. The trouble is that, unlike such issues as whether demand elasticities are defined as positive or negative and whether an exchange rate is taken to be the dollar price of the peso or the peso price of the dollar—which are simple ones—the issues raised by the different usages of the real exchange rate are complex. Moreover, the problems involved are not widely appreciated, so that people who are thinking in terms of one concept may well find unintelligible or downright stupid the things that are said by others who have a different concept in mind. So complex and intertwined are the issues that I am supremely confident of only one thing: Despite the best efforts of myself and others, much confusion will surround the concept of the real exchange rate for a long time to come.

I have been chastened, also, in writing this paper by the fact that all too recently I myself used the above concepts more or less interchangeably, at times explicitly listing concepts (a), (c), and (d) as three guises in which the real exchange rate appears. How fateful that I should now come forward as a defender of concept (b) and as an advocate of yet another concept, (e), double deflation using an index of the world prices of tradables as the foreign deflator and a general index like the CPI as the domestic deflator! But so it is.

The first task (or test) that I would require of a concept of the real exchange rate is that it correctly replicate simple textbook cases of exchange rate determination. This is done admirably by the concept $(E/\bar{p}_d)$, so long as the general price level in the rest of the world is taken as given.

In figure 11.1 I dealt with six disturbances, assuming a flexible exchange rate and a monetary policy that held the general internal price level $\bar{p}_d$ constant. They were the imposition of a general tariff, the imposition of a general export tax, an inflow of capital spent on tradable goods, an inflow of capital spent on nontradable goods, a rise in the world price of a country's exports, and a rise in the world price of a country's imports.

These cases gave the familiar and expected answers, but in the process it was underscored that (for the flexible rate case, at least) the exchange rate is a price that is set *in the market for foreign exchange.* The units that are demanded and supplied are dollars of foreign exchange. To link this fact to the demand for imports and the supply of exports, we must measure the quantity of each individual import and export good in units that have a given value (say, one dollar) in the world market. Based on this assumption we can construct demand and supply curves for foreign exchange and determine the equilibrium exchange rate. One key result was that the demand and supply curves for foreign exchange shift when the world prices of import and export commodities change, causing changes in the nominal exchange rate for a given $\bar{p}_d$.

Figure 11.2 presented my first explicit introduction to the real exchange rate. I there explored the process of adjustment to disturbances like those in figure 11.1, only now under the assumption that the nominal exchange rate was fixed. Here, as is well known, the adjustment process works through monetary expansion and contraction; identical results to those of the first figure are obtained, however, when the price of foreign currency is expressed as $E/\bar{p}_d$. In figure 11.1 the adjustment is in the numerator of this expression; in figure 11.2 it is in the denominator.

The concept $E/\bar{p}_d$ is exceedingly robust. Using it one can handle essentially all types of disturbances originating in the domestic economy and basically any relevant disturbance originating abroad (since the only channels through which foreign disturbances would enter the picture are movements of capital and changes in the world prices of tradable goods and services). The only flaw I find in using $E/\bar{p}_d$ as the general and definitive concept of the real exchange rate is the fact that its equilibrium value falls (signifying an appreciation of the peso or other local currency) when there is a general world (or dollar) inflation. Where world (or dollar) inflation is not an intrinsic part of the picture (for example, in any and all theoretical analyses of the consequences of domestic policies and other domestic disturbances), $E/\bar{p}_d$ is, I believe, the correct concept to use.

Where world inflation is the problem (or an integral part of the problem), the concept of the real exchange rate can be made more nearly symmetrical by introducing a world-price deflator $\bar{p}^*$ along with the domestic price deflator $\bar{p}_d$. The real exchange rate concept then becomes $\bar{p}^* E/\bar{p}_d$. This is a natural extension of the original concept; when the real value of the dollar is not changing, we can treat the basic demand and supply as being for the dollar's worth of foreign exchange. When the real value of the dollar is changing, basic demand and supply will be for the *real* dollar's worth of foreign exchange.

But note that if we fail to introduce $\bar{p}^*$ into the expression for the real exchange rate, the consequences are not cataclysmic; we simply obtain an expression that could be denominated "the real peso price of the dollar, uncorrected for dollar inflation." This type of index has in fact been widely and quite successfully used in cases of countries experiencing very rapid inflation.

Of the alternative concepts of the real exchange rate mentioned at the outset of this section, the one I consider most vulnerable is p_t/p_n, the ratio of the price level of tradables to the price level of nontradables. Taken at face value, this index simply gives the wrong answer too much of the time. The right answers to questions concerning the real exchange rate are those represented in figure 11.1. Of the six disturbances there considered, the concept p_t/p_n does well for only two: a capital inflow spent on tradables (for which the supply of tradables would shift to the right by the amount of the capital inflow and the demand would shift likewise, leaving p_t/p_n unchanged); and a capital inflow spent on nontradables (adjustment to which would require that an excess demand for tradables be generated, causing a fall in the equilibrium level of p_t/p_n). An import tariff and an export tax would each have an ambiguous effect on the price level of tradables, since one component of it (the price level of importables) would rise under either of the two disturbances, while the other component (the price level of exportables) would fall. Whichever one of these two dominated, the effect on p_t/p_n would be the same under either a general import tariff or a general export tax that introduced the same gap between the price levels of importables and exportables, respectively. As the analyses of figures 11.1 and 11.2 show, however, the real exchange rate must unequivocally fall in the case of a general tariff and rise in the case of a general export tax. The concept p_t/p_n therefore *cannot* give the right answer in these cases.

A similar conclusion can be drawn with respect to changes in the world prices of specific tradable goods. A rise in the world price of exports (alone) must cause a fall in the equilibrium real exchange rate. Yet since exportables are an important component of tradables (they could be much more than half or much less than a half, even with balanced trade, because of the existence of domestic consumption of exportables and domestic production of importables), the effect of a rise in export prices might cause the index p_t/p_n to rise, or to fall, or to remain the same. Here again p_t/p_n does not lead us to the correct answer.

We have seen that the effect of a rise in import prices on the demand for foreign currency (and hence on the real exchange rate) will depend on the price elasticity of import demand, the effect being nil with unit elasticity, negative under elastic demand, and positive under inelastic demand. The elasticity of import demand does not even come into play when one considers the ratio p_t/p_n; this ratio *must* rise if the world prices of imports rise while those of exports remain the same. Thus, p_t/p_n once again gives the wrong answer.

In my view, two correct answers out of six is not good enough. Even worse, an extension of the analysis to cover other types of domestically imposed distortions—such as quotas, price supports, and domestic taxes and subsidies—would reveal still further failures of the p_t/p_n concept to predict reliably what would happen to the nominal exchange rate under conditions of a stable general (or for that matter a stable nontradables) price level.

The use of the ratio p_t/p_n has yet another defect: it diverts attention from the necessity of measuring both the demand for and the supply of tradables in dollars' worth. (Actually, if this is done, and if p_t is explicitly defined as the internal price at the border [that is, without tariffs, taxes, or subsidies] of a dollar's worth of tradable goods, the p_t/p_n ratio can be rehabilitated.) The p_t/p_n concept focuses attention on tradables and nontradables as two bundles of goods and services competing for the interest of demanders and for the application of resources by suppliers. One's instinct is to treat those bundles symmetrically, when what is called for instead is an asymmetric treatment. One is also inclined to treat tradables as a single bundle, when familiar disturbances require the separation of importables from exportables and often the breaking down of these categories into individual commodities or groups.

In general the p_t/p_n concept can be amended to produce the right answers when it is employed. Two basic elements are involved here. First, exportables and importables must be expressed in units of "dollars' worth." When this is done, and for "properly defined" curves, the excess-demand curve for importables becomes the demand curve for imports, the excess-supply curve of exportables becomes the supply curve for exports, and we are back in a framework of the supply and demand for foreign exchange. But we must work hard to "define properly" the demand and supply curves of importables and exportables. In general we must make beforehand the necessary corrections so that the tradables price reflected on the curve is the border price of a dollar's worth of tradables. Thus, for a tariff the demand for and supply of exportables would remain untampered with, but the height of the supply and demand curves for importables could be reduced by the amount of the tariff. There would be an outward shift of the supply of importables and an inward shift of demand, with the result that the supply curve of tradables (importables plus exportables) would shift outward; and the demand curve inward, producing a fall in the equilibrium real exchange rate (p_t/p_n in this modified framework). For any disturbance being analyzed, it is possible to find the necessary shifts of the supply of and demand for exportables or importables, or both, that will result in the correct final result. The underlying principle here is that the equilibrium p_t in the p_t/p_n ratio must always be the border price, net of import tariff, gross of export tax, gross of import subsidy, net of export subsidy, and so on. It must always be what an import buyer pays per dollar's worth of a (hypothetical if necessary) nondistorted import good, or what an exporter receives for selling a dollar's worth of a nondistorted export good. Once this is done, the p_t/p_n framework is rehabilitated. I doubt, however, that the result is worth the effort, since other means exist of reaching the same conclusions more directly and simply.

The other concepts of the real exchange rate are more easily employed. To use the nominal exchange rate divided by an index of wages and salaries is just like using $E/\bar{p}_d$, with the general internal price level being represented by the wages and salary level. (Actually, the corrected p_t/p_n ratio, just discussed, substitutes p_n for $\bar{p}_d$ in the same way.) None of the above are corrected for foreign inflation—which for solving many analytical problems is not necessary and which may not be necessary in dealing with particular practical ones.

If one is to correct for foreign inflation, I do not believe that deep theoretical considerations enter seriously into the choice of the index to be used. Foreign CPI indexes and foreign GDP deflators have been widely used, particularly in tandem with domestic price deflators ($\bar{p}_d$) based on the same concept. Since the nontradables of the rest of the world have little connection to a given developing country's economy, I prefer to use as a foreign price deflator $\bar{p}^*$, which explicitly concentrates on tradable goods. And I prefer a general dollar-price index to one that is based on a country's own tradables weights. For practical reasons I prefer a dollar-price index that is quickly and readily available. The U.S. wholesale price index meets this criterion, as does a weighted average of the wholesale price indexes of major trading nations, converted to a dollar basis using the exchange rates of their respective currencies vis-à-vis the dollar.

An alternative would be to use for $\bar{p}^*$ the tradable component of the U.S. GDP deflator or a weighted average of the corresponding components of the GDP deflators of the major trading nations (once again converted to a dollar basis using the prevailing exchange rates). Indexes based on GDP (or GNP, as the case may be) deflators probably have greater conceptual clarity, but they are not available monthly and are quite slow to appear. Of the options available for precisely defining the composition of $\bar{p}^*/\bar{p}_d$, I would at the one extreme opt for the U.S. wholesale price index as representing $\bar{p}^*$ and the country's own consumer price index as representing $\bar{p}_d$. This option is useful for work that requires readily available easy-to-use, and monthly data. At the other extreme I would consider an index constructed from agricultural, mining, and manufacturing components of the U.S. GNP deflator for $\bar{p}^*$ and the individual country's own total GDP deflator for $\bar{p}_d$. This option is appropriate largely for time-series work that requires annual data. It should be clear that these are preferences, not choices determined by profound analytical dictates. In other words, there is much room for fruitful debate over and experimentation with different indexes.

A final note concerns the design of empirical work aimed at explaining movements over time in the real exchange rate. The analysis of this paper suggests a partial list of explanatory variables that might be useful; it also carries warnings that certain variables might not be useful at all, and still others only in restricted cases. An ideal list of explanatory variables would certainly include net capital inflow spent on tradable goods, net capital inflow spent on nontradable goods, the world price level of a country's exports, the world price level of its competitive imports, the world price level of its noncompetitive imports, the average strength of tariffs and other restrictions inhibiting import demand, and the average strength of export taxes (subsidies) and other policies inhibiting (or promoting) export supply.

The above list is only partial, as I have limited it to items explicitly discussed in this paper. Nonetheless, it clearly shows how difficult is the task of empirically explaining movements in the real exchange rate. We rarely have breakdowns as to the types of goods on which a country's foreign borrowings are spent, yet we know that only the part spent on nontradables should influence the real exchange rate. In examining small countries we usually can obtain world prices for a few principal exports, but import prices are difficult to come by, especially if we want to classify them into competitive or noncompetitive imports (or other categories that distinguish groups with different import demand elasticities). We usually have average receipts from import tariffs, but we have little clue as to the strength (and the variation over time) of nontariff barriers. The story is similar with the incentives (particularly the disguised ones) that countries often give to certain export activities.

The list is interesting for the variables it includes, and it is also sobering in light of how difficult it is (in many cases) to approximate the actual variables one has to use to the desired ones. But the woes of empirical workers are familiar, particularly those related to the failure of actual data series to measure what one really wants.

Let me therefore end on a more positive note. The above list intentionally excludes the terms-of-trade (the ratio of export to import prices) variable in favor of separating it into components. The lesson is to avoid trying to work with this variable as an explainer of real exchange rates changes. The list explicitly includes export taxes as variables causing the real exchange rate to rise; these have been extremely important (and variable over time) in a number of countries (among them Argentina and Uruguay), but to my knowledge they have not been used in real exchange rate regressions. Also useful are the concept of net foreign borrowing as a separate argument in the demand functions for different categories of goods and the concept of the fraction of foreign borrowing spent on tradables as being important in determining its ultimate effect on the real exchange rate. These observations, derived from analyzing the underlying concept and measurement of the real exchange rate, may ultimately be of use in empirical investigations that attempt to explain its variations.

Appendix: Impact of a Rise in P_j^* on the Real Exchange Rate

Analysis of Substitution Effects

This is not the place for an extended treatment introducing further complications to the above analysis. But I cannot avoid examining at least in passing the situation in which the demand for imports of the good whose world price changes is not independent, say, of other tradables prices. The issue at stake is standard in the demand for composite commodities, and it is much like the difference between long-run and short-run marginal cost curves. Assuming gross substitutability in all relevant respects, we will have, at any viable equilibrium position (i) a demand curve ($\bar{D}\bar{D}$ in figure 11.4) for imports of j that assumes all other tradables prices move together with that of j (that is, tradables prices move as the exchange rate moves) and (ii) a demand curve (D^*D^*) for imports of j that assumes only p_j^* moves, while other import prices remain constant at their previous level. Assuming that import j is a gross substitute for the rest of the tradables, we find that D^*D^* will be more elastic than $\bar{D}\bar{D}$.

Consider A' in figure 11.4 to be a point like A' in figure 11.3a. Imagine having started from a point like A in figure 11.3a, with that equilibrium being disturbed by a rise in p_j^*. There would be a curve like D^*D^* and one like $\bar{D}\bar{D}$ through A; the two demand curves depicted in figure 11.4 are the "remappings" of these original curves as a consequence of the rise in p_j^*. Likewise, A' is simply the remapping of the original point A. Any adjustment involved must take off from this point. Since only p_j^* has changed, it would seem at first glance that the new equilibrium would be at C. But one must ask what is the meaning of the distance (CF) between D^*D^* and $\bar{D}\bar{D}$ at this point. Obviously, this distance

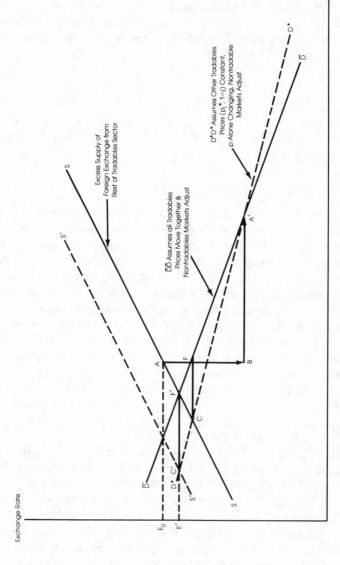

Exchange Rate

S

S'

Excess Supply of
Foreign Exchange from
Rest of Tradeables Sector

$\overline{D}$

$\overline{D}\overline{D}$ Assumes all Tradeables
Prices Move Together &
Nontradeables Markets Adjust

D* D* Assumes Other Tradeables
Prices (p_j^*, $i = j$) Constant.
p_j Alone Changing, Nontradeable
Markets Adjust

E_0

E'

A

F'

D* C'

F

C

B

A'

D

D*

S'

S

Fig. 11.4 Foreign exchange spent on imports of good j.

represents the additional substitution that takes place against good j, when other tradables prices are held constant rather than moving up from A' pari passu with p_j^*. But if people are substituting away from j and toward other tradables, the excess supply curve of foreign exchange arising out of these other tradables markets will shift to the left. Thus, point C is not an equilibrium point, as it is on the old excess supply curve, but not on the shifted one.

Actually, the new equilibrium must be at C' (neglecting income effects). Remembering that the units of tradables are being measured in "dollars' worths"; the extra substitution (at a given price) away from good j and toward other tradables must cause the demand for those other tradables to expand by a like amount. This in turn causes the excess supply curve of other tradables to shift to the left by the same amount. The distance $C'F'$ is thus at one and the same time the leftward shift in the excess supply curve of other tradables *and* the extra substitution in demand of favor of these other tradables because only p_j^* (not all tradables prices) has risen. The end result of the whole process is that the equilibrium exchange rate falls from E_o to E'. It is thus exactly as if one had moved up on $\overline{D}\overline{D}$ from A' to F', neglecting entirely the fact that it was only p_j^* that changed and forgetting entirely about D^*D^* and $S'S'$.

Thus, we need be concerned with only one demand curve for imports of good j—that represented by $\overline{D}\overline{D}$. When p_j^* changes, this curve will be remapped, as shown in figure 11.3a, but no serious complexities are introduced by the changing of only one (or any subset) of the world prices of importable goods. Demand curves will be displaced, downward or upward depending on their elasticities of demand at the points in question, but we do not have to bring in new concepts of demand to take care of the case of nonindependence.

The same story holds for the supply of exports. One can visualize a supply curve of exports of good k, built on the assumption that all tradables prices move together, and another built on the assumption that the other prices are held constant, while only p_k^* moves. The difference between these two curves at an exchange rate like E' will be (for a rise in p_k^*) the substitution (in demand, for present purposes) against good k and in favor of other tradables—something that does not occur if all tradables prices move together. One of the two supply curves will be like D^*D^* in being based on the assumption that only the price of k rises, while the prices of other tradables remain fixed. Along this supply curve and the old excess demand curve for tradable goods other than k, there will be a point analogous to C. This will not be an equilibrium because it fails to take into account that any substitution away from k and toward other tradables will shift to the left, by a like amount, the excess demand for foreign currency generated in that set of markets. Thus, the new equilibrium will be at a point like C' where the extra substitution away from good k is just offset by the rightward shift in the excess demand for foreign exchange. Again, in short, one can operate with the supply-side counterpart of the demand curve $\overline{D}\overline{D}$ without having to concern oneself with the counterpart of D^*D^*. Substitution effects among the tradables end up cancelling themselves out.

Analysis of Income Effects

It remains to speak about income effects. These are dealt with explicitly in figures 11.5a and 11.5b. I have just shown that we can work with tradables demand and supply curves built on the assumption of a pari passu movement of all tradables prices, so far as substitution effects are concerned. The course of prudence is to thank God for this bit of largesse (in clarifying our thoughts and simplifying our tasks), and build our analysis of income effects around it. Once we realize this, a neat trick can be brought into play. Rather than work with excess demand and excess supply curves of the D^*D^* type, why not continue to work with $\overline{D}\overline{D}$ and its supply-side counterpart? We know that if p_j^* (for an import) rises, the induced change in real income (measured in dollars) is $-M_j dp_j^*$, where M_j denotes imports of good j and dp_j^* denotes the percentage change in the world price of j (recall that all tradables are expressed in units whose price is one dollar). This change in income will be spread among commodities in accordance with the respective marginal propensities μ_i of the society to spend on each of them. Since some of them are exportables and some importables, the consequence is that both the compensated excess demand curve and the compensated supply curve will be shifted by the income effect. This is a painful thought, especially since any given equilibrium real exchange rate can be the result of a number of different disturbances, each of which have different effects on the real income of the society.

Now for the trick. Instead of trying to incorporate the income effect of a given disturbance into the excess demand and supply relations we are dealing with, why not insert it as a wedge between the two compensated curves? In that case we need only break down the income effect into two fractions: μ_t spent on tradables, and μ_n spent on nontradables.

Figure 11.5a is built like figure 11.3a, except now we know that we can work with SS as it stands and with the remapped $(\overline{D}\overline{D})$ in seeking the new equilibrium. Some of the change in real income will result in reduced spending on tradables other than j. This will cause SS to shift to the right by an amount equal to $(\mu_t - \mu_j)M_j dp_j^*$. It will also lead to

5a

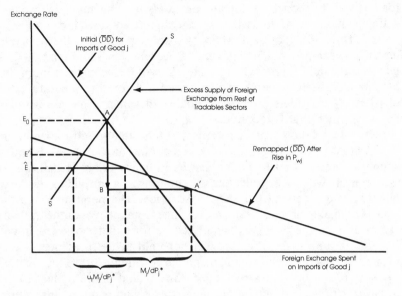

Exchange Rate

Initial ($\overline{DD}$) for
Imports of Good j

S

Excess Supply of Foreign
Exchange from Rest of
Tradables Sectors

E_0

A

Remapped ($\overline{DD}$) After
Rise in P_{wj}

E'

$\hat{E}$

B

A'

S

$u_1 M_j / dP_j^*$

M_j / dP_j^*

Foreign Exchange Spent
on Imports of Good j

5b

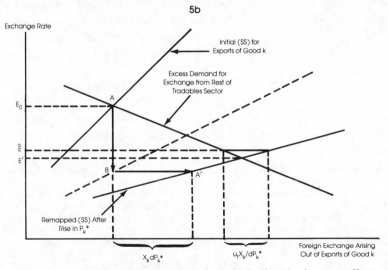

Exchange Rate

Initial (SS) for
Exports of Good k

Excess Demand for
Exchange from Rest of
Tradables Sector

E_0

A

$\hat{E}$

E'

B

A'

Remapped (SS) After
Rise in P_k^*

$X_k dP_k^*$

$u_1 X_k / dP_k^*$

Foreign Exchange Arising
Out of Exports of Good k

Fig. 11.5   Real exchange rate analysis including the income effects of
changes in import or export prices.

less spending on good j itself. This will cause the import demand curve for j to shift to the left by the amount $\mu_j M_j dp_j^*$. The sum of these two shifts is always $\mu_t M_j dp_j^*$, whatever the import good we happen to call good j. Thus, if we know $\mu_t M_j dp_j^*$, we know the size of the wedge to insert between SS and $\bar{D}\bar{D}$ in figure 11.5a, and this is enough to tell us where the equilibrium exchange rate, $\hat{E}$, will be, after accounting for income effects. (Of course, we will need to know the separate value of μ_j in order to determine the equilibrium value of the abscissa, in cases in which that is required.)

Figure 11.5b shows the counterpart of this situation for a rise in the world price of export good k. The remapping of the excess (export) supply curve of good k is done just as in figure 11.3b. Recall that at A' exporters would be replicating the situation at A, providing the same quantity and receiving the same peso price. The point at which the excess demand curve for foreign exchange from the rest of the tradable sector crosses the remapped supply curve for exports of k would call for equilibrium at E'. But this will not hold in the presence of real income effects. Properly, the demand curve would shift to the right by $(\mu_t - \mu_k)X_k dp_k^*$, and the remapped (SS) would shift to the left by $\mu_k X_k dp_k^*$. But we can obtain the same equilibrium result by inserting a wedge equal to $\mu_t X_k dp_k^*$ between the excess demand curve and the remapped (SS). When this is done, the equilibrium exchange rate $\hat{E}$ results.

Notes

1. This paper is explicitly designed as an introduction; I have attempted to make it accessible to students and to other readers with limited formal training in economics, as well as to seasoned professionals in the field. Although the last group may find much of the expository material familiar, I believe that the analysis as a whole enables us to see more clearly than we have been able to from the literature to date some of the main issues surrounding the concept and the measurement of the real exchange rate. A more extended exposition of some of this material can be found in Harberger (1985).

2. This point will be treated in more detail in section 11.4.

3. Once again, for further elaboration of the relevant analysis, see section 11.4.

4. There are some interesting technical relationships among the elasticities of demand for imports and for tradables in general. These are briefly explored in the appendix.

5. This is what is done in mathematical treatments of most general-equilibrium problems. The other general-equilibrium tradition has its roots in international trade theory; it deals with a relatively small number of identifiable commodity groups, one of which perforce ends up being chosen as the numeraire. This choice is what we are concerned with here.

Selected Bibliography

Arriazu, R. H. 1983. Policy interdependence from a Latin American perspective. *International Monetary Fund Staff Papers* 30 (March): 113–63.

Calvo, G. and Rodriguez, C. 1979. A model of exchange rate determination under currency substitution and rational expectations. *Journal of Political Economy* 85 (June): 617–25.

Corden, W. M. 1981. The exchange rate, monetary policy and North Sea oil: The economic theory of the squeeze on tradeables. *Oxford Economic Papers*, Supplement (July): 23–46.

Dornbusch, R. 1974. Real and monetary aspects of the effects of exchange rate changes. In *National monetary policies and the international financial system*, ed. R. Z. Aliber. Chicago: University of Chicago Press.

———. 1976. Expectations and exchange rate dynamics. *Journal of Political Economy* 84 (December): 1161–76.

Edwards, S. 1984. The external sector in developing countries. *Princeton Essays in International Finance* no. 156 (December). Princeton: International Finance Section, Princeton University.

Frenkel, J. and Rodriguez, C. 1981. Exchange rate dynamics and the overshooting hypothesis. IMF Departmental Memo no. 81/88 (December). Washington, D.C. International Monetary Fund.

Harberger, A. C. 1982. The Chilean economy in the 1970's: Crisis, stabilization, liberalization reform. In *Economic policy in a world of change*, Carnegie-Rochester Conference Series on Public Policy, eds. K. Brunner and A. Meltzer. Amsterdam: North-Holland.

———. 1983. Dutch disease: How much sickness, how much boon? *Resources and Energy* 5 (no. 1): 1–20.

———. 1985. Elements of real exchange rate analysis. Washington, D.C.: Economic Development Institute, World Bank, April. Photocopy.

———. 1985. Lessons for debtor country managers and policymakers. In *International debt and the developing countries*. A World Bank Symposium, eds. J. Smith and J. Cuddington. Washington, D.C.: World Bank, March.

Harberger, A. C. and Edwards, S. 1982. Causes of inflation in developing countries: Some new evidence. Paper presented at the 95th Annual Meeting of the American Economic Association, New York, December.

McKinnon, R. I. 1973. *Money and capital in economic development*. Washington, D.C.: Brookings Institution.

———. 1982. The order of economic liberalization: Lessons from Chile and Argentina. In *Economic policy in a world of change*. Carnegie-Rochester Conference Series. Amsterdam: North-Holland.

Mussa, M. 1982. A model of exchange rate dynamics. *Journal of Political Economy* 90 (February): 74–104.

Nunes, L. 1984. Optimal capital accumulation and external indebtedness in a two sector small economy model. Ph.D. dissertation. Chicago: University of Chicago.

Obstfeld, M. 1980. Imperfect asset substitutability and monetary policy under fixed exchange rates. *Journal of International Economics* 10:177–200.

Penati, A. 1983. Expansionary fiscal policy and the exchange rates. *International Monetary Fund Staff Papers* 30 (September): 545–69.

Rodriguez, C. A. 1982. Gasto publico, deficit y tipo real de cambio: Un analisis de sus interrelaciones de largo plazo. *Cuadernos de Economia* 57 (Universidad Pontificia de Chile) (August): 203–16.

Sachs, J. 1982. The current account and the macroeconomic adjustment process. *Scandinavian Journal of Economics* 84 (no. 2): 147–59.

Salter, W. E. 1959. Internal and external balance: The role of price and expenditure effects. *Economic Record* 35 (August): 226–38.

Sjaastad, L. 1983. International debt quagmire: To whom do we owe it? *The World Economy* 6 (September): 305–24.

van Wijnbergen, S. 1984. The "Dutch disease": A disease after all? *Economic Journal* 94 (March): 41–55.

Comment   Carlos Díaz-Alejandro

An admiring connoisseur of smorgasbord is selective. Faced with Harberger's rich table, I will dwell on just two of his servings: the definition of the "world dollar price level" relevant for developing countries (LDCs), and exchange rate policy differences among LDCs and between LDCs and developed countries.

Defining the world dollar price level relevant for LDCs is far from an unimportant or easy matter. Debates over imported inflation, exchange rate policy, and the real cost of servicing the external debt have gained in acrimony in recent years, partly due to the use of different yet plausible statistics for that price level. In Argentina and Chile, for example, those who defended government policies during the years 1978–80 argued that the world price level relevant to those two countries was rising at an annual rate of 30 percent per annum (more than double the inflation in U.S. wholesale prices), so that persistent local inflation, a sluggish pace of domestic currency devaluation, and heavy borrowing abroad were easier to explain and justify.

Carlos Díaz-Alejandro was a professor of economics at Columbia University before his death in 1985.

Since 1972 severe changes in relative prices in the world economy have indeed generated a rich menu of candidates for the world price level, depending on how different goods and services are weighted. For long-term trends this is, of course, less of a problem than for exercises involving two or three years. The already mentioned two-year period, 1978–80, during which some of the most adventurous Southern Cone policies were implemented, coincided with particularly turbulent and confusing fluctuations in international relative prices.

Table C11.1 collects a variety of indicators for dollar inflation during the period 1972–83. Over the whole 11-year period there is a clustering between 7 and 11 percent per annum, using the most plausible indicators. But international dollar prices for LDC imports, including oil, seem to have risen more than price indexes for the U.S. economy. A difference of a couple of percentage points per annum can, of course, cumulate to a very significant gap over 11 years. Export unit values for Argentina, Brazil, and Chile show an inflationary trend distinctly lower than that of the U.S. price indexes and, a fortiori, than that for their imports. Note that the simple averages for import and export price inflation in those three Latin American countries over the 11-year period are very close to the U.S. measures of inflation. For all nonoil LDCs, the simple average of export and import inflation works out only a shade higher than that for U.S. wholesale prices, a generalization that can be extended to the domestic inflation of two classic, *very* open, small Latin American economies, Haiti and Panama, which have maintained rigid pegs to the U.S. dollar for many years. Over the long term the U.S. wholesale price index does well as a measure of dollar inflation, even for international prices, supporting Harberger's suggestion.

In short periods of only two years, however, we are in trouble. Table C11.1 documents the turbulence and unevenness in dollar price behavior during the periods 1972–74 and 1978–80. Although the U.S. wholesale price index did show more sensitivity than U.S. consumer prices and the GNP deflator, it lagged behind most international dollar prices during those two-year periods. But apologists for Southern Cone policies grossly exaggerated that gap for 1978–80. Given the numbers in table C11.1, it would be difficult to argue that the international dollar inflation relevant for the Southern Cone during 1978–80 went beyond a range of 18 to 22 percent per annum. Interestingly, a higher number could be justified for international inflation (and its gap vis à vis that in U.S. wholesale prices) during 1972–74. Note that in Haiti and Panama annual inflation during 1978–80 remained in the 11 to 15 percent range, somewhat lower than during 1972–74.

Of all subperiods shown in the table, 1974–78 exhibits the most 1960s-type, placid behavior. Inflation measures cluster. Only the collapsing Argentine and Chilean dollar export prices deviated much from the 7 percent per annum norm.

Table C11.1   Selected Indexes of Annual Rates of Dollar Inflation, 1972–83, in Percentages

Index	1972–83	1972–74	1974–78	1978–80	1980–83
Nonoil LDCs' import unit values	11	34	7	20	−2
Argentine import unit values	10	32	9	11	−2
Brazilian import unit values	12	34	6	24	0
Chilean import unit values	11	27	10	22	−2
Industrial countries' *export* unit values	8	22	8	14	−4
Nonoil LDCs' export unit values	9	34	6	16	−5
Argentine export unit values	6	35	−3	20	−7
Brazilian export unit values	6	30	5	9	−7
Chilean export unit values	5	41	−5	21	−11
Western Hemisphere export unit values	10	37	7	15	−5
Industrial countries' *import* unit values	10	31	7	21	−4
U.S. wholesale prices	9	16	7	13	4
U.S. consumer prices	8	8	7	12	7
U.S. GNP implicit price deflator	7	7	7	9	6
Panamanian consumer prices	7	12	5	11	5
Panamanian wholesale prices	11	20	9	15	7
Haitian consumer prices	11	19	7	15	9

Sources: Data on Argentine, Brazilian, and Chilean import and export dollar unit values obtained from worksheets of the United Nations Economic Commission for Latin America, courtesy of Andres Bianchi. Data on the U.S. GNP implicit price deflator obtained from U.S. Council of Economic Advisers, *Economic Report of the President* (Washington, D.C.: GPO, 1984), table B-3, p. 224. All other data obtained from International Monetary Fund, *International Financial Statistics,* Yearbook 1984, and January 1985 (Washington, D.C.: IMF, 1984 and 1985). The Yearbook 1984 does not present a Western Hemisphere import unit value; such a series is presented in the January 1985 *International Financial Statistics,* starting in 1979. "Nonoil LDCs" refers to line 201 in the *International Financial Statistics;* "Western Hemisphere" refers to line 205; "Industrial countries" refers to line 110.

The most recent subperiod, 1980–83, presents a remarkable picture: international deflation coexisted with mild U.S. inflation. Again the U.S. wholesale price index behaved closest to international prices, yet a significant gap remained, as during 1972–74 and 1978–80, but with a different sign. It is tempting to speak of U.S. inflation catching up with the higher international price inflation of 1972–80, or perhaps more accurately, of international deflation during 1980–83 wringing out some of the 1972–80 "excess" international inflation. What is more certain is that if one is calculating ex post real interest rates on the Latin American debt, a gloomier view emerges when using some weighted sum of international prices than the already dismal picture one would obtain using U.S. price indices. The real devaluations of Latin American currencies during 1980–83 would appear somewhat less dramatic if international dollar prices were used in the analysis (a point echoing stylized facts of the early 1930s). On the other hand, the nonimported component of the domestic inflations in Latin America would loom larger for 1980–83.

Numerous puzzles remain. Even during short periods Haiti and Panama tend to follow U.S. price trends more than international price trends. This is particularly striking during 1980–83. Either their economies are not as open as they used to be, or the international price indexes have peculiar and unbalanced weights (note that Haiti and Panama have very different per capita incomes and, presumably, different consumption and production baskets, yet their price trends are similar). On balance, this evidence leads me to accept Harberger's recommendation for using the U.S. wholesale prices, even for short periods, although I do so with some misgivings and pleas for further research on the international dollar price level relevant for different types of LDCs.

Recent experiences in Latin America and elsewhere have reinforced the argument that exchange rate policy should differ between LDCs and most developed countries. Freely fluctuating exchange rates with substantial convertibility, an attractive option for most developed countries, remain out of reach for the majority of LDCs, except during short transitions or for the most advanced countries. Credible options for LDCs wishing to have a national currency seem limited to traditional fixed pegs to one currency or to a basket of major currencies, or to passive crawling pegs, for the larger LDCs.

Fuzzy but venerable optimum currency area considerations still carry weight for numerous very small LDCs, many with long traditions of price stability. Freely fluctuating rates among developed countries have complicated the choice of peg for these LDCs and have introduced some inevitable flexibility in their effective exchange rates. But *some* peg and *some* convertibility vis à vis at least one major currency remain the cornerstones of the credibility of national cash and coins, as well as of confidence in domestic banks. In these LDCs the relevant policy change may be either having a pegged nominal rate or having no national currency at all.

But what should keep larger LDCs with a long tradition of monetary autonomy, and often of monetary excess, from adopting freely fluctuating exchange rates with substantial convertibility? The simplest answer is that a majority of these countries are in a near-permanent state of policy experimentation, the success of which crucially depends on the real effective exchange rate and on the rate of devaluation. Those experiments typically include transitions toward less protectionist commercial policies, lower rates of inflation, and more efficient yet safe domestic financial systems. A truly flexible exchange rate regime would imply a substantial liberalization of capital movements.

This combination generates large changes in real effective exchange rates even in developed countries; in LDCs with thin future markets and shallow and shaky banking, financial, and political institutions, one would expect even greater exchange rate gyrations, which would threaten trade liberalization, inflation control, the stability and efficiency of the domestic financial system, as well as the reliability of signals emanating from the price system.

Because the real effective exchange rate is such a crucial variable for LDCs engaged in policy experiments, I feel uneasy about Harberger's pessimistic assessment of attempts to establish systematic empirical links between that variable and such at least partly exogenous variables as the terms of trade and capital movements, whose often violent fluctuations are a source of shocks to LDCs. Policy makers groping for a real effective exchange rate compatible with a more open and stable economy would gain much from knowing how that variable relates at least to the expected terms of trade and to "normal" capital movements.

The inability of preannounced nominal "active" crawling pegs to credibly deliver on a real effective exchange rate compatible with trade liberalization, stable capital flows, and the nimble adjustment of domestic relative prices to outside shocks has doomed "tablita" experiments. One can imagine a world in which the tablita would simultaneously reduce inflation, generate quickly the real exchange rate compatible with trade and financial liberalization, and coexist with orderly capital flows. Copper, corn, and coffee exporters, with long histories of domestic inflation and abrupt policy changes, are most unlikely ever to live in that world. Betting on the tablita is a very risky business for them.

Bailouts during the 1982–85 period have shown that one cannot expect the threat of losses and bankruptcies to be a major disciplining element keeping private capital inflows into LDCs near optimum levels. After this experience lenders will expect LDC governments explicitly to guarantee and therefore to control private as well as public borrowing abroad. In this sense, international lenders are imposing the use of exchange controls even on those LDCs disliking them; once inflows are regulated it appears inevitable to do so with capital outflows also. If exchange rates are roughly "correct" and if domestic inflations are below levels that make "currency substitution" too tempting, those controls may be accompanied by relatively few distortions and could provide some insurance against shocks and unwarranted panics. The danger, of course, is that they will be used as substitutes to desirable adjustments in the real exchange rate or to buttress extravagant levels in the inflation tax on domestic currency. One returns to the old truism that no exchange rate system can do well if fiscal and monetary policies

are out of control, while most exchange systems will do reasonably fine if fiscal and monetary policies are prudent and are expected to remain so.

Finally, it may be noted that multiple exchange rates have experienced a revival during 1982–85 in Latin America—not so much as a mechanism to tax exporters or to prevent further terms-of-trade deterioration, as during the 1930s, but as devices to bail out externally indebted private firms and public enterprises. Cheap dollars have been delivered and promised to those firms to keep them from bankruptcy and to keep their foreign creditors from blacklisting all domestic borrowers. The fiscal cost of these subsidies may be quite large.

Comment   Mohsin S. Khan

Harberger's paper is certainly a wide-ranging and comprehensive piece. It would really not be too much of an exaggeration to say that it gives us just about "everything we ever wanted to know about real exchange rates," and perhaps more! In analyzing the various questions regarding real exchange rates, Harberger brings in his unique blend of economic intuition, technical skills, and a remarkable ability to synthesize and simplify some fairly complex arguments.

The first part of the paper comprising sections 11.2 and 11.3 goes through a very standard partial-equilibrium treatment of the determination of nominal and real exchange rates, respectively, and shows the effects on these of a variety of shocks. There is very little to take issue with in the almost textbook approach, as Harberger himself recognizes, adopted here; and its usefulness lies in the fact that it is all put together in one convenient place. What surprised me, and this will probably strike other readers as well, is that there is no mention whatsoever of any of the current work or thinking on the subject of exchange rates. Although we may not have learned very much in this area, the voluminous literature on the subject is certainly worth a few words. The one other reservation I have about the specific analysis in those two sections is that it leads Harberger to argue for a particular definition of the real exchange rate, and I believe such an inference cannot necessarily be made. I will pick up this point later in this comment.

The paper, despite its breathtaking scope, does exhibit some additional weaknesses. In certain instances Harberger skirts some difficult issues and ignores existing work on the subject, while in others he is

Mohsin S. Khan is a division chief in the Research Department of the World Bank. The views expressed here are the sole responsibility of the author.

too cavalier in pressing his point. A major omission I found is the absence of any discussion of *effective* exchange rates, whether nominal or real. The paper focuses exclusively on *bilateral* exchange rates, and it would have been preferable to round out the picture by some analysis of effective exchange rates. There are several important issues that need to be addressed here, such as the choice of the base period, the weights to be used, and the choice of price indices. Without any discussion of effective exchange rates, which are after all the relevant indicators of a country's international competitiveness, the paper does tend to lose some of its relevance for policy.

There are essentially three specific areas where I found myself particularly uncomfortable with Harberger's analysis: the definition, measurement, and, determination of the real exchange rate. I will deal with these in turn.

Definition of the Real Exchange Rate

Let me state at the outset that I agree with Harberger that there is a great deal of confusion in the literature regarding the appropriate definition of the real exchange rate. I would not, however, go along with him in his claim that since a particular definition ($\bar{E}/p_d$) is able to replicate the results of his model, it is therefore the correct one. Rejecting a definition that has become quite popular in recent years, namely, the ratio of the price of tradables to nontradables (p_t/p_n), because it yields ambiguous answers is, I believe, too hasty. The world may well be more complicated than Harberger's model would lead us to believe, and thus the fact that the response of the real exchange rate to a certain type of shock is not clear cut is hardly surprising. Indeed, if one considers a model with tradable (importable and exportable) and nontradable goods, one can still obtain the same, or at least similar, answers, provided certain conditions, such as gross substitutability in demand, are met. For example, the imposition of a uniform tariff on imports in a Dornbusch-type model would lead to an appreciation of the real exchange rate (a fall in the domestic currency price of foreign money).[1] There is no ambiguity here, although in the case of other types of shocks there may well be.

At any rate, this alteration in the model turns out not to matter much in the final analysis because of the way the real exchange rate that Harberger prefers is actually defined, $\bar{p}^*E/\bar{p}_d$. To use Harberger's own words, the foreign price index, p^*, is an index of the "dollar prices of tradable goods somewhere on the high seas." If the domestic price index, p_d, is highly correlated with the price index of nontradable goods in the home country, and if one truly has good reason to believe that it would be in

most economies, then $p^*E/p_d = p_t/p_n$. In essence, one has gone through a fairly convoluted exercise to get back to square one.

The Measurement of the Real Exchange Rate

Following Harberger's framework I will also divide my comments into the following: first, the appropriate domestic price deflator; and second, the world price deflator.

The Domestic Price Deflator

There is really no dispute on the relative merits of using the consumer price index (CPI) or the whole price index (WPI) to construct the real exchange rate. The CPI is often the only reliable price index available in developing countries, and the fact that it is a better measure than the WPI is certainly fortunate. To the reasons given in the paper on why the CPI is preferable, I would add that it is also a better indicator of overall labor costs in the economy. But the CPI is also not free of problems, particularly in developing countries. For example, it is a meaningful proxy only for short-run changes in relative costs; it does not directly reflect profitability of the primary producing sectors; and its coverage tends to be concentrated in the urban areas of the country. When using the CPI, one therefore has to weigh these negative features against the advantages when using the CPI.

The paper also appears to argue that the GDP deflator is in some sense an ideal index and that it would be the one to use were it not for the fact that it appears with a significant lag, and then only on an annual basis. It should be noted, however, that the GDP deflator also has problems. First of all, it is truly relevant mainly for long-run developments in profitability. Second, the way in which the GDP deflator is computed (as the ratio of current to constant-price value added) can cause major errors, since the imputation of value added at constant prices for certain types of goods and services may not be sufficiently reliable for most developing countries. Finally, the GDP deflator may exclude certain types of costs, such as the costs of nonmanufacturing intermediate inputs in the manufacturing sector.

All these points are, of course, well known, but they should be kept in mind when picking a domestic price index to deflate to a nominal exchange rate.

The Foreign Price Deflator

Fewer problems are posed by the choice of the foreign price deflator that one should use in defining the real exchange rate. I am less sanguine than Harberger regarding the use of the foreign price level in the calculation of real exchange rates because most developing countries do not have such high rates of inflation that one can ignore foreign price changes. I suppose Harberger has in mind such countries as Argentina, Bolivia, and Brazil, rather than developing countries in general. But I believe one will almost always have to bring foreign prices into the picture.

I have three basic points to make regarding the foreign price deflator. First, I think that one ought to use a country-specific index rather than a general international price index, as suggested by Harberger. Consider his own example of a country that is an oil importer. A change in the price of petroleum products may have a small effect on the "world" price level, but as we saw in the 1970s, it can have a dramatic effect on an individual country's import price level. It is really not too difficult to calculate a weighted average of partner-country wholesale price indexes for individual developing countries, so why not do so?

Second, suppose one has followed Harberger and decided to work with a single index. Would it then matter a great deal whether one used the U.S. wholesale price index or some type of weighted average of the wholesale price indexes of countries that make up, say, the SDR basket? In fact, Harberger calls for the construction and publication of such an index using SDR weights. I am not sure how much mileage one would get from this, as these two price series are likely to be closely related, if only because the U.S. series would have a relatively large weight in any basket. To illustrate this point I ran a regression relating a weighted average of the consumer price indexes of all the industrialized countries (Pw) to the U.S. consumer price index (Pus).[2] Using quarterly data for the period 1976–84, I found:[3]

$$\log Pw_t = -0.096 + 0.993 \log Pus_t$$
$$\quad\quad\quad (1.41) \quad\quad (88.52)$$

($\bar{R}^2 = 0.996$; Durbin-Watson = 2.49).

Though one would not want to take this regression too seriously, it does show the tight fit between the two series. I suspect the result for wholesale prices would be similar, and so I am not convinced that much would be gained by going the weighted-average route.

Finally, Harberger ignores the work that has been done on price indexes for tradable and nontradable goods. Such series have been constructed by Clements (1980) for the U.S. and by Goldstein and Officer (1979) for a number of industrialized countries. The methodology outlined in their papers is fairly straightforward and can be easily used to construct a series for the price of tradables, if indeed that is what one wishes to have.

The Determinants of the Real Exchange Rate

Harberger also tends to be much too pessimistic about the possibilities of modeling the real exchange rate for developing countries. Here I think he is influenced by studies on Latin America, and specifically those dealing with countries in the Southern Cone. Aghevli (1981), for example, has shown that one can specify and estimate such a model for a number of Asian countries. In general, there is ample evidence that relating the real exchange rate to variables such as money growth, inflation, and fiscal deficits produces fairly good fits in time-series analysis. Of course, shocks, whether real or nominal, also play an important role; one therefore should not assume that these models will necessarily be appropriate for prediction purposes. Rather than throwing up one's hands in despair, I would argue for more research on this topic. Perhaps no fundamental law will emerge, but identifying any empirical regularities in the behavior of real exchange rates would still represent an important step forward.

Notes

1. See Dornbusch (1974).
2. The data on these indexes are reported regularly in *International Financial Statistics* (Washington, D.C.: International Monetary Fund). The index for the industrialized countries is calculated using GDP weights.
3. The values in parentheses are t-ratios. The equation was corrected for second-order autocorrelation in the errors.

References

Aghevli, Bijan B. 1981. Experience of Asian countries with various exchange rate policies. In *Exchange rate rules: The theory, performance and prospects of the crawling peg*, ed. John Williamson, 298–318. New York: St. Martin's Press.

Clements, Kenneth W. 1980. A general equilibrium econometric model of an open economy. *International Economic Review* (June): 469–88.

Dornbusch, Rudiger. 1974. Tariffs and nontraded goods. *Journal of Political Economy* (August): 117–85.

Goldstein, Morris, and Officer, Lawrence H. 1979. New measures of prices and productivity for tradable and nontradable goods. *Review of Income and Wealth* (December): 413–27.

Contributors

Liaquat Ahamed
Room E-422
The World Bank
1818 H Street, NW
Washington, D.C. 20433

Joshua Aizenman
Graduate School of Business
University of Chicago
1101 East 58th Street
Chicago, Illinois 60637

Jacques R. Artus
Room 9-3000
International Monetary Fund
700 19th Street, NW
Washington, D.C. 20431

Stanley W. Black
Department of Economics
Gardner Hall 017A
University of North Carolina
Chapel Hill, North Carolina 27514

Mario I. Blejer
Room 6-321
International Monetary Fund
700 19th Street, NW
Washington, D.C. 20431

William H. Branson
Woodrow Wilson School
Princeton University
Princeton, New Jersey 08544

Guillermo A. Calvo
Department of Economics
3718 Locust Walk
University of Pennsylvania
Philadelphia, PA 19104

Armeane Choksi
Room N-623
The World Bank
1818 H Street, NW
Washington, D.C. 20433

Jorge Braga de Macedo
Woodrow Wilson School
Princeton University
Princeton, New Jersey 08544

†Carlos Díaz-Alejandro
Department of Economics
International Affairs Building
Columbia University
New York, New York 10027

425

Rudiger Dornbusch
Department of Economics, E52-564
Massachusetts Institute of
  Technology
Cambridge, Massachusetts 02139

Sebastian Edwards
Department of Economics
University of California,
  Los Angeles
Los Angeles, California 90024

Stanley Fischer
Department of Economics,
  E52-280A
Massachusetts Institute of
  Technology
Cambridge, Massachusetts 02139

Jeffrey A. Frankel
Department of Economics
University of California, Berkeley
Berkeley, California 94720

Jacob A. Frenkel
Department of Economics
University of Chicago
1126 East 59th Street
Chicago, Illinois 60637

Manuel Guitián
Room 5-100
International Monetary Fund
700 19th Street, NW
Washington, D.C. 20431

Ravi Gulhati
Room B-1211
The World Bank
1818 H Street, NW
Washington, D.C. 20433

James A. Hanson
Room F-518
The World Bank
1818 H Street, NW
Washington, D.C. 20433

Arnold C. Harberger
Department of Economics
University of Chicago
1126 East 59th Street
Chicago, Illinois 60637

Louka T. Katseli
Center for Planning and Economic
  Research (REPE)
Athens, Greece

Mohsin S. Khan
Room 9-300
International Monetary Fund
700 19th Street, NW
Washington, D.C. 20431

Kathie L. Krumm
Room N-630
The World Bank
1818 H Street, NW
Washington, D.C. 20433

Constantino Lluch
Room S-12-053
The World Bank
1818 H Street, NW
Washington, D.C. 20433

Richard C. Marston
2300 Steinberg-Dietrich Hall
Wharton School
University of Pennsylvania
Philadelphia, Pennsylvania 19104

Michael Mussa
Graduate School of Business
University of Chicago
1101 East 58th Street
Chicago, Illinois 60637

Maurice Obstfeld
Department of Economics
3817 Locust Walk
University of Pennsylvania
Philadelphia, PA 19104

Stephen O'Brien
Room A-313
The World Bank
1818 H Street, NW
Washington, D.C. 20433

Sarath Rajapatirana
Room I8-105
The World Bank
1818 H Street, NW
Washington, D.C. 20433

Marcelo Selowsky
Operations Policy Staff
The World Bank
1818 H Street, NW
Washington, D.C. 20433

Sweder van Wijnbergen
Room N-631
The World Bank
1818 H Street, NW
Washington, D.C. 20433

John Williamson
Institute for International Economics
Suite 620
11 Dupont Circle, NW
Washington, D.C. 20036

Author Index

429

Subject Index

Absorption:
  analytical approach, 372–73
  balance of payments and, 298
  effects of, 297, 329
  income and, 222, 225
Adjustment policy, 2–6, 43, 152
Advance deposits, 150, 157
Africa, 293, 348. *See also specific countries*
  agricultural problems, 1
  BCEAD system, 349, 350, 352
  CFA group, 349
  classification of countries, 348
  consumer price index, 356
  East African common market, 293
  Franc Zone, 348
  nominal vs. real rates, 356t
  Sterling Zone, 335
  West African Monetary Union, 8–11, 333–67
Agricultural exports, 145, 267
Allocation, 158, 346
Announcement effect, 303
Arbitrage, 203–4
Argentina, 144–47, 201, 414–15, 422
  banks in, 177
  capital controls in, 215
  debt of, 4
  exchange rates in, 151
  inflation in, 28, 30–34
  liberalized economy of, 6–7
ARI process, 309
Arms market, 82

Asset market, *See* Money market
Attitudes. *See* Expectations
Auction markets, 145
  devaluation and, 154
  prices and, 302
  taxation and, 154
Autoregressions, 31

Balance of payments, 4, 48–52, 365
  absorption and, 298
  analytical methods, 372
  automatic adjustments, 357
  capital controls and, 67–70
  crises and, 13–14
  deficits in, 41, 207
  devaluation and, 297, 301
  domestic credit and, 207
  energy crisis and, 137
  equilibrium models, 52–67, 73
  multiple exchange rates and, 166
  speculation and, 4
  surplus, 8, 45, 217, 235
Banking, 186. *See also specific countries, systems*
  bonds and, 196–97
  deposits, 7, 184, 188, 193, 200
  central, 7–8, 39–40, 145, 349, 350, 352
  crawling peg and, 203
  commercial LCDs, 19
  credit process, 3, 18, 19, 27–28
  deposits in, 7, 183–84
  financial intermediaries, 199